Hoover's Secret War against Axis Spies

J. Edgar Hoover, circa 1945. *New York World Telegram & Sun Collection, Library of Congress*

Hoover's Secret War against Axis Spies

FBI Counterespionage during World War II

Raymond J. Batvinis

University Press of Kansas

Published by the University Press of Kansas (Lawrence, Kansas 66045), which was organized by the Kansas Board of Regents and is operated and funded by Emporia State University, Fort Hays State University, Kansas State University, Pittsburg State University, the University of Kansas, and Wichita State University

Library of Congress Cataloging-in-Publication Data
Batvinis, Raymond J.
Hoover's secret war against Axis spies / Raymond J. Batvinis.
pages cm
Includes bibliographical references and index.
ISBN 978-0-7006-1952-8 (alk. paper)
1. World War, 1939–1945—Secret service—United States. 2. United States. Federal Bureau of Investigation—History—20th century. 3. World War, 1939–1945—Secret service—Great Britain. 4. World War, 1939–1945—United States. 5. Espionage—United States—History—20th century. 6. Intelligence service—United States—History—20th century. 7. Hoover, J. Edgar (John Edgar), 1895–1972. 8. Internal security—United States—History—20th century. I. Title.
D810.S7B352 2014
940.54'8673—dc23
2013046775

British Library Cataloguing-in-Publication Data is available.

Printed in the United States of America
10 9 8 7 6 5 4 3 2 1

The paper used in this publication is recycled and contains 30 percent postconsumer waste. It is acid free and meets the minimum requirements of the American National Standard for Permanence of Paper for Printed Library Materials Z39.48-1992.

To Maryalice

CONTENTS

ACKNOWLEDGMENTS

There is an old aphorism that describes life as a journey on a winding and often bumpy road. You think you know where you're going but more often than not you don't. Over the past decade, since I started a second career as a historian, I've discovered that the journey of life and the writing life are very similar. One tries to make a plan, have a goal in mind, start out with enthusiasm, carefully trek along, often slip off the trail or go down dead-ends, turn around again, go back to the main road, start over, and hope you make it to your destination wherever that may be. This has been my experience, anyway. It is always fraught with frustration but also filled with fun. I wouldn't have it any other way.

I suspect that all writers will agree with me that the greatest pleasures of the writer's journey are the people you meet and the adventures along the route. And I have been blessed over the five years of this project to experience both. There are more than I can even recall, but I'll try my best.

A special appreciation goes to Mary McFarland of the Franklin and Eleanor Roosevelt Institute for her assistance in the processing of an Isador Lubin/John G. Winant Research Grant, which helped offset my travel and living expenses at Hyde Park.

Our world could not function without the selfless dedication of archivists and librarians. I start with the staff of the Franklin D. Roosevelt Library for their remarkable generosity of time and infinite patience guiding me through FDR's wartime life in papers and photos: senior archivist Robert Clark, the late Karen Anson, who sadly succumbed to cancer in 2010, Virginia Lewick, and Matt Hanson. Elsewhere, I was ably assisted by Alicia Vivona and Spencer Howard, archivist technician at the Herbert Hoover Presidential Museum and Library; Sophie Chevalier-Forget, historian at the Royal Canadian Mounted Police; James Wintel, research librarian in the Music Division of the Library of Congress, who assisted me in my hunt for information about Alexander Semmler; Norman Davis, the head of the Englewood, New Jersey, Historical Society; Bob Woodworth of the Natick,

Massachusetts, Historical Society; Judith Clark of the San Marino, California, Historical Society; and the staffs of the Tennessee Historical Society, the Hawaii Historical Society, the British National Archives, the Library of Congress, the National Archives and Records Administration, the Naval Historical Center, the FBI Academy Library, the Chester Nimitz Library at the United States Naval Academy, the J. Edgar Hoover Foundation, the Aldeman Library at the University of Virginia, the George C. Marshall Library in Lexington, Virginia, the Hornbake Library at the University of Maryland, the American Catholic History Research Center and University Archives at the Catholic University of America, the National Law Enforcement Officers Memorial, the Society of Former Special Agents of the Federal Bureau of Investigation, and the Radio & Television Museum in Bowie, Maryland.

Particular thanks are extended to the staff of the FBI's Freedom of Information Section, whose thankless toil is often met with the question "Why did they redact that?" In fact, such reviewers are an essential cog in the wheels of our democracy, balancing the nation's need for secrecy with the citizen's right to be informed.

Some of the most important breakthroughs occur by accident. That's what happened one day while I was having lunch with a good friend and historical storehouse, Dan Mulvena. While discussing the recent publication of the Guy Liddell diaries, he casually mentioned the rich collection of diary entries that remained unpublished. Within days Dan reproduced them for me. The story they tell and the gaps they fill are fascinating.

One of the blessings for a historian is the professional and personal friendships with scholars who have devoted their entire lives to a particular field. In my case, I have been fortunate to know Rupert Allison, a historian of intelligence and a highly regarded British writer who offered immeasurable support to me and this project. Available for a question or a theory at any time, Rupert always expanded on his answers by offering different approaches, which more often than not were spot on. I am very grateful for his help. Christopher Andrew, former chairman of the History Department at Cambridge University, graciously allowed me to partner with him on a panel at a London conference on the occasion of the publication of his official history of the British Security Service. Thad Holt, who broke new ground with *The Deceivers,* gave graciously of his time, discussing his work while pointing me to key documents in his papers lodged at the U.S. Army Historical Center. In the process we have become good friends as well as colleagues.

My gratitude is also extended to the archival and graphics staff of the Newseum in Washington, who let me tag along while they took measurements of Hoover's office suite for a display they were planning to honor the one hundredth anniversary of the FBI. The dozens of charts and photos of everything from parquet floors to doorknobs proved very helpful. In that regard, I want to recognize my frame-maker pal from Stuart, Florida, Peter Craft, for introducing me to Bill Adair, a world-renowned picture frame restorer and owner of one of Washington's secret treasures, Gold Leaf Studios. After patiently educating me on the beauty and complexity of Greco-Roman architecture and design, Bill suddenly announced that he was a "Cogswellian" and then introduced me to the mindless hilarities of a Cogswell Society luncheon. (Great lunch—terrible jokes.) Their motto: "Temperance, I'll drink to that."

I also want to recognize a good friend, Keith Redmond, who lives in Paris and accompanied me on a wonderful "Redmondian" walking tour of the city, locating historical sites used by the Abwehr during the war and ensuring quality photos; and my wife, who accompanied me on my historical journey south from Paris through southern France by train to Barcelona, Spain, in an attempt to capture the feel of intelligence officers and agents alike in their missions to the United States through the Iberian Peninsula.

Very special appreciation goes to Ernest Porter, Lean Lecari, daughter of Dwayne Eskridge, and Amy Bertheaux, daughter of Art Thurston, for their personal recollections as well as family photos and correspondence; Melvin Barrett for his insights into life in Honolulu in the months after the Japanese attack; George Grotz and the members of the San Francisco chapter of the Society of Former Special Agents of the FBI; Larry Langberg, the late Art Thurston, and Dennis Flinn, who generously allowed me to interview them; Ian Chadburn for his reminiscences of his father, Fred Chadburn; Ileana Semmler for assistance in the research of her father's musical career; Gerry Richards, a former FBI agent and owner of Richards Forensics Services, who analyzed Dwayne Eskridge's seventy-year photo of the Honolulu radio room; and Linda James and Sally Jenkins of East Hampton, New York, who shared their reminiscences of Dudley Roberts over cool drinks on Sally's patio.

I have been greatly assisted by a series of bright and talented interns from the Institute of World Politics in Washington, D.C. I want to particularly recognize Mike Watson from the University of Virginia, David Ferkulak, a graduate of Cedarville College in Ohio, and Drew Sotelo from the

University of South Florida. I also want to recognize Allison Hogarth, one of my students at George Washington University, who discovered some new information concerning the Bernard Kuehn case.

Today the "Benson House" in Wading River, New York, serves as the administrative offices for the DeWolfe Center, a summer camp and conference center, operated by the Episcopal Diocese of Long Island. A study of this type could not have been completed without a visit to the site, which once bulged with radio equipment and technicians whose only mission in life was to deceive the Germans. When Kathleen Loomis Ward, the center's director, learned of my interest she quickly arranged a luncheon for my wife and me in the sun room overlooking Long Island Sound, followed by a tour where I took dozens of photos. For me it was a shining lodestar for my further research.

Douglas Waller has written an excellent biography of General William Donovan entitled *Wild Bill Donovan.* His insights into the wartime Hoover-Donovan relationship proved valuable to me in shaping a clearer understanding of Donovan and the tempestuous and fascinating relationship between these two men. Jim Burns, son of the late Hawaii governor John Burns, was of inestimable help. He patiently answered incessant questions, offered permission for reproducing relevant portions of his father's oral history, and provided insights into his father's years with the Honolulu Police Department, particularly as head of the Espionage Bureau and his relationship with Robert Shivers.

I also want to honor the memory of Jim McGuire, a wonderful person who significantly influenced me in many ways. Jim dedicated his life to public service, first as a Marine Corps officer, nearly three decades as a Special Agent of the FBI (1950–1979), and later as an official with the Smithsonian Institution. He was the quintessential American, who served faithfully for years as the Society of Former Special Agents' history committee chairman.

Thanks go to Cynthia Kwitchoff, owner of CJK Creative, who took my vague ideas for informative charts and graphs and turned them into eye-popping art forms. She is an artistic genius. I also acknowledge the help of Paul Rickenbach, former mayor of East Hampton, New York, who arranged for me to interview Sally Edwards and Linda James.

Mike Briggs, executive editor of the University Press of Kansas, believed in this project from the start and shepherded my proposal through the often tortuous review process. I offer my sincere thanks to him and his excellent staff for helping to make this book a reality.

This story could never have been written without my wife, Maryalice. For the six years it has taken to complete this manuscript she has been at my side, offering me encouragement and support and often taking up the slack of other duties while I read or pounded away at a keyboard. Only a poet could find the words to describe Mary's importance in my life. This book is dedicated to her.

ABBREVIATIONS

Abwehr	German Military Intelligence
BSC	British Security Coordination
C	Chief of the Secret Intelligence Service (MI6)
CCS	Combined Chiefs of Staff
COI	Coordinator of Information
DOJ	Department of Justice
FFF	Free French Forces
G2/MID	Military Intelligence Division of the War Department
ISK	Decrypted Abwehr Machine Cipher Wireless Traffic
ISOS	Decrypted Abwehr Hand Cipher Wireless Traffic
JCS	Joint Chiefs of Staff
JSC	Joint Security Control
LCS	London Controlling Section
LRC	London Reception Center
MI5	British Security Service
MI6	British Secret Intelligence Service
ONI	Office of Naval Intelligence
OSS	Office of Strategic Services
PCO	Passport Control Officer
RCMP	Royal Canadian Mounted Police
SA	Special Agent
SAC	Special Agent in Charge
SIS	FBI, Special Intelligence Service

Hoover's Secret War against Axis Spies

INTRODUCTION

It was October 23, 1943, when Guy Liddell stood before a gathering of his senior British counterintelligence colleagues to offer a top-secret assessment of Germany's appreciation of the challenge it faced from the British Security Service (MI5) and across the Atlantic from the FBI. Liddell was no ordinary counterintelligence officer. In fact, he was a talented veteran of MI5 with more than twenty years of investigative experience against both German and Russian spies. One highly regarded British intelligence historian described him many decades later as "an exceptional intelligence officer in every way."[1]

By 1943 Liddell had served three years as the head of B Division, handling espionage investigations and the fascinating collection of human sources who were playing a pivotal role in the legendary Double Cross System. Two years later he would take over as MI5's deputy director general, a position he would hold until his retirement in 1953. The timing of the October 1943 meeting was propitious. Washington and London had been partners in war for almost two years. Just a year earlier, U.S. and British forces stunned the Germans with surprise landings along the North African coast, starting a campaign that ended months later with the collapse of Hitler's vaunted Afrika Corp. Sicily had already been cleared, with fighting growing more intense as the Allied troops doggedly slugged it out with German forces on the boot of Italy. At the same time plans were underway in London for the cross-channel invasion of Europe sometime in the middle of 1944.

Relying on all available sources (and there were many), Liddell explained that, surprisingly, the Abwehr (German military intelligence) had a very low opinion of the British Security Service, which was then brilliantly deceiving them on a daily basis and would continue to do so until the end of the war. In the next breath he doubtlessly shocked his listeners with the observation that the Germans considered the FBI "a far more formidable obstacle than the British secret service." The reason for this strange dichotomy was what Liddell described as the FBI's "smash and grab" approach, resulting in "huge headlines in the press" that wended their way back to Berlin. On the other hand, the Germans seemed "fairly satisfied" with their performance in Great Britain, an opinion that Liddell attributed to MI5's policy of keeping them "as far as possible in the dark."[2] Liddell's striking remarks are significant not merely because they were offered by an Allied counterintelligence specialist working within his own long-standing organizational tradition, but because just five years earlier FBI missteps and a bumbling investigation of the long-running Guenther Rumrich espionage ring led to public ridicule of FBI director J. Edgar Hoover and his gang of G-men for allowing dozens of spies to slip out of the United States to safety in Europe.

So what was the deeper reason behind Germany's assessment? Part of the answer lies in my first book, *The Origins of FBI Counterintelligence,* which examined the Bureau's development in 1938 from a small law enforcement organization to a counterespionage service and then into a counterintelligence service, following the president's May 1940 order to begin wiretapping embassies and consulates and a second secret order to Hoover two months later creating America's first foreign espionage service without congressional knowledge. Reform began with the recognition of the need for a new intelligence structure to handle the rapidly changing espionage realities facing the country. For example, in June 1939 the Interdepartmental Information Conference, the forerunner of today's Intelligence Community, was established along with the Plant Protection Program, also a forerunner of the modern Industrial Security Program. New liaison relationships were formed between the military, the FBI, and foreign partners like the Royal Canadian Mounted Police (RCMP) as well as Mexican and British intelligence officials. The General Intelligence Division, closed down in 1920 in the wake of American outrage over the mass arrests of alien radicals by Attorney General A. Mitchell Palmer, was restored. The FBI's Identification Division, which held hundreds of thousands of fingerprint records, exploded in size when new military draft laws and the need for new defense workers led to the fingerprinting of millions of Americans. For the most part these initiatives were in place when the Japanese attack on Pearl Harbor ushered the country into the Second World War.

The Rumrich failure, the new initiatives, and the FBI's education in the handling of the complex details of double-agent matters all culminated in the summer of 1941 with the surprise arrest of thirty-three German espionage agents, breaking the back of Abwehr intelligence in the United States. This single act, which reversed German views of U.S. counterintelligence in one stroke, was hammered home again a year later when the FBI rounded up eight hapless saboteurs delivered to American shores by German submarine, making headlines around the world.

But this is not a story of international competition, nor some type of analytical survey measuring who was better or worse, who won the war or who contributed more to Allied success in the shadowy game of espionage and deception. It is an examination of the early days of international counterintelligence cooperation, and it requires readers to keep in mind a couple of important facts as they move through this study. First, the counterintelligence structure of Britain and the United States are reflections of their nations' histories (in the Second World War there was also the matter of geography) and the governments they serve. For example, MI5 emerged out of a military structure during the first decade of the twentieth century, while FBI counterintelligence was woven into a law enforcement culture. MI5, as a counterintelligence service, had no authority to conduct criminal investigations or make arrests. The FBI could do both and still does so today. MI5 was a secret organization for most of the twentieth century, while the FBI was and still remains a public sub-cabinet agency of the Department of Justice. During the Second World War the British press was subject to far more restrictive censorship than American newspapers, which law enforcement relied on in many ways.

This is, in fact, a two-part story of two very different counterintelligence cultures with little understanding of the other, struggling to form an often painful alliance that eventually defeated the German intelligence services. It also extends the narrative beyond *The Origins of FBI Counterintelligence* with the story—much of which has never before been revealed—of the continuing progress of a counterintelligence service that now faced the harsh realities of a world at war.

The details are drawn from a wide variety of sources. Rare manuscripts, government documents, private papers, and photos drawn from Canada, Great Britain, France, and the United States, together with interviews of some of the main players, serve as the core of a fresh appreciation of the FBI's complex role in the war. The book takes a new look at the complicated (and poisonous) relationship between Hoover and William Stephenson, the head of British Security Coordination (BSC), MI6's American center of operation, with new revelations from the eighteen opaque months when Stephenson ran intelligence operations in a still-neutral America, as well as from the war years, during which Hoover tried to limit BSC to the role of liaison service. Among the new revelations is Hoover's role as Stephenson's communications link with London, the harsh consequences of botched BSC mischief, and rumormongering by some of BSC's leading officials. Further complicating the situation was the little known internal MI5–MI6 friction, and Hoover's struggle to cope with the problems posed by these rivalries. The book lays out for the first time why Hoover sent an FBI survey team to London in the summer of 1942, followed months later by the surprise installment of his own man at the American embassy in London to deal directly with MI5 officials, bypassing MI6 and BSC. This led to FBI access to Ultra, the British code name for its penetration of the encrypted German communication system known as Enigma, a success Hoover had been aware of for some time but to which he had never previously had access. Hoover later credited British code breaking as one of the FBI's most important counterintelligence assets in the battle against German espionage in the Second World War.

When I wrote *Origins,* I wanted to describe the Special Intelligence Service, a foreign espionage service that was virtually unknown to the general reader and poorly understood by modern-day intelligence professionals and historians. The story of the SIS is a long one, beginning eighteen months before the Pearl Harbor attack and concluding two years after the surrender of Japan. *Origins,* however, touched only on SIS's prewar days of trial and error when Hoover was struggling to set up the system. This book picks up some of the threads of these beginnings by recounting many previously unexamined features of its wartime growth, operating techniques, and investigations not only in Latin America but in Europe, Africa, and Asia as well.

Conventional wisdom among intelligence historians today is that the Double Cross System involved a collection of MI5 double agents deceiving the Germans from the British Isles. Scores of books and articles have been written about the exploits of this wonderful cast of characters, particularly Juan Pujol, a diminutive Spanish pacifist with the code name Garbo who offered the Germans a symphony of bewilderment and confusion while leading an orchestra of imaginary sources. For his implausible accomplishments he received both the Iron Cross from Adolf Hitler and the Order of the British Empire from King George VI. Englishmen look back proudly, and rightly so, on the genius behind the stunning surprise of Wehrmacht high command when Allied forces landed on the Normandy coast, followed by their continued belief in Garbo's equally audacious lie that the attack was merely a diversion covering a larger invasion yet to come.

While this part of the Double Cross story looms large in our collective memory of the war, it is still only a part of the story. In fact, the Double Cross System was an Allied undertaking that incorporated deception-minded professionals on both sides of the Atlantic. In the summer of 1942 British and American military officials, working with the FBI using American-based double agents, started sending intelligence to the enemy, both useful and worthless and laced with reports designed to confuse the Germans as to the date, place, and time of the invasion of Europe.

For the first time, five FBI double agents who participated in the famed Double Cross System are examined. There was a flamboyant larger-than-life playboy who expected others to pay his bills while he became the central figure in a famous dispute that poisoned the relationship between Hoover and Stephenson. Another was a world-famous French flyer with orders to infiltrate the American aircraft industry. Then there was a lecherous Dutchman who remained bottled up in London oblivious to the fact that the FBI had convinced his German bosses that he was in Washington mingling with wartime leaders. A fourth was an electric shop owner who had once worked as a Dutch double agent, and the last was an Argentine businessman who cooperated with the Abwehr simply to escape from Europe and join the Allies as an informant; he became one of the war's most important deception sources.

Like Garbo communicating by radio to Lisbon, the five transmitted across the Atlantic Ocean to Hamburg. Like Garbo they amassed nearly a dozen imaginary sources, working at key military facilities from New York to San Francisco, passing U.S.- and British-approved lies. Also, like Garbo they feigned complete loyalty to the Nazi cause, all the while pestering them for more and more funds to finance their work and pay their sources. The Abwehr's desperate efforts to get funds to them through cutouts in South America, and even through submarines using jewelry and rare stamps passed through other FBI double agents, would have been almost comical had the stakes in terms of human lives and treasure not been so deadly serious. In the end, what is equally fascinating is that right up to the last days of the war in Europe the Germans were still expressing their appreciation to them for their loyal contributions to the Fatherland.

Unlike Garbo, however, the FBI's double agents provided information to Allied planners that altered the course of history forever. At the same time that America's leading scientists and engineers were recommending the pursuit of the atomic bomb to President Roosevelt, three FBI double agents had informed them of Germany's interest in America's atomic weapon's program and the identities of the men leading the effort. It was this startling intelligence that tipped the balance for these scientists in favor of urging the president to move forward on the unprecedented and world-changing project.

This is a story that has never been told—one the writer hopes will contribute to a better understanding of the FBI's World War II counterintelligence and foreign intelligence saga, and that lays the basis for a larger, longer, and what was potentially a deadlier cold war yet to come.[3]

CHAPTER ONE

A Remarkable Weekend

Washington, D.C.
Saturday, December 6, 1941
3:10 p.m.

The nation's capital was growing colder as the late afternoon light slowly gave way to darkness. Shops along Pennsylvania Avenue were still open for last-minute weekend purchases. Childs Restaurant, home of the forty-cent Blue Plate Special (pot roast, mashed potatoes, and string beans—no substitutions), still claimed a few customers, probably guests at nearby hotels who mingled in odd conglomeration with stately new government office buildings. Pennsylvania Avenue, the now ghost-like grand thoroughfare, anchored at opposite ends by the White House and Capitol Hill, now had only a passing Chevrolet or LaSalle, an occasional trolley lazily rolling along its centerline, and a few pedestrians, hats pulled down tight on their heads, faces invisible behind turned-up coat collars, battling frigid winds that whipped around building corners and sliced down the gray sidewalks. The few hardy souls who braved the elements were finishing weekend shopping at the Woodward & Lothrop, the venerable department store in the city center, now open a half-hour later as Christmas approached; others headed home for the evening after a half-day of work, perhaps anticipating a night on the town; perhaps dinner at the Viking on Thirty-first Street NW, billed as Washington's "Smartest Supper Club" with its always popular "Saturday Special"—only eighty-five cents. For moviegoers there were the hilarities of Abbott and Costello in *Keep 'Em Flying* at RKO Keiths, or more dramatic fare at the Metropolitan with *They Died with Their Boots On* (7:00 and 9:30 showings) featuring Errol Flynn and Olivia de Havilland; more high-brow entertainment could be found at the Wardman Park Theater on Connecticut Avenue above Rock Creek with a live performance of Shakespeare's *Troilus and Cressida.* Whether it was a theater for a play, a movie house showing Hollywood's latest production, or more exotic pleasures at one of the city's many burlesque palaces, Washington was still a small southern town marked by provincial thinking and a gaping racial divide. While in London during the German Blitz, James Reston of the *New York Times* remembered Washington as "a pleasant place if you lived in the 'right' part of town and didn't read or think." Decades later a Washington newcomer, a young reporter fresh from North Carolina named David Brinkley, probably felt at home describing Washington as "a town and a government entirely unprepared to take on the global responsibilities suddenly thrust upon it."[1]

During the 1930s Pennsylvania Avenue's appearance significantly changed with the construction of a one-square-block building that would serve as the new home for the Department of Justice. Situated between Pennsylvania and Constitution Avenues and Ninth and Tenth Streets, the building dominated the eastern edge of the seventy acres that became known as the Federal Triangle. The building's south side facing the Great Mall housed the Department of Justice, with FBI headquarters and its Washington field office on the north fronting Pennsylvania Avenue. Completed in 1935 after five years of work, the 1.2 million square foot, steel-frame structure covered with Indiana limestone was designed by the Philadelphia architectural firm of Zantzinger, Borie, and Medary in a blended neoclassical revival and art deco style characterized by red roofing tiles, large soaring colonnades, a great hall, and a majestic foyer set off with a spacious interior courtyard that offered natural ventilation and illumination. The building's interior was a unique integration of art and sculpture topped by concrete ceiling mosaics. The wall murals depicting the history of the American experience were done by well-known American artists such as George Biddle, a former classmate of Franklin D. Roosevelt and brother of Francis Biddle, the nation's attorney general.[2]

J. Edgar Hoover sat at his neat wooden desk clearing off some last-minute paperwork before ending his day. The forty-six-year-old FBI director worked in a fifth-floor office suite overlooking massive stone columns arching the back side of the new National Archives, the official repository for America's two most precious political statements, the Declaration of Independence and the Constitution, along with millions of government records extending back to the nation's founding. From his desk he could see the imposing dome of the Capitol, which undoubtedly conjured up memories of the Eastern Market neighborhood just a few short blocks beyond, and Seward Square, the home where he was born and spent the first forty-three years of his life. It was only a twenty-minute walk from there, yet light years away in terms of how far he had ascended the ladder of Washington's political power structure.

Formal entrance to the director's office was through a door and narrow passageway carefully guarded by Hoover's longtime personal secretary, Helen Gandy. Two years younger than her boss, the New Jersey native first arrived in Washington in 1918 in search of work. Following some secretarial courses at a local business college and George Washington University, she joined the Department of Justice, where she soon took a job as Hoover's typist and later his personal secretary. "Miss Gandy" (she never married) oversaw her domain with a steely efficiency, personally escorting visitors into Hoover's formal office where the always nattily dressed, modest-sized gentleman rose from his large imposing desk at the room's far end and then gently moved his guest to one of the easy chairs in front of an immense fireplace at the office's south end where they could relax and chat.[3]

Hoover's ceremonial office was cavernous. A first-time visitor got the immediate sense of an enormous presence that both dwarfed and intimidated. Covering more than one thousand square feet of floor space, the perpendicular room was commanded by a heavy, dark, imposing wooden conference table in the room's center, with smaller chairs and side tables ringing the walls for the aides and bag carriers of the many generals, admirals, politicians, and dignitaries with important business with the director. Ochre-colored walls rose to a height of twenty-four feet; one side was embedded with three coffin-like shelves holding leather-bound law books interspersed with mementos from Hoover's twenty-four years at the Justice Department, reminders of just who occupied this space. Three massive Palladium-style windows, bordered by gold-pleated, stiletto-like, floor-to-ceiling drapes, dominated the equally striking wall facing Ninth Street, engulfing the room with morning sunlight; in good weather they could be thrown open to flood the great space with fresh air. Eye-catching fluted pilasters (non-load bearing) soaring upward to the ceiling and strategically sited throughout the office only enhanced the sense of size and space. Illumination was provided by three Etruscan-style brass lamps suspended from the ceiling by slender thread-like chains. At the base were rare, translucent, paper-thin bowl-shaped shades composed of salt, alum, a form of potassium sulfate, and alabaster quarried near Volterra, an ancient city in Italy's Tuscan region, which suffused light throughout the large space with a soft luminescent glow. Complementing this sense of size and strength was a vast parquet floor designed in an equally luminescent moiré pattern with each piece of ammonia-fumed, quarter-sawn oak specially hand-fitted with craftsman-like precision to highlight the right-angled annual rings of the wood.[4]

A massive oak desk with a modest left-side cabinet for correspondence trays and a telephone allowed Hoover to swing back in an overstuffed chair and gaze out the window while chatting with some important caller. Standing as silent sentinels behind his chair were two large pedestaled American flags with the Department of Justice seal on the wall above.[5]

In photographs and newsreel images taken over the years, Hoover is often seen at his desk in front of two large oak doors. They led to a much smaller, rather simple, triangular-shaped room with a small window and a private lavatory that Hoover always used as his working office. There he met with his top advisors and other Justice Department officials, reserving the large office strictly for conferences and official visits. Through a door off this confidential office marked "Private," the director could quietly slip out for meetings down the hall with the attorney general or to his nearby private elevator, always ready to whisk him to the basement garage where his personal chauffeured limousine would await him.[6]

Nineteen days before Christmas 1941, the FBI director sat at the pinnacle of a fast-growing federal agency that probably even amazed him. Born on New Year's Day in 1895, he was a Washingtonian to the core. Raised just blocks from Capitol Hill, Hoover worked as a young man at the Library of Congress while completing his law degree in 1916 and an advanced degree in law a year later, both from George Washington University. After passing the District of Columbia bar exam he entered the employ of the Department of Justice the following July. After a year of service there his name, John E. Hoover, was suddenly altered in the name of efficiency. The momentous change occurred for the most mundane bureaucratic reason—confusion over mail delivery with another, more senior employee named John E. Hoover. Since the future FBI director was so new, his name was forever changed to J. Edgar Hoover.[7]

At the start of the 1920s Hoover, then only a low-level staff attorney, weathered the national backlash of the so-called Palmer Red Raids, the roundup of aliens and radicals on flimsy legal grounds instigated by A. Mitchell Palmer, President Wilson's attorney general. In May 1924, President Coolidge's newly appointed attorney general, Harlan Fiske Stone, appointed Hoover to the position of acting director of the Bureau of Investigation (changed to the Federal Bureau of Investigation in 1935), with orders to reform a service infested with incompetency, inefficiency, and corruption.[8] Over the next seventeen years, through a combination of iron will, ruthlessness, raw intelligence, hard work, political savvy, and some very good luck, he transformed the FBI, expanding its investigative mission from anti-trust matters into a new role as nationwide crime-fighting weapon with rapidly expanding authorities in the field of national security.[9]

The accidental discovery in February 1938 of a large, well-organized German espionage ring operating in the United States followed by a botched FBI investigation led Hoover to refocus the FBI toward counterespionage. These efforts received a boost in June 1939 when President Franklin Roosevelt centralized counterespionage policy by ordering all cabinet departments to report allegations of sabotage, espionage, or subversion in their departments to the FBI. Hoover soon found himself chairing a secret coordinating committee with the Department of State and the armed forces. FBI reach soon extended beyond U.S. shores with investigators secretly dispatched to China, the Soviet Union, and most Western European capitals. Hitler's invasion of France in May 1940 led to White House orders for FBI electronic surveillance of the embassies and consulates of Germany, the Soviet Union, Spain, Japan, and Vichy France, followed two months later by another presidential order for Hoover to establish America's first organized clandestine foreign intelligence service in the nation's history—the Special Intelligence Service. Seventeen months later, as 1941 receded into history, an increasing number of Hoover's agents were moving into Latin American capitals with orders to infiltrate national governments in hopes of carrying away useful secrets for Roosevelt and his policy makers.[10]

Hoover was exhausted. It had been a pretty rough week for him, with one crisis hitting right after another. On Tuesday, December 2, the notorious head of the crime syndicate Murder Incorporated, Louis "Lepke" Buchalter, whom Hoover had personally arrested in August 1939, was sentenced to Leavenworth Prison for murder.[11] The next day Edward Tamm, Hoover's number three man, quietly visited Congressman Martin C. Dies at his Capitol Hill office to reveal an FBI investigation which had uncovered Dies's receipt of a bribe for allowing Jewish refugees into the United States through Cuba. The dumbstruck Texas Democrat, a vocal critic of the FBI, never made another accusation against Hoover or his organization again.[12] The next day Hoover ordered an investigation of a catastrophic leak of military secrets when simultaneous articles appeared in the *Chicago Tribune* and the *Washington Times-Herald* that morning accusing the Roosevelt administration of lying to the American public about trying to avoid war with Germany. Reporters had gotten a verbatim copy of the War Department's top-secret "Rainbow" war plans, comprising five hypothetical war situations (each designated by a color) prepared by the Joint Board of the United States Army and Navy at the insistence of the president. Rainbow Five, the last in the series and classified as top-secret, served as the basis for America's strategy in World War II by outlining in detail the plans for a U.S. alliance with Great Britain and France in offensive military operations against the Germans throughout Europe and Africa.[13] For the next two days FBI agents and military officials traced the security of the documents, with Hoover personally interviewing Navy Secretary Frank Knox, Admiral Harold Stark, the chief of naval operations, and Richmond Kelly Turner, a rear admiral who authored the navy's portion of the plan.[14] While quietly threatening rogue congressmen and chasing war-plan leakers, Hoover also had other official duties to address. On Thursday afternoon he hosted the twenty-eight-year-old Prince Pedro Gastao of Orleans Braganza, a claimant to the Brazilian throne as titular Emperor of Brazil and head of the Petropolis branch of the Brazilian Imperial House.[15]

On Friday, December 5, with Dies silenced, the leak investigation in full swing, Edward Tamm met with William Donovan, whom the president had appointed Coordinator of Information (COI) in June 1941. Starting from scratch, Donovan, a World War I Medal of Honor winner and Wall Street lawyer, rapidly began assembling a collection of academic specialists in geography, area studies, history, and political science to examine raw intelligence collected by various government agencies and then to mold it into useful analytical reports for policy makers. As his staff grew, so did the necessity for security clearance investigations. Tamm and Donovan signed a memorandum of understanding mandating FBI background investigations on each of Donovan's staff members.[16]

Since arriving at ten o'clock that morning, Hoover had met with Tamm and D. Milton "Mickey" Ladd, his assistant director for national defense. He spoke by phone with Attorney General Francis Biddle in Detroit, Percy "Sam" Foxworth, the head of the FBI's New York office, presidential press secretary Steve Early, the legendary Washington columnist Drew Pearson (probably calling for an update on the Rainbow 5 investigation), and Associate FBI Director Clyde Tolson, who was visiting his family in Cedar Rapids, Iowa.[17]

By three o'clock, after a final review with Tamm, his desk cleared by

Miss Gandy, Hoover donned a heavy woolen coat, slipped out the back door through an ever-darkening hallway to his elevator, and headed for the basement where his chauffeur waited to take him to a plane bound for New York City.

Honolulu, Hawaii
Sunday, December 7, 1941
1–2 p.m.

Robert L. Shivers, the Special Agent in Charge of the FBI's office in Honolulu, screamed into the telephone. Bombs were dropping, there were deafening explosions, noise beyond description, pedestrians on the street frantically scrambling in all directions, and in the distance plumes of black acrid smoke slowly rising over the navy's great anchorage at Pearl Harbor, filling the air with an odor of burning oil that gently floated toward Honolulu—just six miles away.

Shivers suddenly had a lot on his plate. As he stood (probably crouching) in his office at the Dillingham Building in Honolulu, his every effort was directed at notifying Hoover that America was under attack. Five thousand miles away a switchboard operator at FBI headquarters immediately relayed the call to Room 2501, Hoover's regular suite at the Waldorf-Astoria. In stunned silence Hoover sat riveted as Shivers's clearly shaken voice crackled out the news that the "Japanese are bombing Pearl Harbor." To allay any doubts, Shivers stuck the telephone receiver outside his office window so Hoover could hear for himself, across eight time zones, the horrific sounds of the opening salvo in America's new war. Shivers then reaffirmed the worst for his boss: "There is no doubt about it, those planes are Japanese. It's war."[18]

Washington, D.C.
Sunday, December 7, 1941
3:50 p.m.

Shivers called again. This time he spoke to Crawford "Kit" Carson, the head of the Special Intelligence Service at his office in Washington, telling him that the attack had ended, but that early reports were bad: two battleships sunk, one badly damaged, the local airbase in shambles with planes smoldering on the ground, hundreds dead and injured, and the territorial governor declaring an unlimited emergency. Shivers, together with Office of

Naval Intelligence, the army's Military Intelligence Division, and the local police, were cordoning off the Japanese consulate. And Shivers would be in his office, available via the continuously open telephone and radio, for the foreseeable future.[19]

Washington, D.C.
Sunday, December 7, 1941
6:44 p.m.

Hoover was in his private office on the telephone with Charles Fahy at the White House. Born in Rome, Georgia, in 1892, Fahy had attended the University of Notre Dame and Georgetown University, where he received his law degree in 1914. After service as a naval aviator (winning the Navy Cross) during the First World War, Fahy began a law practice in Washington, later opening an office in Santa Fe, New Mexico, before returning to Washington to work for the Roosevelt Administration in the 1930s, eventually becoming Solicitor General of the United States. After just thirty-seven days on the job, he suddenly found himself filling in during these intense early hours for Attorney General Francis Biddle, whose speech to the Slav-American Defense Savings Committee at Detroit's Masonic Temple had been interrupted by news of the attack; Biddle was soon en route to the capital aboard an army plane.[20]

Earlier that day Fahy was at home napping after attending church and a midday dinner when he received a call informing him that Admiral Harold Stark, Chief of Naval Operations, had just called the DOJ with news of the attack. Arriving at the attorney general's fifth-floor suite, now a makeshift command post, he learned that Roosevelt had called him at home. When Fahy telephoned the White House the president told him simply, "I want you to do what you feel necessary to be done there," then related his concerns for the protection of the Japanese embassy and consulate officials from possible retaliation by angry Americans. Shortly after passing these orders on to Tamm, who was already coordinating FBI activities while Hoover was returning from New York, Deputy Secretary of State Sumner Welles called Fahy requesting FBI activation of wiretaps on the Japanese embassy and consulates "to pick up what information was possible." This, too, was passed to Tamm. The remainder of the afternoon was spent huddled with Fahy's new legal team, putting the final touches on Proclamation 2525, "Alien Enemies—Japanese," prepared by FBI and Justice Department officials weeks earlier.[21]

At the time of Hoover's call, Fahy was impatiently sitting outside the White House's second-floor family residence for a few moments with President Roosevelt so that he could sign the necessary documents authorizing the arrests of thousands of Japanese aliens throughout the nation during the hours ahead. The solicitor general could only tell the FBI director that his waiting would continue.

Immediately following the news of the attack, Tamm notified all FBI field offices nationwide to "proceed immediately" with arrangements for arrests of dangerous Japanese aliens and to begin coordinating with the local immigration authorities who would then take custody of the individuals. SACs were told to await the president's go-ahead before acting and thus ensure that Washington had the names of every person scheduled for arrest. Field offices were given two hours to comply with these orders.[22]

Hoover was impatient; he needed to know the status of the president's signature on the proclamation. At 7:03 p.m. he called the White House again. Fahy and Francis Shea, his assistant attorney general, were then entering the family quarters, where they found the president in bed propped up by pillows, pen and pad in hand, surrounded by the First Lady and their oldest son, James, a Marine Corp captain. Roosevelt's only words of greeting were "It's pretty grim, Charlie!" In silence Fahy placed the documents gently on Roosevelt's lap. Years later he recalled that moment for historian John Toland. After dolefully affixing his name, Fahy remembered, the weary president, with so many details running through his mind, looked up at the men and reminded them of a remaining requirement: for the secretary of state to affix the great seal of the nation to the documents. After they declined the president's invitation to attend an emergency cabinet meeting scheduled for later that evening, Roosevelt ordered them to ground all private aircraft for fear that the "Japanese might well get up and destroy some of our planes." As they left the room FDR issued one final order. "Now get done what needs to be done, and I'll take care of seeing the appropriate papers are signed." The meeting lasted ten minutes.[23]

Eight minutes later Fahy called Hoover from a White House phone. The warrants were signed; the dragnet could begin. Three minutes later Hoover updated Edward J. Ennis on Fahy's White House mission. A former counsel for the Immigration Service, Ennis now served as the Justice Department's head of the Alien Control Program. Eighteen minutes later Shivers was again on the phone (the first of two conversations with Hoover that evening) updating the boss and getting the go-ahead for the roundup.[24]

For Hoover, the next three hours were a blur of calls and an unrelenting flow of FBI and Justice Department officials in and out of his small office. Orders were issued canceling all annual leave, FBI offices were placed on a twenty-four-hour schedule, working with the local police, increased protection was mounted at the Japanese embassy as well as all consulates throughout the nation, all civilian aircraft were grounded, and commercial air carriers were asked to refuse seats to Japanese passengers or to accept packages from Japanese for fear of sabotage. At 7:33 p.m. Shivers again spoke for fifteen minutes with Hoover, reviewing the unfolding magnitude of the catastrophe, the appalling destruction at Pearl Harbor, and army air installations along with the growing tally of dead and injured, and assuring him of the health and safety of the FBI's local staff. Shivers then assessed the probability of a possible Japanese uprising in the Hawaiian Islands and the growing fear among the local population that the attack was only the prelude to a Japanese amphibious invasion at any moment. Hoover called James Roosevelt at 7:48 p.m., updating him on Shivers's report (an open telephone line between Honolulu and Hoover's office was continually manned throughout the afternoon and evening), followed six minutes later with a call to Frank Knox for the same purpose. A Republican, Knox had been a private who followed Theodore Roosevelt up San Juan Hill during the Spanish American War, later serving as a major during the First World War before making a fortune as owner of the *Chicago Daily News*. In 1936 he ran for vice president on the Republican ticket with Alf Landon, losing in a landslide to Roosevelt. Now serving as secretary of the navy, he was at the White House awaiting the start of an emergency cabinet meeting scheduled for 8:30. Knox warned that Germany and Italy were planning to declare war on the United States, leading Hoover to suggest the immediate arrests of German and Italian aliens now that authorizing documents had been signed by the president. From a "psychological point of view," he said, it would be better to do so now rather than risk a reoccurrence of sabotage as happened in the days leading up to World War I. Knox agreed to bring the matter up with the president. Shivers and Hoover again spoke for four minutes, at 8:59 p.m. Four minutes later William Donovan called for an update (the first of two calls from Donovan to Hoover that night). At 9:30 p.m. Hoover dispatched a note to Assistant Secretary of State Adolf Berle apprising him of the actions taken that evening.[25] Finally Biddle, fresh from the cabinet meeting, called Hoover at 9:42 p.m. from a White House telephone (in the first of two conversations that evening) for an update lasting almost forty minutes and again for six minutes at 10:31 p.m. It was probably during these conversations that Hoover learned of Roosevelt's verbal instructions, temporarily appointing him to serve as the head of censorship.[26]

Everything that could be done that fateful night was done. President Roosevelt's signature on Executive Order 2525 had been flashed to every FBI field office across the land, setting in motion a nationwide dragnet marking the opening hours of the FBI's role in the Second World War. It was 11:45 p.m. Hoover's men were now fanning out, knocking on doors, ringing doorbells, and making arrests. It was the start of a process that would result in more than twelve hundred Japanese aliens in INS custody over the next forty-eight hours. For the FBI director it had been a momentous day. There was nothing else to do now but go home and get some rest. He was going to need it. Hoover's war had only begun.[27]

CHAPTER TWO

Jones and Stott

When the FBI was founded in 1908, America's common 3,000-mile border with Canada made cross-border information exchanges with the Royal Canadian Mounted Police (RCMP) a routine matter. During the First World War, joint investigations of sabotage and suspicious munitions factory fires became common practices. Later, when Congress passed the Federal Extortion Statute in 1932 along with laws federalizing state and local crimes such as bank robbery, car theft, fugitive investigations, and extradition matters, cooperation with Canadian police authorities dramatically increased. One such case involved William Dainard, a drifter, hobo, and kidnapper of nine-year-old George Weyerhauser, son of a wealthy timber magnate, who was arrested following a lengthy hunt by FBI agents and Canadian authorities. Over the years Hoover's frequent meetings and conferences with RCMP commissioner Stewart Wood produced bonds of friendship and collaboration, which led to a 1935 agreement for the attendance of Canadian Mounties at the newly created FBI National Police Academy, where senior police officials mingled with colleagues from around the nation while studying modern investigative techniques. These modest beginnings led to secret understandings between the two men for the exchange of counterespionage and subversive information, couched as criminal intelligence that quietly sidestepped State Department restrictions.[1]

The same could not be said for FBI-British relations before the Second World War. The only instance of direct contact occurred in April 1938 when Special Agent Charles Ager attended an intensive six-week police sergeant's course in London where he studied British policing methods. His comments on MI5, MI6, and the Special Branch of Scotland Yard were so superficial that they took up only half a page of a five-hundred-page report that he prepared for Hoover on his experiences.[2]

State Department officials in Washington controlled FBI-British contacts by requiring the passage of all information through the American embassy in London. Adding to this restrictive system was the department's refusal to pass FBI requests they considered too politically sensitive for foreign eyes while at the same time assigning British investigative inquiries to its own agents. In April 1938 the head of MI5's counterespionage branch, Guy Liddell, visited Washington in the hope of encouraging closer liaison with an equally eager FBI based on recent MI5 assistance in breaking the Guenther Rumrich espionage case. Liddell had much to share with Hoover's people including mutually useful data covering Soviet, German Italian, and Japanese activities. The difficulty, Liddell later observed, was how to do so "without causing offence to the State Department, with whom we have been in touch via the Counsellor of the American Embassy here since the war."[3]

What local liaison Hoover did have with the British was concentrated on Captain James Paget, a forty-nine-year-old retired naval officer with no intelligence experience, assigned to the British Consulate at Exchange Place in Lower Manhattan. Paget served officially as the Passport Control Officer (PCO) handling visa matters in the United States with a staff made up of an MI6 officer named Walter Bell, a secretary, and a clerk.[4]

Since the end of the Great War, MI6 had used PCOs in consulates around the globe for collecting intelligence without attracting local police attention. Unlike intelligence officers under commercial or academic cover, PCOs enjoyed diplomatic immunity, which protected them from arrest, allowed storage of sensitive documents in relative safety, and made possible secure communications with London. As the usefulness of the PCO cover diminished with the reduction of maritime restrictions throughout the 1920s and 1930s, it nevertheless remained, in the words of the official historian, the "primary cover used by SIS in the field" in the years leading up to the war. Nevertheless, James Dunn, the assistant secretary of state responsible for political relations, remained insistent that Paget channel all government contacts through the State Department.[5]

In the fall of 1939 London established the British Purchasing Commission (BPC) in New York City to manage government contracts with American companies. Part of this decision was based on the troubling memories of sabotage and the difficulties encountered in safely shipping war supplies across the Atlantic during the First World War. British officials still went pale when recalling the massive June 1916 blast that destroyed the vital Black Tom Island shipping depot along with hundreds of other mysterious factory fires and explosions throughout the United States and Canada that slowed the shipment of desperately needed war supplies to British and French ports. Harking back to these old fears was the British dread of disruption from a new generation of subversive elements, millions of isolationists, Irish extremists, German Americans sympathetic to the Nazi cause, and communists dominating the National Maritime Union. Compounding London's dilemma was America's indifference to England's plight. "The American authorities were not concerned to take any special measures for protection of British property," one official later remembered, "and while the British Purchasing Commission was technically responsible for preventing sabotage, it was equipped to do little more than minimize the risk in factories turning out war material for Britain."[6]

Hamich Mitchell was a British businessman who arrived in New York in the fall of 1939 with a full BPC portfolio including service as the commission's security officer. Having no familiarity with America or with counter-sabotage, Mitchell soon outlined a series of imaginative proposals that he planned to share with the FBI. One idea called for the creation of an "undercover branch of the British service" that would work side by side with local railroad police safeguarding the thousands of miles of rail tracks crisscrossing the nation while collecting "sabotage information for passage to the FBI." In March 1940 Mitchell offered his plan to R. P. Kramer, a supervisor in the FBI's newly established National Defense Division. Quickly dousing Mitchell's ardor, Kramer explained that British agents secretly working with local U.S. police agencies while America remained a neutral nation was unacceptable. He then gave the British businessman a civics lesson about the American system of government, the U.S. police structure, and the FBI's nationwide authority and responsibilities for investigating sabotage matters. Federal, state, and local law enforcement were governmental functions, Kramer explained, while railroad detectives were either railroad employees or private security officers hired by railway companies to investigate railroad-related crimes and protect freight shipments to U.S. ports. Unilateral activities into this area of American commerce by a foreign intelligence service, friendly or otherwise, Mitchell learned, would be at cross-purposes with U.S. policy and only attract FBI "interest."[7]

Kramer then described the FBI's Plant Security Program: an initiative started in the fall of 1939 requiring agents to conduct top-to-bottom inspections of American defense plants with deficiencies recorded and sent to the War and Navy Departments. When Mitchell asked for the names and locations of these factories, Kramer referred him to the State Department and the military services for authorization before any coordination or release could be made. When Mitchell complained about his difficulty vetting BPC employees, Kramer offered help by explaining the FBI's close relationships with local police agencies throughout the United States, a suggestion that encouraged Mitchell to pursue a similar line of inquiry in Canada with the RCMP. After the meeting Kramer recommended passing Mitchell's name to Percy Foxworth, the FBI's man in charge of the New York office, who could "orally and privately" receive information that would "undoubtedly" benefit the Bureau's own intelligence work. He then suggested informing SACs throughout the country about BPC and Mitchell's new responsibilities.[8]

Days later Hoover discussed Mitchell's visit with Adolf Berle, the assistant secretary of state for Latin American affairs who doubled as the State Department's liaison for intelligence matters. Berle was a New Yorker and a former child prodigy who still holds the distinction as the youngest graduate from Harvard University with a college diploma, having matriculated at the age of fourteen and going on to earn both a doctorate in economics and a law degree by the age of twenty-one. After wartime service as an intelligence officer in France, he joined the military staff supporting the American delegation at the Versailles Peace Conference. It was during these months of service that his long-standing antagonism toward the British was forged as he watched firsthand London's efforts to frustrate the emergence of new democracies in Central Europe. In the early 1920s he joined the faculty of Columbia University as a professor of economics after a brief stint in private law practice. *Modern Corporations and Private Property,* Berle's 1933 landmark examination of contract law, quickly caught the attention of President-elect Franklin D. Roosevelt, who invited him to join his new administration as a member of a "Brain Trust" that he was putting together to seek innovative solutions for relieving the Great Depression.[9] Meanwhile, on matters relating to foreign policy, Berle discouraged any idea of a secret British-FBI relationship, warning that any "combined counter-espionage and secret intelligence unit . . . should be ours and not foreign."[10]

Hoover didn't need a reminder about unauthorized FBI-British contacts. First, the Interdepartmental Information Conference, the government's new intelligence coordinating system, was less than a year old, and there were many questions of policy yet to be worked out. Second, what kind of apparatus did Mitchell have in mind? What would it lead to? Hoover played no role in foreign policy formulation, and any communication between the FBI and a foreign intelligence service outside diplomatic channels would raise serious State Department objections.

Hoover still recalled his severe State Department upbraiding in December 1939 when Dr. Walter Engelberg was found murdered in his Brooklyn home. A career German diplomat then serving as a First Secretary at the German consulate in Manhattan, Engelberg was murdered by Ernest Kehler, a twenty-four-year-old boxer, who was arrested six days later in Toronto. At his trial Kehler denied any involvement in Engelberg's death, claiming that the victim was a secret Nazi opponent who was "purged" by German agents on Hitler's orders. Prosecutors, fearing that the two men may have quarreled over an espionage matter, asked the FBI to check with London through Paget's office for any record on Engelberg. MI5 quickly produced information showing that he was, in fact, a loyal Nazi with "high party connections" who informed on his colleagues for German intelligence. Later he performed similar snooping duties at posts in Austria and Italy. When the State Department learned of the exchange, Hoover was roundly scolded for failing to use State Department communication channels.[11]

Further evidence of Berle's attitude occurred in June 1940, when the British government offered Sir Eric Holt-Wilson's assistance to the American government in establishing an American Central Security Service. Born in 1875, the Harrow-educated Holt-Wilson joined the army after graduating from the Royal Military Academy at Woolwich. In 1912 he entered the newly formed Imperial Security and Intelligence Service, where he spent the next twenty-eight years investigating all manner of counterintelligence and counterespionage issues. By 1940 he was serving in "near anonymity" as the deputy director of MI5 when Winston Churchill, the new prime minister, sacked him and his boss, Sir Vernon Kell, in the erroneous belief that they had ignored the danger of German fifth columnists.[12]

Prompting the British offer was an American study of Fifth Column activities in Great Britain commissioned by Joseph Kennedy, the U.S. ambassador. Kennedy assigned the task to an embassy staff member, Harvey Klemmer, who began working closely with the recently fired Holt-Wilson. Despite his new civilian status Holt-Wilson generously accommodated Klemmer over the next several weeks by carefully tracing MI5's history, its inner workings, operational tactics and methods, and laws and policies governing the service, along with realistic assessments of the minimal threat from Fifth Column groups in the British Isles. So won over was Klemmer by Holt-Wilson's briefings that in his report praising the security service's work he told Kennedy that the "English have done a very smart thing in connection with counter-espionage which might well be copied in the United States." The goodwill spawned by the report led to an MI5 offer for

Holt-Wilson, at sixty-five years old still in good health and reluctant to retire as a consultant to the Americans in the construction of its own security service. Kennedy forwarded Klemmer's findings to Washington with Holt-Wilson's agreement to visit Washington to work side by side with Hoover and his staff.[13] Both the report and the offer of assistance were peremptorily dismissed by State Department officials (Hoover was never informed of the report or the MI5 offer), who claimed that measures were already underway for improving the security setup within the U.S. government. Berle recorded these approaches and offers as examples of "intrigue behind the back of the State Department and even the President designed to further extend British influence inside our own government."[14]

While Berle was blocking cooperation, a historic shift in FBI-British intelligence relations was taking place through separate channels. On April 16, 1940, only weeks before the surprise German invasion of France, a Canadian businessman named William Samuel Stephenson made a courtesy visit to Hoover. The meeting was arranged through Gene Tunney, the legendary American heavyweight boxer and close friend of both men.[15]

No two men were more different than Hoover and Stephenson. The FBI director, then forty-five, was born and raised in Washington and had never lived or worked anywhere else. He was a lawyer with a degree from George Washington University, a law enforcement officer, and a government bureaucrat who had built the FBI into a modern nationwide crime fighting service in under than two decades. He was an army lieutenant colonel who had never served a day of military service; he rarely left Washington and never traveled outside the United States except for occasional official meetings in Ottawa. His buttoned-down, no-nonsense leadership style demanded absolute loyalty from his staff at all levels, clear lines of communication with other government agencies, and an insistence on written memoranda of understanding defining which agency was responsible for what duties. As the new counterintelligence chief responsible for ferreting out foreign intelligence gathering, propaganda, covert actions, and foreign propaganda, it made little difference to him what country or government was involved.[16]

Stephenson was a year younger than Hoover. After completing high school he joined the Canadian forces, fought in France, and spent a year in a British hospital recuperating from a gas attack. After returning to combat as a pilot he was shot down and imprisoned by the Germans. By the end of World War I Stephenson was a wounded veteran who proudly held the Military Cross and the Distinguished Flying Cross. Back in civilian life he launched a remarkable business career that made him a multimillionaire with financial interests throughout the world. Stephenson had a maverick style with a penchant for cutting corners and no qualms about going behind someone's back to achieve his objective of controlling everything. During the Roaring Twenties and the Depression-wracked thirties he bought a land development company in British Columbia called British Pacific Properties; Sound Film Studios, which exploited the explosion of moviegoer interest in "talkies"; Sheppardton Film Studios, one of the world's largest movie production companies (many World War II strategic deception tricks were created there); Pressed Steel Company, producer of ninety percent of Britain's car bodies; General Aircraft Limited; and Alpha Cement Company, one of Britain's largest producers of cement.[17]

Stephenson's growing fortune led him into social circles that read like a *Who's Who* of British business, arts, and government. Among the many prominent visitors to his London home were Sir Charles Hambro, a leading City of London banker; film executive Norman Loudon, a Scotsman, who made a fortune in the camera business and later produced films such as *French Without Tears* (1939); and Sir Alexander Korda, renowned director of the films *The Private Life of Henry VIII* and *Rembrandt*, both starring the film legend Charles Laughton. He also numbered American and British literary and film personalities such as H. G. Wells, George Bernard Shaw, and Greta Garbo as friends, as well as aircraft pioneers Reginald Mitchell, designer of the British Spitfire; Frank Whittle, one of the great minds behind the invention of the jet engine; Henry Acres, the renowned Canadian hydro-electric engineer who worked for years in Africa; and Eugene Dawson, a world-renowned American geologist.[18]

To help support his far-flung enterprises and his London backers, Stephenson quietly formed a "shadowy organization" in the 1930s called the British Industrial Security Service (BISS). It was an informal intelligence system staffed by a loose network of contacts and secret sources strategically placed in major European capitals who kept Stephenson supplied with reams of internal economic data information about his competitors, their secret business deals, and insights into the rapidly shifting European political climate, all of which could affect his own business planning. Faced with growing German militarism in 1938, the small and increasingly stretched MI6 began relying on business sources like BISS for economic intelligence. In July 1939, with war just two months away, Stephenson contacted MI6 to place BISS "entirely at the disposal of HMG." The hard-pressed chief of

British foreign intelligence, Stewart Menzies, only accepted the offer with the proviso that he be given the identities of BISS sources. This requirement soon proved a major embarrassment for both men when it emerged that some of Stephenson's sources were, in fact, MI6 officers supplying information "to supplement their income."[19] The value of BISS's information evidently trumped Menzies's humiliation sufficiently enough for him to overlook his staff's disloyalty in order to absorb BISS resources into MI6.

Menzies, as the new head of MI6, having replaced the ailing Arthur Sinclair in September 1939, was interested in fostering closer Anglo-American intelligence relations. His vague plan called for expanding MI6 presence in the United States through cooperative ventures with both official services such as the FBI and what he referred to as "less formal authorities."[20] For some puzzling reasons that have never been adequately explained, Menzies chose Stephenson rather than a trusted confidant as his personal emissary to carry out this extraordinarily sensitive mission. The new MI6 head knew little about the United States; he had no familiarity or, for that matter, interest in its governmental structure, economy, or culture. Furthermore, Menzies had no American friends to speak of, nor had he ever visited America. Stephenson was a Canadian and, unlike his new boss, had frequently visited the United States over the years for business and pleasure, where he had collected a wide range of American friends and contacts who could prove useful to MI6.[21] In any event, Menzies dispatched Stephenson to America with orders to open up a communications channel with Hoover in anticipation of establishing a direct line to President Roosevelt and the potential for "wider ranging connections" which could offer, in the words of one British historian, "the useful opportunity for feeding the Americans with information that Churchill thought they should have."[22]

Exactly what was discussed between Hoover and Stephenson at their April 16 meeting still remains unclear today. From the scant records on the British and U.S. sides we know that Stephenson told Hoover that changes were underway in MI6 representation with Paget's departure and the assignment of a new PCO with a mandate to launch a new secret channel of communication with the FBI. The wary Hoover, who was probably eager for improved relations, did nothing to discourage Stephenson's proposals but at the same time did caution him about the State Department's extreme sensitivities in such matters. In his subsequent report Stephenson told Menzies that Hoover wanted him to remain in the United States as the "SIS Chief's personal representative," an apocryphal claim that one British expert believes may have been inspired by his "ambition and desire for personal aggrandizement."[23] After getting the green light from the White House, Hoover got to work, first by assigning himself the alias Henry E. Jones (reversing his initials) and then assigning the code name "Stott" for passage of information between himself and Menzies. A MI6 officer in New York serving as the FBI's British point of contact would transmit Stott's information to Henry E. Jones through one Sam Eldridge, the alias assigned to Sam Foxworth, Hoover's man in charge of the New York FBI office. Day-to-day management of the new relationship was turned over to Hoover's confidential assistant, Stanley Tracy, working out of the director's office suite.[24]

Within days Hoover met with Major General Edwin Watson, who gave the president's go-ahead to the Hoover-Stephenson relationship.[25] Menzies was pleased with the success of Stephenson's initial foray. "I like the suggestion of you being my personal contact with Jones at Washington," Menzies cabled on May 11, "but it is considered that you return to London first of all for consultations and instructions." Weeks later when they met in London, Stephenson, in a burst of hyperbole, offered the MI6 head a glowing description of his discussions with the FBI chief. Hoover had unique access to the White House: President Roosevelt supported this initiative and was eager to cooperate with Stephenson. So persuaded was Menzies of the potential value of this arrangement to both MI6 and the Foreign Office that on June 3, 1940, he told his Whitehall bosses of his decision to permanently assign Stephenson to New York as his personal representative. "I have appointed Mr. W. S. Stephenson to take charge of my organization in the USA and Mexico. As I have explained to you, he has a good contact with an official who sees the President *daily.* I believe this may prove of great value to the Foreign Office in the future outside and beyond the matters on which that official will give assistance to Stephenson."[26]

When Stephenson returned to New York in July 1940, one of his first tasks was a request to Tracy for Hoover's help in handling BSC's radio communications. Menzies, Stephenson claimed, wished to transmit confidential information from the prime minister to President Roosevelt using Hoover as a channel and bypassing the British ambassador. The matter was of such delicacy, Stephenson coyly explained, that Menzies could not officially make such a request but would immediately set up a system at London's end if the director thought such a procedure "desirable." Hoover wasted no time making his decision; a communications system would be set up for the transmission of intelligence information between the two service chiefs, but the

FBI could not act as a conduit for passage of diplomatic messages between the two leaders.[27] With Hoover's restrictions now in place, FBI technicians soon got to work on the construction of a secret radio system that Stephenson used for the next year.[28]

The job of designing and building the secret Washington-London radio link was turned over to FBI agent Richard Millen, a two-year veteran with an advanced degree in physics from Indiana University and a former college professor. Millen had no inkling about the purpose of this new station. His orders were simple: locate it within fifty miles of Washington, D.C., spend no more than fifty dollars per month in rental costs, and ensure a capability of "transmitting Morse Code signals over long distances including London, England." Within weeks Millen found a tiny and barely habitable summer cottage with no running water, indoor plumbing, or heat (it did have a coal-burning stove for cooking) near the remote half-mile-square village of Chesapeake Beach, Maryland. Nestled on an obscure western bluff called Randal Cliff 109 feet above the Chesapeake Bay, Millen's new radio station was a mere eighteen miles south of Annapolis and thirty-five miles southeast of Washington. Under the watchful eyes of suspicious locals, the cruddy little bungalow, so long abandoned, was suddenly overrun by a small army of tight-lipped workmen who spent days and nights stringing telephone wires and installing electricity with the help of the local power company while others carried a seemingly endless supply of cartons into the tiny shack that now bulged at the seams. The boxes contained the finest radio equipment available. Communicators assigned full-time to the station sat in front of state-of-the-art, German-made Hammerlund SP-600 receivers, called "Super Pros," which also sent outgoing messages through 450-watt Hallicrafter HT-4 transmitters.[29]

If Millen had any remaining doubts about the importance of the place, they soon vanished when Hoover ordered the installation of a special encrypted copper land-line teletype machine in the tiny kitchen linking the cottage to Stephenson's new thirty-sixth-floor headquarters at Rockefeller Center in New York City. As the months went by and the volume of message traffic increased, two additional teletype machines, a 1,000-watt RCA transmitter and a 1,000-watt Temco transmitter, were added along with an emergency electrical generator to prevent a sudden disruption in the flow of messages. Following the installation of the antenna and some additional testing, the first message from Hoover's new radio station, codenamed "CIR" and using the call sign WFBA, was successfully transmitted at midnight on March 26, 1941, to HMG Communications Center (XQR) at Waddington in Buckinghamshire, England. Within months Bay Station, as it was called, added a second circuit for transmitting and receiving messages from Camp X, the new BSC training site situated in Canada on the banks of Lake Ontario. The security-conscious Millen, always wary of prying eyes, cleverly obscured the station's real owner and purpose by situating it near a cluster of antennas used by the Naval Research Laboratory for radio testing.[30] The only public whiff of the station's existence arose in the weeks before Pearl Harbor when the *Washington Star* published a brief article hinting at the site's true occupants. "Proof of the value of the locality as a radio center," the reporter wrote, "is the fact that a few hundred yards north of the new laboratory [Naval Research Laboratory] there is a set of 'mystery' radio towers, said to be operated by another Federal agency."[31]

Once on line, Bay Station operated around the clock with encrypted messages traveling by hard wire from BSC in New York to Bay Station for transmission to London with encrypted incoming messages from London forwarded to New York. The rapidly growing volume of message traffic in 1941 forced a major adjustment in Bay Station's work environment. David Sherrill, a FBI radio technician and a former Marine Corps communicator, his assistant, Jim Corbett, and others moved into the cramped bungalow on a permanent basis, creating an endless and almost claustrophobic existence of sending, receiving, eating, sleeping, sending, receiving, and so on. Living and working conditions were an other-worldly existence of freezing winter temperatures and blistering summer heat coupled with an endlessly noisy and frenzied amalgam of machines clacking, technicians tapping, and tape spewing everywhere, all in an effort to keep pace with dozens of messages handled on a daily basis. Decades later a history of the station recorded one "three-week stretch early in the operation [when] a noisy Big Ben alarm clock portioned out 'sleep' periods" between shifts."[32]

In addition to supplying BSC with a communications channel to London, Hoover also shared some recently developed technologies with his new partner. They included miniaturized eavesdropping devices for easier concealment along with cameras that snapped photographs without shutter noise. Stephenson reciprocated Hoover's help with censorship experts from the British postal system, teaching FBI agents the art of opening and resealing letters and packages without detection. In the fall of 1940 Stephenson arranged for Foxworth, the recently appointed head of the FBI's new Special

Intelligence Service, to meet with MI6 station chiefs during a secret fact-finding trip he took throughout Latin America. Additional arrangements were made for two senior FBI officials to visit England for three months in the fall of 1940 to study the full array of plant protections programs, wartime urban and rural policing, and the role of the Special Branch, as well as MI5 and MI6 procedures.[33]

In January 1941 Stephenson returned from meetings in London with added responsibilities and the new title of director of British Security Coordination.[34] His new portfolio included representing the interests of MI5, MI6, BPC, the Special Operations Executive, and the Ministry of Economic Warfare, management of MI6 coverage in Latin America, and the vitally important British Imperial Censorship centers in Bermuda, Jamaica, and Trinidad. The three islands were choke points for all mail and travel between Europe and the Western Hemisphere. Highly skilled postal censors, working around the clock in absolutely secrecy, looked for evidence of espionage by carefully examining letters and packages that had been whisked off transatlantic planes and ships. Using everything from the naked eye to sophisticated laboratory tools they checked for secret writing, known aliases, Abwehr mailing addresses, suspicious handwriting, innocuous or senseless correspondence, microdots, and other tell-tale signs of spying. When technicians got a hit they recorded the information for future reference, copied the letter, resealed the envelope, and returned it to the aircraft waiting to take it to America or Europe. Censors then reported the find to BSC in New York for FBI investigation. Among Bermuda's more significant contributions before U.S. entry into the war was the discovery of an espionage ring run by Fred Ludwig, an Ohio-born American of German background using the alias "Joe K." Bermuda also proved useful during the latter stages of the probe of the Frederich Duquesne espionage ring as well as German espionage networks in Mexico and Latin America. So essential was British censorship to FBI operations that Hoover assigned an agent to Bermuda in November 1941.[35]

Looking back today after the passage of more than seven decades, it is clear that the Hoover-Stephenson relationship, which started with such promise, was doomed to collapse from the start. The original agreement between a law enforcement officer and government bureaucrat, on one side, and the new BSC boss, a businessman and maverick, on the other, was verbal and never codified, making it subject to the most liberal interpretation on both sides. Menzies's original charge to Stephenson included obscure instructions to investigate "enemy activities, to institute adequate security measures against the threat of sabotage to British property and to organize American public opinion in favour of aid to Britain."[36] Achieving these goals led Stephenson to relocate Paget's operation at the old British consulate to a larger and swankier address on the thirty-fifth and thirty-sixth floors of the International Building at Rockefeller Center in midtown Manhattan. From the four-member staff he inherited, the BSC director steadily built an empire over the next two and a half years of more than eight hundred officers, analysts, typists, secretaries, file clerks, and security guards based largely in New York and Washington, with representatives scattered at consulates throughout the country.[37]

Stephenson's American odyssey, described by one author as a study in "relentless duplicity," soon raised Hoover's suspicions. Shortly after his arrival he began a campaign to discredit anti-British newspapers while feeding pro-British material to friendly media sources, all in violation of the Foreign Agents Registration Act passed two years earlier.[38] In early 1941 BSC took secret control of WRUL, ostensibly an independent Boston radio station, for use in broadcasting carefully slanted reports carrying a positive British theme. Another concern was the snatching of British seamen off U.S. streets by BSC agents.[39] Faced with Communist Party inducement for British seamen to abandon their ships in American ports, Stephenson considered kidnapping a politically acceptable risk. In a report sent to Hoover in June 1941 he described how his agents in Baltimore had placed two British seamen in "irons and were bringing them to New York where they would be placed on a British ship for a return to a prison camp in England."[40] In March 1941 FBI agents confiscated a notebook left behind on a commercial airliner by an American named Verne Tomkins. A close look revealed a number of cryptic handwritten notations describing senior FBI officials such as "E. J. Connelley—In charge of the Bridges investigation. Very unpopular" and "R. B. Hood—Los Angeles, in charge. Not to be trusted." Tomkins later told FBI agents that he was a private investigator working for BSC. After initially disavowing Tomkins, Stephenson lamely retracted his claim, admitting that he had received information from him on "two or three occasions" under a different name.[41] New questions arose about suspicious BSC investigations of American citizens for reasons not shared with the FBI. One such case arose when Major John Maude, a Stephenson deputy, asked Hoover for State Department information concerning an American woman named Katrina Sergeant, a wealthy New Yorker who resided at Manhattan's Sutton Place.[42]

Hoover's growing skepticism of Stephenson only worsened following reports of BSC eavesdropping on Americans' telephone conversations in violation of federal law and U.S. policy. His fears were confirmed in September 1941 when a lengthy BSC study entitled "Vichy French in the United States," containing the names of Americans suspected of Vichy French sympathies, was delivered to him. The bases for these charges, Hoover learned, came from "individual observers, from documents intercepted by censorship and from a series of mechanically recorded conversations."[43]

One particular target of BSC eavesdropping was Jean Louis Musa, a naturalized American citizen who was born and raised in Europe. Musa was a businessman and personal secretary to Gaston Henry-Haye, the Vichy French ambassador sent to Washington by President Pierre Laval following France's collapse in the summer of 1940. Hoping to discredit Henry-Haye, BSC began watching Musa in search of opportunities to exploit his access to Henry-Haye. At the same time the FBI's New York office was investigating Henry-Haye, the BSC secretly arranged for Musa's use of an office suite at Rockefeller Center so they could easily tap his telephone conversations with Henri-Haye.[44]

The final straw for Hoover came in the summer of 1941 when President Roosevelt appointed William J. Donovan as his new Coordinator of Information (see chapter 14 for full details of the Hoover-Donovan relationship). Donovan's duties were to head a government organization with responsibility for "analyzing the information that came in from everywhere and reporting it in a coherent fashion directly to the president." Stephenson quickly began currying favor with Donovan, who reciprocated his overtures. The two men originally met in the summer of 1940 when Roosevelt sent Donovan to London to report on England's fighting capacity. The fact that Stephenson viewed Donovan as one of those Americans that Menzies described as an "unofficial contact"[45] ensured his access to the highest levels of British officialdom by urging a whirlwind of briefings by the right people. Over the ensuing months the two men, who shared remarkably similar backgrounds, developed a close bond based on mutual need. Stephenson saw Donovan as an American with White House access and strong influence on the president: Donovan pursued the BSC head's assistance in his new role as COI and later in setting up the Office of Strategic Services (OSS). For Hoover, the final betrayal in this already muddled drama came when Stephenson bypassed the FBI director by turning over his U.S. sources to Donovan and assigning a BSC officer to assist the COI in recruiting and training Americans for special operations overseas.[46]

December 7, 1941, abruptly changed the FBI-BSC intelligence relationship. No longer was America a neutral power that needed secret British courting through its intelligence organs. America was now a belligerent power. British intelligence that had informally operated in the United States under the radar for the past sixteen months would now have to adjust its behavior to the new wartime realities. Hoover and MI6 would have to form a new "liaison" partnership based on openness, honesty, and a complete information-sharing arrangement. This would require some difficult adjustments, which would come swiftly and explosively in the next three months.

CHAPTER THREE

The Balloon Went Up

"Exceedingly disagreeable" and "absolutely intolerable." That was how Undersecretary of State Sumner Welles described Stephenson's BSC when he called in the new British ambassador, Viscount Halifax, to his State Department office on February 18, 1942.[1] The tall, stoop-shouldered, sixty-year-old Edward Frederick Lindley Wood, First Earl of Halifax, born on the family estate in England's West Country, was an aristocrat to the core who inherited his father's title following the deaths of his three older brothers. His grandfather once served in the British cabinet as secretary of state for India. A withered right arm from birth was no impediment to pursuit of his two passions, riding horses and fox hunting, both of which he did at every opportunity. After completing Eton he attended Christ Church College, Oxford, where he completed a degree in modern history. Later he became a Fellow at All Souls College, a position he held until 1906. In 1910 Halifax won election to the House of Commons representing the Conservative region of Ripon for the next fifteen years. The First World War interrupted his political career when he enlisted as a captain in a local regiment, the Queen's Own Yorkshire Dragoons. In 1925 he was appointed Viceroy to India, serving in Delhi until 1931 when he returned to London to take up new duties as Secretary of State for War, Lord Privy Seal, and Lord President of Council. In February 1938, following the abrupt resignation of Anthony Eden, Halifax was appointed as Foreign Secretary by Prime Minister Neville Chamberlain, a position he held until the sudden death of the popular Marquess of Lothian in December 1941, upon which Prime Minister Winston Churchill named him ambassador to Washington. The new ambassador arrived in regal style in January 1942 aboard the new British battleship *HMS George V,* which cruised up Chesapeake Bay to Annapolis, Maryland, where, in a rare departure from traditional diplomatic protocol, President Roosevelt boarded the great warship to personally greet the new ambassador.[2]

Halifax was "by no means a natural candidate" for his new role as Britain's senior diplomatic representative to Washington, wrote his official biographer.[3] His four years at the helm of British foreign policy while Hitler gobbled up Europe raised a faint odor of appeasement in the nostrils of his new American hosts. His utterly aristocratic demeanor coupled with a well-deserved reputation for snobbery made his early days in Washington very difficult. A series of calamitous public relations gaffes, including sensational newspaper photos of the ambassador fox hunting in the nearby Virginia countryside while his countrymen suffered at home, only reinforced these impressions. When one British wag who had just returned home from the United States was asked how the new ambassador was getting along, he responded, "Oh, he's doing famously! His popularity has risen from zero to the freezing point."[4]

State Department suspicions went far beyond Halifax's personality and foibles. President Roosevelt's long-serving secretary of state, Cordell Hull, had just weeks earlier threatened to resign over the belief that the British government, particularly Churchill, had "double-crossed him." Hull's feud began shortly after the prime minister's arrival in Washington on December 22 for the start of the Acadia Conference, convened to address for the first time joint military policy. When concern was raised about an important radio antenna array on the islands of St. Pierre and Miquelon, two small fishing islands of no strategic value off the coast of Newfoundland under Vichy French control, Canada, Britain, and the United States agreed to postpone any decision to seize them until after further discussion. Days later Admiral Emile Muselier, head of Free French Naval Forces and commander of a small French flotilla assisting Canadian naval forces in the region, suddenly seized the islands under orders from his superior, Charles de Gaulle, the head of Free French Forces. Two weeks later speaking in Ottawa, Churchill heaped scorn on the Vichyites, which, for some unknown reason, caused Hull's "rage to mount to hurricane proportions" and led to "some blunt conversation" between the two men.[5] Hull later wrote: "As for myself the refusal of the president to bring more pressure on Mr. Churchill to clarify the relations between Great Britain and the United States with regard to de Gaulle and Vichy was one of several factors that almost caused me to resign as Secretary of State in January 1942. I so seriously considered resigning that I penciled out a note to the President tendering my resignation."[6]

It was in this atmosphere that Welles complained to Halifax that Stephenson's men were "shadowing a high official of the United States Government" at a moment when congressional legislation was pending that could have a far-reaching impact on British government representation in the

United States.[7] It was a Senate amendment to the Foreign Agents Registration Act introduced by Senator Kenneth McKellar, a conservative Tennessee Democrat and early New Deal supporter, now an opponent of the president over his creation of the Tennessee Valley Authority. If passed, the amendment would have forced the British government to register Stephenson's organization and its personnel with the Department of Justice by amending the Foreign Agents Registration Act passed in 1938. The bill was designed to

> protect the national defense, internal security and foreign relations of the United States by requiring public disclosure by persons engaging in propaganda activities and other activities for or on behalf of foreign governments, foreign political parties, and other foreign participants so that the Government and the people of the United States may be informed of the identity of such persons and may apprise their statements and actions in light of their associations and activities.[8]

The flare-up originally began on February 13 when Edward Tamm notified Adolf Berle that a BSC operative named Payne was seeking embarrassing information on him for passage to U.S. newspapers in the hope of forcing him from the State Department. The recent month-long surveillance of Payne began when a source reported his attempt to recruit him for information. Through the source, the FBI played Payne along with worthless information about Berle that would satisfy BSC without attracting suspicion from the Bureau. Using aliases such as "Dillon" and "Berhardt," Payne also directed the source against a Danish newspaper reporter who was under FBI investigation for passing information to the Germans about British merchant ship movements, withholding information about an individual under FBI investigation for embezzlement, and another person suspected of selling identification of Nazi spies to the New York City police. Other more onerous orders included tracking the activities of Percy Foxworth, the head of the FBI's New York office and one of Hoover's deputies.[9]

Armed with overwhelming evidence, Hoover ordered Foxworth to question Stephenson about Payne. The surprised BSC boss explained that Payne was assigned to his "uptown" office; he had known the source for a year but had been under Stephenson's instruction to avoid contact with him. In an effort to smooth over the problem, he then offered his full assurances that Payne would have no further contact with the source. On February 8, 1942, Foxworth again spoke to Stephenson; this time informing him that the investigation had further revealed Payne's attempt to smear a senior

Edward Allen Tamm. Hoover's number three man and manager of the FBI's day-to-day wartime investigative operations. *FBI*

U.S. government official, which the FBI found "obnoxious" and outside the scope of BSC's mission. Foxworth then ordered his removal from the United States. Boxed in with nowhere to turn and hoping to avoid worsening a bad situation, Stephenson complied. Twenty-four hours later Payne was in Canada.[10]

Berle's duties included intelligence liaison with the military services, the Department of Justice, and the FBI. In recent weeks he had been following congressional action on the McKellar bill. The British opposed the measure, fearing that its passage would jeopardize their intelligence activities. Berle, a supporter of the bill, viewed it as a necessary step in formalizing the British-American intelligence relationship now that the two countries were allied in common cause against the Axis. No purpose was served by further prewar British skullduggery before Pearl Harbor when they were "naturally looking out for themselves." Even more worrisome, Berle warned, was the ever-present possibility that British intelligence could quickly turn from spying on the Germans to eavesdropping on the United States, a concern to which America, "as a sovereign country, would be bound to object."[11]

The day after Tamm's briefing, Berle called a British embassy official into his office to complain about BSC's outrageous behavior. In light of the "superior importance of the present crisis," Berle wanted to "bury the incident as rapidly as possible in complete oblivion and to forget about it myself." Doing so, however, meant getting the ambassador's "personal word" that BSC would be brought under control and no further incidents would occur. When nothing was heard after three days, Berle issued another request for assurances with his guarantee that the incident "as far as I am concerned is closed."[12]

After ten days of chilly British embassy silence, Biddle entered the fray by hosting a meeting in his DOJ office suite to discuss the next step. Making up the group was Major General Raymond E. Lee, head of the army's Military Intelligence Division, Admiral Theodore Wilkinson, the new director of the Office of Naval Intelligence, Hoover, and Berle. Reiterating a concern voiced to Biddle two weeks earlier, Hoover explained that BSC's unchecked activities, which were contrary to the "community of interests" then existing between the United States and Great Britain, could create a whole range of disastrous consequences to a wartime alliance still in its infancy. Aside from posing a potential danger to U.S. intelligence and counterintelligence operations, they could expose U.S. officials to severe criticism if BSC's mistakes or carelessness became public knowledge. After citing the Payne incident, Hoover warned that avoidance of such a problem required a major change in BSC's relationship with the new wartime U.S. government that necessitated "strong and complete administrative control and supervision . . . over the activities of the British Intelligence Service operating in this country." For Hoover this meant tightening the restrictions on activities of all foreign intelligence services in the United States while limiting them to a "purely liaison" function. All expressed serious concern about BSC's status in the United States: its ballooning secret intelligence organization, its use of "undercover men" and "unscrupulous informants," and its transmission of thousands of encoded cables monthly through an FBI-controlled radio station. While all agreed that protests would have little effect on the British, the consensus was, nonetheless, for Biddle to kick the matter up to the White House for the president's consideration. Berle later recorded the hope that Roosevelt would approve a request for a meeting with Halifax where Biddle could "protest against the situation most vigorously."[13]

At the February 18 meeting Halifax told Welles that Stephenson had nothing to do with Payne's actions but ordered him out of the country when he learned of his behavior. Welles crisply replied that the FBI discovered Payne's actions, the FBI brought the matter to the BSC head's attention, and Hoover ordered his departure. Unwilling to allow the matter to drop, Welles then insisted on a "round-table conference" where Halifax together with other government agencies could attempt a resolution of the issue. Three weeks later, Halifax with Sir Ronald Campbell, his Deputy Chief of Mission, met with Biddle and Berle at the State Department. Biddle opened the discussion by noting that the "President and the Cabinet were both unhappy" about the BSC's status and were anxious for adjustments. Among the changes offered by the attorney general was the limitation of BSC "to a strictly liaison role, which included the probability of a new man to head it." Digging in his heels, Halifax told the attorney general (Hoover's boss) that the BSC was "working in the closest harmony" with the FBI and undertaking no action without Hoover's authorization. Berle then placed a telephone call to his FBI director for clarification. Mincing no words, Hoover relayed through Berle to Halifax that he did not know what Stephenson and his staff were doing, that he was rarely informed of their activities. BSC officers illegally tapped telephone conversations of Americans and grabbed British sailors out of bars in U.S. port cities, forcing them back onto British ships for internment in England. He too reminded Halifax that the FBI brought the Payne incident to the attention of Stephenson and Hoover, who gave orders for Payne's departure from the United States to the BSC chief. When Halifax asked if Stephenson should remain as head of BSC, Hoover demurred, claiming that while he had "pleasant personal relations with Stephenson . . . [he] did not, however, feel [he was] on terms of such confidence with the organization or with Mr. Stevenson [*sic*] as to make close working relations possible." Faced with these new facts, Halifax acknowledged that his "mental structure" was altered by the revelations of FBI and BSC disharmony. Perhaps in an effort to distance himself from the BSC, Halifax explained that the British intelligence system was headed by Stuart Menzies, who was under the nominal authority of the Foreign Office but not a public figure. He answered to Foreign Secretary Anthony Eden, who "did not usually interest himself much in the matter." Biddle, who had started the meeting, now ended it by insisting that Halifax provide him with a list of all the men and women employed by BSC together with a detailed statement of activities engaged in by BSC. Biddle closed the meeting with the observation to Halifax that the statements made by Stephenson (to Halifax) that BSC was simply a liaison service "simply did not correspond to the facts."[14]

At the ambassador's insistence, the three men met again a week later at the British embassy. Halifax conceded a "wide diversity" of views between Hoover and Stephenson and then stunned his two listeners by saying that the BSC had done nothing "except with the direct authority and cooperation of American officials," concluding that this must be "taken as established fact." Biddle and Berle "looked a little blankly at each other" at Halifax's dismissal of Hoover's position, leading the attorney general to explain that the Department of Justice was the sole authority in this matter working through Hoover, who knew little of what Stephenson was doing and could not be said to have approved it.[15]

When the ambassador insisted on his point, the attorney general questioned the size of BSC's American operation by asking him why the FBI radio set up in Maryland with British intelligence headquarters in London was sending and receiving two to three hundred messages a week. Halifax replied that "quite frankly, he did not know." When questioned about Stephenson's claim that these cipher messages were kept from the FBI because they contained highly confidential messages between Churchill and the president, Halifax said that Stephenson denied ever making such a statement to Hoover. Biddle then produced a July 1941 FBI report in which Stephenson claimed this very reason for refusing to supply the codes to American officials. When Halifax insisted on the continuation of the secret radio communication, the attorney general insisted on receipt of decrypted copies of these messages by the Department of Justice. Halifax politely responded that such messages were none of the attorney general's business. An angry Biddle warned the ambassador that this radio station was set up and operated by the FBI for the British as a gesture of "American hospitality—American license and that it could be terminated at anytime." When Halifax cited the diplomatic principle recognizing that messages of this sort could be sent without interference, Berle reminded him that the United States had always recognized an embassy's right to send encrypted communications but not in the FBI/BSC situation. Halifax replied that Colonel Donovan claimed this right in Britain, to which Berle countered that unlike Stephenson, Donovan's operation in London was attached to the embassy, which was responsible for their messages. In his continued efforts to parry, the ambassador noted that many of these issues had been cleared with Colonel

Donovan and indicated his surprise that the Department of State was not aware of this fact. Biddle responded that it was unnecessary for him to consult with Donovan because he was responsible for foreign espionage while internal security rested with the Department of Justice. Halifax rejected the attorney general's claim, charging that Donovan did have internal jurisdiction through his efforts to recruit personnel for overseas assignments, his use of British intelligence personnel, and the fact that British intelligence personnel were on Donovan's payroll. An increasingly exasperated Biddle retorted that his charter did not cover internal espionage operations and furthermore did not permit the British to conduct investigations on American soil without the knowledge and authorization of American government officials. In the end no agreement was reached except that BSC should act in strictly a liaison capacity and that Hoover and Stephenson should meet to straighten out matters between them.[16]

On March 19, four days before the Senate Judiciary Committee began considering McKellar's bill, Hoover and Stephenson met to hammer out matters. After some tense discussion Hoover set forth the requirements for BSC's operating parameters in the United States. Stephenson agreed that BSC would act only in a liaison capacity through the FBI and provide a complete list of all their employees and informants updated on a regular basis to the Department of Justice. All information collected by BSC which was of interest to the British together with information concerning South and Central America and the Caribbean would also be passed to the FBI. Finally, Hoover insisted that in view of the FBI's continued role in serving as BSC's radio communicating service, the full *en-clair* text of all messages must be provided as well. While Stephenson agreed to all these points, it is doubtful that either man believed they would be fulfilled.[17]

After returning to London from a trip to the United States in late March 1942, one of Ned Reid's first priorities was a visit to MI5 headquarters for a chat with his cousin, Guy Liddell. Forty-year-old Edward James Reid (Ned to his friends) was born in 1902 into a world of privilege and wealth. His father was James Reid, the personal physician to Queen Victoria; his mother was the daughter of the fabulously wealthy merchant banker Edward Baring, the first Baron Revelstoke. Queen Victoria's son, the future King Edward VII, offered himself as Ned's godfather; a few years later Ned served as a page for King George V. After graduating from Cambridge University in 1922 he joined Baring Brothers, and a year later he became a second baronet on the death of his father, followed three years later with his election to a

D. Milton Ladd. FBI agent who served as assistant director of the Bureau's National Defense Division during World War II. *FBI*

Baring directorship and a partnership in 1928. During the war his facility in the German language together with his remarkable financial acumen proved very valuable for British intelligence. At the time he met with Liddell in March 1942, Reid was acting in the highly sensitive role of financial advisor to MI5.[18]

Guy Liddell was, in the words of one renowned historian, "unquestionably . . . the pre-eminent counter-intelligence officer of his generation, respected by his adversaries and admired by his subordinates."[19] He was born in London in 1892, one of three sons born to Captain Augustus Liddell, an officer of the Royal Artillery, and his wife, Emily. All three Liddell boys were educated at the University of Angers in western France, where they acquired fluency in both French and German. Entering the Great War as a private, Guy rose to officer rank, winning the Military Cross for bravery in battle. In 1919 he joined London's Metropolitan Police as a counterintelligence officer in the Directorate of Intelligence, serving under the legendary Sir Basil

Thompson, a former prime minister of Tonga, the director of Dartmoor Prison, and a power grabber who was fired in 1921 for planning a domestic intelligence service that he hoped would absorb the responsibilities of Scotland Yard's Special Branch and MI5. In May 1924 Liddell coordinated the police raid on ARCOS, the Soviet trading organization in London. In 1931 he transferred to MI5 when Parliament passed the Treaty of Westminster. His growing concern about the Soviet espionage threat was confirmed when his source, Olga Gray, gained the confidence of Sir Percy Glading, head of the British Communist Party, and learned about his recruitment of espionage agents who transmitted confidential Woolwich Arsenal documents through him to Moscow. In 1940 Liddell became director of B Division, MI5's counterespionage element, replacing Brigadier Jasper Harker. His boss, David Petrie, director general of MI5, years later described him as "a storehouse of a vast amount of knowledge on all aspects of security past & present & in him the Service has for years had an invisible asset of value above that of any Registry."[20]

Colleagues and friends of Liddell were fairly consistent in their descriptions of his personality. He was an outgoing man with a garrulous personality who loved parties, an excellent dancer who could amuse friends with an Irish jig when gently encouraged. As a gifted cellist, he played for his own personal enjoyment and relaxation from the pressures of his work. For years he was a member of a quartet which played regularly around London. His devotion to the instrument so was deep that decades later he still joked about keeping three cellos hidden at strategic locations throughout the United Kingdom so one would always be available if war forced his evacuation from London.[21]

His life changed in 1926 when he entered a calamitous marriage to Calypso Baring, the eldest daughter of Lord Revelstoke (the son of Baron Revelstoke, thus making Guy and Ned Reid cousins by marriage). It was a union which produced four children before Calypso abandoned Guy with the children for California, where she moved in with her half-brother Lorrilard (Larry) Tailor. With no family, Liddell became an increasingly lonely figure isolated from friends, living in the London house he had shared with Calypso at Richmond Court, Sloane Street, and plunging more and more deeply into his MI5 duties to fill his time and relieve his depression.[22]

Reid had been in New York for weeks working with BSC in connection with the British Treasury and Special Operations Executive, all the while witnessing the battle that was brewing between Stephenson and Hoover. Reid described Stephenson's operation and his relationship with Donovan, which was very close. On the other hand his dealings with Hoover and key State Department officials were severely strained and rapidly deteriorating. Reid explained that the rift had been simmering for months, but when the FBI discovered Payne's investigation of Berle, the "balloon went up."[23]

Liddell, who was eager for improved sharing arrangements with the FBI, started planning a trip to the United States to make his own assessment of the Hoover-Stephenson relationship. By December 1941, MI5 was growing increasingly confident that Germany had no active spies on British soil, and those agents on the continent preparing for intelligence missions would be quickly caught thanks to Intelligence Service Oliver Strachey and Intelligence Service Knox. (For a description of ISK and ISOS, see chapter 9.) By April 1942, Thomas Argyll Robertson, a senior MI5 officer and head of B1(a) who managed all double agents, could categorically claim this as a certainty. An essential feature of an effective double agent program was the careful passage over a long period time of valid information cleverly mixed with fabricated data in order to mislead, redirect, and confuse the enemy service. To accomplish this complex task the British government set up what became known as the Double Cross System at the start of the war. The Twenty Committee emerged out of the Wireless Board (or W Board), originally formed in September 1940 at the suggestion of the Director of Military Intelligence to direct the dissemination of false information to the enemy. It was originally composed of the three Directors of Military Intelligence, MI6, MEW, and MI5 as represented by Guy Liddell, who as head of B1(a), the counterespionage branch, played the largest role. W Board members were senior ranking officers with many and varied responsibilities, a dilemma which often absented many of them from meetings where important decisions were required. This led to the creation of the Twenty Committee to act as a subcommittee made up of members of the War Office, General Headquarters (GHQ), Home Forces, the Home Defense Executive, Air Ministry Intelligence, NID, MI6, and elements of the Air Ministry responsible for dummy airfields and targets, with MI5 serving as the chairman and corresponding secretary for the committee. In March 1942 the committee made the monumental decision that no information destined for passage to the Germans should be sent without first being considered by the committee. The Twenty Committee, which held 226 meetings during the war, remained in existence until June 1945. "It thus exercised a steady and consistent supervision of all double agent work throughout the last four and half years of the war."[24]

In January 1941 the Twenty Committee began meeting weekly to review

Guy Liddell. Legendary British counterintelligence officer who relentlessly lobbied for direct MI5 relations with the FBI. *British Crown Copyright*

the activities of controlled German agents and then decide "what information could safely be allowed to be passed to the Germans, and what could not—in other words to assess the probable gain of a proposed release against the loss involved in supplying a particular piece of information to the enemy." It acted as a clearinghouse where the work of the double agents was compared to ensure consistency and reconcile the information needs of the key ministries relying on the system.[25]

Liddell arrived in the United States in late May 1942 for a personal six-week survey of BSC, with particular attention to improving the flow of information between MI5 and the FBI. His first visit to America was in the spring of 1938 when he met FBI officials concerning Gustave Rumrich, a

U.S. army deserter involved in a major German espionage ring. On June 3 Liddell, together with BSC's Washington liaison, Walter Bell, initiated a series of discussions with FBI officials beginning with Edward Tamm, the FBI's number-three man and assistant to the director. Born in St. Paul, Minnesota, in April 1906, Tamm had spent much of his early life in Montana where his father worked as an agent for the Chicago, Milwaukee, and St. Paul Railroad Company. After high school he briefly attended Mt. St. Charles College in Helena, worked as a railroad clerk during the summer, and then went on to the University of Montana at Missoula for pre-legal courses in anticipation of law studies. In 1928 he entered Georgetown University, graduating fourth in his class two years later with his law degree. In June 1930 he was awarded second place for the Charles Hamilton Prize with his essay on legal ethics. Six months later he joined the FBI as a Special Agent. In 1948, following his nomination for a federal judgeship by President Truman, Tamm explained his decision to join the FBI to a Senate panel as a matter of economic necessity. "The year 1930 was economically a very difficult year," he testified, "particularly for young graduates of law school. . . . The best offer I could get was [five dollars] a month which I considered long and long [until] the offer was made to me by Mr. Hoover." After three weeks of training he was assigned for two months to San Antonio and then to Kansas City. He was soon promoted to the position of Assistant Special Agent in Charge in New York City, and then moved on to Pittsburgh as Special Agent in Charge before returning to Washington in 1934, where he quickly rose to the post of Assistant to the Director in January 1941, overseeing the day-to-day aspects of the FBI's far-flung investigative work. Tamm met daily with Hoover, often serving as acting director during the latter's absences from Washington and representing him at conferences around the country and at high-level White House meetings. Tamm was even a member of the Justice Department's War Policy Committee along with both the assistant to the attorney general and the solicitor general, Charles Fahy.[26]

Tamm and Liddell had a wide-ranging conversation about enemy alien matters and differences between British and U.S. laws regarding enemy aliens, particularly the newly passed British Alien Order of the Defense Regulations. Tamm expressed surprise at the absence of enemy sabotage. Reports of fires and explosions reaching the FBI were "extremely crude," leading his staff to speculate that these amateurish acts were German efforts to mislead authorities for reasons unknown. Liddell echoed similar MI5 doubts, speculating that while German sabotage was "well conceived and well planned," its efficiency of action was seriously lacking. Liddell met with Kit Carson, the assistant director in charge of the FBI's Special Intelligence Service, created in July 1940. They shared views on the interrogation of the German spy Albrecht Engels, who was arrested by Brazilian police and brought to the United States for internment, and Werner Nicolaus, arrested by Mexican authorities before a similar trip to a U.S. prison camp. Carson eagerly sought Liddell's help in gaining MI5 support for keeping German intelligence agents who had been arrested in South America imprisoned in the United States. Hoover was having difficulty with the Department of State on this issue, and the hope was that MI5 could help strengthen the Bureau's hand in this matter. Worries about the Abwehr's use of the Spanish Consul-General in the United States diplomatic pouch and the growing Allied shipping losses in the Caribbean were also reviewed. Carson attributed the attacks to "extremely" accurate information relayed from agents in the Western Hemisphere to German submarines prowling the Atlantic waters.[27]

The next morning Liddell met with the head of the National Defense Division, D. Milton Ladd, who was responsible for all counterintelligence operations and investigations. Known to his friends as Mickey, he was a confident, stocky, forty-four-year-old lawyer and Bureau veteran of fourteen years who was fairly at ease in his role as the manager of counterintelligence investigations and operations, having been around official Washington for more than twenty years. He was born in 1903 in the frigid, hardscrabble region of Fargo, North Dakota, where the average temperature over the long, cold winter was four degrees below zero, alternating with summers ranging from warm to hot and humid. The eldest of eight children, he attended local schools until his move to the nation's capital at the age of sixteen when his father, Edwin Fremont Ladd, an agricultural chemist, then serving as the president of North Dakota Agricultural College, was elected as a Republican to the U.S. Senate. Mickey began college at George Washington University majoring in chemistry, a pursuit that ended abruptly for reasons unknown in 1924. During his father's Senate career (1921–1926), he learned a great deal about the workings of official Washington as an operator of the subway that ran under the capitol building, as an aide in his father's Senate office, as a clerk on the Committee for Public Lands chaired by his father, and as a physical trainer and woodworking instructor at a local Washington school. In 1925 he returned to the university, graduating with a law degree, and was admitted to the District of Columbia Bar in 1928. Decades later he told a journalist that he joined the FBI in 1928 merely to develop some maturity and with no intentions of making a career at the Bureau. Soon, however, he was hooked because, as liked to say, "when you find something that you love to talk about you might as well stick with it."[28]

Liddell offered him a list of the current cases underway in Britain together with data about codes and secret inks, which Ladd greatly appreciated. Ladd then raised his suspicions about Britain's uncanny knowledge of U.S. secrets, pointing particularly to the B-25 bomber raid on Tokyo led by Colonel James Doolittle just six weeks earlier. Before the raid was launched, BSC requested that an FBI double agent pass information to the Germans about an impending American air attack on the Japanese home islands in the hope of relieving growing pressure on British naval forces in Burma and the Indian Ocean. As Liddell later said, "Tokyo was bombed three days later." Ladd questioned how the British knew about the bombing and where the possible leak may have occurred. Ladd's sour mood was undoubtedly affected by the increasingly hopeless military situation in the Philippines with General MacArthur's desperate defense at Corregidor coming to a tragic end. Adding to his gloom was recognition that the loss would mean the immediate capture and execution of FBI-trained Nisei from Hawaii who had been sent to the Philippines to infiltrate and report on the Japanese population. Ladd complained that no microdots were coming from the United States, nor was there any evidence of Italian espionage surfacing through FBI investigations. After a review of double agent matters, the conversation turned to the cases of two German agents traveling through Gibraltar with plans and photographs, who were later arrested in the United States. Liddell then requested that British authorities be given access to them so that they could interrogate them concerning matters possibly pertaining to British security. With preliminary issues behind them Liddell then got to the heart of his visit: MI5's interest in developing a sharing arrangement "on the broadest possible basis" concerning German and Japanese intelligence issues, a concern that would be dealt with in earnest over the next few weeks of his stay.[29]

R. P. Kramer and Harry Kimball were next on Liddell's agenda. To break the ice Kramer joked that he was of pure German descent and that his grandfather had served as one of the kaiser's bodyguards. Liddell than discussed the workings of the recently developed Double Cross System and the Twenty Committee that was set up to manage the operation. Since the start of the war MI5 had recruited a sizable stable of double agents from the German agents captured trying to secretly enter the British Isles. Yet in the words of J. C. Masterman, MI5 only became "dimly, very dimly" aware that in fact they controlled the entire German intelligence system in January 1941; at the time they were still fixated on the fear that many uncontrolled German spies were still on the loose in the British Isles. From the early days of the war, Liddell explained, the British strategy called for the use of controlled agents to uncover Axis agents. As confidence grew and the need for deception increased before the anticipated fall 1942 Allied invasion of North Africa, B1(a) thinking switched from an emphasis on security to deceiving the enemy. MI5 had already started selecting high-quality agents for passage of believable deception, which would cause Germany and its Italian ally to make erroneous assessments that would lead to incorrect strategic military dispositions. He then went into detail about the origins of the Double Cross, its emergence from the Wireless Board, its makeup, including MI5 case officers who personally worked with the military services representatives, and government ministries that would provide the genuine and fictitious material for passage. Careful and frequent coordination was essential for ensuring that everyone was cognizant of any new German instructions that could signal suspicions of the agent or new or unanticipated moves by the enemy. This type of constant analysis, comparison, and rethinking in a group setting was essential not only at the strategic level but tactically by determining which double agent was best suited for originating certain deception material.[30]

Another essential feature of the system was the agent's living arrangements; the agent's case officer lived with the agent and was responsible for his domestic existence, ensuring that deceptive and accurate messages sent to the enemy were consistent with the agent's personality, intelligence, educational level, and imaginary access. Kimball was quick to grasp the implications of the system and the necessity of securing the cooperation of the military. The meeting ended with Kimball explaining the discovery of microfilm in the toe of Nicolaus's boot describing the plans for an escape device from the latest American submarine. Kimball was pleased by the evidence, which they hoped to use in their struggle with the Department of State over the detention of enemy aliens from South America suspected of connections with German intelligence.[31]

While in Washington, Liddell lunched with Wyndham Bruce, an assistant RCMP commissioner, then serving in Washington as liaison with the FBI. Wyndham Valentine McMaster Bruce was born on May 3, 1887, and

Wyndham Bruce. Assistant Commissioner, Royal Canadian Mounted Police. As the RCMP wartime liaison officer in Washington, he secretly kept Hoover informed about BSC criticisms of the FBI. *Royal Canadian Mounted Police*

joined the Royal North-West Mounted Police in June 1910. Six years later he resigned to accept a job in the Canadian Forestry Service, returning to the force less than a year later with an assignment to Herschel Island in Canada's Arctic region. While still in the Force he volunteered for Canadian military service during the First World War, which led him into the Canadian Special Expeditionary Force and a year-long assignment to Siberia in 1918. For his service Bruce received the British War Medal and the Victory Medal. After the war he started a slow ascent through the ranks beginning with his commissioning as an Inspector in February 1920 and a series of assignments at Brandon, Manitoba; Lethbridge, Alberta; Whitehorse, Yukon; and Fredericton, New Brunswick, where he headed "J Division" as commanding officer of the province. In early 1942 he was transferred to Ottawa headquarters where he was immediately assigned to Washington as the RCMP liaison with the FBI.[32]

"I asked him to tell me quite frankly what the FBI thought of [the British]," Liddell later recorded, prompting Bruce's caution that his comments should remain "strictly confidential" and unattributed. The FBI was very suspicious of the British, particularly BSC, believing they were "cagey" and that they only reluctantly shared information. When the FBI would ask for information about BSC requests for investigation, BSC tended to answer with evasiveness and obscure reasons, which only deepened Hoover's suspicion of British motives. By contrast, Bruce explained, the RCMP completely trusted Hoover, who had always given Commissioner Wood his "fullest cooperation," including direct access to raw FBI files. Liddell appreciated that "in many ways he was quite right" about British caginess, telling Bruce that he hoped his visit could serve as a corrective. When Liddell then asked how Hoover would receive an MI5 offer for a representative assigned to liaison with the Bureau, akin to the RCMP, Bruce suggested that such an offer would be favorably received. Liddell's day ended with a long and leisurely dinner with Carson, who was eager to visit London to study British counterintelligence methods firsthand. Three days of constant conferences with FBI officials made an impression on Liddell. On June 7 he wrote to his MI5 bosses in London urging them to pursue every effort toward a relationship "as free and frank in our exchanges of information as possible."[33]

After an overnight train trip to Ottawa, Liddell and Bell began a series of meetings starting with Stuart Wood, the RCMP commissioner. Their conversations touched on a variety of matters, including detention of enemy aliens and the conflict with the existing Canadian law, double agent cases jointly controlled by RCMP and BSC, and the introduction of the Double Cross concept. He urged Wood to develop four or five high-grade double agents in conjunction with the FBI as an effective tool against foreign intelligence penetration. The FBI could also develop some very good candidates who could then move to Canada for effective counterintelligence coverage in the United States and Canada. Wood grasped the significance of this suggestion, telling Liddell that he would begin conversations with the FBI at the first opportunity.[34]

What Liddell most likely had in mind was Springbok, a double agent who had recently arrived in Canada and whose handler was William Stephenson's longtime friend Tommy Drew-Brook. Springbok was the code name for Hans von Kotze, a German who immigrated to South Africa in 1929. Hoping to avoid confinement as an enemy alien, von Kotze moved to Portuguese East Africa, where his later expulsion forced him to flee to Europe. In July 1940 Kotze was jailed in German-occupied Morocco after his ship was captured by a German raider in the South Atlantic. Only after agreeing to serve as an Abwehr agent in June 1941 was he released and sent to Brazil to set up a cover business supporting the Albrecht Engels espionage network. After receiving orders to move back to South Africa, he volunteered his services to the British in exchange for a British passport after the war and reunion with his wife and children, who were still interned in South Africa. Springbok supplied a wealth of information concerning codes, ciphers, personalities, and the inner workings of the Engels Brazilian ring. When Liddell arrived in the United States von Kotze had only been resettled in Canada for two months; perhaps Liddell was thinking of using him in the Double Cross System that he was discussing with the Canadians and Americans.[35]

On June 16 Liddell was again back in Washington for three more days of meetings with the FBI. This time he began with Edward Coffey, the FBI man in charge of the Laboratory Division, which handled scientific specimen analysis, radio engineering and research, cryptography, and clandestine support (including secret inks, covert photography, and concealment devices). Liddell shared insights with him about a "very ingenious" hand code used by Dr. Hilaire Anton Weber, posing as a Dr. Westerlinck, a Dutch ship's physician from Antwerp and agent of the Abwehr's naval division who first came to MI5's attention in 1940 in Lisbon for encouraging desertion among sailors in exchange for return to their homes. Weber and his family were removed from a ship sailing to the Belgian Congo in April 1942 and taken to London, where the ingredients for secret inks were discovered during a routine search of their luggage. Upon arrival Weber quickly confessed, offering the possibility of his use as a Double Cross agent. They also shared code data and a book entitled *Elementary Crypto-Analysis* by Helen Fouche Gaines, which the American Photographic Publishing Company of Boston published in 1939 and which the FBI seized from a German spy. Arrangements were quickly made for distribution of this material to British censorship points.[36]

Liddell was next escorted into an unproductive meeting with Hoover, whom he characterized as a cordial, nonstop-talking "prima donna type" whose mind seemed fixated on relations with other government departments. That evening over dinner, Kimball, "bursting with keenness and longing to come over to England," confided that he had already taken steps toward planning a Double Cross System as suggested by Liddell and was interested in Ladd visiting London as a remedy for his suspicions and improving FBI-MI5 relations. Liddell concurred, believing that "if [Ladd] could be convinced of our sincerity I think things would go better." The next morning he toured the FBI training facility at the Marine Corp base in Quantico, Virginia, followed by a second meeting in Tamm's office where the two men initialed a five-point sharing agreement. Without reference to other parties, both services would exclusively exchange confidential information: the exchange of names and references in microdots and secret writing, the exchange of traffic in all double-agent cases of mutual interest, collaboration in running double agents, and finally the right to interrogate persons of mutual interest.[37]

Before his departure for home, Liddell met in New York with Percy Foxworth, FBI agent George McSwayne, who was handling the Dusko Popov double agent case (see chapter 10), and Benjamin deForest Bayle, BSC's director of communications and second in charge of the organization. The thirty-nine-year-old Bayle, known to all as Pat, was born in London, Ontario, and grew up in Moose Jaw, Saskatchewan, where his father was a medical officer. As a boy isolated in a remote region of Canada he helped start 10AB, Moose Jaw's first amateur radio station, broadcasting church services and other events. Having no interest in a legal career despite having earned a law degree at the age of twenty from the University of Saskatchewan at Saskatoon, he enrolled in the electrical engineering program at the University of Toronto, where he so excelled that he was asked to teach fourth-year students while still in his third year of study. After graduation he stayed on at the university as a professor for the remainder of the decade while also serving as a consultant for the National Electric Corporation (NEC). When the war started, the NEC assigned him to design specialized antennas and bomb racks for planes using classified French blueprints covertly obtained by the FBI.[38]

His growing reputation as a radio engineering expert soon caught the attention of British intelligence officials, who arranged in November 1941 for his travel to London where he met Stewart Menzies, the head of MI6. Visits were soon arranged to Bletchley Park where he observed firsthand the cryptographic attack on the Nazi Enigma then in full throttle. Gordon Welchman, one of Britain's great cryptographic heroes and head of the legendary "Hut Six," which broke the German army and air force ciphers, viewed Bayle as an "exuberant person with an infectious enthusiasm" and with special skills in communications security. Years later Welchman still fondly remembered how Bayle taught him "about the technology of communication and [how Welchman] taught Bayle about Bletchley Park's problems." Welchman quickly got Bayle's signature on the Official Secrets Act before sending him to New York as William Stephenson's new head of communications. His principal mission required him to harden BSC's ciphers in the wake of the new war which began on Sunday, December 7, 1941—Bayle's first day on the job. Over the next six months, Bayle discouraged Stephenson's telephone use for confidential communications "because he knew everyone would be listening." As voice scramblers then in use "weren't worth a damn," Bayle immediately made Stephenson's communications with Washington impregnable by introducing encrypted teleprinters and one-time pads.[39]

Bayle confided to Liddell his concerns about BSC "reluctance" to divulge ISOS, which was creating "a very uncomfortable" atmosphere with the FBI. Liddell learned that Bayle had told the FBI about ISOS "in strict confidence" and had told Stephenson that he had done so and was "quite ready to stand the racket" if his revelations were discovered by London. Liddell then assured him that upon his return to London he would request that Bayle take over responsibility for MI5's account within BSC and would recommend a colleague, Cyril Mills, as his assistant to pursue the Double Cross idea with the Americans.[40]

After taking the overnight train from New York to Montreal, Britain's head of counterespionage took off for home on July 8. In full flying suit he lay on a mattress in the bomb rack of an unpressurized B-26 Liberator, a mask over his face connected to an oxygen tube next to four other passengers. Remaining awake for the entire flight was a matter of life or death; falling asleep could result in a coma if he disconnected his oxygen line by rolling over. Despite the seemingly endless hours lying on his back, awake and immobile, he could console himself knowing he had achieved an agreement with the FBI and now had a better sense of BSC. All in all a "satisfactory" outcome—if "it can be lived up to by both parties."[41]

CHAPTER FOUR

Rothschild Is Coming

Back in London, Liddell found little relief after his exhausting eight-week mission to the United States and Canada. The first order of business was catching up on key developments while he was away. A top priority was a new double agent code-named "Arabel" by the Germans whom MI5 spirited into England on April 25, 1942, on a special flight from Lisbon. Arabel was Juan Pujol Garcia, a diminutive, thirty-year-old Spaniard who wished only to serve the British cause by working for the Germans in the grand hope, as he later wrote, of fighting "against all tyranny and oppression."[1] After his initial rejection by MI6 in 1941, Pujol concocted the outrageous idea of approaching the Germans in the belief that spying for them would make him more attractive to the British. For more than a year he fed the Abwehr a steady diet of fantastic lies and fabrications about British naval dispositions, which cost the German armed forces a fortune in wasted time and resources. Unbelievably, despite these continuous failures, German faith in Arabel and his information remained unshakeable.

MI5 first learned about this mysterious source in October 1941 when Bletchley Park code breakers decrypted a German message describing his successes in England operating three important sources at the strategic ports of Liverpool and Glasgow, with another in the west country. After months of turning England upside down, MI5 came to the startling conclusion that he wasn't in England at all, but actually alive and well and living quietly in Lisbon. Now safely under MI5 control with a new British code name, Garbo, Pujol would become over the next two years the central figure in a large cast of imaginary characters that would supply a vast catalogue of truth and lies, culminating later in a brilliant deception that would save the lives of thousands of soldiers and sailors on the beaches of Normandy.[2]

Between briefings and meetings, Liddell concentrated on a trip report containing his impressions of the American officials he encountered and the Anglo-American intelligence relationship. He confirmed for both Petrie and Menzies that the friction between the FBI and BSC was bad and steadily worsening. Hoover's frustration stemmed from the paucity of information he was receiving from London as well as the impression that Stephenson "did not trust" the FBI.[3] Faced with what he viewed as an irreversible situation, Liddell urged serious consideration of assigning an MI5 officer to BSC or, secondly, the establishment of an independent MI5 relationship with Hoover. Also high on his agenda was continuing the pressure on the Americans to employ double agents to mislead the Axis regarding Allied military plans. In a note to his diary he recorded importance of this tactic and the need for the FBI to begin coordinating with MI5 in the use of double agents by encouraging "the Americans to see the value of the double-cross system and to urge the FBI to greater activity." Mindful of his promise to Ladd and Kimball assuring them of MI5's honesty and candor, Liddell turned for help to one of Britain's most creative geniuses, Ewen Montagu.[4]

Montagu was a forty-two-year-old barrister, yachtsman, and Trinity College and Cambridge graduate who spent a year at Harvard in the 1920s heartily enjoying Jazz Age speakeasies while touring America from coast to coast in a private rail car, meeting and befriending an infinite number of Americans from all walks of life. Too old for active military service, he joined the Royal Naval Reserve in 1938 only to be later called up for active duty when Admiral John Godfrey, the director of naval intelligence, personally selected him for his staff. By 1942 Montagu was at the heart of the British secret intelligence establishment, responsible for selecting deception material for passage to the enemy in coordination with MI5, Bletchley Park, the service departments, and the prime minister. In the run-up to the Allied invasion of Sicily in July 1943, he teamed with his colleague Charles Cholmondeley to fool the Germans by creating the imaginary Major William Martin, which Montagu described a decade later in his book *The Man Who Never Was* and immortalized on film three years later.[5]

Liddell asked Montagu to prepare a memorandum on deception for the FBI with complete details of MI5's sources and operations. Montagu's willingness to share such sensitive British secrets with the foreign counterintelligence service of an allied country had deep personal motives for him. First, his wife was in New York working for BSC and, second, as he later wrote, "I felt a great deal of gratitude to Americans for their kindness to me and felt I should repay it in some small measure."[6] When Petrie learned of Liddell's initiative he objected to giving such detailed information to the foreign counterintelligence service of another country with no restrictions on what Hoover would do with the information. After calming his boss down, Liddell acknowledged that it was a bold step which carried "considerable risk," but he emphasized MI5's need to educate the Americans "in the value of the double-cross system since we should become more and more dependent on their co-operation."[7]

On August 21, 1942, the debate over the sharing memorandum became moot when Liddell received a shocking BSC request for arrangements for two FBI officials intent on visiting London at the "invitation of MI5." "I do not quite understand what this means," Liddell wrote, "unless it is the result of a general invitation which I gave them when I was in Washington, DC." In any case, "we will be pleased to have them." Three days later Harry Kimball and Lawrence Hince, accompanied by Walter Bell, arrived for a three-week stay.[8]

Kimball wasted no time outlining the purpose of his visit. Following their discussions two months earlier, the FBI wanted more information about the Double Cross System, sabotage, British methods for handling refugees, alien registration, passports, visas, and the unique role of Special Branch. Kimball also brought a mandate to discuss "the affairs of [the FBI] with [Liddell] and to explain Mr. Hoover's grievances" about British representation in the United States. He told Liddell that when President Roosevelt appointed William Donovan as his Coordinator of Information in 1941, Stephenson had turned over all his agents "with the connivance" of American authorities to him instead of the FBI.[9] Worse yet, Stephenson had since continued operating these agents on Donovan's behalf. Kimball criticized BSC's intelligence-gathering operations against the Spanish embassy in Washington, using a source who routinely reported their activities to the FBI. Hoover, according to Kimball, was exasperated with Stephenson and wanted nothing more to do with him. Another Kimball objective was to press for direct liaison with MI5. After explaining that his service had "nothing to hide," Liddell expressed a similar MI5 desire to arrange a "complete exchange of information with the FBI" while warning the FBI man that there were "certain sources of information which [MI5] had access but . . . was not at liberty to disclose without the concurrence of SIS."[10]

MI5 threw the doors open for the American visitors. Kimball spent considerable time with Robin "Tin-eye" Stephens, the commandant of Camp 020, or B1(e) as it was known within the Security Service. The nickname "Tin-eye" (which was never mentioned in his presence) derived from his ever-present monocle, which some wags suspected him of wearing while he slept. At forty-two years of age, Stephens had spent fourteen years with the Indian Army and later in the Judge Advocate-General's office before joining MI5. He did a stint as a journalist and was the author of a couple of law books despite a failed attempt at a law degree. Among his other talents was a knack for languages. Over the years he had become fluent in German, French, and Italian, together with passable Somali and Amharic and Urdu good enough for him to qualify as an interpreter. His many travels throughout the world had strangely infused him with many prejudices instead of enlightenment. In his world, Belgians were "overweight, weeping romantics," the French were corrupt, and Polish Jews were "shifty," while Icelanders were simply "unintelligent." Tin-eye reserved a particular dislike for Germans. Idiosyncrasies and prejudices aside, Stephens was a "remarkable judge of individual character" who constantly drilled into his interrogators the lesson that "national characteristics in spies [were] inconclusive" and that counterintelligence officers must treat "each spy as an individual case . . . a very personal enemy."[11]

Stephens tutored Kimball on the two most important steps in the process of identifying German spies and deploying the Double Cross System. The first was the London Reception Center (LRC), opened in January 1941 at the Royal Victoria Patriotic School in Wandsworth, where aliens arriving from enemy territory were screened. Over the course of the war B1(d), as it was designated, processed approximately 33,000 refugees, scrutinizing their documentation, closely questioning them for personal background information, their family connections and friends, how they escaped from German-occupied Europe, and so on, and then meticulously compared their story with information gleaned from earlier LRC interrogations. By relentless questioning, re-questioning, checking, cross-checking, and rechecking, certain stories broke down and the lies revealed themselves, leading inevitably to the detainees' confession. The LRC, in the words of Sir Dick White, who later served as director general of MI5 and chief of MI6, separated the "sheep from the goats," with the goats moving on to Camp 020 under suspicion of serving the Abwehr.[12]

Camp 020 housed the "incorrigibles," both men and women who underwent rigorous interrogation in a prison-like environment. Stephens, who prohibited physical abuse, had no qualms about the use of psychological tactics. Inmates routinely experienced all sorts of mental and emotional pressure such as intimidation and personal isolation: all designed to create a sense of both helplessness and hopelessness, leading the inmate to conclude that confession was the only option. At that point MI5 would decide on the next step: imprisonment, execution, or use as a Double Cross agent.[13]

Harry Kimball. FBI agent and the National Defense Division's Espionage Section Chief. Kimball secretly visited London in August 1942 where British counterintelligence officials introduced him to the Double Cross System. *FBI*

Hoover's men received a thorough tutorial from fifty-one-year-old John Masterman, the chairman of the Double Cross Committee. A scholar educated at the Royal Naval Colleges at Osborne and Dartmouth and at Worcester College, Oxford, Masterman spent four years in the notorious Ruhleben internment camp during the First World War following his arrest in August 1914 at the University of Freiburg, where he had been studying. After the war he returned to academic life, teaching modern history at Christ Church, Oxford, where he routinely enjoyed the pleasures of cricket, field hockey, and tennis. Masterman offered Kimball a strategic overview of double agentry, relegating the first principles of daily management to Thomas Argyll Robertson, the head of B1(a) and the officer in charge of all of MI5's double agents. Known to all by his initials, "TAR," the thirty-three-year-old Brit, who was born in Sumatra and raised in England, attended the

Royal Military College at Sandhurst before joining the Seaforth Highlanders. His first assignment after joining MI5 in 1933 was to assess the mood of British sailors in the aftermath of the Invergordon mutiny by mingling with them in local pubs. From this humble start he matured into a highly skilled counterintelligence officer and "one of the Security Service's ablest agent runners."[14]

Robertson explained to Kimball that an important principle was to volunteer nothing through the agent. A double agent's "first duty" was to respond only to questions posed to him. In this way counterintelligence avoided enemy suspicion while guiding subsequent questions in a direction most favorable to achieving counterintelligence goals. An important corollary to this rule was the need for the double agent to supply imaginative, yet plausible reports on his day-to-day secret life behind enemy lines, logical reasons why he did or did not have access to valuable intelligence, incorporating mundane problems and crises that disrupted access to information or put it out of reach altogether. By feeding the enemy a steady stream of accurate and verifiable information, the counterintelligence service could, almost imperceptibly, maneuver the Abwehr into requesting their agents to supply information on topics which could prove useful for counterintelligence deception.[15]

Robertson also emphasized the importance of a double agent for investigating links between belligerents and neutral countries such as Spain, Portugal, Sweden, and Switzerland. Kimball and Hince learned about a Spanish espionage network involving a German agent named Miguel Piernavieja del Pozo, who arrived in London on an intelligence mission in August 1940. Posing as a journalist and observer for the Instituto de Estudios Politicos, del Pozo contacted a retired Swansee police inspector posing as G.W., whom the Abwehr thought was a "fanatical Welsh nationalist" and expert saboteur. G.W. had previously volunteered his help to MI5 when another double agent, code-named "Snow," had promised his German handler to bring a Welsh saboteur to a meeting on the continent. Both returned to England with money, instructions, and full German confidence. G.W. met del Pozo at his London flat identifying himself as a German agent working for Angel Alcazar de Velasco, a close friend of Ramon Serano Suner, the Spanish foreign minister and brother-in-law of Spain's leader, Francisco Franco. G.W. received £35,000 for details of the Welsh Nationalist movement and aircraft production, which he later turned over to the hall-porter at the Spanish embassy.[16] In a very short time, Kimball learned, G.W. painted a full and complete picture of Spanish espionage in the British Isles, leading MI5 to comment on the "remarkable fact that in the few months between September 1941 and February 1942, we . . . gained not only a general outline but a fairly precise picture of the [Spanish] Espionage network in our country."[17]

Next on the FBI list was Victor Rothschild, MI5's head of counter-sabotage who peppered Kimball for details about the eight Nazi saboteurs arrested by the FBI in June while patiently offering him insights into British counter-sabotage policies and programs. Kimball had earlier given Liddell a summary of the case, but Rothschild was keen for particulars about the case including saboteurs' backgrounds and biographies, training, and technical knowledge of the sophisticated sabotage equipment they brought with them. Kimball and Hince also received a series of MI6 briefings, the nature of which still remain unclear today.[18]

A final Kimball assignment before his return home was a personal audience with the MI6 chief, Stewart Menzies. Again, the particulars of this meeting are unknown except to note that Kimball made clear in his remarks the "grievances of the FBI." By the time they returned to the United States on September 14, both Kimball and Hince had pronounced themselves pleased with the visit and hopeful that matters would proceed "more smoothly" from then on. A final note on Kimball's historic visit came from Liddell, who summed up his own bleak view of future MI5-FBI cooperation by pointing directly to Stephenson's need to end his practice of running agents in the United States and refrain "from carrying out operations on his own in J. Edgar Hoover's territory." In despair he concluded, "I rather doubt, however, whether he will."[19]

In the weeks following Kimball's return to America, Rothschild chomped at the bit for a chance to examine firsthand the FBI's recently acquired bonanza of Germany's most advanced sabotage equipment. The cache of explosives dug up on the beaches at Amagansett, Long Island, and Jacksonville, Florida, contained seventy-three different items, including large yellow blocks of TNT, fuse lighters, thirty-caliber blasting caps, and fifteen wooden boxes filled with an assortment of detonators which Earl Connelley, the head of the investigation, called the "most impressive" collection of sabotage equipment he had ever seen.[20]

Rothschild sought David Petrie's authorization to visit Washington for consultations. When Petrie wired New York for Rothschild's travel clearances, he learned that Stephenson had rejected the request, claiming that Hoover considered his visit inconvenient at that time. Weeks later, when Rothschild bumped into Stephenson at a London hotel, the BSC boss denied any knowledge of his request for a visit, nor sending any message blocking his travel. When Petrie learned of the conversation he promptly dispatched a "strong letter" to Menzies, who then informed Liddell "off the record" that Stephenson had, in fact, sent the message in his personal cipher turning down the trip. After ordering Rothschild to pack his bags, the now furious Petrie sent a flash message to Stephenson informing him simply that "Rothschild is coming."[21]

Nathaniel Mayer Victor Rothschild was born to William Rothschild and his wife, the former Rozika Edle von Wertheinstein, in 1910. The affable young aristocrat attended Harrow and later Cambridge University, where he read physiology, French, and English while developing a wide range of friendships that included three classmates who would later become notorious in the annals of espionage as traitors spying for the Soviet Union: Guy Burgess, Anthony Blunt, and Kim Philby. Rothschild, Burgess, and Blunt were members of The Apostles, a university society of intellectuals then dominated by young Marxists, which decades later cast a shadow of suspicion over Rothschild because of his links with the so-called Cambridge Five spy ring. At the age of twenty-six, Victor inherited his family's barony and a lifetime seat in the House of Lords on the Labour Party benches. Recruited into the Security Service in 1940 by Guy Liddell on the recommendation of his assistant Anthony Blunt, Rothschild set up B1(c), the first counter-sabotage unit in MI5's history (with personal funds) in a Wormwood Scrubs prison cell. From there he managed its explosives laboratory for the remainder of the war. More than half a century later the official history of the Security Service characterized him as a man of "extraordinary bravery" who routinely risked his life defusing German bombs, a skill aided, in part, by his careful dissection of frog's eggs and sea life while an undergraduate. So scrupulous was Rothschild at keeping records that in one instance he disarmed a bomb buried in a crate of Spanish onions on a British dock—all the time "meticulously recording his every move by field telephone in case he was killed in the attempt." For this act of gallantry he received the George Medal, an award initiated by King George VI in 1940 to honor civilian "acts of great bravery."[22]

In 1940 MI5 entered into an agreement authorizing MI6 to represent the Security Service's interest in the western hemisphere. Since then MI5, and particularly Rothschild, had been embroiled in a bitter dispute with MI6 over the very poor flow of sabotage information between the two services and especially with Stephenson's BSC in New York. Whenever reports of sabotage in the United States came to his attention, requests to MI6 for further information were often delayed or ignored, creating, in Rothschild's view, a serious "lack of confidence owing to the paucity of information" passed to MI5. There was "practically no information about the various important cases which had been running in the United States," he bitterly complained, because it "sticks in the [Section V—MI6's counterintelligence branch] bottle-neck," which set itself up as the judge for "what concerns New York and London."[23]

Rothschild arrived in Washington in November 1942, where he was warmly greeted by his old friend Harry Kimball. It did not take long before he began opening up about the Security Service's struggle with MI6, including BSC's claim that the FBI had no interest in meeting him. Kimball denied the charge, explaining that Hoover, who was interested in expanding the liaison with MI5, would have insisted on arranging a program for Rothschild or any MI5 official interested in visiting.[24] Throwing discretion and caution to the wind, Rothschild viciously attacked Stephenson's trustworthiness and motives, charging that suspicions of MI6 "caginess" ran so high within MI5 that both he and Liddell never believed that FBI objections to his visit ever existed. Stunned FBI officials listened in silence as Rothschild blasted BSC for its bloated staff, its limited understanding of intelligence matters with little to do, and for harboring "extremely poor feeling by the ranking officials of Mr. Stephenson's staff in New York and Washington toward the Bureau" while courting William Donovan, because Stephenson believed he had "the President's ear." Even greater scorn was heaped on Menzies, whom Rothschild considered a weak leader with strong political contacts whom he used to offset an absence of ability. "He couldn't be a division chief in either of our organizations," Rothschild charged, "and he definitely has certain of the high-ranking influential officials in London fooled."[25]

Rothschild presented his hosts with specimens of German explosives and other material which FBI laboratory officials described as "exceedingly good." He described MI5's modest laboratory devoted strictly to the study of secret inks and its limited photographic processing capability that forced reliance on Scotland Yard's more advanced laboratory. Along with the full range of strengths and weaknesses of his counter-sabotage section, he described how technical examinations of suspected sabotage devices were conducted by carefully vetted private corporations such as the Anglo-Iranian Oil Company, which looked for the presence of sand, soaps, and other abrasives in oil; actual explosives were analyzed in university laboratories. Other British sabotage concerns included chemical and biological

Thomas Argyl "TAR" Robertson. MI5 officer and manager of the famed "Double Cross" sources who educated Harry Kimball on the strategies and tactics of the system. In 1945 Robertson was awarded the Distinguished Service Medal by President Truman for his wartime contributions. *British Crown Copyright*

warfare targeting British food stocks through the introduction of the so-called Colorado Beetle, a serious threat to potatoes, eggplants, and tomatoes, which the Germans were reportedly considering for release into the British countryside. British authorities were also making preparations for German bacteriological sabotage, which was "treated as being of the highest level of secrecy in England."[26]

The important relationship between the sabotage investigator and industrial plant security officers throughout the British Empire was also reviewed in detail. MI5 officers, carrying the title "Defence Security Officers," maintained their own staff and conducted their own inquiries while sabotage investigations in Great Britain were carried out by the police in areas under civilian control. In rare instances, special sabotage investigations had been conducted in those parts of the British Empire under military control, such as Gibraltar, where serious German and Italian sabotage was suspected.[27]

The Double Cross System, Rothschild noted, also offered opportunities to collect information about enemy sabotage techniques. In one memorable case MI5 created a phony explosion aboard a ship towed into Gibraltar in an attempt to build up a source in the eyes of the Abwehr. Local British consuls ill-equipped to protect shipping from sabotage relied on specially trained counter-sabotage squads from England traveling to Gibraltar to accompany British merchant ships destined for Spanish ports. Their focus was the prevention of Spaniards from boarding a British merchantman "with any object which might conceal a bomb, unless that person demonstrates to the guard that everything he brings on board is not a bomb." They had strict orders to prevent swimmers, small boats, or divers from approaching the ship by shooting anyone refusing an order to halt. "It may be a violation of international law," Rothschild blithely noted, "but we are prepared to take the consequences in view of the extreme dangers to British merchant shipping in Spanish ports from German saboteurs." He then confidentially mentioned "utmost secret" sources, a reference to German radio communications decrypted at Bletchley Park and passed to MI6's Section V. MI5 could not take action on this vital source of intelligence without MI6's authorization.[28]

While Rothschild was conferring with RCMP officials in Ottawa, Charles Ellis, Stephenson's principal assistant, and another MI6 officer, Walter Wren, met Wyndham Bruce for lunch in New York in an attempt to learn details about Rothschild's visit. Meeting FBI agent Arthur Thurston days later, Bruce confidentially related the details of his meeting with Ellis and Wren, describing Ellis's criticisms of FBI methods and tactics, which he claimed made it impossible for BSC to share information for fear that it would be "undoubtedly released to the newspapers." Bruce dismissed Ellis's claims by accusing BSC of a duplicity which accomplished nothing except to build FBI distrust and enmity toward them and the entire British intelligence establishment.[29]

Such BSC attitudes were not new to the FBI. Months earlier Bruce had related a similar story to Ladd about a lunch with Ellis, Wren, and Bell when Liddell visited Washington in June 1942. The thirty-three-year-old Bell was a lawyer before his initial MI6 posting to Mexico. His next assignment had been to New York City, where he had served before the war as the second in command to Paget. Bell had developed strong American connections over the years, including marriage to Katherine Spaatz, the daughter of General Andrew "Tooey" Spaatz, a West Point graduate and commander of the Eighth Air Force in England. Frustration over BSC's behavior led Bell to transfer to MI5 in 1943, where he spent the remainder of his career serving as the Security Liaison Officer in Nairobi, Nassau, and Delhi and later as the personal assistant to Sir Roger Hollis, MI5's director general.[30]

After Ellis's clumsy probe about his relationship with the FBI, the wary Bruce bluntly told him that "it appears that you are trying to ascertain what my connection with the Bureau is, and if that is what you are interested in you should ask and I will tell you." After sheepishly acknowledging this, Bruce explained that the RCMP and the FBI had developed a strong working relationship of long standing with the "utmost confidence in each other." When Wren and Ellis expressed BSC's opposite view, Bruce attributed FBI coolness to the sneaky way they had approached the Bureau, which had only weakened Hoover's confidence and trust in them. BSC often withheld vital information when requesting FBI investigations on its behalf, Bruce charged, leading to suspicions that the British did not always "lay their cards on the table and deal openly" with Hoover. Before Ellis or Wren could comment, Bell looked at them and said, "That's just what I've been trying to tell you."[31]

Charles Howard Ellis, known as Dickie to friends and colleagues, was the second son of an English-born clothing manufacturer. He was born in 1895 in Sydney, Australia, to a family that later settled in Melbourne, where he received his early education and learned the oboe sufficiently well to play with the Royal Melbourne Philharmonic Society. Later he worked as a bookseller before arriving in England just two months before the start of the First World War. Soon after enlisting in the 100th Provisional Battalion in 1915, he was promoted to the rank of corporal and shipped to France, where he was twice wounded. In September 1917, Ellis, now commissioned in the 5th Battalion of the Middlesex Division, returned to France and was wounded again. After convalescing in England, he returned to military duty escorting troops to India, acquiring proficiency along the way in Urdu, Persian, Russian, and French. Over the next two years he worked for the British military mission under Major General Wilfred Malleson in an effort to block a German move into Afghanistan and India. Later he fought against the Bolsheviks.[32]

After joining MI6 in 1924, Ellis was first posted to Berlin as Passport

Victor Rothschild. Heir to a family fortune, winner of the George Medal for bravery, and wartime MI5 countersabotage officer who secretly met with FBI officials in the fall of 1942. *British Crown Copyright*

Control Officer and then to Paris as a journalist where he infiltrated the White Russian émigré community, a task made considerably easier with his marriage into a White Russian family named Zilinsky. These connections soon led to his recruitment of a mysterious character named Waldemar von Petrov, a close friend of a pair of White Russian generals named Nilolai Skobline and Prince Turkel, both leaders in the anti-Bolshevik movement. Over a long period of time Ellis picked up a great deal of information from them, particularly from Turkel, who provided insights into the internal affairs of the Nazi Party that he had gained through his close connection with the head of the Gestapo, Heinrich Himmler, and Nazi leader Alfred Rosenberg. Skobline and Turkel were later exposed as Stalin's agents. In 1937 Skobline masterminded the daring abduction of Eugene Miller, the former czarist chief of staff, off the streets of Paris while Turkel figured in a major Russian deception against the Germans after the two countries went to war. Years later a secret MI6 review of the information Ellis obtained from Skobline and Turkel found it to be largely worthless. One knowledgeable British historian surmised that it had either been "faked by the informants or dreamed up by Ellis himself to improve his standing at headquarters." When Ellis fell under suspicion, he shifted the blame to his sources, a ploy which did little to recoup his credibility within MI6. Following his return to London in 1938 with a new English wife, he remained with MI6 but was curiously barred from working at headquarters. Two years later, with Menzies rapidly expanding his organization in response to the growing Nazi menace, Ellis was sent to New York as Stephenson's deputy with the new rank of colonel.[33]

Hoover wasted no time acting on Bruce's report to Thurston. Stephenson was briefed on the allegations (without identifying Bruce) and told that the FBI would have no further dealings with Ellis. The stunned BSC head denied any knowledge of such attitudes, adding that "drastic disciplinary action would be taken" against any member of his staff making slanderous comments.[34] Eighteen days later, Stephenson met with Tamm and Ladd in the hope of easing the crisis. After a lengthy back-and-forth debate laced with repeated refusals for the identity of the Bureau's source, Tamm ended the discussion by explaining simply that Hoover's decision was irreversible.[35]

Now desperate, Ellis tried to plead his case directly to Hoover. After professing his innocence of these "completely fantastic" charges and claiming no recollection of any such conversation, he then suggested that his listener had distorted his comments or had taken them out of context. When Ellis wrote a personal letter to Hoover requesting an opportunity to meet with him, he was immediately rebuffed. There was no need "for me to further express my views about the situation," Hoover wrote. "I am, of course, exceedingly sorry that matters of this kind arise and threaten the very existence of the cooperation which is essential between your organization and the Federal Bureau of Investigation. I do not feel, however, that there is anything further which I can do to make clear my attitude about such matters." Accordingly, Ellis's service with BSC came to an end.[36]

By late November, with American troops firmly lodged on the North African coast and moving east to link up with British forces in Libya, Rothschild was back in London after a difficult Atlantic crossing aboard the *Queen Elizabeth.* Within days he and Walter Bell had reported their impressions to Liddell. The BSC's dire relationship with the FBI was "quite irretrievable." This was not merely Rothschild's verdict but also Bell's, who had the rare opportunity to meet with the FBI director before his departure. This reality forced Liddell to conclude that MI5's only option was the creation of its own communications channel with the FBI through some other means.[37]

CHAPTER FIVE

Art Goes to London

J. Edgar Hoover had reached his breaking point. Charles Ellis had repeatedly disparaged the FBI and then lied when he was called on it. BSC didn't trust the FBI and was double-dealing Hoover; he was getting no current intelligence of value from MI5 through MI6; Liddell's fruitful visit in May and June 1942, Kimball's success in London two months later, and Rothschild's revealing comments to his staff in November had finally convinced him to arrange a direct channel of communication with MI5 bypassing BSC. In mid-November, Hoover abruptly issued travel orders to London for twenty-eight-year-old Special Agent Arthur Thurston to serve as the FBI director's personal representative to the British intelligence establishment.

Arthur McCaslin Thurston, born in Colorado on March 13, 1914, was the son of a second-generation farmer-banker family from Shelbyville, Indiana, about fifty miles south of Indianapolis. Shelbyville, the county seat of Shelby County in Addison Township, was named for Isaac Shelby, an eighteenth-century Indian fighter and Kentucky governor. Art's childhood was a blend of school, weekly Methodist Church services, farm chores, days in the family bank, and mostly doing what he loved best: hunting for deer grazing on the rich Indiana farm land or fishing in the Little Blue and Big Blue Rivers which forked at Shelbyville. Amy, Art's daughter, recalled years later that her father loved nothing more "than being on the farm or on the river in Indiana where he could shoot or tramp through the woods" to his heart's content. After the war when he returned to Shelbyville, he started a standing Wednesday night meeting with a group of friends called the "Varmints," who cooked outside in practically any weather, sharing stories and talking endlessly about "their guns."[1]

After high school he went off to Bloomington for a business degree at Indiana University. Forgoing a scholarship there, he moved instead to Indianapolis where he worked as a bond salesman in the hope of gaining experience in anticipation of returning to the family banking business. One day while eating lunch on a park bench, he fell into a conversation with the local FBI office chief, who enthralled him with tales of J. Edgar Hoover and the exciting life of a G-man. Eager for some adventure, Thurston promptly ditched the bond business and joined the FBI on April 18, 1938, one month after his twenty-fourth birthday.[2]

After training he was assigned to Charlotte, North Carolina, for his first taste of criminal investigations. The work was a steady stream of routine investigations, dealing with all sorts of people, both high- and low-brow, rich and poor, powerful and weak, prominent and obscure, experiences which proved valuable for his later career. Almost a half-century later, Art still proudly recalled one case involving a stolen car which was torched and dumped in a local river. With professional scuba diving still a thing of the future, Art volunteered to free-dive into the river bottom in search of the missing car in the hope of locating the serial number on the engine block. A rugged man and powerful swimmer, Thurston spent hours looking for the car, finally spotting it through the dark, murky water, stuck in the mud. When the car was pulled to shore the number was confirmed on the spot.[3]

His next stop was San Francisco in late 1938, handling a lengthy "road trip" which took him four hundred miles north to Medford, Oregon. There he worked with tribal police departments investigating crimes on the many Indian reservations dotting central and eastern Oregon. It was in San Francisco that he had his first brush with counterespionage. One weekend evening while manning the office telephones he received a strange call from a local hotel operator claiming that Rudolph Huebner, the German consul-general, was routinely meeting at the hotel with soldiers for sexual purposes. The following week Thurston followed Huebner and a soldier onto the Presidio, where he asked a military police officer to confront the pair for identification. Years later Thurston recalled that he was among a handful of agents to attend one of the FBI's first counterespionage schools, where he learned the fine points of diplomatic immunity. Mindful of the lessons he learned, he had the military police front for him so the Germans would never know of the Bureau's involvement. The soldier was court-martialed and Huebner was declared persona non grata and expelled from the United States by the Department of State.[4]

It was in San Francisco that he first met Hoover. The FBI director often visited the West Coast to inspect field offices, meet with office personnel, and relax with the many friends he had made over the years. Thurston served as the director's driver, picking him up and dropping him off at his hotel, taking him to appointments with local officials, as well as spending long hours driving him around Bay Area tourist sites. One regular stop, he later remembered, was San Francisco's Exhibition Hall, where Sally Rand, the notorious actress and burlesque queen known for her outrageous ostrich feather fan dance, performed nightly in a bawdy theatrical revue called *Sally Rand's Nude Ranch;* it was a Hoover favorite whenever he was in the Golden Gate city.[5]

Thurston was promoted to headquarters in the summer of 1940 and assigned to the National Defense Division, an outgrowth of the General Intelligence Division that was reestablished in the fall of 1939, nineteen years after its dissolution in the wake of the Palmer Red Raids. As the division's only liaison man, Thurston made daily rounds throughout the capital, exchanging counterespionage information and meeting officials of various cabinet departments, particularly State, Treasury, and the two military services. A year later he moved again, this time to New York City, working for Sam Foxworth in the FBI's secret Rockefeller Center office developing cover assignments for Special Agents operating undercover in Latin America. He was in this job when Hoover abruptly ordered him to London in November 1942.[6]

The flying boat gently lifted off from the Port Washington terminal on November 15, 1942, for a pleasant and uneventful five-day trip across the Atlantic. His first stop was Bermuda, where he spent a day before moving on to Horta in the Azores and then to Lisbon. With German aircraft ranging from the French coast far out into the Atlantic in search of Allied shipping, Thurston's plane made a wide western swing en route to Foynes, Ireland, where another plane carried him to Scotland. The final leg of his journey was by train, which got him to London on November 19.[7]

Arriving at eight o'clock at night, Thurston was greeted by Robert Coe, a Second Secretary at the American embassy, responsible for coordinating intelligence matters. Riding through a city cloaked in total blackness shocked the impressionable young Hoosier, who was away from his home country for the first time. London was nothing like Shelbyville or even New York City, where only minimal precautions were in place. "The blackout here in London," he later wrote to his parents, "is complete and just a little depressing at first. I thought New York City's dimout was just a little dismal but it is nothing like we have here." Despite the city's dreariness, he soon found himself checking into London's finest hotel, the grand and aristocratic Claridge's.[8]

Early the next morning he made his way to the American embassy located at One Grosvenor Square in the city's fashionable Mayfair district.

Despite its upscale reputation, the square was a scene of violence and destruction that Thurston had only read about in American newspapers. Homes with shattered roofs and walls were still occupied while others, dark, cold and lifeless, remained abandoned since the relentless German aerial pounding of 1940 had forced out the owners. Art gazed incomprehensively at a wartime crazy-quilt of empty lots and sandbags piled six feet and higher, interlaced with endless rows of barbed-wire barricades surrounding hastily built wooden shacks used for shelter and other wartime purposes; one shanty housed a detachment of the Women's Auxiliary Air Force which handled "Romeo," an enormous barrage balloon floating directly over the square.[9]

John Gilbert Winant, America's ambassador to Great Britain, led an embassy staff of nearly four thousand. Born in 1889 to a prominent New York family, Gil, as he was known to all, was a child of wealth and privilege from Manhattan's fashionable Upper East Side. During the First World War he served as a pilot in the fledgling Army Air Corp doing spotter duties over enemy lines. Winant emerged from the war as a highly decorated officer rising from private soldier to a captain commanding an observation squadron.[10]

As a young war hero he easily won a legislative seat in New Hampshire (his adopted state), serving as a liberal Republican pushing for shortened work weeks for women and children, safer working conditions, the abolition of capital punishment, and regulated pay standards. His growing popularity led him to the governor's office, where he became the first politician in the state's history to serve three terms. In 1935 President Roosevelt appointed him to his new Social Security Board. Four years later he moved to Geneva to direct the International Labor Office (ILO), the post he held until his appointment to the London ambassadorship in March 1941.[11]

The U.S. embassy in London was the largest and most important American diplomatic post in the world when Winant arrived. Churchill's secretary John Colville later claimed that it "became little short of an extension to 10 Downing Street" and, like hundreds of other British officials, he "made frequent journeys to [consult with Winant] at 1 Grosvenor Square."[12] From the start, the new ambassador with the tall, lean, and somewhat brooding visage set out to change the American diplomatic tone following the disastrous tenure of his predecessor, Joseph Kennedy, whom the British loathed for his appeasement and defeatism. Winant became an instant idol on the very day he arrived by announcing that "there is no place I would rather be than in England." There were many evenings when he risked his life walking the streets alone in order to share the civilian wartime horrors and to convey to Londoners in an understated way that his country stood with them in their hours of trial. During one air raid he was suddenly overcome one night as he watched the mangled bodies of some nurses being carried out of a collapsed building.[13]

In a stark departure from standard State Department practice, Winant encouraged the assignment of representatives from other government departments and agencies to the embassy in the belief that the complexity of the war in Europe required a wide range of knowledge and skills. Their instructions and authority, in his view, came from their parent departments and agencies: his only stipulations were that he approve all policy moves, the person integrate himself into Winant's working team, and all communications pass through the embassy code room in order to avoid jurisdictional conflicts and overlap.[14]

On the afternoon of his second day on the job, Thurston spent forty-five minutes introducing himself to the ambassador and explaining his mission. Touching on the subject of espionage, Winant recalled his daughter's experience some years earlier at the University of Peru where she was studying Spanish. While in Latin America for the ILO he visited Quito to assess its new hospital service and pension system, with his daughter serving as his interpreter. Before Winant arrived, his daughter had a chance meeting at a diplomatic reception with the German ambassador, who posed "searching" questions that she parried by suggesting that he confer with her father. Winant then mentioned that the ambassador directed a large collection of underground German-Italian propaganda organizations in South America.[15] In May 1941 Winant returned to the United States, carrying sensitive documents from Churchill for the president. Within hours of Winant's arrival, Hoover learned that a German agent operating from the Hungarian legation had taken a room next to his in New York's Roosevelt Hotel; the director immediately assigned an agent to guard the ambassador until his return to London.[16]

Thurston explained Hoover's interest in forming a closer working relationship with the MI5, which thus far had been hampered by William Stephenson and his staff in New York City. Remaining neutral, Winant suggested that perhaps the matter had become a "partisan affair" with both sides "partly to blame."[17] Regardless of the circumstances, the ambassador promptly offered Thurston his full cooperation, assigning him the title of

Arthur Thurston. FBI agent sent by Hoover to London in November 1942 as his permanent representative. In January 1943 British officials introduced him to "Ultra," which he codenamed "Ostrich." *FBI*

"Attache" with Robert Coe designated as the FBI man's informal boss. Until office arrangements could be made, he was assigned a desk in Coe's office where Coe would review reports of his meetings with British officials. Coe was assigned to introduce Thurston to key contacts at Scotland Yard and MI5, with Winant setting up formal meetings for him with Menzies and Petrie. Hoover's man was then assured of a free hand to deal directly with any of the British intelligence agencies and, as for MI6, he could deal with Menzies or any of his staff if he did not wish to deal with Stephenson.[18]

Having no FBI stationery nor letter of introduction from Hoover, Thurston prepared over Winant's signature a note for Petrie, whom Coe described as a formal man from the "old school." It included favorable references to the recent visits of Liddell and Rothschild to the FBI, describing "how welcome they were and how satisfactory their visits were." Hoping to build on these expressions of goodwill, both Hoover and Winant were "most anxious for Mr. Thurston to be in the closest possible contact with the Security Service for the exchange of information pertaining to counter-espionage and security intelligence work."[19] MI5 officials later told Thurston in confidence that Petrie interpreted the ambassador's flattering remarks as an endorsement of his own frustrations with Stephenson, which Thurston later reported were not exactly the feelings of the ambassador, a fact that he chose not to share with Petrie in furtherance of the good cooperation that he was receiving. Thurston spent the next ten days at MI5 headquarters introducing himself, describing his background, comparing MI5 with FBI procedures, meeting staff members, receiving briefings on espionage and treason investigations, and spending a great deal of time with Petrie. For his part, Petrie took a personal interest in ensuring a cordial and cooperative tone, which Thurston later learned was "quite unusual" for him.[20]

Sir David Petrie was a powerfully built Scotsman with a steady gaze and a straightforward, firm, and decisive demeanor. Born on September 9, 1879, at Inveravon, Banffshire, in Scotland, he completed a graduate degree at Aberdeen University before entering the Indian Police Service in December 1900. His spent his first three years there in India's Punjab region, followed by a stint in the Northwest Frontier as an adjutant for the Samana Rifles, the military police force along the Kohat Border. Over the years he rose through the ranks to assistant to the deputy inspector-general of the Punjab Department of Criminal Investigation and senior assistant to the assistant director of the Department of Criminal Investigation, which was directly responsible to the Home Department of the government of India. In 1912 he investigated the failed assassination of the Viceroy of India, Lord Hardinge, resulting in a series of terrorist arrests two years later. In the summer of 1914 violence once again erupted in India when the First World War emboldened Sikh nationalist sentiments. Wounds received in a gun battle forced Petrie's evacuation to London for six months of recuperation.[21]

His next assignment was to Siam as an intelligence officer at the British legation, and then Shanghai, where he recruited a vast network of agents that ranged from Singapore throughout the Dutch East Indies all the way to Japan. As his achievements grew, so too did his honors. He received the Commander of the Indian Empire (CIE) in 1916, the Order of the British Empire (OBE) in 1918, and the Commander of the British Empire (CBE) a year later. In 1920 he returned to India as the director of the Department of Criminal Intelligence, where he investigated M. M. Roy, India's leading Marxist, who was trying to install communist cells throughout the country.

In 1929 he received a knighthood for his service, followed by his retirement six years later.[22]

When Churchill sacked Kell in May 1940, Menzies recommended Petrie as his replacement. After initially turning the job down, he later accepted but only after conducting a thorough examination of the agency. In a report prepared in February 1941 he concluded that the rapid expansion of the service since 1938 (from 30 officers in 1938 to more than 200 in 1940) had produced "haphazard recruitment, inadequate supervision, confusion in the chain of command and general demoralization." Two months later he took charge of the security service with the new title of director-general and a commitment to change. Through a strong personal leadership style and willingness to make tough changes, Petrie turned the security service around.[23] Dick White, an MI5 officer who in later years would head both MI5 and MI6, summed up the feelings of most MI5 professionals at the time by describing Petrie as "one of the best managers I ever met."[24]

One of his major leadership flaws, however, was a reluctance to cultivate influential government bigwigs who could prove useful when interdepartmental rivalries and conflicts arose so often during the war. He was a complete professional who worked hard and briefed himself thoroughly for meetings with senior government officials, yet made "scant effort to cultivate influential people." He possessed "a thorough grasp of practical intelligence work with skills of an unspectacular but effective manager," his biographer later wrote.[25] One very senior official criticized him as a "bad publicity merchant," bewildered by the complexities of Whitehall and seemingly uninterested in the positive effects such relationships could produce for his service and staff. Unlike Menzies, who regularly met with Churchill, Petrie never visited 10 Downing Street, working instead with Desmond Morton, the prime minister's long-serving intelligence advisor. In a March 1943 letter Petrie acknowledged his flaws with some sound reasons:

> I have lived so long abroad that I had comparatively few contacts in London, and I never cared to extend them beyond what was necessary for business purposes. So it is a fact that many people, even some who ought to know better, have only the vaguest idea of M.I.5 and what it does. This certainly does not hurt our work—quite the contrary—but it bears rather hardly on the department and the many able officers it comprises.[26]

Petrie quickly signaled his eagerness to cooperate with Hoover in a variety of subtle yet powerful gestures. He frequently lunched with Thurston, personally introduced him to his entire staff, accompanied him on tours of MI5 installations, and even took him to a "highly secret" espionage trial of a Belgian seaman named Franciscus Winter. Petrie cautioned him to keep the court visit confidential with the promise that he would furnish a summary of the proceedings for transmittal to Washington. Hoover later learned that Thurston was the first American ever invited to such a proceeding. Next Thurston spent a few days at the MI5 headquarters at Blenheim Palace, the ancestral home of the Duke of Marlborough located in Woodstock near Oxford University and the birthplace of Winston Churchill, where he had studied MI5's Registry System. Hoover's new British liaison man also visited a number of port cities where he witnessed firsthand how British immigration and customs procedures operated, and then on returning to London he toured the LRC and Camp 020. In a unique gesture marking a watershed moment in FBI-MI5 relations, Petrie opened up all MI5 files to Thurston along with an office for his personal use. Hoping to deepen this new liaison relationship, the director-general expressed interest in a reciprocal arrangement, with Hoover identifying Cyril Mill, an experienced MI5 officer, then awaiting departure for Canada, as his selection for this assignment. In a letter to Hoover just weeks later, Thurston characterized his MI5 hosts as "extremely cordial and cooperative" in every way possible.[27]

Crowded into a hectic first month of official meetings and visits was a search for permanent quarters in a city where housing shortages were at a crisis level. Thurston found a flat at 17 Grosvenor Street, just a short block away from the embassy. In a stroke of luck he now had two recently redecorated rooms including a living room with a coal-burning fireplace stove, a bath, and a small dining room with a bar. His new home had its own "lift" and a separate entrance with "breakfast served in my room." In a letter to his worried parents, he assured them that despite the conditions in London, he was "reasonably comfortable and not suffering any undue hardships." His maid looked after his laundry, got his morning newspaper, and did everything "but draw my bath." With tongue firmly in cheek and a sly smile on his face, he put their mind completely at rest: "Right now without moving from my chair I can reach the service button that will bring the maid running with tea, ice or a whiskey soda."[28]

He was not alone in the big city: he had some friends from Indiana he could call on for company. One was an old Shelbyville family friend named D. Wray Deprez, a colonel serving in England as the commander of the Indiana National Guard. For additional comradeship he joined the

Royal Automobile Club, an exclusive men's club which offered fine dining, a library with thousands of selections, a well-stocked bar, squash courts, a swimming pool, and a rifle range. One club member who became a particularly close friend was a member of the House of Lords.[29]

Art's warm and straightforward personality and love of the outdoors instantly appealed to the British fondness for hunting, fishing, and tramping through the English countryside. He bought a squash racket so he could stay in decent physical shape and played three nights a week with police inspectors at the London Metropolitan Police Service gymnasium. His regular playing partner was a Special Branch officer named Fred Chadburn, who became a life-long friend. In a letter to his mother he admitted that he was hard on his clothes, particularly his socks, with large holes appearing with surprising regularity. English wool was in very short supply, making decent socks almost a black-market item. Chadburn's wife, Barbara, "a swell gal," took it "upon herself to see that my socks are darned and clothes mended." So critical were functioning socks that he described her "knitting a pair of heavy ribbed grey sox with green [unintelligible] stripes. She put in double heels and toes and they are the nicest sox I've ever had." For the cold damp winter to come she "knit a pair of string gloves for me that are fine." Months later, in a supreme gesture of personal as well as Anglo-American friendship, Barbara and Fred honored Art by asking him to serve as the godfather for their new son, Ian.[30]

Thurston met Stewart Menzies on the first anniversary of the Japanese attack on Pearl Harbor. His visit was prompted by a telephone call late that same afternoon in which Menzies suggested a meeting that evening and offered a car to drive the FBI man to his confidential suite of offices at 54 Broadway. Art was surprised to enter a dark, shabby office building which was poorly lit, overcrowded, and "quite dangerous in places."[31] Guarding Menzies's fourth-floor office was a triad of sentries led by Kathleen Pettigrew, the director's powerful and longtime secretary. Described as a "formidable grey-haired lady with the square jaw of a battleship" and fiercely loyal to "the Chief," Pettigrew had served directors for more than twenty-one years, first as secretary to Mansfield Cummings, the founder of the service, and later his popular successor, Arthur Sinclair, who Menzies replaced in September 1939. Her reputation for discretion was legendary, as was her knowledge of the British government's most sensitive secrets, having typed countless letters from her bosses to a succession of prime ministers. Decades later Ian Fleming, then serving as an MI6 officer, immortalized Pettigrew as his inspiration for Miss Moneypenny, the devoted servant of M, James Bond's inscrutable boss.[32] Custom required that visitors wait in an outer office until a small red light above the entrance to Menzies's office switched to green, indicating that he was free. One then passed through a door of double thickness with multiple layers of padded leather that guaranteed the muffled security of conversations in the heart of MI6's inner sanctum.[33]

Stewart Graham Menzies was born in 1890 to a life of wealth that had been created by his grandfather, the founder of a successful distilling business. Later he used a portion of his new fortune to purchase Haliburton, a large landed estate just north of Queen Victoria's summer residence near Balmoral Castle. His parents, who lived on the fringes of the royal household, rose rapidly up the social ladder during these years, a fact which rumormongers attributed to the widespread suspicion that Stewart was the illegitimate son of the Prince of Wales, who became King Edward VII in 1901.[34]

John Menzies, Stewart's father, was the polar opposite of his own father. His relentless spending habits eventually eroded the family fortune, leaving his wife and children broke when he suddenly died in May 1911. Wasting no time in her efforts to recoup the family finances, Susannah, his widow, suddenly shot to the highest levels of British society when she became Lady Holford upon her marriage to George Holford two months after John's death. At the age of thirteen, Stewart entered Eton College, considered at the time the leading Protestant college for the landed and titled aristocracy. True to his class, he became a skilled swordsman, an accomplished steeplechaser, and a regular at Beaufort, England's most famous fox hunts. Increasingly focused on a future in the military, he abandoned Eton in 1908 to join the elite Grenadier Guards, "an English elite brotherhood" who considered themselves the "finest soldiers in the world." From there he advanced to the rarefied world of prestigious Life Guards of the Household Cavalry, whose only duty was to "guard the king's life, constantly and without intermission." They were a "race apart," according to one author "who acknowledged that they were subject to no ordinary laws and conventions, but did what they thought best or what suited them in most mortal pursuits."[35]

By November 1914 twenty-four-year-old Captain Menzies found himself battling it out with the Germans in the killing fields of France. After sustaining wounds in a gas attack in December 1916, Menzies transferred to the Intelligence Section of the General Staff of the British Armies to work for Major Reginald Drake, a counterespionage professional and founder of

MI5, who used him as his chief spy-catcher until the end of the war. Menzies was soon working with Sir Mansfield Cummings, the head of MI1(c), Britain's wartime intelligence operation. By November 1918 the future head of MI6 was a brevet major, winner of the Distinguished Service Order (Britain's third-highest military order) for gallantry in action, the Military Cross (Britain's second-highest military order) for "conspicuous ability, coolness, and resource in controlling the actions of his regiment and rallying his men," and the Le Croix de Guerre (Lower Order), the symbol of French gratitude.[36] Menzies remained as the head of the military espionage section before transferring to MI6 under Cummings in 1923. Over the next sixteen years he refined both his espionage skills as well as the art of negotiating the more dangerous trails of the Whitehall bureaucracy with skill, slyness, and coolness. In September 1939, not yet fifty years old, he took command of MI6.

When the light above the office door flashed green, Thurston entered the inner sanctum of the most powerful figure in British intelligence. Menzies was cordial to the young FBI man, but "behind the regency elegance and style was a ruthless man, devious and subtle."[37]

Following a few minutes of light chit-chat about Thurston's background and the FBI, Menzies began putting out "feelers concerning Mr. Stevenson [*sic*]" and Hoover's attitude toward the BSC head. Thurston spent some time tracing the history of their relationship, describing BSC's transgressions in the United States that had created an "exceedingly poor impression" in the process. Considerably more time was spent as Thurston catalogued the list of Hoover's complaints that had led to his decision for direct liaison with MI5. When Menzies asked if tighter restrictions on Stephenson could resurrect a better relationship, Thurston quashed the idea, insisting that Stephenson had "damaged himself irreparably and would never be able to enjoy the Bureau's confidence again." Menzies demurred with the claim that he had "almost" reached a similar conclusion but would have to consider matters further before taking corrective action.[38] Thurston next turned to a topic that the British intelligence chief probably never expected. Hoover knew that the British had broken the German Enigma codes and were reading Abwehr messages. Mincing no words, the new legal attaché made it clear to Menzies that any future cooperation with Hoover depended on FBI access to decrypted information relating to espionage in the Western Hemisphere. Thurston assured "C" that Hoover was most sensitive to the security of this vitally important source of information to the future of the Allied war effort. He then offered Hoover's additional guarantees of compliance with any British restrictions regarding their use.[39]

During his first month in war-torn London, Thurston had lived a whirlwind existence of meetings with new British colleagues who took him everywhere and introduced him to everyone. It was no wonder that with Christmas just days away he eagerly looked forward to celebrating the holiday relaxing with American friends. His plans, however, changed when Walter Bell, his old chum from New York and Washington, invited him to Seven Oaks in Kent, about an hour train ride south of London, where Bell's father served as the local vicar. The vicarage was in many ways light years away from his Shelbyville home, with an old twenty- or thirty-room stone house, no central heating, fireplaces in every room, and large, green, well-kept gardens overlooking the village in the valley below. The entire setting, Thurston marveled, "was more typically English than anything I had ever imagined."[40]

Christmas Eve was a relaxed affair with a family dinner around the living room fireplace, the celebrants sipping from a "quart of good whiskey and quart of Sherry wine, much sought after delicacies in ration conscious Britain," which Art had bought at the American embassy store. Everyone took in the joy of the children as they picked from stockings brimming with American chocolate bars, boxes of cookies, and a can of Planters peanuts, again courtesy of Art and the American army post exchange. So thrilled were the little ones that they quickly began calling Uncle Walter's new American friend "American Embassy."[41]

Christmas Day began late after a lengthy sleep-in followed by church services at eleven o'clock, a stop at the pub for a holiday toast (or two) to better times, a sumptuous dinner of mutton roast (fowl was not available), an eight-mile walk through the countryside, and a return to the vicarage, where a second, equally grand late afternoon meal awaited them. Stuffed beyond belief, Art bade his hosts a heartfelt goodbye and boarded the late night train for London. In the morning he would greet his new secretary, Gene Rogers, arriving from Washington. As the train rolled steadily north, Art Thurston could only sit and ponder the arc of his life over the past four and a half years, from tiny Shelbyville to San Francisco as an obscure FBI investigator to Washington, New York, and to London as a diplomat. Musings aside, he still had to face another dreary year of war. What he did not know, however, was a recent British decision that would profoundly complicate his new role as Hoover's man in London.[42]

CHAPTER SIX

Ostrich

Excitement at the White House on January 9, 1943, was electric with final preparations underway for a top-secret, 3,000-mile journey that would take President Roosevelt to Casablanca for a rendezvous with Winston Churchill. Across the Atlantic, Art Thurston was at Glenalmond, the country home of Walter Grimston, the Fourth Earl of Verulam, nestled near St. Albans, a small ancient village about twenty miles north of London. At the start of the war MI6 took over the estate as the headquarters for Section V, its counterespionage branch. Among the few assets that Stewart Menzies controlled was the intelligence produced by the British government's code breakers working at Bletchley Park, a quiet country manor forty miles north of London. It was there that Britain's best minds began assembling in the summer of 1939 to solve the impenetrable riddle of Enigma—Germany's supposedly unbreakable cipher system.[1]

One of Bletchley Park's brightest stars was fifty-four-year-old Alfred Dillwyn "Dilly" Knox, a tall bespectacled Oxford don. Knox, the son of an Anglican bishop, was educated at Cambridge University and later became a Fellow at Kings College, where he numbered Harold MacMillan, a future prime minister, among his many students. Dilly was a man of letters, a classics scholar specializing in Greek studies with a subtle intellect that "danced elegantly among the mazes of cryptography."[2] During the Great War he was a Royal Navy officer assigned as a cryptographer in the Admiralty's famous Room 40 under the indomitable Admiral Reginald "Blinker" Hall. Later he returned to university life only to be recalled to government service in the 1930s to apply his talents to a solution of the commercial version of the Enigma machine that Hitler shared with Generalissimo Francisco Franco during the Spanish Civil War. Decades later, a history of Britain's silent cryptographic war described Knox as a "visionary dreamer" with a mind that "moved like the flash of kingfisher across a pond."[3] By December 1941 Knox had solved the all-important Abwehr machine cipher used to communicate secret messages between European field stations and Berlin. The

British government deemed his remarkable accomplishment so vital to the war effort that the breakthrough was thereafter called Intelligence Service Knox (ISK) in his honor.[4]

Another cryptographic giant was Oliver Strachey. Born in 1874 and educated at Eton and Oxford's Balliol College, Oliver was the brother of Lytton Strachey, the famed literary critic and writer, whose works include *Eminent Victorians* and *Elizabeth and Essex: A Tragic History.* After his First World War service in military intelligence, Strachey began a career with Government Code and Cipher School, concentrating on Japanese naval attaché machine ciphers and Abwehr hand ciphers throughout the 1920s and 1930s. Building on early Polish successes, Strachey and his team solved the problem in May 1940, which became known as Intelligence Service Oliver Strachey (ISOS). Thanks to these two extraordinary Englishmen, Bletchley Park began reading volumes of Abwehr messages by the start of 1942, giving the British a clear advantage in the intelligence war with the Germans.[5]

Messages decrypted at Bletchley Park traveled by landline to Section V at Glenalmond for cataloguing and analysis under the supervision of Colonel Felix Cowgill, MI6's counterintelligence boss. Cowgill was veteran of the Calcutta Special Branch, where he built a solid reputation investigating communist subversion activities. He had also served David Petrie as Special Assistant at the Central Investigation Bureau in India. Cowgill became the Section V head following Valentine Vivian's promotion to the rank of deputy chief of the SIS.[6] Vivian was also a long-serving officer in the India Police Service and the Central Intelligence Bureau before returning to London in February 1939 to set up Section V accompanied by Cowgill.

On that momentous January morning Vivian introduced Thurston to Cowgill, who began acquainting Hoover's man to MI6's "most secret source."[7] He learned about Ultra (the code name for the British solution of Enigma), its production and distribution, and the important role of the Radio Security Service (RSS) that intercepted German signals through a vast array of antennae ringing the entire coastline of the British Isles. Cowgill described how the RSS transmitted them to Bletchley Park for decryption with the clear text sent to Section V at Glenalmond. Due to the large volume of messages processed daily by the small Section V staff, Cowgill quickly cautioned Thurston that any Section V analytical examination of the messages for leads of value to the FBI could not be rendered. As a solution, Vivian suggested assigning a full-time FBI representative to Section V to handle these duties. Thurston wasted no time acting on the offer. The following day he "urgently" radioed Hoover, requesting the transfer of an FBI agent to London for the sole purpose of sifting through ISOS and ISK. "I am convinced that the work at St. Albans will be extremely valuable to us," he wrote, adding that "an agent who has been trained in the work of Mr. Kimball's office would be able to originate in the United States a number of cases."[8]

How significant were ISOS and ISK? In a report entitled *Theory of Counter Espionage,* X2, the counterintelligence arm of the OSS, described their "incalculable" value for gaining complete counterespionage control of the German intelligence system. Through both sources, the "ideal situation had come close to being achieved" by providing the key to "the innermost recesses of the enemy's espionage system" through a "constant and increasing flow of up-to-date information on the organization of German intelligence and its officials, but also to keep track of agents in the United Kingdom, Western Europe, and to some extent, indeed throughout the world." Through ISOS and ISK, "thousands of individuals became known, their movements, actions, and even thoughts were recorded." Counterespionage operations could "often be conducted with great confidence, and with the assurance that the enemy was being fooled."[9] The FBI was equally effusive in its praise. A top-secret history prepared by Thurston in late 1943 credited it as a "very valuable and unimpeachable source of information."[10]

While Thurston was asking Washington for help, MI6 was awash in intrigue and intraoffice politics. Vivian, the deputy director of MI6's Central Security Service and nominal second in command of MI6, was engaged in a bitter rivalry with Colonel Claude Dansey, Menzies's executive assistant and his head of foreign espionage operations. Fueling these tensions was Dansey's haughtiness (many called him an insufferable snob) and the friction between officers with decades of experience and newly hired temporaries recruited by Dansey from London's many exclusive clubs and universities. Strained relations between MI5 and MI6 only compounded the situation. The security service chafed at Cowgill's stubborn refusal to share any more Ultra material than he believed necessary for MI5's internal security function. Petrie took strong exception to Cowgill's intransigence, claiming that he "ought to be sent away for some time" while Liddell, ever the diplomat, attributed his "narrow and bigoted attitude" to overwork and the strain of guarding his embattled country's most important secret.[11]

Some of Thurston's wartime letters from London to family members survive today. Most offer snapshots of his daily life in England with references to friends, social activities, and prominent personalities among British high society whose paths he crossed. None, however, contain any reference to business travels except for one to his parents at the end of January 1943, describing visits to St. Albans "several times recently." The city was the "capital of England during the Roman Conquest . . . and there are numerous Roman ruins there and an old Roman wall built about the 2nd century AD is still standing." He went on to say that he was "going down there Sunday on a business and pleasure trip and am taking Gene Rogers [Thurston's recently arrived secretary] along so I can show him around."[12] While we don't know if Thurston's decision to include Rogers on his visit to St. Albans was really for sightseeing, it was more likely to do with devising a method for swift processing of ISOS and ISK, which Thurston soon code-named "Ostrich."[13]

Progress on reviewing Ostrich material remained steady for the next two months until General George Strong, the army's assistant chief of staff for intelligence, suddenly clamped restrictions on FBI access to the deciphered messages. George Veazey Strong was a tough guy who came up through the ranks the hard way and took his job seriously. A fifty-two-year-old graduate of Michigan Military Academy and West Point, Strong started out as a young cavalry officer stationed at an assortment of dusty western outposts fighting Indians. Later, after earning a law degree and teaching law at West Point, he began a slow rise through the ranks until General Marshall tapped him as the head of Military Intelligence Division, replacing General Raymond Lee, in June 1942.[14]

Strong tolerated no rivals to his control over all facets of intelligence. He despised William Donovan, calling him an "amateur" soldier who imposed himself on the military with a conferred title of "general." Concern about Donovan's blabber-mouth, his practice of choosing his officers from America's upper crust, and his willingness to hire communists into the OSS led Strong to deny him access to both Ultra and Magic. The incensed OSS head immediately appealed to the White House, only to learn that Roosevelt sided with the military. Later FDR partially amended his ruling in a way that still left Donovan at Strong's mercy by permitting him access to only those messages that the MID boss considered useful.[15]

The general's initial attitude regarding FBI access to Ostrich may have been influenced by Captain Eddie Hastings, an MI6 man working for Stephenson and posted to Washington in a liaison capacity. Hastings confided to Strong that the FBI wanted all Ultra material funneled through its office, an impractical condition the general could not abide. In March

1943 Cowgill informed Thurston that access to diplomatic intercepts were off-limits to the FBI at Strong's orders. To clarify this misunderstanding, Thurston explained the fallacy of these claims to Vivian and Menzies, who offered assurances that FBI access to the source would continue.[16]

In an attempt to resolve the controversy, G. C. Burton, the Bureau's liaison man with the MID, met with Strong. The general explained that both the British and the Army Security Agency were intercepting and decoding this material, with the United States actually acquiring about sixty percent of the product. Speaking "very bitterly," Strong expressed his suspicions of Stephenson and BSC, telling Burton that after recently learning that Hastings had been passing diplomatic intercepts collected by ASA to Stephenson, he threatened to cut the British completely off from the U.S. product. Burton then learned that a BSC representative who had approached Strong seeking a liaison relationship had been curtly dismissed. When the stunned BSC man insisted that the "Prime Minister desired it," Strong suggested that Churchill "take up the matter with President Roosevelt."[17]

Burton told Strong that the FBI had no wish to serve as government conduit for Ultra information between Section V and the American military services. Its only interest was access to Abwehr messages between its agents in the Western Hemisphere and Europe, which was essential for counterintelligence purposes. Strong conceded the point and, after agreeing to inform Menzies of the change, offered Hoover the use of military channels for transmission of any emergency messages with Thurston.[18] Despite these assurances, problems continued. In a follow-up letter to Strong, Hoover complained about British insistence that their denial was based on the original interpretation of Strong's position. Menzies and his assistants, Hoover explained, "insist on interpreting statements made to you by Captain Eddie Hastings, and other British representatives in the United States, as prohibiting them from discussing any case of interest to the Federal Bureau of Investigation in which intelligence from the [Ostrich] source has been used."[19]

In a memorandum prepared for Strong, Thurston explained that

> In cases which the British have developed as a result of their B.J. or diplomatic intercepts, certain difficulties however have been encountered. Sir Stuart Menzies, Director of British SIS (MI6), and his assistant Colonel V. Vivian, have advised the FBI representative on several occasions that while they are anxious to receive all information in the possession of the FBI with reference to these widespread enemy espionage

> operations, and while they are eager to cooperate to the fullest degree, they themselves are prohibited from making available to the FBI any information obtained from the B.J. source as a result of instructions they have received from Major General Strong. They interpret these instructions as precluding both MI6 and MI5 from discussing any case with the FBI in which intelligence of this type has been used even though they may be within the primary jurisdiction of this Bureau.[20]

While the controversy raged on, Hoover moved quickly on Thurston's request for help with the assignment of Special Agent John Cimperman to London in March 1943. Cimperman's new job was not an easy one. By the time he arrived at Glenalmond, strict caveats had been imposed. Italian circuits with Latin America as well as Japanese diplomatic codes called "Black Jumbo" or "BJs" were off-limits. Only Abwehr transmissions dealing with the Western Hemisphere could be reviewed and even these had restrictions. Cimperman could examine the body of the message, recording only names and addresses for submission to Washington. The additional wording of the message which placed the names and addresses in context for the reader's understanding was also denied. Further frustrations involved the prohibition from recording the vitally important preamble that began every German message. In order to make sense of the names and addresses, an analyst required the identity of the message's originator (Abwehr, navy, army, air force, etc.), its destination, together with the call letters, times, and dates. Without these details the value of the Ostrich source was virtually worthless: yet all of these essential items were denied to Cimperman.[21] Decrypted messages collected months earlier which could have proven useful for comparing names, places, events, or simply for clarification purposes were also restricted. Thurston later complained to Hoover that "the only information that this office (Thurston's office in London) could transmit to the Bureau was a brief paraphrase of the contents of the message and the source would be referred to as the 'ostrich source' and under no conditions as a German radio message and the preamble of the message should be utterly disregarded."[22]

The Section V staff at Glenalmond bore full responsibility for executing Strong's order, a flaw in the system that worked to Cimperman's distinct advantage. Cimperman was assigned a desk in Section V's main file room surrounded by shelves and cabinets filled with index cards containing the entire message originally decoded by Bletchley Park. Working side by side with him were MI6 officers, U.S. military representatives, and members of the OSS. Staffing the room was a collection of overworked young filing specialists and a senior clerk who acted as the chief of the section. They were stretched thin handling a myriad of duties ranging from file retrieval to incessantly answering questions and carefully filing the relentless stream of new messages flowing in daily from Bletchley Park. As they had no time to paraphrase every message for Cimperman's examination he was given access to the unedited index cards with the instructions to copy names, places, and dates. Risking complete cutoff from this essential source, Cimperman brazenly and nonchalantly, in full view of everyone, copied entire messages together with the preamble for submission to Washington. A typical message with preamble surreptitiously recorded in its entirety by Cimperman appeared as follows:

> Group II/1A
> Madrid to Berlin
> PFU on 9280 Kcs 2024 GMT August 4, 1943
> . . . Please inform me by W/T whether sets referred to are known at your end and whether you are interested in them. 1) Radio Receiver PHILCO Corporation, type BC (?) 647A, No. 2923. 2) Radio Receiver and Transmitter U.S. 3) Receiver and transmitter for formation flying. (8 corrupt) set, type TR 5043, No. 4741, make BENDIX.
> Virgil
> 1031/223
> Ko. SP
> Cimperman to Hoover 8/5/43[23]

Thurston later described Cimperman's deplorable working conditions: "In so far as surreptitiously obtaining verbatim texts messages is concerned [they] are by no means even slightly satisfactory." Even copying a "short message consisting of only a few lines is liable to arouse undue suspicion and detection."[24] Only current information was examined. No attempt was ever made to ask for old information unless "special circumstances warranted." Such restrictions only reinforced FBI suspicions that MI6 was denying them messages that they were rightly permitted to view. Thurston reported to Hoover that one day Cimperman accidently noticed an Abwehr message lying on a clerk's desk: it was a transmission from Argentina to Berlin about which he was never informed. Thurston later surmised that MI6 was intentionally "not making all intercepts available and undoubtedly are withholding some very good intelligence information from these and possibly other circuits." Inquiries to the Section V staff could "arouse (MI6) suspicion," Thurston feared, leading to a possible "cut off from the material."[25]

Slip-ups in this dangerous and delicate process occasionally occurred with potentially serious consequences. When several cases predicated on Ostrich were "untimely disclosed" by FBI officials in Washington, London was promptly notified and a stinging complaint was flashed to Thurston. "This proved to be very embarrassing," he warned his bosses, "and it was only after additional assurances had been made that the matter was ultimately straightened out."[26]

Wasting no time, Thurston set about making correctives by establishing strict procedure for FBI use of Ostrich material. Beginning in mid-1943 all cables sent to Washington containing Ostrich material carried a strict warning.

> The verbatim text of this message is being transmitted for the information of the Bureau only. It is urgently requested that its possession or contents not be disclosed to any other agency including [presumably G2] or included in any Bureau monograph or other publication. No mention should be made of the date of the message, the point of origin or destination, or of the frequency, nor should it be referred to as a radio communication. It is also requested that the information itself not be used either directly or indirectly solely as the basis for interrogation.[27]

In an effort to further tighten up security, Hoover grudgingly agreed with a British requirement for the transmission of all Ultra messages to the FBI as selected by Cimperman from the Ostrich index cards through BSC via the MI6 communications system. This caused little disruption as both Cimperman and Thurston ignored the agreement by continuing to secretly send the entire message separately to Washington via U.S. diplomatic channels. Over the next three years Hoover instituted additional measures to ensure the security of the Ostrich source such as rigid internal controls, Ostrich access lists at FBI headquarters, and orders to London to keep Ostrich records at the embassy at an absolute minimum. The system continued to function in this manner until the end of the war in Europe.

Gradually a wide variety of information made its way to Washington that was valuable to FBI operations. On August 13, 1943, for instance, Thurston reported a Lisbon-to-Berlin message describing a conversation with an American army colonel named James L. Guion. "In a conversation with

Col. James L. Guion in the staff of Admiral Leahy, a U.S. Russian Bureau of Coordination has been set up in Moscow since the middle of July and that Adm. L. sent Col. D. M. (or N.) Hauseman for this purpose." Cimperman sent many reports of messages identifying Abwehr name traces on Spanish and Portuguese citizens with no particular indication that they were destined for the Western Hemisphere. One message sent to Hoover in February 1945 addressed to "Vaulka" expressed interest in "Jose Maria Unzela, born 1925 in Miranda Del Ebro, Spaniard candidate for commission on merchant ship, lives Miranda Del Ebro." Others carried more significance, such as a Lisbon-to-Berlin message reporting the arrest by Portuguese police of Robert Lerch, a repatriated German previously living in Argentina who was asking to be placed in touch with British authorities. FBI records listed Lerch as an employee of the German embassy who had previously worked as a wireless radio operator for the military attaché. Other messages carried great weight for FBI operations throughout the war, as will be seen in upcoming chapters.[28]

CHAPTER SEVEN

A Fool's Errand

Despite his struggle for access to Ostrich, Thurston made significant progress in advancing the FBI's hitherto strained relations with the British. Valuable information concerning espionage, sabotage, controlled enemy agents, Double Cross techniques, profiles of Abwehr officials, their tactics and strategies, Camp 020 interrogation summaries—all began flowing across the Atlantic to the FBI in Washington. Thurston was briefed on espionage investigations in Spain, particularly the work of Jose Brugada Wood, code-named "Peppermint," an MI5 source inside the Spanish embassy in London who vastly improved British understanding of Axis capabilities and limitations. As for Petrie, he could not have been more pleased with the possibilities that Thurston's presence offered him for an expanded relationship with Hoover. Thurston's direct contact with Menzies and his staff only added to his growing workload, especially with the opening to Ostrich that now meant increasing trips to Glenalmond.[1]

In December 1942 Cyril Mills, an MI5 officer whom Thurston had met shortly after his arrival in London, was sent to Canada to handle Springbok and another double agent, Watchdog. Mills's grandfather, Halford Mills, had been a prominent and well-to-do undertaker who was considered the "pioneer of embalming." In addition to operating a string of funeral parlors, he also ran a funeral carriage company while publishing a professional newsletter, the *Undertakers Journal.* Cyril's father, Bertram Wagstaff Mills, wanting nothing to do with cadavers, rejected the family business, choosing instead to run his own circus. For years the famous Bertram Mills Circus performed throughout the British Isles, thrilling audiences with live animal acts, clowns, and performers. Cyril attended Harrow and studied engineering at Cambridge. An adventurer who flew his own plane, he entered the oil business after university and traveled across the world before returning home to join his father's firm. Managing a circus was uncharted territory for him, a career move that meant "taking a gamble of going into something for which I had no training and to which I might be totally unsuited." Mills quickly showed a flair for the business, taking control of everything from ticket sales to the complexities of safely shipping valuable wild animals across the English Channel for shows in Paris. At the outbreak of the war he closed his business and joined MI5, where he remained a staff officer until the summer of 1945. Betting successfully on his countrymen's hunger for a return to simple family pleasures after such a long war, Mills became a very wealthy man when he took his privately owned circus public by adding new investors. Years later his personal fortune ballooned again after joining the Lloyds of London insurance market as an underwriter.[2]

Based in Ottawa, the audacious Mills traveled regularly between New York, Montreal, and Washington, meeting frequently with FBI officials and forming close working relationships along the way. His brief, received before his departure from London, was simple and direct—be candid and straightforward with American and Canadian authorities but exercise discretion about the precise nature of "Most Secret Sources." His openness was rewarded in kind. Describing himself as the longest-serving MI5 officer in North America, he discovered that officials relaxed around him and were willing to engage him in an honest dialogue. Among his initial discoveries was confirmation of BSC's calamitous relationship with both the FBI and RCMP. Mills routinely heard "nothing less than little digs" directed at Stephenson and BSC, which in RCMP circles, he cautioned, "practically represents H.M. Government." They referred to BSC "as fools and some as knaves," an impression that was all the more puzzling to him because he never heard from the RCMP "a single word against the FBI or any of its representatives although most other forms of Americanism come in for plenty of criticism." Reinforcing his growing concerns were comments made by Stewart Wood, the RCMP commissioner, who described for Mills his personal difficulties with BSC. Wood confidentially told Mills that Hoover shared a great deal of information with his staff, adding the proviso that none of it go to BSC without prior Bureau approval. As for Wood's own relations with BSC, Mills found them "so bad they scarcely could be worse, and beyond the hope of repair."[3]

Mills's frequent visits to BSC's New York office left him bewildered. As a canny business owner with an eye for financial statements and bottom lines, he was surprised to discover a bloated and inefficient bureaucracy with hundreds of personnel performing little meaningful work. Stephenson's professional staff received harsher criticism. Some of them were lazy with little to do; others were "polished nincompoops" whose only qualifications for their assignments were influential "friends at court."[4]

After carefully reviewing the transatlantic information flow, Mills found that the bottleneck was not necessarily BSC but rather Felix Cowgill, the head of SIS's Section V, who stubbornly refused to release information which he felt should not be shared. This criticism of Cowgill was undoubtedly influenced by the larger tensions between Cowgill and MI5 over B Division's discovery that he was withholding all ISOS and ISK decrypts that mentioned double agents including Garbo. MI5 was not alone in these feelings. Ewen Montagu had little regard for Cowgill, accusing him of possessing a "psychological inability to inform anyone of anything that he can possibly avoid." Weighing in against his own boss was Kim Philby, the head of Section V's Iberian branch, who complained that Cowgill's failure to distribute decrypts more widely threatened to produce distorted and incorrect appreciations of the enemy.[5]

Mills's conversations with the FBI were equally sobering. Hoover's staff had little regard for Harford Montgomery Hyde, BSC's man handling the MI5 account, claiming he had no background in counterintelligence matters. Hyde, who was very close to Stephenson and politically well connected, would be Stephenson's choice in March 1943 to assemble a self-serving, two-hundred-page chronicle of the organization's accomplishments, *Report of British Security Coordination in the United States of America.* Mills learned that all FBI reports destined for MI5 were sent through BSC, as well as directly to Thurston in order to guarantee delivery. At the same time important issues requiring action on either side of the Atlantic were exclusively handled through Thurston. Mills warned Petrie about the hopelessness of the situation, noting that the FBI/BSC relationship was so poisoned that the assignment of any MI5 officer to serve under Stephenson, replacing Hyde, would be "doomed to failure." Mills went on to note that "until we face up to this frankly we shall get no improvement. On the contrary, I fear that our continued association with Stephenson is bringing no little credit and the sooner our work can be detached the better it will be for it." Mills described Hoover's eagerness for the permanent assignment of an MI5 officer to Washington in a liaison role serving as Thurston's counterpart with an office and access to raw FBI files.[6]

At the same time that FBI discussions with Mills were underway about permanent MI5/FBI liaison in Washington, MI5 sounded out Thurston on the same issue. The question in London, however, centered on the possibility of the FBI accepting an MI5 officer under Stephenson's control. Thurston explained that relations with the BSC would never be completely severed because, in fact, the FBI needed this line of communication in order to acquire vital information. On average, ten to twelve items concerning espionage cases in South and Central America were exchanged daily. BSC also had several important sources which the FBI could not ignore, as well as an extensive card-index file built up over many years on Latin American matters. There was also a British Caribbean censorship product which had uncovered a number of German espionage agents in the Western Hemisphere as well as MI6 reports from stations in the Eastern Hemisphere. MI5 had similar needs from the FBI, which included information concerning double-agent cases, updates on German espionage agents captured by the FBI, Abwehr sabotage equipment, communications, and tradecraft methods studied by the FBI under the censorship arrangements then in effect. Guy Liddell, a participant in these discussions, complained that with Thurston in London and no MI5 representative in Washington, the information flow would eventually devolve into a one-way street in Washington's direction. Unless the Security Service assigned an experienced officer inside the FBI building to "ferret around," Liddell warned, the current exchange setup would gradually settle into a lopsided relationship consistent with the way things were before Thurston's arrival. Looking beyond the Secret Service's immediate needs, Liddell hoped to cement strong ties with Hoover and his FBI while there was still a serious wartime need, rather than after the emergency passed. The "FBI will remain after the others fade away after the war," he warned, "and we should lay the groundwork for the future." Information needs and long-term relationships were not the only problems. From a practical standpoint there was the question of how liaison with the FBI would work. The assignment of an MI5 officer under Stephenson would be cumbersome, as BSC's downtown and uptown offices already had separate liaison with local and Washington FBI officials. Yet based on his experiences and Mills's reports, Liddell concluded with certainty that the FBI would never trust an MI5 officer serving under the BSC banner.[7]

In his haste to move the process along, the inexperienced Thurston prematurely cabled Hoover, reporting MI5's interest in directly assigning a representative to the FBI. Adding to his misstep was an endorsement of the idea by Ambassador Winant, followed by the Department of State's official imprimatur, all before senior British officials had a chance to consider the matter. When MI6 officials learned of Thurston's actions they were stunned. Vivian sent a stinging memorandum to Petrie, accusing him of instigating Thurston's actions in order to cut across MI6 lines of responsibility. The clearly blindsided director-general quickly chided Thurston for getting "too far ahead" in the matter, reminding him that the agreement signed between MI5 and MI6 in 1941, assigning Stephenson as MI5's representative in America, remained in effect. Yet despite his professed concern over this interagency dust-up, Petrie could not have been more pleased with the opening that Thurston's presence in London offered him for expanding the FBI-MI5 relationship even further.[8]

Within weeks of becoming prime minister, Winston Churchill formed a highly secret subcommittee of the War Cabinet called the Home Defense (Security) Executive, better known as the "Security Executive" under the chairmanship of Lord Swinton, previously Sir Philip Cunliffe-Lister, a Conservative politician and a former air minister. Its original mandate was to address security matters, focusing on flushing out Fifth Columnist groups. Two months later Swinton turned his attention to MI5 with instructions to reform the organization along business lines by introducing modern technology to its antiquated filing system. The Security Executive's membership was balanced with officials from various ministries including the War Office and the Home Office, along with Petrie for MI5 and Vivian. On April 9, 1943, the Security Executive convened at Kinnaird House under the chairmanship of Duff Cooper, who had succeeded Swinton in June 1942, to address the question of MI5's representation in Washington.

Cooper was born in 1890 in London to a prominent surgeon who specialized in remedying the "sexual problems of the upper class." After schooling at Eton and Oxford he joined the diplomatic service, later serving as a subaltern in the Grenadier Guards during the First World War in France, where he was wounded and decorated with the Distinguished Service Order. After the war he rejoined the diplomatic service and in 1920 he married Lady Diana Manners, the beautiful daughter of the Duke of Rutland. Two decades later as a member of the House of Commons, Churchill appointed him to his cabinet.[9]

With Desmond Morton, Churchill's long-serving intelligence advisor in attendance, the Security Executive concluded that "a representative in direct contact with the F.B.I. appeared to be required" for MI5 as BSC was not meeting the Security Service's needs in the Western Hemisphere. As a former SIS officer, the hostile Morton frequently disparaged the Security Service, even while MI5-controlled double agents "were achieving unprecedented success in deceiving the enemy." In his opinion, "MI5 tends to see dangerous men too freely and to lack that knowledge of the world and sense of perspective which the Home Secretary rightly considers essential."[10] Cooper instructed Petrie to send an officer to the United States to survey the situation with the final decision for a transfer to be worked out between the MI6 and MI5 leadership. He also ordered Vivian to New York to inspect Stephenson's operation, with particular emphasis on personnel reductions in BSC's counterespionage section. Cooper warned Vivian that if BSC had outlived its usefulness, then SIS should carefully weigh whether the title of "British Security Co-ordination and the position of Director should continue and, if so, by whom it should be held." If he found such to be the case in respect to Stephenson, then "possibilities would arise of his leaving the service of the S.I.S."[11]

Given the extreme sensitivity of this mission, Petrie acted cautiously in choosing the man to represent his interests in the United States. In the end he chose Geoffrey C. Denham, an old friend and colleague from his days in the Indian Police. In the years before the First World War, Denham worked closely with Petrie in the investigation of the Alipore conspiracy, a botched attempt on the life of a British magistrate by radical Indian nationalists which had resulted in the death of a woman and her daughter. Denham's work led to the arrests of thirty-three suspects, most of whom were convicted a year later. In 1915 he was assigned to Canada, where he probed a series of sabotage bombings along the west coasts of the United States and Canada, organized by Franz von Bopp, the German consul-general based in San Francisco. Explosives hidden on ships sailing from Tacoma and Seattle exploded along with suspicious fires in Canadian Pacific Railway tunnels in British Columbia. Denham frequently visited San Francisco, where he assisted the Bureau and the local U.S. attorney in the successful prosecution of von Bopp and others on conspiracy charges. Later Denham moved to Singapore where he worked for two years as the police commissioner before retiring to a private business in Java. When war was declared in 1939, Denham joined MI6 in Burma, Singapore, and India before Menzies ordered his return to London in early 1943. In Denham, Petrie had a confidant and a richly experienced law enforcement officer with decades of criminal investigations under his belt. He had worked with the old Bureau of Investigation before the war, could speak the language of the FBI, and Petrie wanted the FBI director to know it. Denham "is an exceptionally competent" law-enforcement professional, Petrie wrote in his letter of introduction to Hoover, whose "knowledge of intelligence matters, particularly Japanese activities, in the Far East is probably far more up-to-date and extensive than that possessed by any but a very few officers today."[12]

On the evening of June 4, 1943, Denham and Vivian boarded the RMS *Queen Elizabeth* at Southampton for the perilous high-speed run across the Atlantic. Unsurpassed in size for more than half a century, the liner had been secretly refitted for military use in Singapore and had been employed ferrying troops and German prisoners captured during the North African campaign across the Atlantic. Taking a zig-zag course and cruising at a top speed of twenty-six knots, she easily outran enemy U-boats.[13]

Cimperman and Thurston had learned a great deal about Denham from MI5 and from their conversations with him. Aside from his impressive résumé, Mickey Ladd, the head of the FBI's National Defense Division, learned that Denham's main asset was his close friendship with Petrie. His assignment was to assess the possibility of MI5 taking over full responsibility for counterespionage operations in Canada and the Caribbean, establishing direct liaison with the FBI and bypassing BSC, with Cyril Mills acting as Petrie's personal representative in Washington. Adding to the mix was Denham's resentment toward MI6 and Menzies, for reasons unknown, which apparently dated back to when he had worked for the service years earlier. As Thurston noted, the best thing in the FBI's favor is Denham's "extreme dislike" for MI6 and, by extension, BSC.[14]

Seven days later, Hoover launched a charm offensive when the *Queen Elizabeth* passed Ambrose Light, through the Lower Bay and into quarantine in New York. Waiting for Denham was Harry Kimball, who, since his visit to London ten months earlier, had been reassigned to the New York field office. Kimball escorted his guest off the ship to a waiting Coast Guard vessel which quickly hustled him to the pier, past a cursory immigration check, to a waiting car which whisked him uptown to Grand Army Plaza, where the FBI had arranged for him to stay at the luxurious Plaza Hotel overlooking Central Park. Hoover ensured that full courtesies were extended to this most important British visitor throughout his visit to the United States. An appreciative Denham was surprised by his reception. Hoover's men "have been kindness itself," he recalled, claiming the FBI had been "put to the test and found them not wanting and without reserve, though I must confess I was warned by everybody that such co-operation was most unlikely."[15]

Denham opened his meeting with the FBI by asserting he was his own man and not working for Stephenson. His task was not made any easier when Ladd brought up a recent incident involving British handling of espionage agents traveling between Europe and the Western Hemisphere. New information had revealed German use of Trinidad as a route for infiltrating agents into the Western Hemisphere, a clue that proved valuable for both the FBI and the British. The previous January, the FBI's man in Trinidad, Joseph Holmes, had reported that the British had arrested Hans Alfredo Laski, Joaquim Martinez, Francisco Jose Javier Pacheco y Questa, Pacheco y Questa's wife, Viviana, and Fernando Lipkau Balletta, all trained German spies sailing across the Atlantic to fulfill their Abwehr missions. The arrests had been made in the hope of seizing their cipher material, which could add to the already extensive British understanding of the German agent communication system. More recently, however, agents intercepted at Trinidad, such as Juan Gomez-Lecube, who had been bound for Panama, carried no cipher material, casting serious doubt on the wisdom of the arrests. Ladd complained to Denham that Martinez, who had worked for two years as a German agent in Spain and Argentina, could have offered valuable clues about the Abwehr's Latin America operations. In Pacheco's case, he was a Cuban, traveling with his wife, bound for Cuba. Laski was headed for Venezuela, equipped with mail drop addresses in the United States, while Balletta, a Mexican, was en route to Detroit with a mission to find work at the Chrysler or Ford factories to collect production statistics on tanks and armored vehicles for passage to Abwehr mail drops in Mexico. Having been intercepted, the five had been placed on the SS *Masskerk,* which stopped briefly in New York before continuing the voyage to Great Britain where they had been interned. Having received permission from BSC, the FBI were interviewing the five between April 11 and 15 when BSC abruptly suspended the interviews, citing London's desire "to interview the prisoners . . . without same having been previously interviewed by Bureau representatives." Assurances were given, however, that the interrogation results would be relayed to the Americans.[16]

Galled at the loss of five potential sources of valuable information who might have contributed to the FBI's developing double-agent program, which Liddell had encouraged just a year earlier, Ladd had learned about

Cowgill's obsession with security from Thurston, who had accused the SIS officer of burning "a message before it was decoded in the interest of security." Correctly surmising that the five had been compromised by decrypts, Ladd told Denham that the arrests had not been based on information from German agents jailed in England, as MI6 had claimed, insisting that this fabrication was nothing more than a cover story intended to protect the true sources, ISOS and ISK. Denham then tried to calm the FBI man by assuring him that upon his return to London he would encourage a proposal that future German spies should be allowed to continue their journeys unimpeded so the Bureau could be given advance notice of their arrival. Over the next few days, as tensions relaxed, relations improved considerably through a series of frank and open discussions which included a rare opportunity for extensive conversations with Hoover, whom Denham later characterized as "undoubtedly a real personality worthy of admiration."[17]

On June 23 Vivian paid a courtesy visit to Ed Tamm. Vivian, known simply as "V.V.," had been born in London in 1886, one of nine children of two famous artists, the portrait painter Comley Vivian and his wife, the miniaturist Elizabeth Farquhar, both of whom had been exhibited at the Royal Society of the Arts and the Royal Academy. At the age of twenty Vivian had joined the Indian Police Service, where he served for twenty years. He had received steady promotions in the Punjab's criminal intelligence department and had been transferred to Delhi Intelligence Bureau, where he took over as assistant director. Later he served with the Indian Army in Palestine and Turkey and was decorated with the MBE. By 1920 he held the rank of major in MI-1c, SIS's War Office cover designation for the Secret Intelligence Service, then headed by the legendary Mansfield Smith-Cumming. For his concentrated study of the Pan-Islamism threat and communist subversion in Turkey and Persia, he would receive the CBE.[18]

Vivian returned to London in 1925, where he continued his work on communism and anarchism as the head of SIS's newly established Section V. One biographer described him as a professional amply suited for the role "both by experience and temperament," bringing to his post "habits of meticulous case work and attention to detail acquired in India." In 1933 Vivian uncovered the first hints of Stalin's purges through the investigation of Johann Heinrich deGraff, a senior Comintern agent recruited by the SIS station in Berlin. Felix Cowgill replaced him as head of Section V when he was made Menzies's deputy.[19]

Tamm listed his difficulties with Stephenson and BSC, and Vivian explained the purpose of his visit as surveying BSC's performance while insisting that MI6 wanted only goodwill in its relationship with the FBI. At the same meeting he told Tamm that he was opposed to a direct MI5 and FBI liaison. Bluntly dismissing his claim of interest in improving MI6's links with the FBI, Tamm warned that Hoover was encouraging direct relations with MI5 for reasons outlined by Thurston to Menzies months earlier. After their meeting ended in stalemate, Tamm told Hoover that Vivian was "very frankly upset" over the possibility of a direct MI5 relationship with the FBI, characterizing it as "unconstitutional" under the British system.[20]

From Washington, Denham traveled to Ottawa to confer with Stuart Wood, a meeting that was a reunion of sorts as both men had worked together nearly a quarter-century earlier when Wood had served in the North-West Territory and Denham had been investigating German sabotage in Regina. Wood's insights about Stephenson reinforced his earlier conversations with Ladd and Hoover, leading the bewildered Denham to conclude that Stephenson had "in some way or other entirely estranged some people over here who are of the utmost importance to us." Days later, back in New York for scheduled meetings with Stephenson, Denham learned that the BSC director had unexpectedly flown to London. Furious, Denham cabled Petrie that Stephenson had made himself unavailable for consultation, a snub that left Denham with "only one thing to do and that was to leave him out of consideration."[21]

Stephenson's deputies were in no mood to offer generous cooperation and, according to Denham, had tried to "put me on the spot," taking a literal interpretation of the resolution for a "speedy" handover of MI5 responsibilities to him at once, a ploy the wily Denham dismissed as a deliberate attempt "to make things difficult." The notion of such a quick change was, in Denham's view, quite absurd as he had no funds, no office space, no budget, no nominee for the assignment, and, most important, no final approval from Petrie and Menzies.[22]

By the end of July everything changed. When Denham and Vivian had arrived in New York on June 15 they had been in accord that separate representation would take place based on the recommendation of the Security Executive. Up to July 9 Denham had still believed that both he and Vivian were in complete agreement. On July 19 Vivian made an unexpected visit to the State Department where he discussed the matter with Adolf Berle, informing him that the matter was still an open question with "no binding decision" having been made.[23]

On July 30, with Denham still in the United States, the Security Executive meeting at Kinnaird House heard Vivian (now suddenly back in London) describe his "unstinted praise" for Stephenson and BSC, and reviewed his letter to the Security Executive accusing Denham of "fishing in troubled waters" by spending too much time with the FBI.[24] Vivian received support from Edwin Herbert, the director of Imperial Censorship and a member of the Security Executive. Born in London in 1899, he had been educated at Queen's College, Taunton, before joining the Royal Naval Volunteer Reserve in 1917 as a signalman. Later he earned a law degree at London University and entered private practice until 1925, when he joined Sydney Morse, one of the City's most prestigious firms, and became a senior partner. In 1940 Churchill appointed him director-general of the Postal and Telegraph Censorship Department, which he had built into a "highly efficient machine" that exercised control over both enemy and neutral mail and other means of communication through inspection facilities in Bermuda and Vancouver. One biographer called him a man of "characteristic personal courage" who had flown to America immediately after the Japanese attack on Pearl Harbor to offer the American director-general designate for censorship his advice and encouragement. Herbert and Stephenson shared "complete confidence" in each other, a status shared with Herbert's deputies Charles des Graz, a former chairman of Sotheby's, and William Hill-Wood of the London banking firm Morgan Grenfell, who supervised censorship in the Western Hemisphere from headquarters in New York. Herbert's work was rewarded in 1943 with a knighthood followed by the U.S. Medal of Merit at war's end.[25]

Herbert and Vivian described Hoover as a schemer whose strategy was aimed at creating a direct relationship with MI5 to use as a wedge between MI5 and MI6, for the purpose of driving the British out of the United States. Accusing Hoover of selfishness and pettiness, Herbert claimed that he had refused to supply the American censorship authorities with a list of known Abwehr cover addresses for fear that they would become known to the OSS.[26] Petrie found Herbert's argument absurd, on the grounds that Hoover was on record about the critical importance of British censorship to the FBI. During his many discussions with the British, Hoover had characterized it as one of the most effective tools for identifying German and Japanese spies in the United States and Latin America. Driving the British out of the United States made even less sense considering the extraordinary value of Ultra to the FBI. Petrie then reminded the Security Executive that when he had previously discussed MI5's direct liaison with Stephenson, no objection had been posed.[27]

Richard Butler, Petrie's personal assistant since 1940, and a former London lawyer, openly challenged Vivian's vote of confidence for BSC without access to his written report as requested by Duff Cooper months earlier. The Executive still had no information about the BSC Registry system, which was reportedly in complete disarray, about the number of staff employed, and the endemic infighting. Unanswered questions still remained about the "suitability of some of the officers there for the intelligence functions which they are supposed to be carrying out."[28] Even more worrisome for Butler was the explanation to Hoover about any change of decision concerning a direct relationship. An awkward explanation would have to be offered not only to Hoover but also to the American ambassador, the Foreign Office, the Dominions Office, and the Colonial Office. Just as Butler was recommending that Cooper order a further report before placing any weight on Vivian's views, Thurston received a cable from Hoover dated August 13 informing him that Stephenson had returned to the United States with "full control over British intelligence interests and that Mr. Denham has been recalled to London." Hoover demanded an explanation.[29]

In the end Menzies and Stephenson won the battle. Vivian, who had not objected to such a move while traveling with Denham, strongly opposed the decision and, together with the support of Herbert and Desmond Morton, persuaded Cooper of the dire consequences that would ensue for British interests in the Western Hemisphere. Insisting on the need for British unanimity, the Security Executive abruptly reversed course, ruling that no MI5 officer would be assigned to the FBI in Washington. In a cable to Denham explaining the decision, Cooper offered his regrets, claiming that the unanimous decision of the Security Executive was based on the views "expressed by all who have recently returned from the U.S. including Herbert of Censorhip [*sic*] and Vivian . . . as to the grave unwisdom of dividing our representation there."[30]

The issue of MI5 representation in the United States remained the subject of heated discussion over the next two months. Cooper's view was that a role for Mills, similar to Thurston's, was possible with Stephenson's full agreement; but without his full cooperation Stephenson would make "life impossible for Mills." Liddell disagreed, believing that after everything that had occurred over the years, Stephenson could not affect MI5's relations with the FBI. After much debate, a compromise of sorts was reached which kept the counterespionage account with BSC while offering an opening for direct MI5 meetings with the FBI in Washington. Cyril Mills was authorized to travel to Washington for meetings with Hoover and his staff, and joint visits of FBI and MI5 officers between London and Washington were approved as the need arose.[31] In the end, however, everyone recognized that a direct relationship between the FBI and MI5 was a dead issue despite the overwhelming need for change. Cooper nonetheless had closed the door on the topic in a dismissive fashion. At a meeting on September 27, Cooper issued his final edict to Petrie:

> In the future there will be no special representative of M.I.5. in Washington. Mr. Denham will complete his tour in the Caribbean and then return and report. Mr. Mills will return to Canada on special M.I.5. work. M.I.5's relations with F.B.I. will in future be restricted to communication through Mr. Thurston and, possibly, to special visits as in the past. Such visits will only take place with the knowledge and agreement of B.S.C.[32]

Denham was completely nonplussed when he was suddenly ordered to return to London after learning of the decision to retain the status quo. In a blistering series of cables he complained that he had been asked to return to London from India to take on this mission. After fully briefing himself on the situation, he had undertaken an exhausting transatlantic voyage, under harrowing conditions, only to learn that a decision had been made without his input or report. For reasons far beyond his grasp he had been left with the feeling that he had, in the end, been dispatched to America on "a fool's errand."[33]

Denham had an additional dilemma. While in Washington he had informed the FBI director that a change was underway, and accordingly he felt honor-bound to personally explain the sudden shift in policy to Hoover. Thurston, of course, routinely had kept Hoover updated on the debate, passing on details received from his Security Service colleagues. Liddell, who was fully aware of this, had urged Petrie to tell Hoover of the final decision as soon as possible, and the letter they produced, which took on new urgency, was a truly team effort. The original draft prepared by Richard Butler with some editing by Liddell was followed by discussion with Cooper. In his first draft Butler had inserted, at Denham's request, a line that he was continuing his tour of the Caribbean area but wished to personally express his appreciation for Hoover's hospitality. Cooper rejected this line, reasoning that Denham would be an unnecessary supplement to Petrie's official statement concerning London's decision. Another fear was that Stephenson would object if he thought Petrie had authorized Denham's visit, which might be interpreted as an unfortunate revival of ancient disagreements. After completing the letter on Wednesday, September 29, Butler traveled more than a hundred and thirty miles by train to Cardiff, where Petrie signed it at his country home near Llanover, a tiny rural town at the base of the Black Mountains.[34]

Tinged with apology and disappointment, Petrie summarized the new plan for Hoover. The "Security Executive is the body to which is submitted for discussion and advice all problems touching on security or intelligence work in which there may be a conflict of departmental interests," he wrote, and while it is "unnecessary to burden you with the details of these discussions . . . it was thought desirable to arrange for Mr. Denham to cut short his tour and come back to London to report." Petrie then noted that after Denham's arrival "further discussions took place, and it has now been agreed that the Security Service shall in future have no special representation in the U.S.A."[35]

Recognizing the continued importance of a close alliance between the two services, Petrie offered his assurances that all future exchanges would be through Thurston. Signaling his appreciation for an FBI presence in London, he told Hoover "how delighted we are to have Mr. Thurston with us," characterizing him "as one of the family" at MI5. Petrie concluded that he was "confident that such friendly relations, which it is my earnest wish to see developed as far as possible, will be of very great advantage to our common war effort and also to our work thereafter." While conceding that he was "somewhat disappointed" over the change, Hoover nevertheless signaled his disregard for BSC by making Bureau records available to Mills whenever the need arose, and by turning to him when matters of "mutual interest" arose. In closing, Hoover urged Petrie to have "Mr. Mills do likewise whenever you have occasion for him to take up some matter personally with this Bureau."[36]

The endgame occurred when Denham, who was in New York resuming his trip to the Caribbean, expressed a desire to meet Hoover to extend his appreciation for his hospitality, and his hope for continued goodwill between the Bureau and the British services. Evidently he had not received word of Cooper's ban on such a meeting. When Stephenson ordered Denham to meet the FBI officials only in the company of a BSC representative,

Denham refused, claiming that he didn't need a "watch-dog" as he was neither a government employee nor under Stephenson's control.[37] Denham cleverly agreed to be accompanied by Stephenson himself to Washington, confident that Hoover would never talk to the BSC chief. Naturally, Stephenson turned down the offer and Denham eventually cooled down, but not before he had sent a personal note to Hoover offering his apologies that they could not meet. "I must say I regret that I am not in a position to work more closely at Washington," he wrote, "but Sir David Petrie's letter will have explained how circumstances have altered."[38]

Denham did, however, travel to Washington where, in a scorching act of indiscretion, he unloaded his feelings about the entire matter to G. C. Burton, a supervisor assigned to the FBI's Espionage Section. Emphasizing MI5's earnest desire to work with the FBI "frankly and openly," he launched into a tirade about the "rather low caliber" of BSC personnel. He said that Stephenson "surrounded himself with incompetence," ignoring British wartime interests and instead advancing his own agenda by making important contacts that would assist his business prospects in the years to come. "He believes that Stephenson will be knighted for his activities during the war," Burton later wrote, which "will cloak him with considerable prestige." This will offer him access to a "dozen or more directorships in large American companies with which he has made contacts" while acting in his official capacity for the British government. Denham ended his diatribe with the charge that MI6 had adopted a rather "high-handed attitude" toward the FBI, which he characterized as "not unusual." He offered it as an illustration of the "pettiness" of MI6 personnel, which derived from their "false sense of self-importance" as a result of their control over the product of British code-breaking, and Menzies's privilege of direct personal access to the prime minister.[39]

Was Denham simply an old man whose time had come and gone? Or had he and Petrie simply been outmaneuvered by wilier and more skillful Whitehall bureaucrats? Were his remarkably indiscreet remarks, particularly to an American intelligence officer, who had no business hearing such comments concerning MI6 and Stephenson, really accurate? Was Menzies thinking of his own interest while ignoring, even demeaning, a liaison service to which he only wanted to extend goodwill? Did the BSC director surround himself with second-rate personnel? Was Stephenson playing a double game, leveraging and enhancing his relationships with important American industrialists and businessmen under British intelligence cover in the hope of further enriching himself after the war? Or was he, as so many have claimed, Intrepid, the quintessential man of mystery, secretly pursuing an Allied wartime agenda at some very high level of policy with the full countenance of both governments? Whatever the truth of Denham's outburst, and Cooper's decision to keep Stephenson in place, one indelible fact stands out: the die was now cast. For the remainder of the war all meaningful FBI liaisons with MI6 and MI5 would be routed only through Hoover's men now embedded at the American embassy in London.

CHAPTER EIGHT

South of the Border

At the same time Denham was complaining to FBI officials about the intelligence service of his own country, J. Edgar Hoover sat at the top of America's only civilian foreign espionage service.

The idea for an American foreign espionage operation originated in early May 1940 with a flurry of Washington meetings following the surprise German invasion of France, when officials suddenly became concerned about a potential German and Italian threat to Latin American governments. By early June an agreement had been reached between the MID, ONI, and the FBI on the scope, activities, and jurisdiction of American foreign intelligence collection. Assistant Secretary of State Adolf Berle then took the matter to the president, who issued a top-secret verbal order creating America's first foreign espionage service and delineated the regions of the world for intelligence coverage by the military and the FBI. Roosevelt's June 24 directive assigned Hoover to collect "foreign intelligence in the western hemisphere on the request of the State Department," with the army handling Europe, Africa, and the Panama Canal region and the navy covering the western Pacific region and Asia.[1] The directive cautioned that any "proposed additional foreign intelligence work should not supersede work now being done" by the FBI which "might be called in by the State Department on special assignments outside the American hemisphere under special circumstances."[2]

By July 1940 Hoover had created the clandestine Special Intelligence Service (SIS) and appointed Percy Foxworth as its new leader. All assignees initially posed as businessmen in the countries of interest. A month later, through the assistance of Nelson Rockefeller, grandson of the legendary John D. Rockefeller, Foxworth established a fictitious business firm, the Importers and Exporters Service Company, in a one-room office manned by an FBI clerk at 30 Rockefeller Plaza in New York. The company, which posed as a research firm conducting surveys of Latin American markets, business prospects, and trade opportunities, soon proved impractical. It had been created too fast and with little thought. Undercover agents going to Latin America had no business literature for local customers, no training for their assignments, no knowledge in the language of business, nor any U.S.-based associates to refer potential business prospects. Suspicions only deepened when visitors to the Rockefeller Center office found one lonely person sitting at a desk in a cold, antiseptic workplace who couldn't answer the most basic questions. Years later in an internal history, the FBI acknowledged these failings, describing the Importers and Exporters Services Company as "more of a nuisance and detriment than an advantage" when a constant stream of salesmen, business investigators of various types, and advertising solicitors visited, hoping to speak to someone in charge. As for Hoover, he called it an "embarrassment."[3]

Initial funding amounting to more than $400,000 came directly from a confidential fund buried in the 1940 military appropriations budget and controlled by the president alone. Part of the effectiveness of the SIS program in the years before America's entry into the war was its complete secrecy.

> A request by the Bureau for funds from Congress for SIS operations would perforce be made a matter of public record available to any person who desired to see the request and the resultant compliance thereto. Therefore the necessary funds were obtained from the confidential fund allotted by the Congress annually to the President of the United States for confidential unvouchered expenditures. This fund is administered by the Bureau of the Budget for the President and there is no requirement of law that the reasons underlying the expense be made a matter of public record.[4]

By September 1940 seven agents had been dispatched to Brazil, Cuba, Mexico, Peru, Uruguay, and Venezuela.[5] A few months later that number doubled with agents either permanently assigned or traveling throughout Latin America on intelligence missions. One original SIS man, Gus Jones, a sixty-year-old Texan who joined the Bureau of Investigation in 1916, had worked for twenty-five years on every kind of investigation imaginable, from one end of the country to the other. One memorable assignment occurred in 1935 when Hoover assigned him to head the security team on the train carrying the nation's most dangerous convicts to Alcatraz, the newly opened federal penitentiary on a rocky outcrop in the middle of San Francisco Bay. Jones was the Special Agent in Charge of the San Antonio Division in 1939 when he began working with the Mexican police. Along with cross-border criminal investigations, Jones worked closely with Colonel Alvaro Basail, the assistant chief of Mexico's Secret Service in the formation of a radio patrol in Mexico City, the first of its kind in Latin America.[6]

In September 1940, Ambassador Josephus Daniels made Jones a "civil attaché" at the embassy in Mexico City in response to his growing concern about German subversion in the country. Jones remained in this post until 1943 when he was reassigned to Bermuda. Years later he recalled that "from 1939 to 1943, I was privileged to collaborate with Mexican officials whose duties were to investigate and control the actions of foreigners who were engaged in activities that were inimical to the best interests of Mexico and the American hemisphere."[7] Another SIS officer was Special Agent Edgar Thompson, who for five years before the war worked in Colombia and Brazil training local army and police officials in counterespionage. He had found himself posing as a businessman with no training, explanation, or backstopping in his new role.[8] The product of these FBI agents-turned-businessmen was predictably negligible "in the beginning and for some time thereafter quite small and of little value," according to a later history of the service. Unfamiliarity with the local language, customs, and culture posed serious problems. With "a very poor pretext for clandestine operations and the widening of his circle of acquaintances," undercover agents found themselves isolated, a condition only worsened by a prohibition against embassy contact and no American expatriates who could be trusted or approached for help.[9]

Hoover's undercover agents also had major difficulties transmitting information to Washington quickly and safely. All had been hastily trained in the use of secret ink for letter writing, a procedure that was often slow, inefficient, and dangerous. The information hidden between the lines of a routine letter was often vague, superficial, and lacking the necessary detail for policy formulation. Agencies generally "took no action" on these often isolated and uncorroborated reports, but they did send them to the local ambassador and diplomatic staff. "The almost invariable result would be a diplomatic dispatch or cable reply . . . denouncing the authenticity of the original information supplied by the undercover agent." In one instance a local embassy staff member tried to identify the agent and the source of the information. Later frictions emerged between the SIS and embassy staff members when the quality of these reports slowly improved. As Washington policy makers began taking them more seriously, embassy specialists became defensive, viewing SIS work as a "reflection upon their own efforts in the intelligence field."[10]

The "difficulty being caused by the British" also slowed SIS progress. The British postal censorship with stations at Bermuda, Trinidad, and Jamaica kept a very close watch on mail moving in and out of Latin America. So skilled were they that in a matter of months SIS secret writing messages were being investigated by MI6 for the "bona fides" of the writer.[11] Codes and ciphers proved equally worthless when Latin American laws began requiring the registration of codes used in international cablegrams.

By late 1940 FBI and State Department officials recognized that coordination between undercover agents and the local diplomatic staff required the presence of an FBI agent in the embassies to support the undercover agent. A major obstacle to such an initiative was the resistance (despite Jones's appointment) from the State Department and, particularly, local ambassadors. Their view was that FBI agents would pose a danger to intergovernmental relations. They had no diplomatic training, no experience working in foreign countries, nor any language skills or familiarity with Latin cultures. Even more worrisome was a constant fear of diplomatic blowback on the United States if the FBI's new role became public knowledge.[12] Spruille Braden, the ambassador in Bogota, broke the impasse in November 1940 when he requested an FBI agent to handle "subversive activities investigations and the coordination of intelligence activities in Colombia."[13] Braden was a forty-seven-year-old Montana native who made one fortune digging for copper and another as a shrewd stock investor before his appointment to Colombia in 1939. From the start Braden was frustrated by the shortage of information on local conditions, in particular the extent of Nazi influence on political life and commerce. Colombia was also important to both the United States and Germany as a source of wolfram, a rare strategic mineral used as a hardening alloy for other metals in weapons such as artillery projectiles.[14]

As a businessman and mining engineer, Braden was trained in solving problems. He was not a professional diplomat with institutional State Department biases. As a visionary facing a serious challenge, he quickly began pestering Washington for any insights into what he faced in his new job. "I stormed around Washington for a month," he later remembered, "about the importance of having adequate intelligence in Colombia." He wanted the "low-down," as he put it, "on Nazi fifth-column activities and how to set up an efficient counter-intelligence." "Desperate straits" is how he later described his predicament: a danger that only worsened as Nazi propagandists increasingly began threatening his life and that of Eduardo Santos, Colombia's president.[15]

Around November 1940 Braden convinced Santos to form his own intelligence and security apparatus with U.S. assistance. In his view, such an organization working side by side with the Americans would be a powerful force against Nazi infiltration. Santos and Braden's plan made it "vital to maintain . . . [an] intelligence liaison" between the embassy and local police officials. After "great difficulty" Braden received State Department agreement for Hoover to detail a man permanently to his staff. One of Hoover's best operators, M. Clair Spear, arrived in Bogota in February 1941 and began working with Colombian police officials for the next seventeen months.[16] In April 1942 Spear's success led to augmentation of his staff with Richard Godfrey, and in June with Donald Clegg. The following August, Spear was replaced by Special Agent Charles Morgan. Also in 1942 Braden began augmenting his FBI Bogota contingent with FBI agent Jack Lee at the consulate in Barranquilla, James McMahon in Medellin, and Sidney Amdur in Bucaramanga. Decades later Braden called Spear an "excellent man" whose "exemplary" work opened the floodgates for FBI agents moving into embassies throughout Latin America, as well as London, Lisbon, and Madrid. At its height in October 1943, the SIS had more than 700 employees operating overseas including 350 FBI agents, Special Employees, radio operators, secretaries, and stenographers.[17]

In January 1942 President Roosevelt strengthened the SIS mandate with a budget increase of $100,000 and agreement with the military over the FBI's role in South America.[18] By July 1942 Hoover and Foxworth began modeling the attaché office on domestic FBI field offices, making each attaché, in effect, a Special Agent in Charge with "responsibility for all administrative supervision under the Bureau's direction of all work performed in the particular country involved." Building on the domestic practice of sending nationwide instructions to field offices, the SIS referred to the sequentially numbered communications to embassies as "Memorandum to all Legal Attachés." Soon unmarried male stenographers began training for embassy assignments to handle the day-to-day office routine. Twenty-five agents a month were recruited and by the summer of 1942, 152 Special Agents and Special Employees were serving in Latin America.[19]

Building on Spear's success, Hoover responded to a request from the Bolivian government in June 1942 for his agents to inspect local tin mines for evidence of sabotage. The Plant Protection Program originally started by Hoover in the fall of 1939 was a cooperative effort with the ONI and MID using a group of specially trained FBI agents to inspect industrial plants doing war work throughout the United States. These top-to-bottom surveys scrutinized every aspect of factory processes, from personnel to proper lighting to document handling to cafeteria conditions. The FBI's inspection of tin mines in 1942 soon resulted in an agreement with the U.S. military to begin training Latin American government officials in the inspection process. With FBI agents beginning to be assigned to embassies as "Security Officers," eighteen agents traveled from the United States to Latin America in January 1943 for an intense four-month mission to inspect factories and train local inspectors. The team examined 104 companies, installations, ports, and organizations with a total of 150 separate branches requiring physical security. Among the companies studied were the American Building and Refining Company in Bolivia, Companhia Paulista de Estradas de Ferro in Brazil, Gulf Oil and Royal Dutch Shell Company in Venezuela, and Ecuadorian Balsa Wood in Bolivia. Fourteen Brazilian seaports, such as Rio de Janeiro, Bahia, Maceio, and Recife, were also examined.[20]

The success of these surveys led to an increasing number of State Department requests for security studies of a far more delicate nature. Just how safe were American diplomatic installations from local counterintelligence penetration? To answer this important question, Hoover sent technically trained agents overseas under the guise of embassy code clerks on temporary assignment and diplomatic couriers. During the war, they traveled not only to Latin America but to England, Scotland, Sweden, Finland, Spain, and Portugal. In May 1945, with the war in Europe at an end, they made technical inspections in Holland, France, Switzerland, Poland, and Germany.[21]

The results were often startling. Typical of the findings was an inspection in August 1943 of the many offices making up the American embassy and consulates in Spain, Portugal, and Spanish Morocco. In Spain, taps were discovered on the telephones of the ambassador, deputy ambassador, military attaché, and head of the Office of War Information, along with the consulate telephones in Barcelona and Bilbao. They were also discovered on the private hotel phones of the military attaché and his assistant, a vice-consul's residence, and the private home of the economic attaché. Findings at Tangier were no different; six taps were uncovered. Particularly unsettling was a discovery on the consulate phones in Valencia, Malaga, and San Sebastian, as well as in the home of the American consul in San Sebastian: microphones in the phones for operation even when not in use. FBI personnel were not immune. One tap was found on the "unlisted telephone assigned to the radio room utilized by the office of the Legal Attache" in Rio de Janeiro and another on his home phone.[22]

Additional help for SIS agents soon came from American citizens recruited in the United States who had business acumen and a willingness to assist the FBI. Hired as "Special Employees," they traveled to Latin America under their true names and representing their own companies. Their role was to work for the undercover agent, spotting potential sources and then casually introducing them either to the undercover agent or someone else who then introduced the target to the undercover agent (to deflect attention away from the Special Employee) for direct assessment and recruitment as a source. In addition to spotting and assessing, they routinely violated local laws by receiving secret information from the undercover agent for transmission to Washington "through an appropriate drop-box in New York."[23]

One such volunteer was a wealthy thirty-year-old businessman named Dudley Devore Roberts. Born in 1910 to a Park Avenue physician and his wife who was the daughter of Henry Steele, president of General Chemical Company, young Dudley followed his grandfather's path by pursuing a Wall Street career as an investment banker. Before the Second World War he founded Roberts & Company, which later merged into Kidder-Peabody & Company. Polio, which he contracted as a young man, disqualified him from military service, so he joined the FBI as a Special Employee in 1942 and worked for the next two years in Mexico.[24]

Herbert Hoover Jr., son of the thirty-first president of the United States, also served with the SIS. Born in London on August 3, 1903, Hoover earned an engineering degree at Stanford University in 1925 and a graduate degree in business from Harvard three years later. In 1929 he joined Western Air Express and Transcontinental, two of the nation's pioneering airlines, as a communications engineer. Six years later he formed the United Geophysical Company (UGC), serving almost two decades as the company's first president and as chairman of the board. Based in Pasadena, California, UGC pioneered new instrumentation and technologies for charting sub-surfaces and field studies for mining and oil companies such as Anaconda Copper and Standard Oil. Hoover's endlessly inventive mind produced dozens of new patents for such technologies as mass spectrometers, range-finders, stable seismic-wave amplifiers with automatic volume control, and a geophysical prospecting receptor circuit. The demand for UGC's advanced seismographic methods of geophysical exploration to locate new mineral and oil deposits throughout Latin America provided excellent cover for undercover agents, with the name Herbert Hoover offering instant credibility.[25]

As a teenager Hoover became interested in the new technology of radio; at the age of nineteen, he was so skilled that he began contributing articles for the new radio journals springing up throughout the country. "Mr. G. M. Best, our technical Advisor, has called my attention to your success with a tuned radio frequency amplifier, non-regenerative, for reception of 200 meter signals, by the use of separate heterodyne oscillators," wrote the editor of *Radio,* a magazine for amateur radio fans, to Hoover. "He and we both believe that a description of your equipment would be of great interest and value to many fellow workers in the radio field." A year later Hoover proudly cabled his father in Washington that "on a wavelength of .76 meters I worked New Zealand last night."[26] Hoover allowed his huge homestead near Los Angeles, which was already bristling with radio antennas, to be available for the FBI's use throughout the war. By January 1942 he had received a license for a land radio station based in Washington, D.C., which also proved useful to the FBI.[27]

One key to SIS success was strong emphasis placed on the development of informant networks and on local police liaison. Agents openly affiliated with the FBI began training local police in the tactics of counterintelligence such as surveillance, interrogation, interviews, surreptitious searches, and so on. While many local police officials worked closely with agents, liaison was often uneven or in some cases nonexistent. In Mexico, for example, there was no formal police liaison in the matter of counterintelligence. Good results were still obtained, however, when senior police officers were placed on the FBI's payroll as informants. This proved "invaluable in connection with the Bureau's overall intelligence coverage and work."[28] Surveillance was also conducted through FBI informants in local post offices, telephone companies, steamship lines, airlines, customs offices, and other government departments. Some were even recruited in presidential palaces where SIS agents acted as special advisors. Diplomats, professional and business groups, and refugees, especially those with German, Italian, or Japanese backgrounds, also offered excellent sources of needed information. During one three-month assignment in Buenos Aires, Special Agent Joseph Campisi, operating in an undercover role, developed an informant network from local Jewish groups, many of whom had escaped Nazi persecution in Europe. Later he added to his success when he was appointed security advisor to President Enrique Penaranda of Bolivia. Some informants were indirectly recruited. When William Horan was assigned to Asunción, Paraguay, he lived with a German Jewish couple, and later with the son of a Colgate University graduate whose father was the former president of Paraguay.[29]

Not every informant operation went smoothly. Occasionally, the FBI was victimized by so-called professional informants. These "very troublesome and dangerous" creatures caused "untold confusion waste, and harassment by the furnishing of inaccurate and frequently fictitious information concerning enemy activities."[30] Careful analysis and cross-checking of their reports through embassy channels frequently revealed that the informant, or an accomplice, was peddling the same intelligence to other buyers. When discovered, the bogus source was followed by "special so-called surveillance" informants, who soon exposed his fraud using a variety of creative techniques. Through "telephone and the mail surveillance, bribery of the informant's mistress, etc., it was almost invariably possible to completely expose the spurious nature of the informant's data within a comparatively short period of time," an FBI internal history later recorded. With evidence in hand, the source was "appropriately denounced and with regard to the more troublesome ones neutralized with the assistance of the local police or internment authorities."[31]

To successfully recruit a source, one must have "access" to the person. A target of information can live and work anywhere—in large cities or rural areas, major industrial concerns or corporations, state, regional or federal government, and small villages that depend on ranching, farming, or mining for their livelihood. These factors and many more dictated what type of American companies the FBI used for cover purposes. To meet this challenge the SIS covers drew from an almost infinite variety of businesses. They included popular magazines, credit organizations, news associations, commercial investment houses, stock brokerage firms, shipping lines, and motion picture companies, just to name a few. Hoover approached dozens of American businesses for help in providing his undercover agents with plausible cover jobs.

Charles Merrill, a founder of the famous financial brokerage firm that bears his name, allowed a number of agents to pose as account executives. FBI agents first attended SIS training in Washington and then enrolled in the Merrill, Lynch, Pierce, Fenner & Beane training course, leading to a brokerage license and a seat on the New York Stock Exchange. One of these agents was Kenneth McCorkle Crosby, a lawyer from Tennessee who got his Merrill Lynch credentials and was then assigned to Buenos Aires, where he set up the company's first office in that country. To make his undercover role easier, he carried a personal letter from Merrill to Leo Welch, the head of National City Bank's Buenos Aires branch, informing him of Crosby's real role; within days Welch was introducing the young account executive to Argentina's most important business and government personalities.[32]

The SIS found RKO Pictures and the Walt Disney Studios very valuable for traveling in rural areas and particularly the jungles of Brazil. Before the war Disney had produced a number of wildly popular animated movies for Brazilian audiences. Through Philip Reisman, a Disney vice president in charge of the company's export division, an undercover FBI agent collected valuable intelligence posing as a company researcher traveling through the country looking for native animals and birds for future Disney productions.[33] Latin American publications also proved helpful. *La Hacienda* was a highly regarded Spanish-language agriculture magazine published in New York City with a Latin American circulation of more than 20,000 subscribers. Agents posing as magazine researchers could ask questions in small villages and remote regions of South America without arousing local suspicion. Armour Meat Corporation allowed agents to visit the pampas where vast cattle ranches abounded while Anaconda Copper offered SIS agents access to otherwise off-limit mining regions.[34]

Media and journalistic covers were also supplied by the Hearst Magazine Corporation, the owner of *Cosmopolitan,* International News Service, *Liberty Magazine, Newsweek,* and other major publications. Hearst used undercover agents for researching short stories and feature articles, as well as acquiring articles for *Cosmopolitan* from South American writers. Agents traveled widely, asking questions on all sorts of topics of intelligence value while developing valuable contacts who in most instances were unaware of the end use of their information. Journalist Fulton Oursler, owner of the International News Service and editor of *Liberty Magazine,* covered Hoover's agents as freelance writers, allowing them to go anywhere and meet anyone while freeing them from actually writing articles. "This cover is most elastic," it was later noted, "as the amount of time required depends entirely upon the Bureau representative and further, the Bureau representative can make any number of inquiries under this cover as there is no prearranged subject matter for him to cover."[35]

Another Oursler creation was American Editors Syndicate, which he formed with journalist Bernard McFadden. Oursler had befriended Molinas Campos, a South American cartoonist, whose work he previously featured in *Liberty Magazine.* This connection led Oursler to constantly think about other plausible Latin American literary possibilities for SIS use. The SIS also relied on the J. Walter Thompson Advertising Agency to travel widely doing surveys about radio listening habits, all in a constant effort to develop informants and collect intelligence.[36]

To access corporate and financial records of Latin American firms, the SIS relied on New York firms such as American Financial Underwriters Corporation (AFUC) and Dun & Bradstreet. AFUC serviced American industry by reporting on export markets and potential buyers in Latin America, while Dun & Bradstreet offered wide latitude for undercover agents to discuss sensitive business issues, examine financial statements, and assess corporate leaders for their willingness to secretly assist Hoover and his men.[37]

Penetration of the shipping and export industry was aided through the Moore-McCormick Lines, and Smith, Kirkpatrick & Company, which engaged in general import-exports. The undercover agent with Smith & Kirkpatrick had no official duties except to connect potential customers with the main office in New York. The agent working for Moore-McCormick in Brazil posed as the owner's representative, which offered the freedom to pursue potential intelligence targets under the guise of legitimate business. Although the war had brought commercial shipping to a virtual standstill, there was plenty of room for creative cover opportunities. Instead of actually doing business, shipping companies simply sent young executives to Latin America to familiarize themselves with the region's languages, customs, and culture so as to be well placed for resumption of trade at the war's end.[38]

Not all covers proved successful. Proctor & Gamble Corporation, one of the nation's largest manufacturers of soap products, allowed agents to conduct business surveys throughout Latin America. This cover was later discontinued when soap exports ended with America's entry into the war. Perhaps the most creative cover was assigned to Frank Garvey, a young lawyer from Babylon, New York, and a scratch golfer. Garvey posed as an indolent playboy idling away his time schmoozing the wealthy and powerful at Latin America's swankiest holiday retreats while dodging military service in the United States. His assignment was successful until one day he overplayed his cover: his victory in a golf tournament became international news, prompting a wrathful Hoover to reassign him to new SIS duties in Mexico and Chile.[39]

The synergy between the undercover agents and FBI agents in the embassy soon became clear. Undercover agents now had safe local support for passage of valuable, time-sensitive intelligence acquired from an informant. The legal attaché routinely met the undercover agent in a dark alley, street corner, or restaurant, where he grabbed the material and quickly took it back to the safety of the embassy. A summary was then quickly sent to Washington over State Department radio channels while the original awaited later shipment by diplomatic courier.

FBI agents, posing as State Department couriers, carried diplomatic bags from embassy to embassy throughout Latin America, delivering mail together and such items as new codes, equipment for the SIS Network, special instruction for legal attachés, and so on. For FBI officials conducting periodic inspection tours, the cover was helpful in deflecting attention from the real purpose of their visit. One inspector, who became a legend in the FBI's SIS, was Myron Gurnea. Ken Crosby, who escaped from Argentina and was later assigned to Mexico City as the legal attaché, recalled how the Mexican federal police once put on a display of their pistol-firing skills. When one expert asked for a volunteer to have a cigarette shot from his mouth, Gurnea stunned the crowd by quickly raising his hand. Hoover's man survived the shot with a much shorter cigarette dangling from his mouth and, according to Crosby, in return received an unspoken guarantee that the FBI would receive everything it asked for from Mexican police authorities. Another SIS man posing as a courier was Louis Beck, a Wisconsin native with graduate and law degrees from the University of Southern California. Fluent in Russian and German, Beck undertook a confidential mission to Moscow in July 1940 posing as a State Department clerk to survey the porous security at the American embassy. Two years later, while carrying diplomatic mail throughout Latin America, he was again ordered to Moscow to pose as an army captain at the request of General George Marshall. His assignment was to examine the destructive rift between the army attaché and General Phillip Faymonville, then the head of the Lend-Lease Mission.[40]

Embassy radio channels soon proved inadequate for SIS purposes. State Department communicators were routinely alerted to an FBI message with the preamble "Hoover" and Hoover's name again at the end of the message. To guard against nosy eavesdroppers, Hoover established the Confidential Radio Network (CRN), which later became known simply as the SIS Network. Gradually, FBI radio technicians began installing equipment in all embassies throughout Latin America with the exception of Argentina, where encrypted messages were routed through Montevideo, Uruguay, for radio relay to Washington by FBI radio.[41]

Typical of these stations was the FBI radio setup in Santiago, Chile, operated without Chilean government knowledge. The equipment was concealed inside a filing cabinet drawer camouflaged by a row of paper binders. A tiny button released the drawer exposing the radio. While the system functioned effectively, it often produced "a lower signal level as a result of this added security." In the tradeoff of signal strength for security, the latter always trumped the former, with the concealed antenna running up the elevator shaft next to the power lines to the roof, causing what was later recorded as "considerable electrical interference."[42]

Working conditions for the radio operator greatly varied. In Bogota the radio station was in a small back room of an old house on embassy grounds that doubled as the stenography pool. The FBI operator also processed SIS film using an embassy bathtub for washing negatives and making prints. In Quito, at 10,000 feet above sea level, and with generally mild weather, the station experienced few transmission problems. Situated in the penthouse of the embassy, with a carpeted floor and drapes that absorbed sounds, the station created a relaxed atmosphere for the operator.[43] There were, however, serious security concerns. During the time of its operation no physical security could be afforded to it or the technicians.[44] In a memorandum to Hoover, one Bureau official expressed concern that German agents had discovered the radio and were watching it.

> The radio operators are in a particularly dangerous position at this point due to the fact that they are actually violating the laws of the country and technically would be subject to charges of operating an illegal radio station and most possibly espionage. . . . Due to the circumstances under which they operate, it is not possible to afford them armed protection and there would be no recourse should these operators be killed by anyone.[45]

A number was assigned to each radio station, as were special one-time pads for encrypting messages. By the end of 1942 SIS stations were communicating directly with Washington and stations throughout Latin America. Atmospheric problems soon emphasized the importance of Lima as a relay point for all transmissions below the equator, including Santiago, Montevideo, Buenos Aires, La Paz, and Asunción. Traffic between Washington and Bogota, Havana, San Jose, Quito, San Salvador, and Lima was direct, with the Bureau's station in San Diego and San Salvador used in emergencies.[46]

Neutrality and tight government surveillance of American officials in Buenos Aires made SIS operations particularly tricky in Argentina. In one instance, Special Agent John Thomas, an undercover agent, was arrested and imprisoned by the police on charges of espionage. Resisting strong interrogation to reveal his true identity, Thomas stuck to his cover story until Spruille Braden, now assigned as ambassador, arranged for his release. The dangerous nature of the work, the constant threat of discovery, and the need for speedy exfiltration of FBI personnel and sources, particularly in Argentina, made quick escapes across the border to Uruguay absolutely essential. One of these routes was known as "Crandall's Navy," a fully gassed and outfitted speedboat docked in Buenos Aires harbor always ready for the short run across the River Platte to the safety of Montevideo.[47]

On October 21, 1942, Andres Elay Pigrau, the Peruvian consul-general in Barcelona, Spain, was arrested by British authorities in Trinidad while en route to Buenos Aires on a German espionage mission. During his interrogation, Pigrau revealed the existence of a previously unknown espionage courier system using Editorial Falangista Española (EFE), the Spanish Falange news service controlled by General Friederich Wolf, the German air attaché in Buenos Aires, and Johannes Becker, the local Sicherheitdienst representative. The Germans had become increasingly concerned about disruption of contact with its South American agents if the Argentine government severed diplomatic relations with the Nazis, a calamity that would leave EFE as Germany's only espionage and sabotage cover. Five months later another German agent, Joaquin Baticon Martinez, arrested in Trinidad and taken to New York, corroborated Pigrau's story to the FBI, leading to the SIS's investigation of the "most extensive espionage and smuggling ring" in the Western Hemisphere.[48] The EFE investigation soon uncovered Manuel Perez Garcia, a German agent and former Falange police officer employed by the Spanish embassy in Buenos Aires, who supervised the shipment of contraband and information between South America and Europe. Armed with enough evidence for Garcia's arrest, Hoover warned the British in July 1943, which promptly removed him at Trinidad from a ship en route to Spain where he was to retrieve a cipher machine for the head of the Abwehr station at the German embassy in Buenos Aires.[49]

Another crippling setback occurred in August 1943 when the SIS recruited two sources in the EFE's courier network. One was Jesus Aguilar Fernandez, a courier aboard the *Cabo De Buena de Esperanza,* who had left the ship in Buenos Aires to serve as the chief liaison officer with Jose Valles, a Spanish consular employee, and Garcia's replacement as the new head of the EFE. The other, also a courier, was Ramon Queveda, who carried contraband across the Atlantic. Both men were soon supplying a gold mine of inside information about the network with minute details concerning its size, makeup, priorities, transit schedules, and leadership. Among its leading personalities were E.J.F. Langer, a major smuggler of strategic materiel, Jose Mella, the manager of the Siemens-Schuckart branch in Buenos Aires, and Ramon Castillo, a plain-clothes detective with the Argentine Maritime Police. Both sources supplied the SIS with weekly lists of confidential documents destined for Berlin, together with photographs of documents passing to and from Europe. They also identified Jose Olivaro del Rio, a radio operator working on the Spanish ship *Habana*. Although Ostrich had previously revealed his Abwehr connection, there was insufficient independent evidence to allow the British to take him into custody. Fernandez and Quevada remedied this problem when they told the SIS of a package of coded messages given by Valles to Olivaro for delivery to the Germans, together with two ounces of platinum, a rare metal used for specialized industrial processes. After a "routine" search of Olivaro's belongings when his ship docked at Gibraltar on October 19, 1943, he was interned in England where he disgorged additional insights into EFE's illicit activities. After learning that the spy ring supported itself through drug smuggling to Europe, SIS agents began squeezing off EFE's income source by replacing the drugs with worthless imitations.[50]

The FBI called the Clog investigation the "largest and most important espionage case handled by the SIS during the war."[51] Based in Mexico City, the ring involved more than fifty conspirators in Mexico along with dozens of others spread out through Argentina, Colombia, Uruguay, Brazil, and Chile. In a slight twist on normal procedure, the ring was actually composed of three separate components answering to Abwehr stations in Cologne, Hamburg, and Berlin. The Abwehr considered Mexico a safe haven as the country had no espionage laws and only weakly enforced censorship laws. With no surveillance on them, German agents created a vast network of Mexican spies up and down both coastlines who supplied valuable information about raw material production and, most critically, details of ships leaving Mexican ports, which they relayed to Berlin for retransmission to U-boats lurking in the Caribbean. This information was initially sent to Germany over the cables of the Mexico City branch of the German Bank using a sophisticated cipher called Sudemax. The actual messages transmitted to Berlin, code-named "Sudermo," were then decoded and relayed to the

Abwehr. Both Sudemax and Sudermo ended when the Mexican authorities began tightening commercial code regulations under U.S. pressure as the Second World War approached.[52]

The Abwehr first tipped their hand in 1940 when Hamburg radioed an FBI double agent on Long Island, New York, asking for his assistance in retransmitting messages between a secret low-powered station in Mexico and Germany.[53] Investigation led to the discovery of the ring leaders, Karl Friedrich von Schlebrugge and George Nicolaus, code-named "Max," two Mexican citizens of German background who were sending secrets to Hamburg through Carlos Retelsdorf, an amateur radio operator and coffee planter who owned a farm in an out-of-the-way region of Veracruz. Based on the evidence laid out by Hoover, the State Department pressured the Mexican government to force von Schlebrugge's departure for Germany on a Japanese ship in April 1941. Simultaneous with Schlebrugge's departure, Nicolaus's spying career came to an unexpected end also. His end came not through sophisticated intelligence but rather a woman, Maria Teresa Quintilla, Max's landlady and jilted lover who denounced him to the Mexican government as a German spy. Two months later the government revoked Retelsdorf's license, ending his radio broadcasts. It took another year before the government arrested and interned him.[54]

With no official channel of communication or clandestine radio, the Clog ring turned to microdots, tiny photographs no larger in size than the dot over the letter "i" or a period at the end of a written sentence. Reading microdots was a simple procedure requiring only a microscope, but producing them was a far more complicated matter involving larger equipment available only in Germany. The man behind this new initiative was Arnold Karl Franz Joachim Ruge, a Mexican of German origin, who studied the technique in Berlin before returning to Mexico in August 1940 with the training necessary to produce a limitless number of microdots. Soon after his arrival, Hans Burandt, an official in the German embassy, secretly offered him the use of the microdot equipment that had been shipped to Mexico through the diplomatic mail.[55]

Ruge's microdots system worked well until British censors in Bermuda discovered a microdot hidden on an eastbound letter dated December 6, 1941, and postmarked in Mexico. Following an SIS investigation, the microdot transmission of secret defense information ended when Mexican police jailed Ruge in May 1942. Months later Hoover learned that the wily Ruge was once again on the loose, having bribed a prison official to help him escape. Ruge quickly resurrected the Nicolaus spy network, with microdots once again flowing across the Atlantic. In pursuit of the Clog ring's new leader, the SIS this time changed tactics; instead of alerting the Mexican government with its evidence, causing the ring to go underground, SIS agents quietly began identifying and dismantling the network's structure. Through constant surveillance Ruge's movements, habits, finances, friends, family, and sources were scrupulously monitored. FBI informants and double agents determined its collection procedures, the nature of the information acquired, and details of the microdot transmission and schedules. Over the course of the investigation the SIS painted a complete picture of Ruge's operation and co-conspirators. One was Edgar Hilgert, a German agent of Mexican origin who collected military information for the Hamburg Abwehr station. Another was Franz Wilhelm Buchenau, who worked for the station in Cologne. Over the next three and a half years of the war, without informing the Mexican government, the SIS investigation of the Clog ring had neutralized twenty-four members.[56]

Another important reason for the confidential nature of the Clog investigation was SIS use of Ostrich information. The Joint Chiefs of Staff (JCS) objected to any sharing of evidence with Mexican officials for fear that a leak could send a signal to the Germans that their codes had been compromised. On August 1, 1946, eight months after being shown the FBI's evidence, Mexican police began arresting the Clog conspirators. Many of them, having been tipped off only days earlier, quickly went into hiding. Edgar Hilgert was found hiding at a remote ranch in a remote area near Pueblo, Mexico. As for Ruge, after he threatened to kill anyone who tried to arrest him, police returned to his home where they discovered that he had killed himself.[57]

Like most governments with espionage systems, the Japanese government relied heavily on intelligence officers operating under diplomatic cover. In Buenos Aires two Japanese diplomats, Tomiya Koseiki, an embassy secretary, and Shozo Murai, an intelligence officer under cover as a civil attaché, ran the so-called JAPSA Network. It was a widespread espionage and sabotage ring recruited mainly from ultra-nationalist groups and the Japanese émigré communities that had lived in South America for decades. SIS knowledge of the JAPSA Network came from a disgruntled JAPSA agent, resentful of his treatment by his bosses, who walked into the SIS station in Buenos Aires offering his services as a double agent. After identifying

Koseiki and Murai as the ringleaders, the source sat for hours cataloguing the names of ring members while laying out details of its strategy and methods. The two Japanese intelligence officers controlled Carlos Santa Cruz, a Chilean who had moved from Santiago to Buenos Aires in the spring of 1942. Santa Cruz had been a member of the Chilean Union Nacionalista before moving to Argentina, where he posed as a correspondent for the Union Nacionalista publication, *Veinta Naciones*, and the Japanese propaganda magazine *Mirando al Oeste*. Carlos corresponded with Alberto Santa Cruz, his cousin, born in Tokyo, who lived in Santiago and edited *Veinta Naciones*.[58] SIS interception of correspondence between the cousins soon implicated Inez Pobate Ortega de Santa Cruz, Albert's mother, who acted as a mail drop for espionage information about Allied shipping, particularly the names, characteristics, armaments, cargo, and destination of the vessels in Buenos Aires harbor destined for Koseiki and Murai.[59]

The identities of espionage agents weren't the only SIS success in defeating the JAPSA Network. Investigators confiscated more than a hundred sheets of stolen official U.S. embassy document paper that was later authenticated by the FBI laboratory. Months of surveillance and informant coverage led to the discovery of the clever tactics used by the ring to sabotage British and American ships leaving the harbor of Buenos Aires. It was a simple plan involving statues and religion. Operating through paid intermediaries, Koseiki and Murai prepared tiny incendiary devices with delayed fuses designed to ignite once the ship was well out at sea. To conceal them they fitted them into statues of the Virgin of Lujan, a local religious icon, depicting an apparition of Mary memorialized in the Basilica of Argentina in Buenos Aires and sold as souvenirs to seamen. The investigation continued until May 5, 1944, when Argentine police deported Santa Cruz to Chile, where the SIS soon turned him as a double agent.[60]

Italian espionage in South America never posed a serious threat to the Allies. Even before Benito Mussolini brought Italy into the war in 1940, no preparations had been made for long-term productive intelligence gathering. Underfunded and poorly trained intelligence officers in embassies throughout South America had few sources of any quality while producing little information of value for European war fighters. Their efforts during the three years of fighting before Italy's surrender in the summer of 1943, an FBI history later recorded, proved "relatively futile," a "commentary on the inefficiency of the Italians as organizers and collectors of intelligence."[61]

One case that symbolized this view was the case of Andreas Angel Bonzo. Born to Italian parents in Chivilehoy, Argentina, Bonzo returned to Italy in the 1930s where he joined the Italian army. His Spanish fluency, his family contacts, and his connections throughout Argentina's Italian community led to his selection for a secret mission back to his country of birth. Bonzo underwent intensive training in the months before he sailed to Buenos Aires in May 1942 accompanied by his radio operator, an Italian military engineer named Zeffarella using the alias of Jose Carlos Trotti. His efforts over the next year were marginal at best. He recruited three agents who managed to produce decent information, particularly about Allied shipping, but which proved worthless when it arrived in Rome too late for timely action.[62]

As Allied troops in Sicily in the summer of 1943 pushed German and Italian troops northeast toward Messina and across the Straits of Messina to the temporary safety of Italy, the Italian embassy in Buenos Aires, seeing the handwriting on the wall, turned off the money flow for Bonzo and his band of hapless spies. Refusing to accept the reality of Mussolini's death and the collapse of Italy, Bonzo decided to personally contact Italian authorities to clarify his position as Italy's chief of intelligence in South America. After departing for Spain on August 14, 1943, aboard the SS *Monte Albertia,* Bonzo was arrested by the British at Trinidad and interned in London, where he provided MI5 with a full confession.[63]

Italy's collapse reduced Allied interest in its intelligence activities in Argentina. Within weeks of U.S. recognition of the new Badoglio government, Arthur Carey, an FBI's legal attaché, contacted the Italian embassy's new intelligence boss. Soon, a productive relationship began to flourish, with Carey acquiring large volumes of information including itemized lists of cases, agent identities, and, more importantly, details of German operations and joint intelligence operations.[64]

As the war progressed, the FBI expanded beyond Latin America. In early October 1943 Special Agent Frank Ampirin posed as an army officer in Algeria and later Italy conducting counterespionage investigations. Another FBI agent under military cover was Arthur Avignone, who followed combat troops up the boot of Italy conducting investigations and collecting documents for use in later trials against Ezra Pound, the famed American poet who broadcast propaganda messages for the Italian government. Frederick Ayer, General George Patton's nephew, and Donald Daughters, an All-American football player from Harvard, entered Paris in August 1944 and later moved on to Berlin, where they worked with military intelligence officials pursuing treason and espionage investigations. Nicholas Alaga spent a year in Manila after the Philippine liberation in July 1945, while others such as Alex Hurst and Fred Spangler went to Tokyo. In March 1945 Frederick Tillman arrived in the Philippines and then moved on to Tokyo until he returned to Washington in September 1946. In all, approximately fifty agents were assigned throughout Asia and Europe until 1947, when the passage of the National Security Act transferred the functions and duties of the SIS to the newly created Central Intelligence Agency.[65]

CHAPTER NINE

The Man from Buffalo

One of the key contributors to Hoover's headaches with William Stephenson was his close relationship with William Donovan. Bill Donovan shared little in common with Hoover except for one thing: their birthdate. Donavan, a Buffalo native, was born on January 1, 1883, twelve years before his future nemesis entered the world in the front parlor of the family home just blocks from the U.S. Capitol building.[1] The oldest of Tim and Anna Donovan's five children, Will, as the family called him, grew up in a home filled with a love of reading and a Catholic tradition centered on St. Bridget's Church. Will's intellectual pursuits came from his father, a lean, tea-totaling railroad worker who devoured American and English biographies, together with the works of Shakespeare, Dickens, and the great Irish poets. In his later years Bill proudly lined the shelves of his Manhattan apartment with hundreds of his father's books. Tim's other passion was a zest for politics and the local Republican Party, much to the displeasure of every Democratic Irishman in Buffalo's First Ward. One Donovan biographer later quipped that Tim became party leader because he was the only member.[2]

After grammar school Donovan attended St. Joseph's Collegiate Institute followed by three years at Niagara University before completing his senior year in 1905 and a law degree three years later at Columbia College in New York City.[3] Donovan returned to Buffalo where he married, started a family, and opened a law practice he later merged with the city's leading firm, headed by the redoubtable John Lord O'Brian. As a member of the firm O'Brian, Hamlin, Donovan, and Goodyear, Bill Donovan moved into big-time local law and politics, representing many of city's most important business personalities.

Donovan's first diplomatic assignment occurred by accident in February 1916 when he took leave of his firm to embark on a humanitarian mission, helping Poles and Germans displaced by the fighting in Central Europe. Warwick Greene, director of the War Relief Commission created by John D. Rockefeller with a $100 million endowment, encouraged Donovan to persuade German authorities to allow the distribution of desperately needed food, such as powdered milk, wheat, and flour, all the while heeding Greene's warning to observe "strict neutrality in word and act."[4] Ignoring orders, Donovan soon expanded his brief by scrounging clothing from Paris and emergency medical supplies from neutral countries, all the while hectoring the Germans to improve conditions for the more than four million soldiers housed in squalid POW camps. Under his humanitarian cover he traveled widely throughout the war zone in the hope of witnessing the fighting firsthand. In one case he spent weeks on the Balkan Front with an American Red Cross virologist who was delousing Bulgarian soldiers to prevent the spread of typhus and studying mountain warfare tactics. By the time he returned to the United States in June 1916 he had a clear picture of the fighting, the enormity of the daily slaughter, and, most importantly, a grasp of what the Americans forces would encounter a year later.

No sooner had he settled down than he abruptly set off again for McAllen, Texas, to join Troop 1, his local National Guard unit, which had merged into the 1st Cavalry Division. Donovan was in Europe when the War Department issued a call for state militias to join General John Pershing, commander of the U.S. forces, in tracking down the Mexican revolutionary Pancho Villa. After President Wilson recognized Villa's political rival, Venustiano Carranza, as president of Mexico in January 1916, Villa set off on a murder-and-mayhem spree throughout Mexico and across the border into the American southwest. In Chihuahua he hijacked a passenger train, singling out and murdering nineteen American passengers. Two months later he struck again, this time leading 1,500 troops into Columbus, New Mexico, killing nine more Americans. Nine months later Donovan and Troop 1 were back in Buffalo with a combat record marked only by boredom and tedium.[5]

Within months of President Wilson's declaration of war on April 6, 1917, Donovan was again in uniform. In July the "Fighting 69th" Infantry Regiment of the New York National Guard, made up mainly of Irish Americans, was incorporated into the 42nd Division. During his service in Mexico Donovan had witnessed the 69th in action and came to admire its élan, fighting qualities, and traditions that dated back to the American Civil War. After enlisting in October 1917, Major Donovan took command of the First Battalion, which soon left Montreal for a two-week voyage to England. History records that Donovan's *nom de guerre* "Wild Bill" derived from his constant presence under fire with his men at the front, where he showed remarkable daring and leadership in the face of great danger. By war's end, as a "superior officer who has shown brilliant military qualities," he had won both the Croix de Guerre and the Distinguished Service Cross (DSC) for leading his division for "four days all the while under shell and machine-gun fire from the enemy who were on three sides of him," yet "persistently and repeatedly counter-attacked." For wounds sustained near Landres and St. Georges, he received two Purple Hearts, a bronze oak leaf on his DSC, and America's highest award, the Medal of Honor. Even the Italian government recognized his achievements by bestowing the Merito di Guerra on him. After a year of combat, "Wild Bill" had amassed more military awards than any other American in the 42nd Division and most likely in the entire American Expeditionary Force. In May 1919, after mustering out of the army, Colonel William Donovan quietly returned home to Buffalo and his law practice following an uproarious New York City homecoming for the Fighting 69th.[6]

A year after taking office, President Warren Harding appointed Donovan to the post of U.S. District Attorney for western New York. Wasting no time, the energetic Donovan and a hand-picked team of prosecutors began a series of wide-ranging political corruption probes which led to the convictions of a major narcotics-smuggling ring, their local police protection, and powerful local political officials, including Buffalo's mayor, Frank X. Schwab, who was jailed for violating the Volstead Act.[7]

In April 1924, after succeeding to the presidency upon the death of President Harding, Calvin Coolidge replaced the disgraced attorney general Harry Daugherty with his old Amherst College classmate and dean of the Columbia University Law School, Harlan Fisk Stone. Based on his war record, his Republican Party credentials, his anti-corruption image, and his crime-buster reputation, Donovan accepted his old law school professor's invitation to come to Washington and take charge of the Justice Department's Criminal Division. Stone's new chief prosecutor now suddenly found himself on a collision course with J. Edgar Hoover, the man who would play such a critical role in his life when the world was once again at war almost twenty years later. As acting director of the Bureau of Investigation since his appointment by Stone in May 1924, Hoover reported directly to Donovan. Hoover was everything that Donovan was not. Hoover was a reserve lieutenant colonel in the army's MID who had never left Washington; Donovan held the Medal of Honor. Hoover was a reserved, distant, and cautious government bureaucrat while Donovan was outgoing, garrulous, and

Sir William Stephenson receiving an award from William Donovan, the head of the Office of Strategic Services. Stephenson was a businessman, a maverick, a spymaster, the legendary head of British Security Coordination and Hoover's nemesis. *New York World Telegram & Sun Collection, Library of Congress*

impulsive. Hoover was rigid, a workhorse, and a dogged manager who created a strict hierarchical structure he commanded with absolutely authority. Donovan cared nothing for office routine, rules, established procedures, or the chain of command. One OSS colleague later described his management style as putting "a lot of men in a pen and letting them fight it out on the theory that the strongest ones would emerge at the top."[8]

All the evidence suggests that these two polar opposites took an instant dislike for each other which only intensified as the years went on. One reason for their enmity certainly was Donovan's recommendation in December 1924 against appointing Hoover as permanent director, a suggestion Stone ignored. Another was the political fallout resulting from Donovan's disastrous decision to criminally charge the Democratic senator from Montana, Burton K. Wheeler, with practicing law while serving as a public official with intent to defraud the government. Wheeler, like Donovan, was also a maverick; he first won his Senate seat in 1922, then broke with his party two years later to campaign as Robert La Follette's vice presidential running mate on the Progressive Party ticket. Following their defeat, Wheeler returned to the Democratic Party, serving two more decades in the Senate. With fellow Montana senator Thomas Walsh serving as his defense attorney, a federal jury in Great Falls heard the evidence and then pronounced Wheeler's innocence after ten minutes of deliberation. Blame for the fiasco promptly fell squarely on Donovan, who was lambasted by his Washington political enemies for reckless prosecution. In the spring of 1925, after Coolidge elevated Stone to the Supreme Court, Donovan was quietly shipped to the Justice Department's Civil Division, where he enforced anti-trust laws for the next four years.[9]

Donovan's DOJ career ended when President-elect Herbert Hoover passed him over for attorney general, the cabinet post he most coveted. After five years in Washington, Buffalo's bitterly disappointed favorite son suddenly found himself out of government and a civilian once more. Instead of returning home to Buffalo, however, he moved to New York City where he started his own law practice with offices at 2 Wall Street in Manhattan's financial district and another in Washington at the newly opened Shoreham Building. Over the next few years with Depression-related litigation exploding across the nation, Donovan, Leisure, Lombard, & Irvine grew into a legal powerhouse, making him a very wealthy man by the end of the decade.

Donovan came to President Roosevelt's attention with the surprise appointment in 1940 of Republican Party stalwart Frank Knox to his cabinet as secretary of the navy. Knox was a veteran of Teddy Roosevelt's Rough Riders and a newspaperman who later became the publisher of the *Chicago Daily News*. The two men first met in 1936 shortly before Knox joined Republican presidential nominee Alf Landon as his running mate in an election that Roosevelt won in a landslide. Donovan helped put Knox on the ticket and later served as one of his advisors. In the late 1930s his paper's editorial position backed Roosevelt's rearmament policy and the sale of arms to England. In 1939, following a White House conference on the congressional embargo of arms sales, he demanded repeal of the law, charging that there was nothing in international law forbidding a neutral country from selling arms to belligerents. Months later when Knox arrived in Washington, he was hosted by Donovan at his Georgetown home while preparing for his Senate confirmation hearings. Donovan, also an internationalist and a believer in the need for a stronger American role in world affairs, had recently testified before the Senate Military Affairs committee in support of the president's proposed military draft legislation.[10]

No one really knew if Great Britain would survive in the summer of 1940. While girding the British people with soaring rhetoric for the trial they would soon face, Prime Minister Winston Churchill had no strategy for combatting the awesome German power just a few miles away across the English Channel. As for the underfunded U.S. military intelligence agencies, their reports on this vital question were often contradictory and of little use to the White House. It was in this atmosphere of uncertainty that Knox dispatched Donovan to London in July 1940 for a firsthand assessment of British "Fifth Column methods" in the wake of France's collapse just weeks earlier.[11]

Quickly sensing Donovan's importance to Britain's U.S. interests, Stephenson framed the importance of the visit to Menzies by noting that he was "personally representing Roosevelt, Hoover and [Harry] Hopkins." Due in large part to the SIS chief, Donovan's visit was a resounding success. Upon his arrival in London on July 16 he received unprecedented access "befitting a high level visitor" to the cream of British policy making.[12] Senior Admiralty and air staff officers briefed him on all manner of technical issues concerning ships and aircraft while escorting him through shipyards, aircraft assembly plants, and airfields lined with fighter squadrons then mauling the Luftwaffe in the Battle of Britain. Government economists bombarded Donovan with reams of facts and figures on everything from industrial production to farm output. When not busy with military officers and bureaucrats he was hobnobbing with MI5 and MI6 officials who supplied him with confidential details on Fifth Column activities and overseas intelligence and propaganda operations. Menzies personally offered Donovan insights about his agency's work (no mention of Ultra) and his belief that the nation could defend itself. Donovan was thoroughly impressed with what he witnessed, so much so that he ended his visit with promises to lobby hard for the "closest co-operation" between the FBI and MI6.[13]

After briefing the president upon his return in August 1940, Donovan began a furious lobbying campaign starting with a nationwide radio broadcast over the Mutual Broadcast System in which he warned the American people to begin preparing themselves for war or face the fate of the "nations of Europe that have fallen." Together with Edgar Mower, a foreign correspondent for Knox's *Chicago Daily News* (Mower accompanied him to

London), Donovan penned a "wildly exaggerated" series of articles describing a well-financed German propaganda and sabotage program originating in Europe that was burrowing its way through a network of agents and Nazi sympathizers inside the United States. The charges were wholly fanciful, but, in the words of a Donovan biographer, FDR's belief in it led to orders for Hoover "to ruthlessly investigate Nazi, fascist, and communist subversion in the country."[14]

Building on this triumph Stephenson began cultivating Donovan over long lunches, reinforcing the importance of the good he was doing for the British cause and planting the seeds in his mind for an American intelligence agency constructed along the lines of MI6 which he would lead. Following Roosevelt's reelection, the president again dispatched Donovan on an expanded fact-finding journey to London and then on to the Mediterranean region. Describing Donovan as "presently the strongest friend whom we have here," Stephenson again pressed Menzies to afford this important presidential emissary every amenity, including a "completely frank" discussion with the prime minister before he returned to America, in order "to repeat his good work of last occasion and to combat forces of appeasement here which are gaining ground again." Such an audience could, in Stephenson's inflated view, contribute "very largely to our obtaining all that we want of the United States."[15] Menzies quickly took the lead by once again lobbying everyone with any influence throughout the military and the Whitehall establishment. Among those buttonholed was Foreign Minister Anthony Eden, who learned that Donovan had more influence with FDR than "Colonel House had with [Woodrow] Wilson." Stephenson's strong endorsement produced a luncheon meeting at 10 Downing Street with Churchill, who issued orders afterward to extend "every facility" to Donovan, "who has influence with the President" and "who has been taken fully into our confidence."[16]

From his office in Washington the ever-wary Hoover closely followed Donovan's latest London visit through reports from Hugh Clegg and Lawrence Hince, two senior agents who were in the British capital at the same time studying MI5, MI6, and wartime policing methods. By the time Donovan landed in New York in March 1941, Hoover's London report was on the president's desk, a fact which only fueled the FBI director's ire after learning that Donovan was "running round passing himself off as the first to discover intelligence's Holy Grail."[17]

As a man of action, Bill Donovan had little interest in leading a spy service. Following his return to the United States in early 1941, he essentially abandoned his legal career to devote himself full-time to lobbying Washington for a return to military life. As U.S.-German relations continued to deteriorate, the fifty-eight-year-old lawyer passed an Army physical exam in May 1941 in the hope of commanding a combat division. The British, however, had other plans for him. Stephenson began an intensive lobbying effort to convince administration officials of the importance of creating an intelligence service that would work closely with MI6, all the while continuing to pressure Donovan that he should lead the new organization. Assisting Stephenson were Admiral John Godfrey, the head of British naval intelligence, and his aide, Lieutenant Commander Ian Fleming, who began making the rounds of official Washington singing Donovan's praises to anyone who would listen. On June 5 they spent three hours with Hoover "studying Bureau methods and discussing matters of mutual interest."[18] Stephenson eventually convinced him to take the job by emphasizing that he could shape the new service into his own image with a structure made up of men he romantically described as "calculatingly reckless with disciplined daring."[19]

Donovan discussed the concept with his friend Knox, who quickly passed it on to Roosevelt. What until then had been a secret, unofficial, back-channel initiative quickly leaked throughout official Washington. Hoover and the military tried to quash the plan, claiming that it would interfere with the considerable progress made since June 1939 when the president ordered all cabinet departments to provide any espionage, sabotage, and subversion reports to the FBI. Weeks later Hoover, together with MID and ONI officials, formed the Interdepartmental Information Conference to coordinate their investigations and policy formation. Thousands of records were being created on dangerous aliens (Custodial Index) who would be taken into custody in the event of war. Thousands more espionage, sabotage, and subversion investigations were also underway. Counterespionage training schools were being set up for FBI personnel, formal liaison with RCMP officials was underway, Hoover had reestablished the National Defense Division after a twenty-year hiatus, and a new Plant Protection Program was established to survey the security of industrial research facilities and factories producing weapons for the military services. Further complicating matters was the FBI's year-old Special Intelligence Service, which was sending agents in undercover roles throughout Latin America to conduct foreign espionage.[20]

The president liked the idea and asked Donovan on June 10 to send him some details. Cloistering with Stephenson, Donovan hastily produced a document entitled "Memorandum of Establishment of Service of Strategic Information" that outlined a new analytical organization under a "Coordinator of Strategic Information" responsible to the president and assisted by an "advisory panel." Opening with the lines "Strategy without information upon which it can rely is helpless" and "Likewise information is useless unless it is intelligently directed to the strategic purpose," Donovan and Stephenson argued for a "central intelligence organization which would itself collect, either directly or through existing departments of Government, at home and abroad . . . relevant information . . . on potential enemies," concentrating on their armed forces, diplomatic secrets, economic intentions, and citizens' morale. It would collate information scattered through the many agencies of government for analysis by military specialists, as well as by carefully trained academics drawn from American universities and colleges. Its essential purpose, Donovan concluded, was the creation of a mechanism to provide the "President, as Commander-In-Chief, . . . accurate and complete enemy intelligence reports upon which military operational decisions can be based." The new agency would include a propaganda section capable of mounting a "psychological attack against the moral and spiritual defenses of a nation" using "radio as a weapon."[21] On July 11 Roosevelt created the new position of Coordinator of Information, with Donovan serving as its unpaid director.[22]

Hours later Stephenson proudly cabled the good news to Menzies:

> Donovan saw the President to-day and after long discussion wherein all points were agreed, he accepted appointment. He will be co-ordinator of all forms [of] intelligence including offensive operations equivalent SO2 [part of Special Operations Executive]. He will hold rank of Major General and be responsible only to the President. Donovan accuses me of having 'intrigued and driven' him into appointment. You can imagine how relieved I am after three months of battle and jockeying for position in Washington that our man is in a position of such importance to our efforts.[23]

Flush with $450,000 from the president's unvouchered secret Emergency Fund, the new COI set up his office in a three-story granite office building atop Navy Hill overlooking the Potomac River at the corner of 25th and E Streets. Within weeks a high-powered staff composed of academics and the politically well connected began trickling into the new space. The Librarian of Congress, Archibald MacLeish, opened the library's collections, while James P. Baxter, the president of Williams College, moved to Washington to take over as head of the research and analysis section. Estelle Frankfurter, Justice Felix Frankfurter's sister, signed on to analyze the dizzying array of government reports that would soon be flowing in; Marine Corps captain James Roosevelt would handle interagency liaison; and David K. E. Bruce, a lawyer, world traveler, and Andrew Mellon's son-in law, would manage intelligence collection. Other more senior staff members included William Whitney, a lawyer assigned to London, and Donovan's World War I friend, Edward Buxton, as his assistant director and organizer of a group to interview foreigners for intelligence. To keep a strong hand on the direction of the new COI organization, Stephenson reassigned Dick Ellis from New York to work with Donovan. Ellis, Stephenson was convinced, "had had a lot of experience in this type of work and could undoubtedly be of considerable assistance to Donovan."[24] As one author insisted, Donovan had "no intention of operating a small agency confined to sifting through other agency's reports and correlating them for the President." By the end of December the COI had nearly six hundred people on his payroll.[25]

After more than a year of FBI assistance and cooperation involving BSC, Stephenson's growing coziness with Donovan only served to infuriate Hoover. Nevertheless, the COI was now a reality, with the White House's blessing, and the FBI, like the military, had no choice but to tolerate it. Over the next year he watched cautiously as the COI grew in helter-skelter fashion, adding historians, geographers, area specialists, economists, and scores of specialists with little regard for their politics or ideological leanings. Some of Hoover's suspicions were frivolous, like the groundless belief that Donovan was scheming to take over Special Intelligence Service operations in Latin America. Others, like the increasing number of employees with Communist Party connections, were very real. In the years to come most of Donovan's people served honorably with postwar careers marked by major success. Some, however, went on to ignominy when American cryptographic successes against Russian one-time pad communications exposed them as Soviet spies.[26] Eleven months after its founding, President Roosevelt's Military Order of June 13, 1942, transformed the COI from a civilian agency into a military intelligence unit with the creation the Office of Strategic Services "under the jurisdiction" of the JCS. Donovan remained at the helm with the new rank of major-general.[27]

BSC's internal history written at the end of the war claims that during the war OSS had as many as 22,000 people on its roles ranging from "professors to screwballs, movie producers to communist fellow-travelers, missionaries' son's to stockbrokers, college presidents to ex-governors of states, and charwomen to the left-at-home wives of servicemen."[28] The hatred that eventually developed between Hoover and Donovan can be traced back to the antics of one of those screwballs, a man named Donald Chase Downes, an American whom supporters and friends viewed as highly literate, an ideal and amusing companion, and a superb cook, while others found him an insecure and indiscreet intelligence officer and a "fat, worthless bastard."[29]

Downes was born in Catonsville, Maryland, on September 30, 1903, to Joseph Lodowick Downes and his wife, Effie Chase. His early education was in Baltimore, the Kent School in Connecticut, and then at the prestigious Philips Exeter Academy in Massachusetts. After dropping out of Yale College in 1923, he taught school in Cape Cod before returning to Yale in 1930, eventually earning a bachelor's degree in June 1935. For the next five years he taught history and English at the Cheshire Academy in Connecticut while becoming proficient in Spanish, French, and German during summer sojourns to Europe. Following Cheshire's closing in 1940, Downes launched a new career in intelligence work. Through his brother, Willard, a naval lieutenant commander, he met Captain Samuel Moore, acting director of naval intelligence, who offered him a reserve commission and pointed him in the direction of British Intelligence.[30]

Downes soon found himself in Istanbul teaching English on weekdays to Turkish army and navy officers awaiting training in the United States, and spying on weekends. Boarding the Orient Express on Friday evening with memorized instructions, he traveled to Sofia to meet some British sources, and then returned with the results on Sunday evening. After six months, MI6's confidence in his work gradually diminished, with his handlers assessing him as an "insecure" officer who would "most likely create problems" for them in the future. His Turkish odyssey with MI6 ended abruptly when they discovered that he had recruited his own source in Sofia without permission while supplying his British reports to the American naval attaché. Accordingly, Downes suddenly found himself back in the United States.[31]

Once again out of work, yet eager to build on his Balkan adventures, Downes sought out Dick Ellis in New York. After accepting employment with BSC over coffee at a Rockefeller Center restaurant, he began working closely with Stephenson's deputy and Donovan's close friend John Pepper. Downes soon found himself enrolled in a two-week British training course studying "mapping, fieldcraft, weapons, demolitions, communications, and cipher," along with the "rudiments of unarmed combat and what the British more straightforwardly called silent killing."[32] The Yale historian Robin Winks later concluded that "Downes, an American citizen, in contravention of any number of American laws, became a spy for the British intelligence, with the goal of undermining anti-interventionist organizations by demonstrating, if he could, that they were unconscious dupes of Nazi Germany."[33]

Ernest Cuneo, a savvy New York labor lawyer with strong Democratic Party connections and close ties with the Oval Office, joined the OSS in 1942 as its liaison with the White House and the FBI. Always wary of Downes, Cuneo brutally assessed him as impetuous and thoughtless, "a rogue elephant," a "born loser" living in a giddy euphoria of plots and mystery. Cuneo had developed a strong relationship with Edward Tamm, which later grew into a warm personal friendship that lasted until the end of their lives. On one occasion the ever-plotting Downes threatened this relationship when he asked Cuneo to arrange with Tamm for a drop-address in Buenos Aires. Through Tamm's efforts, Downes sent two agents to Argentina where they were soon compromised. Undeterred, he then compounded this disaster by using the FBI's original and narrow authorization to set up additional letter drops in Caracas and Havana. When he learned of the fiasco, Cuneo washed his hands of him, believing that he was out of control and "running amok."[34]

Following the Pearl Harbor attack, Downes transferred from BSC to the COI and began working in Washington. Once again, with his new training and spectacular imagination running wild, he set his sights on stealing codes and ciphers from the four neutral embassies of Spain, Vichy France, Portugal, and Turkey. Downes's actions were clearly in violation of American law as well as Donovan's agreement with Hoover that his officers would not operate in the Western Hemisphere. Ignoring this dictum, Downes pressed on with "child-like guile," using the flimsy rationale that an embassy (Spain, Portugal, Turkey, Vichy France) was foreign soil, thus giving OSS "technical grounds on which to proceed."[35] In March 1942 Bruce authorized the mission with particular focus on the Spanish embassy in the belief that it was sending the Germans confidential American aircraft information and falsifying oil and gas statistics in order to refuel German submarines at sea.

Beginning with the Vichy French embassy, Downes spent months leading a team of burglars into the building copying thousands of documents, only to learn later that other sources had earlier supplied the same material to U.S. and British authorities.[36] Undeterred, he next turned his attention to the Spanish embassy in late summer of 1942, using compromised staff secretaries to duplicate confidential documents and report on the comings and goings of embassy officials. For months Downes and his men roamed the embassy halls after dark, breaking into file cabinets and copying more than 4,000 documents in the process. An increasingly worried Donovan, who kept himself informed of the operation, repeatedly warned Bruce that the break-ins were "very much against the law" and "if you get caught we're in terrible trouble."[37] Ignoring his boss's concerns, Downes continued his nocturnal adventures until one night the entire operation ended when they were spotted by a neighbor who called the police. At the same moment, in November 1942 when Victor Rothschild returned to London after his visit to Washington and Thurston was shipping off to London as well, the mortified OSS director, who could do nothing to save Downes, ignominiously shipped him to North Africa to support the Allied invasion. Adding to this humiliation was his renewed fury toward Hoover after President Roosevelt ordered him to turn his sources and his domestic burglary operations over to the FBI.[38]

The final straw for Hoover occurred in late 1943 when the JCS began imposing strict limits on sharing information with the Soviets in the belief that they already had a vigorous espionage network in the United States. On December 27, 1943, Donovan was in Moscow meeting with Lieutenant General Pavel Fitin, head of the foreign intelligence directorate of the NKVD (Russian intelligence), and his English-speaking assistant, Colonel Alexander Ossipov. Wearing civilian clothes, the dark-skinned Ossipov, with wavy brown hair, brown eyes, and sallow complexion, looked like a "ringer for Boris Karloff."[39] Unbeknownst to Donovan, Ossipov was, in fact, Gaik Ovakimian, a senior NKVD officer who had posed as an engineer before the war at Amtorg, the Soviet trading company in New York. In 1942 the FBI reported that Ovakimian, known as the "wily Armenian," had received a Soviet government scholarship for study at the Rockefeller Institute, a position that had offered him direct access to many of America's leading scientists. Later he assisted the Spanish communist Ramon Mercader in the murder of Leon Trotsky with an ice axe in his fortified Mexican compound. Two months after the FBI had arrested him for violating the Foreign Agents

Registration Act, he quietly returned to Moscow when the charges were dropped in the wake of the German invasion of the Soviet Union.[40]

Fitin slyly asked Donovan if he had come with an offer of cooperation, or did he have "some other intentions"? Hoping to gather information on Russia, Donovan joked that he did have other intentions. Fitin, one writer later noted, had the same idea, which was why "one of the NKVD's best penetration agents sat in the room with him."[41] Without any approval from the JCS, Donovan and Fitin agreed to an exchange of missions, with OSS officers assigned to Moscow and a reciprocal NKVD team posted to Washington. Donovan later defended the agreement by claiming that the British had made a similar arrangement.[42] Hoover, however, exploded in opposition, calling the proposal a "highly dangerous and most undesirable procedure," which would only serve the Soviets' real objective of "penetration into the official secrets of various government agencies." As for the British experience, the FBI director warned that the "fundamental purpose of its operations there was to surreptitiously obtain the official secrets of the British Government."[43]

Hoover's opposition was not mere pique, for in August 1943, just four months before Donovan's Moscow meeting, Hoover had received an anonymous letter, later determined to have been written by Vasili Mironov, a disgruntled and mentally unbalanced NKVD officer assigned to the Soviet consulate in New York. It named eleven NKVD officers working under diplomatic cover in the United States, Canada, and Mexico, along with Vasili Zarubin, whom he identified as head of Soviet espionage at the New York consulate since 1941. His wife, Elizabeth, was also named as a senior NKVD officer. Later investigation revealed that Zarubin's vast espionage portfolio had included Martha Stern, formerly Martha Dodd, who, as the daughter of the former American ambassador to Germany, enjoyed high-level contact with the State Department; Laughlin Currie, an economist serving as a White House advisor to President Roosevelt; and several sources inside America's most important secret, the atomic bomb project.[44]

Hoover's investigation confirmed many of Mironov's claims about the eleven officers and some of their sources, such as Andrei Shevchenko, an NKVD officer posing as an aviation engineer for the Soviet Government Purchasing Commission, who collected intelligence while visiting U.S. factories inspecting aircraft destined for the Soviet Union under Lend-Lease. Hoover's men later turned three NKVD sources into double agents, including Boris Morros, a Russian immigrant who worked for Paramount Studios in California and had been handled first by Ovakimian and then by Zarubin.[45] Despite Donovan's furious protests, the OSS/NKVD partnership plan was quietly dropped.

Over the next two years the hostility between Hoover and Donovan continued unabated but with no further flare-ups. Donovan eventually achieved a small measure of revenge over Hoover when he denied him access to the War Room that the Supreme Headquarters Allied Expeditionary Forces set up in London in the summer of 1945 to analyze captured enemy documents. Undeterred, Hoover's men in London still managed to acquire some of the data from their excellent MI5 contacts. In a later report one FBI staff member remembered that through the creation of an "elaborate liaison system . . . all material of importance immediately came to the attention of Bureau representatives in London," a manifestation of Anglo-American cooperation reminiscent of Glenalmond. In one case, an OSS officer "surreptitiously photographed" German handbooks on the Russian intelligence activities for the FBI, which, when later translated, added considerably to the FBI's "knowledge of the international bases of Communism." By late autumn, through the assistance of Winston Scott and Joseph Campisi, both of them navy lieutenants, OSS officers, and former FBI agents, Hoover's London representatives finally reached an agreement with SHAEF officials for complete FBI access to the War Room.[46]

By the time FBI agents began examining Abwehr material in London, Donovan's intelligence career was at an end. President Roosevelt's death ended any influence Donovan may have exercised on the postwar shape of American intelligence. As for FDR's successor, Harry Truman did not see the need for a centralized intelligence structure. Even if he had, it would not have included Donovan. Clark Clifford, a close confidant and advisor to the new president, who had worked on legal matters with Donovan in the 1930s, captured the new president's doubts about the OSS director when he characterized "Wild Bill" as "big, breezy, with a tendency to roll over people." As a Wall Street lawyer and Republican whom the man from Missouri dismissed, perhaps unfairly, as a "self-promoter," Donovan was doomed.[47] On September 20, 1945, Harold Smith, the White House budget director, placed on the president's desk an executive order dissolving OSS along with a "perfunctory" letter of appreciation for Donovan's three years of "capable leadership" of his beloved service. Truman signed both without comment.[48]

CHAPTER TEN

Breach of Faith

Just days before President Roosevelt's appointment of William Donovan as the new COI in June 1941, Sam Foxworth received a telephone call from Adolf Berle's assistant, Fletcher Warren. A cryptic message had been received from London conveying British interest in moving a double agent to the United States to work under FBI control. Foxworth agreed to accept him, and in an instant one of the FBI's most controversial FBI cases was off and running.[1]

The mystery man was named Dusko Popov, code-named "Skoot." He was born on July 12, 1912, into a wealthy Serbian family accustomed to fine homes, servants, yachts, foreign travel, and high-society connections throughout Europe. The family fortune started when his industrialist grandfather founded a successful bank that he later used to finance lucrative textile manufacturing and coal-mining combines. Milorad, Dusko's indolent and indulgent father, lived off his inheritance, frequenting European playgrounds like Monte Carlo and Paris with his many mistresses and family alike. His sons followed his example, playing tennis and water polo, riding horses, and enjoying a separate house that Milorad built for them to entertain their friends.[2]

Dusko's homestead was in the ancient Adriatic coastal city of Dubrovnik, a prewar oasis for the European glitterati. The region's liberal and democratic character shaped Popov's self-assurance, independence, and commitment to "living life to the full." His education was an amalgam of tutors who taught him to speak French, Italian, and German and private schools in Paris, a brief spell at an English boarding school where caning was the rule, back to Paris for his high school years, another two years at the Sorbonne and the University of Bologna, and then to Belgrade, where he finished his law degree.[3]

A turning point in his life, one that had considerable influence on his later service as a British spy, was his postponement of a legal career to pursue a doctorate in law at the University of Freiburg, one of Germany's oldest intellectual centers dating back to the Middle Ages. The unsuspecting Serb entered a troubled campus community filled with intrigue and closely watched by the Nazi police agents for any signs of subversive behavior. As a carefree outsider seemingly oblivious to the threat, he snubbed police surveillance by regularly frequenting Jewish-owned restaurants and shops and speaking openly (and critically) about political conditions in Hitler's Germany.[4] Popov's real problems began when he joined the university's Auslander Club, a foreign student debating society which met monthly to discuss political issues of the day. Hand-picked Nazi informers who had infiltrated the club often chose the discussion topic and then carefully rehearsed their themes along fascist lines. Popov blithely taunted the Nazi snoops with spirited defenses of American and British democracy that humiliated his enemies and tagged him as a troublemaker. Retribution came early one morning when the police raided his room while he stood by in his nightclothes watching helplessly. Finding nothing incriminating, Popov was quickly hustled to the local Gestapo headquarters for eight days of questioning about his contacts and student life. Several months of solitary confinement followed before his friend, Johannes "Johnny" Jebsen, negotiated his release by guaranteeing the young Serb's immediate departure from Germany.[5]

Like Popov, Jebsen was a young bon vivant from a wealthy and well-connected Schleswig-Holstein family that had loathed Hitler and Nazism. When the army began gobbling up young conscripts, Jebsen sought relief from "soldiering" by appealing to a Wehrmacht colonel, Hans Oster, an old family friend who was serving in the Abwehr as the deputy to Admiral Wilhelm Canaris. Oster appointed him a *Forscher*, a German term meaning a combination of researcher, talent spotter, and freelance spy. His new assignment kept him away from danger, allowing him free and uninterrupted travel throughout Europe on family business as long as he remained available for Abwehr assignments. In the summer of 1940 Jebsen recruited Popov for help in identifying French citizens who would collaborate with German intelligence after the fall of France.[6] Months later Jebsen introduced him to a Major Munzinger, an Abwehr officer in the Germany's Belgrade embassy who was impressed with his family background, business connections, English-language skills, and familiarity with Great Britain. Munzinger pitched Popov on the idea of expanding his Abwehr portfolio by collecting political and military intelligence through business visits to London. Popov agreed and within days reported his new assignment to

British authorities in Belgrade. His price for betraying Jebsen and the Germans was payment commensurate with the risk, and the right to refuse any British order that would harm Yugoslavia. After concocting a story for him about a fictitious senior British diplomat friend with excellent London connections, Popov received a list of questions that one MI5 officer later described as "long and interesting." Among the German demands were details of the defenses along England's southeast coast, the identities of commanders, Winston Churchill's political enemies, British officials supportive of an early peace with Germany, and technical requirements about arms production. The questionnaire amounted to a double-edged sword, for as well as offering valuable insights into gaps in Abwehr intelligence appreciations, it posed problems for MI5 in responding without revealing valuable secrets that would aid the Germans. Following Popov's continued stalls and excuses, the frustrated Munzinger ordered Popov to meet his friend and make a personal assessment of the situation. Codenamed "Ivan" by the Abwehr, Popov agreed and left Belgrade for Lisbon, where MI6 spirited him to England on December 20, 1940.[7]

Upon arrival in London he was warmly greeted by MI6 officials who flattered him by introducing him to his new MI5 handlers as a "godsend placed high in the Abwehr organization." A month later, Popov returned to Lisbon carrying a glowing report (created by MI5) that only made his Abwehr controllers eager for more. Accepting everything he said without question, the Abwehr urged him to return to London, this time to set up a new network of British agents who could supply even more information that Popov could deliver to Portugal. A "delighted" MI5 soon began building a circle of interesting sub-sources around Skoot, beginning with Dickie Metcalfe, a former infantry officer, code-named "Balloon" (because of his girth), whose work for a London arms manufacturer offered access to data about new weapons systems. Popov described Metcalfe as a disgraced army officer who had been cashiered from the military for financial shenanigans to cover his expensive tastes and a willingness to break any rule for the right price. Popov's recently acquired Austrian-born mistress, Friedl Gaertner, code-named "Gelatine," was also added. Before the war Gaertner was an MI5 source in London who walked into the German embassy posing as a secret Nazi sympathizer willing to volunteer her services. The final link in the chain was an MI5 double agent code-named "Giraffe." He was a Czech named Georges Graf with previous military service in the French army whom the Abwehr described to Popov as a useful source in England for emergency contact.[8] To avoid any suspicions arising from Popov's easy travel between London and Lisbon, MI5 created a fictitious import-export company called Tarlair Ltd. with Popov listed as its leading sales representative. The Germans accepted Balloon and Gelatine completely, assigning them the code names "Ivan II" and "Yvonne," respectively. With a functioning ring of British double agents now led by the clever Popov, MI5 changed his code name to "Tricycle."[9]

The origins of Popov's Abwehr mission to the United States remain opaque today, despite an impressive collection of books and articles about the case over the years. In his memoirs, written almost thirty years after the end of the Second World War, Popov claimed that during a Lisbon visit in April 1941 the Germans encouraged him to undertake an "extraordinary" mission to America that "would put [the Abwehr] in control of the enemy's American espionage organization when the United States entered the war—as we all felt was inevitable." The FBI, he wrote, "had matters under control and was netting all existing spies," creating a "vacuum" that he was to fill by building a new agent network. The fault with this thesis was that no arrests of any German agents had taken place in America between the winter of 1938 and the date of Popov's supposed conversation in Lisbon. The trap that was being set for the thirty-three members of the Duquesne spy ring would not be sprung until June 1941, two months *after* Popov's alleged Lisbon briefing.[10]

The only available records of the Popov matter are the MI5 and FBI case files. What does exist suggests that Popov received his assignment from his German bosses in Lisbon in January or very early February 1941, and there was no advanced coordination by either MI5 or MI6 with the FBI before his August 1941 arrival in the United States. A brief diary notation recorded on February 5, 1941, by Guy Liddell reveals that Popov was ordered by the Germans to proceed to Paris "in a month's time, in order to undergo a course before being sent to America." Forty days later Liddell cryptically wrote about the "immense difficulties" Popov had encountered trying to obtain a diplomatic visa for Portugal and an "American visa from Portugal and Egyptian visa from New York." Once he arrives in the United States, Liddell noted, he "can get in touch with us in Lisbon and will be contacted both by us and by the FBI in America." Liddell's entry was dated three weeks *before* Popov's rendezvous with the Abwehr in Lisbon. Adding to the mystery is another entry in Liddell's diary dated May 29, 1941, describing Popov's cover as an "import and export merchant" because he could not get

Sol Bloom. Brooklyn, New York, congressman and chairman of the House Foreign Affairs Committee. BSC secretly ordered Dusko Popov to falsely identify Bloom to the Abwehr as one of his sources, infuriating Hoover and further poisoning the FBI-BSC relationship. *New York World Telegram & Sun Collection, Library of Congress*

the backing of "his own Yugoslav Legation to proceed as a representative of the Ministry of Information." Liddell held a meeting with Herschel Johnson at the American embassy on June 4, 1941, where he explained the "whole circumstances," prompting Johnson's cable to Washington. The following day, Warren telephoned Foxworth.[11]

Equally puzzling was why MI5 agreed to Tricycle's move. He was, according to one biographer, the head of Britain's most valuable double-agent network and its "most productive and important" source. His Abwehr questionnaires were very valuable for British war planners, and he also enjoyed high-level German contacts that offered the British important insights into the foibles, behaviors, and personalities of his handlers in Lisbon. At the time he was the only MI5 source who could travel to Lisbon and Madrid for regular personal meetings. Furthermore, his departure from London would cut off the Abwehr's link to Giraffe, Balloon, and Gelatine. So why would they turn him over to a security service whose only previous connection with the MI5 was the Rumrich disaster which ended in such a humiliating failure for the FBI?[12]

The MI5 file suggests that the service agreed to the U.S. move for financial reasons. When the war in Europe began, the British government had hermetically sealed off all legitimate access to the British Isles, making it almost impossible for the Germans to communicate with their agents by mail, telegraph, or radio. Most of their agents were imprisoned, with the few that remained at large running for their lives and incapable of spying. As for travel, visitors from Spain and Portugal were rigidly controlled through a sophisticated customs and immigration regimen at British ports of entry that led to the London Relocation Center or, worse, to Camp 020.[13]

As a consequence, a strange twist of roles occurred, with MI5 now frustrated by Germany's difficulties in sending funds to its agents in England. Adding to this headache was the larger challenge of keeping pace with Popov's profligate lifestyle. The "libidinous Serb playboy," in the words of Ben Macintyre, who was being paid handsomely by the Germans, did not expect reimbursement from the British but did want MI5 to provide him with "wine, women and song." Typical of the Security Service's daily dilemma was one London visit when the bored Popov hinted to his handlers "that a little high-class feminine society would be most acceptable." The challenge fell to Tar Robertson, who arranged through Special Branch of Scotland Yard for a woman to "purely and simply entertain Skoot and keep him out of mischief" while keeping Robertson "informed of the various curious associations which he is making in this country."[14]

MI5 was searching for a way to fully support these agents by arranging for funds to more easily make their way into England. The fairly straightforward and simple solution to the problem which was supposedly conceived in Popov's "supple" mind came to be known as "Plan Midas." Popov convinced the Lisbon Abwehr that he had recruited an unscrupulous London theatrical producer named Eric Glass to open a bank account in New York, where the Germans could wire funds that Glass would transfer to his own

London account for the use of Popov's agents in exchange for a percentage of the funds. Popov convinced the Germans that Glass, portrayed as an Austrian Jew and defeatist, was offering his cooperation in this dangerous scheme in exchange for his safety when the Germans invaded Great Britain. In May 1941, during a face-to-face meeting in Madrid with his controller, Major Ludovico von Karsthoff, the brazen Yugoslav sold Plan Midas to the Abwehr for a ten percent "commission" that he insisted was his due for his effort.[15]

The Pan Am flying boat carrying Popov to America touched down at the Port Washington terminal on Long Island's north shore on August 12,1941, just days after the start of the trial of the thirty-three espionage agents led by Frederick Duquesne in the Manhattan federal court building. Following a cursory customs and immigration inspection, Popov soon found himself in a car en route to Manhattan where the British had arranged for his stay at the Waldorf Astoria on New York's Park Avenue. Hints of what was to come began emerging the day he arrived. Contrary to the FBI instructions to remain incognito for a few days while checks were made for German surveillance, Popov quickly left his hotel suite, and within a matter of hours purchased a new Buick Phaeton trimmed with a maroon interior and convertible top. Next, he made two telephone calls, one to Billy Rose's Diamond Horseshoe nightclub, the second to Ben Marsden's Riviera, a "well known nightspot and . . . gambling house on the New Jersey side of the Hudson."[16] Making matters worse were startling reports from FBI sources at the Waldorf Astoria that the hotel management already suspected him of being an important "British spy," having overheard him talking "too freely" to guests "who were not aware of what the situation was as to his entry into the United States." Soon dissatisfied with his Waldorf accommodations, he abruptly moved north a few blocks, paying $36,000 in cash for a luxury apartment at 530 Park Avenue next to Christ Methodist Church on the corner of East 61st Street. For his new home he also added a new decor and a full-time Chinese servant.[17]

Six days later, Popov had his first meeting with Earl Connelley, an FBI assistant director and inspector and one of Hoover's key officials. A twenty-year veteran who had spent the last ten years traveling the country heading practically all of the FBI's major cases, Connelley was then in New York overseeing the Duquesne prosecution.[18] Together with the BSC's Dick Ellis, who supplied a personal history of Popov's relationship with the British up to October 10, 1940, Connelley grilled Popov for three hours in a

Igor Cassini. A prominent Washington, D.C., society columnist and brother of Oleg Cassini, the famed fashion designer, who Dusko Popov falsely characterized to the Abwehr as his confidential source on BSC instructions. *New York World Telegram & Sun Collection, Library of Congress*

Manhattan hotel room.[19] Popov explained he would pose as a representative of the Yugoslav government-in-exile and as an avid British supporter sent to the United States to act as a propagandist attacking American anti-interventionists as dupes of the Nazis. His duties would involve cooperating with the British Ministry of Information, the British Library of Information in New York, and other "agencies of Great Britain." He then produced a letter of introduction signed by General Dusan Simovitch, head of the Yugoslav government in London, and addressed to the Yugoslav minister to the United States, along with additional documents attesting to his "confidential mission." As for the Germans, they believed that he landed the job through influential family connections through whom he could arrange contacts in the United States. In fact, he knew no one in America, he explained, but planned to inflate his "social prestige and connections" in the hope of convincing the Abwehr that he could "render valuable services." The Abwehr, who were thrilled with the possibilities of his new assignment, urged him to be aggressive by taking an "attitude hostile to the German government."[20] After outlining his German intelligence training, particularly his course in radio communications, he warned of the anticipated receipt of a cable from the Germans identifying someone in the United States who would provide him with a radio transmitter.[21]

Popov waffled when Connelley questioned him about $70,000 in cash that Customs officers found in his briefcase upon his arrival. He explained that $6,000 had been supplied by the Germans in Lisbon for his operational use in the United States. When his funds ran low, the Lisbon Abwehr would resupply him. Another $38,000 came "through some arrangement with the British authorities" for deposit in a New York bank in the name of someone in London who would subsequently transfer these funds to a London bank.[22] Days later, however, "after some hesitation" Popov changed his story, telling Connelly that the $38,000 was British funds given to him before he left Lisbon. His assignment was to deposit it in a New York bank account as part of a scheme to identify German agents in England by monitoring German transfers from this account to the "Chief German Agent in London in the form of English pounds."[23] The now wary Connelley insisted that Popov maintain a strict accounting of all funds that he received from the Germans and that any payments and support for his services would be paid to him by the FBI. The grandiloquent Serb refused all FBI remunerations, claiming that he only wanted to serve his country by placing himself "entirely at our disposal and direction." Then in a final flourish he insisted that he would do "what we required or directed in each situation."[24]

Special Agent Charles Lanman, a seasoned investigator with years of experience handling sources, was assigned to work with Popov. He began by delving into his background, first carefully reading Popov's British-supplied resume and then gradually pulling additional details out of him through general conversations. The British described him as having the "general appearance of a Slav type with high cheek bones, broad nose bulbous at tip." Facial characteristics included "thick lips, a loose sensual mouth with deep lines running from the wings of his nostrils to the corners of his mouth" and a "sallow complexion after late night, white and blotchy."[25] When the war ended, Popov hoped to return to Dubrovnik to resume his easy lifestyle, perhaps serving as the British consul, a prestigious post to which he "attaches great importance." The report ended with his gratitude for a suggestion "that he might receive a British decoration in recognition of his work for this country."[26] Lanman then took in the challenge that Popov posed to him.

> He is a clever, attractive and courageous young man of whose sincerity and loyalty we are satisfied. Although something of an adventurer he has a great admiration for Great Britain and a deep affection for France and like the majority of his countrymen at the present time is violently anti-German. He has an excellent brain but dislikes work, having been brought up in an atmosphere of comfort and ease. He has a secure position in Dubrovnik and an income equivalent to $12,000 a year, which in Yugoslavia is a lot of money. He likes to lead the life of a playboy and spends a great deal of his time in the presence of women. Yachting is his only other pastime. He drinks only moderately and has great personality and charm.[27]

A signal to Lanman of what was to come appeared in the file's next paragraph.

> While at first he refused to accept payment from the British on any account, as the Germans have paid his exceptionally heavy expenses, the British authorities have provided him with a little money and have generally paid his air expenses from England back to Lisbon. He has been promised by the Germans the important Kollf Agency after the war as reward for his efforts. But he is prepared to leave to us the question of any reward, his principle concern, so he says, being that the war should be won.[28]

Lanman's attention then turned to the eleven German microdots Popov brought with him from Lisbon. They were segmented into four categories: the first, of "great importance," demanded information about American air defenses with a particularly "urgent" need for monthly production figures on fighters, pursuit, training, and civilian aircraft, and where in the British Empire they would be delivered. The second, which had "special importance," concentrated on the Canadian Air Force's development of new aircraft, squadron locations, air training plans, and school locations with types of training conducted at each site (beginning, intermediate, and advanced). Allied shipment of war material, convoy assembly points "with the names of vessels and speeds, if possible," made up the third category.

The fourth and longest section listed fourteen questions about the readiness status of naval and armed forces in Hawaii. The Abwehr wanted Popov to determine the "exact situation" at Hawaii's Wheeler and Wickham airfields, the military's use of civilian airfields, and commercial aviation firms. There were five specific questions asking for sketches of piers, shipyards, fuel facilities, workshops, mooring berths, and floating docks, among others, at the Pearl Harbor naval base. A final question entitled "Special Assignments" requested details about torpedo-protective nets that had recently been introduced into the British and U.S. navies. "To what extent already available in commercial and battle fleet? Use while underway? Average reduction of speed when used? Details of the construction and etc."[29]

On September 26, 1941, Arthur Thurston discussed the Popov case with ONI providing them at the same time with a "summary questionnaire of information that is currently needed by the Bureau in connection with the Popov case." As the Bureau's liaison with MID and ONI, he had experienced considerable difficulty over several months getting maritime and naval material for double-agent passage to the Germans. His efforts had met with repeated resistance from ONI to supply "authentic information concerning the United States Navy as well as misinformation which would not be susceptible to check," Thurston told his bosses.[30] Faced with this new list from Popov, ONI offered Thurston only discouraging claims that it had no material ready for passage, nor was there much chance of getting any in the near future due to a shortage of staff to handle the necessary processing.[31] The real reason, however, was quite different. Navy officials were squeamish about counterintelligence operations, with double agents being particularly worrisome. Thurston found a general attitude among ONI officials that supplying any kind of naval data to the Germans through FBI double agents "would be dangerous."[32] A month later the ONI's director, Captain Alan Kirk, and the Chief of Naval Operation, Admiral Harold Stark, partially broke the impasse by providing a two-page memorandum about torpedo nets described as "not accurate but plausible."[33] One document which went to the heart of German demands concerned the Tiburon Navy Depot, where tests were underway on torpedo nets. ONI officials insisted that the last paragraph be given high priority for passage to the Germans. "Facilities at Tiburon Navy depot are considered far from suitable for experimentation with the 4/8/T/, II (submarine indicator anti-torpedo) net which is now in progress. Among other things the signal flares on these nets have not been proved entirely satisfactory and are in a stage of continuing development.

Isetically, this is a fleet defense problem rather than a Mobile Advanced base Net Defense Force problem."[34]

As instructed by the Abwehr, Popov and Lanman sent six secret writing letters to Portugal between August and October confirming his safe arrival, his readiness for business, demands for additional funds and radio broadcasting equipment, and his discovery of Nicolaus Frolic, a Croatian radio operator whose house in Oyster Bay, New York, could be safely used as a transmission site. Subsequent letters contained tidbits concerning War Department appropriations and army tank construction figures, all sent to different mail drops along with continued demands for much-needed funds.[35] In a letter dated October 25, 1941, Popov and Lanman tantalized the Germans with a description of a multi-volume table of organization of U.S. armored divisions that he was eager to supply his bosses. Lanman's objective was to test enemy capabilities to collect bulky material too voluminous for reduction to invisible lines on a piece of paper. Warning the Germans of the constant danger of holding such confidential information, Popov demanded that the Abwehr send someone to America to retrieve the valuable cache of secrets or for some other German agent in the United States to take custody of the information from him. A third option called for Popov to travel under Yugoslav diplomatic cover with the information to a Central or South American city where the Abwehr would feel safer in meeting him. As a sweetener, they then sent another letter describing light, medium, and heavy tanks, armored cars, and navy facilities in Florida (in response to requirements in Popov's original microdot questionnaire), together with details about naval flight training that had originally been intended for passage in another double-agent case. As in all previous secret letters, Popov signed with his code name "Ivan."[36]

The letters struck home. On October 31 Lisbon cabled orders for Popov to proceed to Rio de Janeiro as soon as possible. Over the next two weeks Lanman familiarized Popov with the G2-supplied charts and tables, created luggage concealments, and arranged for his temporary Yugoslav diplomatic courier status to reduce the chances of any customs and immigration checks along his route. On November 14 Popov left New York for Miami; twelve days later, two weeks before the attack on Pearl Harbor, he departed by plane for Brazil.[37]

A week after the Pearl Harbor attack, Popov arrived in New York aboard the SS *Uruguay*. With the ship in quarantine at Pier 32 in New York's North River, Popov greeted Lanman with some disturbing news. Stored in the ship's cargo hold was a collection of "butterfly trays" that should undergo careful examination before release to their recipients. Popov's information struck a note with Lanman, who recalled that three months earlier E. W. Bavin, a British Purchasing Commission official in New York, had reported his suspicions to Connelley that wooden trays with butterflies pressed under a glass top and sold in America as fashionable serving trays or coffee tables were being used by the Germans as microdot concealments. Manufactured in Rio de Janeiro and labeled "Industra Brasileira Atelier Elizabeth, R.D. Gerardo 44–1⁰ Rio de Janeiro," the trays, sold in a local Brazilian shop, were popular with merchant seaman who brought them into the United States. Popov described seeing a number of them while passing an open door in an off-limits space inside the German legation.[38] Through arrangements with the Customs Service, hundreds of trays were taken to the New York FBI office where they were all disassembled and inspected by Charles Appel, a leading FBI forensic specialist and founder of the FBI laboratory. No evidence of any espionage was uncovered.[39]

In Rio de Janeiro, Abwehr officers questioned Popov about his experiences in New York while pressing him hard about his American contacts. He spent hours with an embassy secretary transcribing, modifying, adjusting, changing, and then retranscribing his dictated notes on the table of military organization he carried from the United States. The final transcript was then separated into two copies: one retained in the legation file and the second carried immediately to Lisbon by a German diplomatic courier aboard a flight operated by the Italian carrier Lati Airlines. After praising him for finding a radio operator, they warned him that mailing radio equipment from Lisbon was too risky. They then ordered him to buy radio parts in New York so he could begin broadcasting at the earliest opportunity. His transmissions were to be beamed to Brazil where a German agent code-named "Alfredo" would relay them to Germany using radio codes that would be sent to Tricycle at a later date. Complaining about the danger and unpredictability of travel to Central and South America, Tricycle insisted on a safer method for moving large caches of data. His Rio contacts then offered the services of an Abwehr agent who routinely sailed between New York and South America. This mysterious spy was described only as a ship captain who had already performed a number of intelligence missions, such as photographing the port of Trinidad used by the British as a travel control and censorship facility. Until the captain arrived for a meeting in New York, Tricycle was to continue sending his secret messages to Lisbon for instructions. Before leaving Brazil, Popov received $10,000 ($156,520 in 2012 dollars) at a local safe house along with two microdots affixed to a piece of paper containing his radio operating instructions, new mail drop addresses, and questions about smokeless cartridges, ship construction, and armaments production, particularly rapid-fire airplane canons.[40]

"Alfredo" was well known to the FBI. He was Gustav Albrecht Engels, the head of the CEL-ALD espionage group, one of six German spy rings (CEL-ALD was the principal ring) operating throughout Brazil. Engels was a business executive with the Allgemeine Elektrizitaets Gessellschaft, an electrical products firm based in Rio de Janeiro. In 1939, he embarked on the creation of a well-funded ($120,000 in 1941 equates to $1.98 million in 2012) and wide-ranging Brazilian espionage network under the overall direction of Herman Bohny, the German naval attaché in Rio.[41] An internal FBI history of SIS wartime activities in Brazil described Engels as "integral to German espionage in the Western Hemisphere and linked to German agents in the U.S." who "served as a relay unit forwarding radio messages between U.S. agents and Germany." Beginning in July 1940, FBI radio technicians started intercepting and decoding CEL-ALD messages, correlating the information and identifying ring members to penetrate the ring through informants. Over a two-year period agents amassed a wealth of intelligence on Engels's mail drops, secret inks, financial records, cover companies, codes and ciphers, and, most importantly, the CEL-ALD leadership and membership.[42]

Since Popov's arrival in America, coping with his lavish lifestyle had become an increasing problem for his FBI handlers. Never having worked for a living, Popov blindly burned through the recently acquired $10,000 to pay ballooning expenses for the upkeep of his Park Avenue penthouse, his new car, a large and ever-expanding wardrobe, nightclub and restaurant charges, and more. In January, with the United States now at war and the FBI busying itself constructing his radio (which it commenced on January 28), familiarizing itself with transmission frequencies, secret writing, briefing the military on the new intelligence collection requirements, and preparing for the arrival of the mystery ship captain, Popov abruptly left town for a vacation in Sun Valley, Idaho.

By March, with Popov once again nearly broke and no word from the Abwehr about any ship captain, Engels radioed Popov with Berlin's assurances that they would send him an additional $15,000 ($211,000 in 2012) if he could assure them that no danger would be incurred in the transfer. FBI technicians immediately radioed the green light: "Your suggestion

OK. Through previous arrangements my funds are not frozen. No danger if money sent by Santos for sale of antiques. For God's sake please hurry." Six days later, a now desperate Lanman reported to Washington that the promised money had not arrived and ND63 (FBI code name for Popov) was "without funds" and needed it "*today.*"[43] Lanman frantically requested a short-term loan of $2,500 ($35,289 in 2012) in order to cover Popov's "obligation to his servants, to his grocer, tailor, florist, and other individuals who must be paid immediately."[44]

Adding to the frustration over Popov's spending problems was a growing tension between the FBI and the British regarding the handling of Tricycle. BSC had little to offer when MI5 in London repeatedly questioned them concerning the progress of the case. Anger first brewed up in March 1942 over an apparent misunderstanding involving H. Montgomery Hyde, the BSC counterintelligence specialist, whom the Bureau accused of encouraging Popov to return to London and once again spy for the British.[45] On the heels of this dustup Stephenson reported what he described as "good evidence" that the Germans now suspected Popov of cooperating with American authorities. These fears were based on a series of factors starting with an intercepted March 12, 1942, message that Berlin radioed Engels (picked up at the FBI radio station in Wading River), asking if Popov's "salary [should] be remitted to his family." Engels radioed the question to Popov with assurances that Jebsen had visited the Popov family in Dubrovnik and found them healthy and well. Based on this report, Stephenson criticized the wisdom of the FBI's demand for money. He suggested that the Germans, suspecting that Popov had come under American control, would be reluctant to send him funds, fearing it was a ploy by the BSC or FBI, who were "anxious to get hold of the money." The FBI, in Stephenson's view, should have insisted that the funds go to his parents instead. Adding to German doubts was the sudden drop-off in quality intelligence from Popov since his return from Brazil and Engels's unexpected arrest in late March. Stephenson then began applying pressure on Hoover for the production of high-grade feed material to rehabilitate Popov's prestige with the Germans, adding that his value to the Allied war effort is "likely to be judged very much by results as past experience shows."[46]

At the same time that the Abwehr was voicing suspicion of their important American agent, a letter arrived from Lisbon which raised serious FBI questions about the strength of the Abwehr's doubts. Hidden in the flap of the envelope were eleven microdots for Popov containing a "Questionnaire," made up of more than 2,600 words. This priceless German smorgasbord included three dots filled with questions (fuel, propulsion, engine design, speed, altitude, etc.) about a new "rocket plane" under development at a laboratory in Langley, Virginia. Others demanded statistics on American exports of raw materials such as iron and steel, ball bearings, and armor plate shipped from U.S. ports along with the "absolute" necessity of supplying dates of shipments. Timely receipt of the destinations of shipments (Asia, Africa, Egypt, Europe) were also required. Popov was instructed to develop informants in various U.S. government agencies where this information could be found.

The next instruction raised terrifying concerns for the small group of scientists who would soon offer their recommendations to President Roosevelt regarding a decision to move forward on the atomic bomb:

> Decay Uran. According to some information obtained there is reason to believe that the scientific works for the utilization of the atoxic [*sic*]—kernel energy are being driven forward into a certain direction in the U.S. partly by use of helium. Continuous information about tests made on this subject are required particularly 1. What process is practiced in the U.S. for sending of heavy uran? 2. When are being made [*sic*] tests with more important quantities of uran? (Universities, industrial laboratories, etc.) 3. Which other raw-materials are being used at these tests? It is recommended to entrust only best experts with this test, and if not available, to abstain from it.[47]

This new series of question encouraged Foxworth and his colleagues in their handling of Popov in New York. The contents of these eleven microdots provided military analysts with a goldmine of insights into German intelligence gaps concerning U.S. readiness, capabilities, and strategic planning so soon after the Pearl Harbor attack. Contrary to British beliefs, Foxworth viewed Engels's arrest as a plus for the Popov case. Certainly the Abwehr would raise questions about how Engels was discovered, questions they most likely could not satisfactorily answer. At the same time, however, Popov remained an important source and one of the only assets they had working in America. Suspicions aside, with America and Germany now at war they could ill afford a major communications break that would force them to find a new radio operator to reconnect with Popov. Foxworth, in sync with Stephenson, believed that careful attention to Popov's radio connection could in time divert the communications of other unknown

German agents to Popov's channel, thus offering the FBI "control over the information being furnished." Second, losing his services would be counterproductive as the Abwehr would only replace him with someone else. Finally, the American awareness of the recent "Questionnaire" offered the possibility that in the future the military could "forecast with a certain degree of accuracy [German] plans and tactics based upon analysis of the information in which they are particularly interested at any time." Accomplishing this objective required Popov to pass genuine information pertaining to the U.S. effort in this country, "which would be plausible but not subject to verification."[48]

Any chance of gathering high-quality feed material from MID or ONI in the spring of 1942 was out of the question. Indeed, by British standards the American military had little organization for anything above the level of two independent services, Army and Navy. Both were independent and "fiercely turf conscious" with no unifying Department of Defense. This same shortcoming applied to joint planners who had no organization similar to the London Controlling Section, which would be manned by specialists skilled in the art of deception. They came instead from the Operations Division (until March 1942 known as the War Plans Division) of the War Department General Staff. Deception, however, was a small part of the much larger planning schemes developed by the military. Adding to Hoover's feed-material frustrations was the fact that until the end of the war the Army was more interested in strategic and operational deception planning than the Navy. Even concerted BSC efforts to encourage British military intervention on the U.S. high command to break free some valuable "chicken-feed" failed due to the Americans' fear of telling the enemy too much.[49]

By March 1942 the FBI still had not received the balance of Tricycle's resume, which they had been promised seven months earlier. Three months later, probably through Guy Liddell's intervention, it was finally turned over along with previously requested information concerning the roles of Giraffe, Balloon, and Gelatine in London.[50] To ease the situation Hoover authorized Colonel Walter Wren to interview the source and to participate in all future meetings with him.

By July 1942, with Popov's spending again out of control (no word on funds had been received from the Abwehr), and little to show for the expenditure of time, funds, and manpower, Ladd decided to turn him over to the British for their use in Europe.[51] Before his departure, however, the lingering question of his financial obligations had to be settled. Throughout the summer, while preparations were underway for his move, discussions between Foxworth and Wren took place concerning Tricycle's expenses, which had ballooned to $18,500 ($261,139 in 2012). When an angry Foxworth warned Wren that the FBI had no further obligation for Tricycle's maintenance, Wren conceded the point with the plea that the "British are anxious for the Bureau to give further consideration to assisting the British in liquidating his debts." By mid-August the final tally had been made: the two sides agreed to split Popov's expenses totaling nearly $10,000, with the FBI's portion coming from the three earlier loans of $2,500 ($35,289 in 2012), $700 ($9,880 in 2012), and $1,800 ($25,408 in 2012). In the end a furious Hoover settled up for $5,000 ($70,677 in 2012).[52]

The summer and fall of 1942 was a watershed period for Hoover's relations with the British. Guy Liddell had visited the FBI, Harry Kimball had undertaken extended discussions with MI5 and MI6 officials in London; Donald Downes Chase was arrested while burglarizing the Italian embassy in Washington for the OSS and BSC: Victor Rothschild's visit exposed MI5's view of MI6 and BSC; Dick Ellis's critical comments about the FBI relayed by Wyndham Bruce ended the FBI's relationship with him, and, finally, Arthur Thurston, the FBI man who provided Popov's Pearl Harbor questions to ONI, was en route to London as Hoover's personal representative with MI5.

In the weeks before Popov's departure for Europe, Lanman and Special Agent George McSwain spent days with Wren preparing Popov's cover story for the Germans, which became known as the "Lisbon Memorandum." The three agreed that Popov would point to inadequate finances as the reason for his return. Despite his failed efforts, Popov's Croatian radio operator remained in the New York area ready to continue work with the equipment now safely stored for security. A new uproar began when Wren asked Lanman and McSwain for the names of prominent Americans whom Popov could identify as his sources of intelligence for the Germans. During these discussions five names were raised: Igor Cassini; Sol Bloom; a man named Robbins who was a close friend of the secretary of war, Henry Stimson; Edward Bacher, the head of the National Defense Committee of the International Chamber of Commerce; and Navy Lieutenant Commander Frank Waldron: all American citizens, all unaware of Popov and this case.[53]

Cassini was born in Russia in 1915 to Alexander Loeisky, a czarist diplomat, and his Russian Italian aristocrat wife, Countess Marguerite Cassini. Cassini, the younger brother of the famed courtier and fashion designer

Oleg Cassini, was a journalist on the gossip beat for the *Washington Times-Herald,* then owned by the Hearst Corporation.[54] The seventy-two-year-old Illinois-born Bloom moved to New York City in 1903, where he became rich in real estate. In 1923 he entered the House of Representatives, following a special election to fill the Brooklyn seat of Samuel Marx, the deceased congressman-elect. Bloom was no ordinary congressman: he was the chairman of the powerful Committee on Foreign Affairs.[55] Wren's plan called for Popov to tell the Germans that Cassini and Bacher provided him with information on aircraft production; Waldron supplied notes on naval conferences, and Bloom "let you [Popov] have War Department appropriation figures. He knew you were connected with the British Government and used the figures in support of his contention that the U.S. were making all possible preparation to intervene." The memorandum read in part:

> Since June you have had no funds to continue buying information from the journalist, Cassini. Igor Cassini is a Russian now naturalized as an American. He writes a column mainly about the private lives of high members of the US administration for the 'Washington Times-Herald.' He is thirty years old–weak face, curly hair, clean shaven. Very anti-British. He boasted to you how he was in the habit of obtaining confidential figures for his paper by bribery—particularly from the War Production Board. You discovered he was open to accept bribes himself by offering him money to publish pro-British material. You then disclosed that you were really as anti-British as he was and arranged to pay him for the production information received. He refused to give you his source but you believed it was really in W.P.B. as his detailed figures accorded with the general figures you got conversationally from your social contacts.[56]

Before Lanman could discuss Wren's proposal with Washington, Popov abruptly departed the United States on October 12, 1942, with Wren's approval to pass the names. Nine days later Wren rationalized his actions by explaining that Popov's scheduled departure for Lisbon had been moved up by several days, "making it necessary to whip the story into final form." At the same time he conceded that he had no FBI authority for permitting Popov to convey these names to the Germans.[57]

Hoover was blind with rage when he learned that Americans would be falsely exposed to the Germans as traitors to the Allied cause by discussing confidential information with Popov. Particularly baffling was the identification of Bloom, one of the most powerful men in the government with significant influence over military budgets. Hoover found portions of the cover story "most objectionable," which would never have been cleared, "as Wren well knew." Hoover then let loose on Stephenson, accusing him of a "serious . . . breach of faith due to his failure to give us the promised opportunity to clear the material." At that point, however, the matter was moot. By the time Hoover's message reached the BSC head, Popov was back in London under MI5's exclusive control. He never returned to America again.[58]

CHAPTER ELEVEN

The Count from New York

Four months after the Pearl Harbor attack, alert British censors in Bermuda intercepted a letter mailed from the United States to Europe. Postmarked in New York City and dated April 6, 1942, the envelope was addressed to Walter Hirzel, an attorney living in Winterthur, a small village in northeast Switzerland near the German border. Analysis of the letter uncovered a secret writing message tucked between the lines of a breezy and innocuous letter offering updates on the mysterious author's day-to-day life in America. The letter's hidden message contained cryptic details about technical matters that could prove useful to German military planners. The "present plane output [is] nearly 3500 monthly," and "it is said emphasis is now on bombers, also transports to Canada and Africa." The author also described the "present lack of skilled labor, slow delivery, propulsion machinery, electric motors, pumps causing long commissioning delays" and the increased use of "a new explosive called Trinitrophenylmethylnitramine," said to be "more sensitive and powerful than TNT when used as a booster charge in bombs and shells."[1]

British censorship technicians ranked among the best in the world at the craft. As recognized masters in this arcane counterintelligence specialty, technicians could easily open envelopes and packages, quickly examine them for evidence of espionage, and then reseal them without revealing any evidence of tampering to suspicious recipients. This was especially true in Bermuda, where censors, operating under great pressure, were required to remove and examine mail from a recently arrived ship or plane and then return it to the same ship or plane before its scheduled departure. This need for speed led to occasional errors, and secret writing messages were often missed altogether; it was a skill, an art form, and sometimes a science, but not an exact science.[2]

While the information in the letter revealed espionage, there was little else in it or the envelope that offered any clues to the author's identity. Based on the nature of the information and the "Gerson" signature at the bottom of the letter, censors theorized that the author could be identical to another unknown spy whom the FBI had been chasing since December 1941. Just weeks earlier, Bermuda censors discovered a similar letter bound for Switzerland, postmarked in New York, and signed "Fred Lewis," which they gave to the FBI for investigation.[3]

Based on analysis of the Fred Lewis letter, investigators produced a sketchy profile of the author as probably a married male who had once been an air-raid warden, tended to his own modest garden, lost his house through a foreclosure, and had once suffered an illness that confined him to bed. He may also have been an amateur inventor who was pursuing a "button patent" and some kind of "camouflaged royalty settlement from South America."[4] When FBI handwriting analysis of the "Lewis" and "Gerson" correspondence revealed two different authors, suggesting the possibility of two separate spy rings in the New York area, the FBI immediately flashed a signal to Bermuda asking them to stay alert for more messages in what now became known as the "Gerson Series."[5]

Wilhelm Albrecht Von Pressentin Gennant Von Rautter was the mysterious author of the April "Gerson" letter to Switzerland. Born in 1899 on a 73,000 acre estate in the sleepy Prussian village of Wilkamm, Germany, near the Polish border, Rautter was the son of Count Earl Von Rautter and his English-born wife, Countess Bertha Von Rautter, previously known as Bertha Brayley-Fisher. From birth to age nineteen Wilhelm lived with his parents, attending a local private school where, he later told the FBI, he had acquired the equivalent of a college education before the age of twenty.[6]

Divided national loyalty abruptly ended his parent's marriage. When the First World War started and Count Rautter joined the German army as a major, the government took over a portion of his estate to house British prisoners of war. Gradually the conflicted countess began offering them aid and comfort, behavior that so outraged her humiliated husband that he soon sought a divorce while pressuring his government to charge her with treason. After the war, mother and son lived for a time in Cologne, working for the YMCA under the authority of the British Army of the Rhine commanded by Field Marshall Herbert Plumer. A year later they moved again, this time to London, while Count Rautter finalized his divorce in a German court. Wilhelm now found himself in a divided world of destitution, living with a resentful mother who had married a German and now returned to England in disgrace.[7]

Now hopelessly unemployed and living off the charity of his mother's family, Rautter left England on an odyssey that would take him across the Atlantic Ocean many times over the next twenty years. Arriving first in Valparaiso, Chile, he took a job as a deckhand on the *Lake Pithia,* a tramp steamer bound for the Port of New Orleans. From there he caught a train to New York City and then on to Sharon, Pennsylvania, on the Ohio border where, perhaps through family contacts, he landed a job for the next six years in the personnel department of the Standard Tank Car Company, which manufactured rail cars for transporting petroleum and other liquids. In Sharon he taught English and citizenship classes in the hope of demonstrating his "Americanism," a noble gesture which failed when a U.S. magistrate rejected his citizenship application after learning that he entered the country illegally.[8]

Hoping to reenter the United States legally under the German immigration quota, Wilhelm quit his job, returned to England for a visit with his mother, and then went on to Germany for a reunion with his father, now remarried and still living on the family estate. In the back of his mind was a nagging concern for his hereditary rights to the family estate. The family line began at the turn of the nineteenth century when Gustave von Rautter, a Prussian nobleman and Wilhelm's direct ancestor, was killed fighting in the Napoleonic wars. Nineteen years later, when Gustave's only child, a daughter named Auguste, married Otto Bernhard Von Pressentin II, the couple successfully petitioned the king of Prussia to allow them to adopt the name "Von Pressentin Gennant Von Rautter" in order to perpetuate the "Rautter" name. More than eight decades later, on the one-hundredth anniversary of the war against Napoleon, Kaiser Wilhelm II granted Christoph Von Pressentin Gennant Von Rautter, Wilhelm's grandfather, the title Graf Von Rautter Wilkamm. As Wilhelm was the third of four boys born to Earl and Bertha, the deaths of his two older brothers in the First World War left Wilhelm as the direct heir to the title of "Count von Rautter of Wilkamm" and the vast Wilkamm estate, a fact bound tightly by history, law, and tradition that his father's disinheritance could not change. How the matter was settled remains a mystery. What is known is that a year later he returned as a legal alien to New York, where he secured a Wall Street job in the Foreign Loan Department of the investment banking firm Dillon Reade & Company, analyzing European and South American loans.[9]

Rautter was young and unattached, with money in his pockets. During these years he lived carefree, drifting from job to job and even making his birthday a regular event by celebrating it on Martha's Vineyard every

August. Four years later, after leaving Dillon Reade for a brief visit to England and Germany, he joined National City Bank of New York and later First Boston Corporation, which sent him to Colombia where he divided his time between Cali and Medellin, conducting financial analyses of the Cauca Valley, a subdivision of the Colombian government. When his contract ended in 1932 he traveled again to Europe for a year, checking on family finances before returning to the United States to a job placement counselor position for the state of New York. Two years later he moved to Washington, D.C., working for the Resettlement Administration where he was responsible for relocating struggling rural and urban families to planned communities. It was a job that later proved useful for German intelligence as it routinely took him to New Mexico, where his fluency in German, Spanish, Russian, French, and Portuguese proved to be a valuable asset. When a reduction in work force ended his three-year federal government career, the nomadic Rautter again returned to a Germany now completely in the iron grip of Adolf Hitler.[10]

In 1938 he returned to America, where he once again resumed his nomadic existence and acquired his U.S. citizenship in New York. After collecting his U.S. passport he again left for Germany on a journey that would forever alter his life. His motivation, as in the past, was his concern for family finances, his father's ailing health, and the nagging fear that his father's "fortune seeker" wife would steal his inheritance. In February 1940, while William Sebold sat for hours in a New York FBI office outlining his recruitment into German espionage, Rautter crossed into Germany where he immediately filled out German police forms listing the purpose of his visit along with personal details and the length of his stay in Germany. At the family estate he found his father older, mellower, in good health, and more disposed to financially aid his ex-wife and son, now a major problem because of the new Nazi restrictions placed on the transferal of money from Germany.[11]

Three months later Rautter received an unexpected letter from Hans Blum, an Abwehr major and owner of Remy and Company, inviting him to meet for a discussion about business opportunities in the United States. A week or so later the two men met in Hamburg at Blum's office where he described his company's chemical export and import business. Blum explained that he had heard that Rautter was returning to the United States and hoped to hire him as his representative with his company's American clients. Blum expressed concern that the sudden eruption of the war with

France and Great Britain would disrupt his company's transatlantic operations, which Rautter could help by maintaining "communications with and the good will of such [American] customers." All his expenses, of course, would be covered by Remy and Company.[12]

A month later, Blum again summoned him to Hamburg for a continuation of their discussions. After some perfunctory business chatter and the drafting of employment contracts, Blum abruptly informed Rautter that German military intelligence had investigated him, found him acceptable, and wished to use him for collecting information in the United States. To soften the blow, Blum downplayed the request by insisting that no one wanted Rautter doing anything that would endanger himself or German–U.S. relations. It was simply a matter of gathering helpful "information as to the war and productive activities of the [United States]." Blum's style, always friendly, soft-spoken, and reassuring, nevertheless subtly betrayed a sinister, threatening tone that would not accept "no" for an answer. Wilhelm later told the FBI that fear for his father, his younger brother then serving in the German army, and his own welfare (there was still his inheritance to consider) forced his agreement to serve as an Abwehr agent in America. Years later when facing espionage prosecution he rationalized his decision by claiming that his family was of noble birth and committed monarchists. An uncle, who served as the last Privy-Counselor to Kaiser Wilhelm II, was also "anti-Nazi, as was his father." With Hitler in charge, however, there was no alternative; one did not challenge the new regime but rather "went along with the German Government as a matter of convenience." His view in the end was that "when in Rome one must do as the Romans do."[13]

Rautter soon found himself in an obscure Hamburg business office studying the basics of espionage. Instructions included the use of secret solutions such as buttermilk, urine, and pyramidon (Blum told him to characterize pyramidon as "Edward" in all his communications and to send his messages to Blum using his code name, "Simon"), a common over-the-counter headache remedy effective for secret writing when combined with pure alcohol. At night in his hotel he practiced his assignments, returning the next day for Blum's critique. Rautter received one hour of instruction (he had no previous radio experience) for ten days on radio construction, along with transmitting, receiving, coding, and decoding using a standard work of fiction. After buying the radio parts in New York City, he was to recruit an experienced operator to handle transmissions. When he was ready to broadcast he was to cable Blum.[14]

Next he studied microdots hidden on common everyday letters sent from Europe and then read them using a local store-bought microscope. From time to time, Blum would send him letters containing microdot instructions and information. If a letter contained no "of" designation in the dateline, then he was to carefully examine all letters "O" appearing in the sixteenth line of the text for a microdot that could be read through a 110- or 125-power microscope. His code name on his secret writing messages to Europe would be "Rogers," and they would be sent to three mail drops: Mr. A. John in Lisbon, Portugal, Mr. Walter Hirzel in Winterthur, Switzerland, and Apartado 1006, Mexico, D.F. Mexico, the last of which he was to use on a regular basis. For his cover as Blum's U.S. business representative he received a thirty-two-page list of chemical companies engaged in business with Remy and Company throughout the United States.[15]

His catalogue of Abwehr requirements was broad but nonspecific. He was ordered to cross the Hudson River on the Brooklyn–Staten Island Ferry, pick out ships of all kinds filling New York harbor, pay close attention to the names, and make mental notes of markings on crates bound for Europe while casually strolling along docks and wharves. Other assignments that took him away from New York included observing factory facilities of United States Steel, Remington Arms Corporations, and the twelve leading aircraft companies such as the Douglas and Boeing companies. Meeting Blum's business contacts offered good cover for his travel up and down the East Coast observing factory sites and picking up intelligence in local bars and restaurants about troop strength, unit designations, military equipment, and specifics on armament production. To help him remember his instructions, von Rautter carried three microdots with the Abwehr's shopping list and radio instructions concealed in his pants cuffs or the lining of his tie. Keeping up the pretense of a business arrangement, Blum paid him a salary during his training period and agreed to send his new agent $300 per month ($4,925 in 2012) through a bank in Mexico. Before departing Germany, Blum gave him $1,200 ($19,700 in 2012) as an initial payment for services and expenses. The following December the Germans paid him an additional $5,000 ($78,000 today) through a bank in Mexico.[16]

After returning to New York City in September 1940 von Rautter quietly rented an apartment in Brooklyn at 18 South Portland Avenue near De Kalb Avenue and Fort Greene Park. His choice of residence was no accident. A year after settling in Brooklyn, American defense preparation led to spiraling growth of the nearby Brooklyn Navy Yard, forcing the city authorities to quickly build housing in the vicinity of Fort Greene for many of the tens of thousands of employees who worked there during the Second World War. Within days of his arrival, as instructed by Blum, he set up a mail drop by recontacting Mrs. Clara Von Der Goltz, then living across the East River at 465 West Avenue on Manhattan's Upper West Side near Riverside Drive. She was an old friend of Rautter who regularly accepted his mail for years due to his often unsettled living and working situation. Von Der Goltz later told FBI agents that she had no knowledge of his espionage or awareness that his mail was anything other than routine letters from his mother, father, or European friends and business contacts. When notified of receipt of a letter, Rautter would retrieve it and then return to his apartment where he would examine it for microdots.[17]

Rautter soon received a message from Blum instructing him to contact Heinrich Ludwig Suhl, a New York businessman with offices in the Singer Building, a Lower Manhattan office complex located at 149 Broadway in Manhattan's Financial District near the future site of the World Trade Center. Suhl lived with his wife and children at 62 Clark Street in the historic Brooklyn Heights section, home to nineteenth-century poet Walt Whitman, civil rights activist W.E.B. Du Bois, and exiled Norwegian writer Sigrid Unset, who lived there during the Second World War. Suhl's home, which was a short subway ride from his office, offered easy observation of the Brooklyn and Manhattan piers where merchant ships routinely lined up to load cargo bound for England. It was also a short walk to von Rautter's apartment on Portland Street.[18]

Born in Dockehard, Germany, the fifty-five-year-old Suhl came to America in 1925, became a U.S. citizen, and grew wealthy over the years as an importer of cork. Blum and Suhl were in the same business, which brought them into regular contact during Suhl's many visits to Germany and Blum's 1938 visit to New York to personally assess Suhl's suitability for espionage. In 1940 Blum officially signed Suhl up as a German agent during a meeting in Lisbon, a decision, Suhl later told FBI agents, he was forced to make out of concern for the welfare of his fourteen-year-old son still living in Germany. Suhl was to act as a paymaster for German agents in the event war disrupted the international movement of funds. The Abwehr plan aborted when a check for $50,000 (more than $820,000 in 2012) that Blum sent to Suhl, drawn on the Lisbon account of a German agent named Herman Zum Hingate, was questioned by American banks.[19]

The FBI's first whiff of Rautter emerged during the Duquesne investigation when FBI technicians set up a secret short-wave radio in a bungalow in Centerport, New York, for William Sebold's radio communications with Hamburg. Convinced that it was dealing with a trustworthy agent, the Abwehr transmitted daily messages for fifteen months starting in May 1940. A routine feature of this radio relationship was occasional disruption and message breaks caused by unpredictable atmospheric conditions over Europe and the Atlantic Ocean. These same problems were worse for the Abwehr in their efforts to contact a well-hidden German spy ring operating in Mexico. As the problems persisted, Hamburg asked Sebold to act as a relay between Germany and the unknown espionage cell. This sudden catastrophic German mistake proved to be a windfall for American counterintelligence. Despite the fact that the initial messages were indecipherable, the FBI radioed its agreement to the Germans. Over the ensuing months as increasing traffic accumulated, cryptanalysts penetrated the cipher revealing the existence of a major German espionage ring operating in Mexico.[20]

In March 1941, Centerport relayed a short Hamburg message informing the Mexican ring that "Bremen [is] asking suspension of sending mail to Rogers." A flurry of eleven strange messages followed over three months, ordering "Fraser" in Mexico to improve the quality of reports coming from the "Count from New York," using "Rogers" in order that the origins of all messages could be "exactly determined." The Mexican ring then radioed Hamburg that "Rogers" had acquired descriptions of three battleships docked in Newport News, Virginia, four in Philadelphia, and another two in New York, all undergoing repair.[21]

At the same time, Sebold was acting as an international radio relay. FBI technicians were reading the coded messages used by Sudermo, the German-South American Bank, for its communications with its various branches and headquarters in Germany. The Rogers and Count mystery only deepened in June 1941 when a Sudermo-Berlin message to its Mexico City branch complained that the Count was having difficulty maintaining contact with Hamburg: "Even report letters risky. How can we write [to] Rogers sometime? Rogers is to direct only urgent reports through you." On June 11, just weeks before the roll up of the Duquesne ring, Sebold relayed a Mexico message to Hamburg, reporting that "Rogers has no more ink. Should I give him a pad?" Within hours Hamburg replied to Mexico's plea with instructions to "carry out orders."[22]

Reading enemy radio messages offers a counterintelligence service an overwhelming advantage. At the same time, however, it can lead investigators down false trails and to wrong suppositions. Facing this classic dilemma, Hoover's men concluded that they were facing two German agents: one code-named "Rogers" and another called the "Count from New York." Pressure to locate them only increased after Sebold relayed a Hamburg message informing Mexico that an "additional forty [micro]dots" were currently en route to Rogers. The arrest of the Duquesne ring, the exposure of Sebold as an FBI double agent, and the end of the Centerport radio site abruptly closed this unique window into the Mexican ring, and, with no logical leads to follow, the names were indexed and stored for future reference. A waiting game now began.[23]

The FBI remained blind until November 20, 1941, less than three weeks before the attack on Pearl Harbor, when its station at Camp Springs, Maryland, intercepted a radio message from a clandestine German radio in Chapultepec, Mexico, advising Hamburg that Rogers was again in Mexico demanding an end to secret writing messages because it endangered his security in the United States. Wasting no time in its response, Hamburg responded a day later that they had no intention of writing Rogers again but demanded his immediate "return to his post." The message ended with the puzzling instruction that Hamburg expects "dispatches to be sent here directly again," suggesting that Mexico would no longer play a part in the espionage communication system.[24]

Between April 1942 and May 1943, British censors on the lookout for Gerson correspondence intercepted twelve secret writing letters bound for known mail drops in Europe and containing information on aircraft production and shipping. One reported that American companies were manufacturing planes at a rate of "3500 monthly," the navy was using "forty shipyards with 275 ways," while the "Allison 2400 H.P. motor [was] reportedly perfected." Another offered data about a Ford Motor Company plant that was building the B-24E bomber. It spans "2,547,000 sq. ft. floor space—3200 long—200 wide, plus 1,200,000 sq. ft. hanger space." Gerson wrote about a Bell Aircraft Company plane "with detachable fuel tanks flying hopwise to England," while just five months before the invasion of North Africa he cryptically (and inaccurately) warned the Germans without further explanation that "many second front assertions are bluff." In December 1942 with Allied troops firmly lodged in Morocco and Algeria and pushing toward Tunisia, Gerson sent a message that again inadvertently confused the Germans about Allied post-North Africa plans when he signaled that "Greece Balkans and other spot plan for next simultaneous attack."[25]

While no specific information can be gleaned concerning the degree of damage that he caused to the Allied war effort, some insights can be gained from the contents of a secret writing message. A wide-ranging array of military and industrial data, bomber designations, types of aircraft and numbers coming off the assembly line, aircraft motor types, sizes, and power generation, fuel tank specifications, information concerning the companies producing them, and descriptions of armaments plants around the country in such places as Clinton, Indiana, and Point Pleasant, West Virginia, were just some of the categories of information he was generating. While Gerson's letters offered British and FBI experts evidence of the damage he was causing to the Allied war effort, he also provided investigators with insights into his dissolving state of mind resulting from the paralyzing fear of discovery that was beginning to grip him. "My fate in your hands," he wrote. "Further mail since unreceivable by me would land with FBI not me and suicide, have warned repeatedly. May have to flee now. If alive will write when possible." After pleading for understanding, he warned the Abwehr of the possibility of being drafted into the army "if not in jail." Possibly in an effort to end his espionage he told the Germans that he was going "through hell"; that "Edward" (pyramidon) was "unobtainable and too dangerous," suggesting instead the use of urine and changing the code name from Gerson to Peel in all future correspondence.[26]

By May 1943, as the last Gerson letter passed through Bermuda's hands, the FBI was no closer to identifying "Gerson," "Rogers," or the "Count from New York" than they were a year earlier. Neither the secret message nor the clear text of the many letters offered any meaningful clues as to the writer's identity. The forwarding addresses were certainly German mail drops in Switzerland and other neutral European countries, but return addresses remained fictitious or not included on the envelope at all. Analysis revealed that the letters were written on a standard quality paper available in thousands of stationery stores around the country. Latent fingerprint examination produced no matches when compared to the tens of millions of records in the FBI's Identification Division. What was consistent in all the letters, however, was the handwriting. FBI experts confirmed for investigators that all the intercepted letters appeared to be written by the same person.

Analysis of the "Gerson," "Rogers," and "Count from New York" cases, particularly the sophistication of the secret writing, together with other information gathered from previous FBI and British investigations, suggested that all three suspects received espionage training in Germany and all three probably arrived in the United States through New York around September 1939. Having no other recourse, FBI personnel in the New York office working with the Customs Service undertook the laborious process of comparing known Gerson handwriting samples with tens of thousands of baggage declarations of travelers arriving from Europe since the summer of 1939. By the fall of 1943, after examining countless declarations, an agent made a tentative match that was then confirmed by FBI laboratory experts in Washington as the handwriting of Wilhelm Albrecht Von Pressentin Gennant Von Rautter. Now confirmed as "Gerson," investigation of Rautter's family background quickly linked him also to the code name "Count from New York." The remaining question was the identity of Rogers. Now that Rautter was identified as Gerson and the Count from New York, his secret writing messages were reexamined for any clues that he may also have been Rogers as well. A closer look at the Gerson signature on the secret writing messages confirmed that what British and FBI experts had thought was Gerson was in fact Rogers, a fact missed due to misinterpretation of Rautter's poor handwriting.[27]

Rautter quickly gave the FBI a full confession following arrest at his Portland Avenue apartment in the early morning hours of January 11, 1944. Later in the day, when he appeared before U.S. Commissioner Jacob A. Visel, charged with espionage, he tearfully exclaimed that he was "forced into [spying] almost at pistol point." Hoping to gather some sympathy, he told Visel that he was "brought into it while on a good will mission, an errand of mercy for my mother." Unmoved, Visel ordered him held in jail in lieu of $25,000 bail ($326,000 in 2012).[28]

Over the next several months Rautter's indictment was delayed as FBI and Department of Justice officials wrangled over charging key members of the Clog ring that was linked to Rautter in Mexico. The Bureau reasoned that while American courts had no jurisdiction over ring members in Mexico, Rautter's overt acts of espionage in the United States could include them in the conspiracy section of the statute. His indictment came on July 25, 1944, and on October 10, 1944, just four months after the bloody invasion of Normandy, he appeared in Brooklyn federal court before Judge Grover M. Moskowitz, a Calvin Coolidge appointee with almost nineteen years on the bench. After listening to him plead guilty, Moskowitz "waived aside" Rautter's cries of regret. "I cannot tell from the record how many of our boys went to their deaths on your information," Moskowitz charged. "I could impose the death sentence, but that might mean that revenge would be meted out to American citizens in Germany. That's the only reason why I hesitate to impose the death penalty." Rautter, now "pale and slumped forward," was "supported" by two deputies as he was led from the courtroom after Moskowitz sentenced him to twenty-nine years in jail.[29]

CHAPTER TWELVE

Japs, Aspirin, and Pep

One day in October 1942, a stocky, well-built Spaniard named Jose Maria Aladren walked into the American embassy in Madrid and asked to speak with an intelligence official. The forty-one-year-old Aladren was born in Madrid to a wealthy land-owning family whose privileged life included summers spent at Biarritz, Cannes, and other luxury European spas. Jose's younger brother was the noted sculptor Emilio Aladren y Perojo, who died in 1944. After a classical Jesuit education which included learning to speak French, Italian, English, and German, he earned a law degree at the University of Madrid, followed by eleven years working at a local insurance company, selling luxury automobiles for the Rolls Royce Company and managing a local tourist agency. During the Spanish Civil War he fought with Francisco Franco's forces as an artillery lieutenant. Later he joined the Spanish interior ministry as the "Chief Censor of Foreign Correspondents," a position he held until April 1942 when he was let go following a governmental shakeup.[1] Months later Japanese intelligence officials approached Aladren with a proposal to send him to the Western Hemisphere as a journalist as a cover for espionage. His Japanese contact man was Angel Alcazar Velasco, a Spaniard well known to the FBI and the British.[2]

One writer has described Velasco as a true Walter Mitty character. Born in 1900 in the small Spanish village of Mondejar, he took up the national pastime of bullfighting, and after turning professional at the age of twenty-eight he was soon fighting bulls in the great rings of Madrid before large crowds who called him "Our Young Gypsy of Madrid." Four years later he suddenly abandoned the sport for the University of Salamanca, where he earned a degree in letters and philosophy and later became an author of note.[3] Velasco's strange mystical creed included a virulent racism and anti-semitism mixed with a belief in astrology, which he viewed as an essential guide for life. His bizarre supremacist views envisioned a world ruled by an elite, reincarnated group of supermen like himself, an ideology that eventually drew him into the Falange Party and then to contact with the Abwehr and enrollment in intelligence school in Germany. After returning to Spain he became embroiled once again in Falange politics and was imprisoned on charges of murdering Jose Castillo, a policeman with anti-Falangist leanings. In a strange twist of logic, Velasco, now a prison inmate, refused to swear loyalty to Franco when the Spanish leader demanded Falange allegiance. When threatened with execution, Velasco quickly began reconsidering his politics. His chance for redemption came when he locked himself in a jail cell following an attempted escape by fellow prisoners, an act that prompted Franco to issue a reprieve from Velasco's death sentence. And for his bravery, the ever-resourceful bullfighter-astrologer was also awarded the Falange Silver Star.[4]

Velasco first came to British attention in September 1940 when MI5 began making inroads into the heart of Spanish espionage in London. In addition, MI6 learned that Miguel Piernavieja del Pozo had arrived in the British capital on an espionage mission posing as a journalist and observer for Spanish Instituto de Estudios Politicos. A month later del Pozo contacted an MI5 double agent code-named "GW" who the Abwehr believed was a fanatical Welsh nationalist recruited for them by another British double agent code-named "Snow." The two men met at del Pozo's apartment, where he gave GW (probably as a test of his bona fides) a talcum powder tin containing £3,500 (£100,000 in 2009) along with instructions to hold the funds until the Spaniard later called for it. GW was also to pass weekly reports to the porter at the Spanish embassy in London on the Welsh nationalist party together with information on arms and aircraft production. During one of their meetings, del Pozo identified Velasco as his boss and a close friend of Ramon Serrano Suner, Franco's foreign minister. In January 1941 Velasco came under direct MI5 coverage following his posting to London (despite speaking no English) as press attaché at the Spanish embassy. Referring to him derisively as a Spaniard of "gypsy extraction," MI5 investigators soon discovered that his crude behavior was resented by his embassy colleagues. At the same time that he was terrorizing his embassy colleagues, he was routinely accepting invitations to "smart London clubs and insisted on paying for drinks; he ate fish with hands at the Savoy" and "gave a demonstration of bull fighting technique at the Turkish baths," making him appear "ridiculous." The Spanish embassy staff could do little else but accept his behavior by relegating themselves to "yes men fearing Alcazar's power in Madrid." When Velasco returned to Madrid, MI5 tried and failed to persuade the

Foreign Office to declare him persona non grata, which feared similar retaliation against British diplomats in Spain.[5]

Aladren's story was relayed to the FBI, which quickly agreed to assist in his travel to the United States in the hope of operating him as a double agent. Aladren was met by FBI agents when he arrived in New Orleans aboard the SS *Marquis de Camillas* on December 16, 1942. His destination was Washington, D.C., where he would pose as a journalist for *El Alcazar,* a Fascist Spanish newspaper founded in 1936 as Franco's principal propaganda organ during the Siege of Alcazar. His job was the collection of military and political intelligence that he would transmit to Velasco in invisible ink or the Spanish diplomatic pouch in order to avoid British or American censorship. Velasco in turn would pass the information to the Japanese in Madrid.[6]

Once in the safe hands of the FBI, Aladren told the agents a surprising story about two passengers aboard his ship named Fernando Kobbe de Chinchilla and his daughter, Beatrice, both of whom he suspected of having links with the Japanese intelligence service in Madrid. Aladren learned that the English-speaking Kobbe, a career Spanish diplomat with more than twenty years of experience, had previously worked in Cuba, Great Britain, and France. Kobbe's defection during the Spanish Civil War to the victorious Franco forces was rewarded in 1939 when he was allowed to return to the Spanish diplomatic corp. Kobbe told Aladren that he was now traveling to Canada to take up duties at the Spanish consulate in Vancouver. Agents learned that during these conversations Kobbe often made oblique references to additional duties that he would perform for the Japanese government in his new assignment.[7]

For years the Spanish consulate was located in Montreal with only a limited presence in western Canada. Spanish diplomatic responsibilities in Canada were supervised by Juan Cardenas, the Spanish ambassador to the United States, with Pedro Schwartz, acting as consul general in Montreal, and his subordinate, Francis Bernard, a Canadian, serving as a part-time vice consul in Vancouver. Following America's declaration of war on Japan, Spain assumed responsibility for handling Japanese and German diplomatic affairs while the British covered Canadian interests in Spain. Like the United States in the months following Pearl Harbor, hysteria about the loyalties of Japanese aliens and Japanese Canadians gripped Canada, leading to their internment and confiscation of their property. Despite a watchful eye,

Canadian authorities found no evidence of espionage or intelligence gathering. Investigation of Aladren's report confirmed that Kobbe was en route to Vancouver to assume the role of full-time Spanish vice consul. Among his new responsibilities was handling the mounting paperwork stemming from the imprisonment by Canadian authorities of thousands of Japanese, as well as other more mundane tasks such as promotion of Spanish cultural interest and bilateral matters.[8]

In fact, Kobbe's real assignment as confirmed by the Ostrich source was collecting information for the Japanese about military shipments to the Pacific theater by casually strolling along docks and wharves while copying down vehicle and crate numbers, shoulder patches on military uniforms, and more, and loitering in bars and restaurants frequented by sailors and merchant seamen.[9] Further troubling for American authorities was the proximity of Kobbe's new office to the top-secret plutonium research facility a few hundred miles away in Hanford, Washington. Kobbe and his daughter first traveled by train to Washington, D.C., where he conferred with the Spanish ambassador and then on to Montreal for further briefings. They then boarded a train for the journey across Canada to Vancouver, where he soon opened a new and fully equipped consulate office at 325 Howe Street in the busy city center.[10]

In the wake of Aladren's reports, Hoover immediately took two steps. He shared information from Aspirin (Aladren's new code name) about Kobbe with the British and RCMP and dispatched Special Agent Frank G. Siscoe, a member of the SIS with previous assignments since January 1942 in Mexico City and Asuncion, Paraguay, to the American embassy in Madrid. Surveillance, both physical and technical, was used for monitoring Kobbe and the consulate along with the development of a unique source. RCMP officers soon focused on Beatrice: a young woman, isolated, alone in a strange land, knowing no one. Through a random series of chance encounters, Beatrice's social life gradually blossomed with new friends who soon began reporting her every word and move to Canadian authorities for the next year. The British Foreign Office closely watched the case with the view of finding a "lever of influence" on the Franco government to continue maintaining its neutrality now that British and American forces were wearing down Rommel's Afrika Corp in Tunisia and Libya. Kobbe offered the British this opening if Spanish foreign ministry complicity in Japanese espionage could be proven.[11]

The British opportunity to confront Franco eventually came through Aspirin. During Aspirin's first eight months in Washington, Velasco communicated only once with him, supplying (through the Spanish diplomatic pouch) microdots with instructions and new batches of secret ink. Aspirin steadily sent Velasco military and political information cleared for passage by the army's Joint Security Control (JSC; see chapter 13) and the State Department, in addition to almost 130 press dispatches and cables containing hidden references for necessary funds to carry on his espionage. In August 1943, Aspirin received a package from Velasco for passage to Kobbe containing $1,000 in American currency ($13,000 in 2012) and microdots that the FBI laboratory determined were mail drop addresses, secret ink formulas, and codes. Aspirin then passed the material on to Kobbe.[12]

Through State Department and FBI channels, photocopies of this evidence was supplied to delighted British authorities, who now had the proof they needed. The concern, however, was that a British challenge to Spain using the Aladren-acquired material could expose the FBI's investigation. After months of British and U.S. discussion, Hoover took the risk. In accord with U.S. authorities, London ordered Sir Samuel Hoare, London's ambassador to Madrid, to confront Spanish foreign ministry officials using the FBI confiscated material as evidence.[13] The sixty-three-year-old Hoare was educated at Harrow and New College, Oxford, before entering politics in 1907. He entered politics in 1907 and by the 1920s had risen to Secretary of State for Air and to Foreign Minister during the 1930s when he negotiated the famed Hoare-Laval agreement. In 1940, the newly elected prime minister Winston Churchill appointed Hoare as the ambassador to Spain with the monumental task of convincing Franco, whom he loathed, to remain neutral in the war.[14]

On January 14, 1944, thirteen months after the start of the Aspirin case, Hoare confronted General Count Francisco Gomez Jordana, a Franco loyalist and Spain's foreign minister. After laying out the evidence against Kobbe and Spain's use of its diplomats in spying for Japan, Hoare demanded that Spain cease such practices, close the Vancouver consulate, recall Kobbe back to Spain, and imprison Velasco for his espionage and violation of Spanish neutrality. Eight days later, without waiting for Jordana's response, the Canadian Department of External Affairs ordered an RCMP raid of Kobbe's Vancouver apartment, where they uncovered the $1,000 (the microdots were never found). After declaring him persona non grata the Canadian government turned him over to the RCMP, which escorted him to Montreal and there placed him in the custody of FBI agents who accompanied him to the SS *Marques de Comillas,* docked at New Orleans. The Kobbes sailed for Spain on February 8, 1944.[15]

Kobbe's expulsion by Canadian authorities raised FBI worries about Velasco's continued trust in Aspirin. Taking a significant risk, Aspirin agreed to return to Madrid to meet with Japanese officials and retest his previous relationship with Velasco. His first step after his arrival in Madrid in March 1944 was a meeting with Velasco, who, still convinced of his loyalty, urged him to return to Washington with no guarantees of money or enhanced communications. In the words of one FBI official, "All Velasco offered were promises." Taking matters into his own hands Aspirin approached Japanese embassy officials, where the question of his money was quickly cleared up. Velasco had hoodwinked the Japanese by pocketing $10,000 a month ($133,000 in 2012), which they gave Aspirin "for the operation of his fictional and real agents in the United States."[16] Siscoe then instructed Aspirin to volunteer his services to the Japanese as their American agent with no Velasco involvement. After some discussion they agreed to his return to Washington, posing as a correspondent for the conservative Spanish newspaper *Ya* with a guaranteed yearly payment of $10,000 ($130,000 in 2012) which he would receive through an unspecified route after his return to Washington.[17] These plans never came to fruition. By the time Aspirin returned to America in February 1945, Germany and its military were collapsing. Franco, reading the handwriting on the wall, turned on his Axis friends by closing all German and Japanese diplomatic missions and arresting Abwehr agents en masse. Any possibility of continued counterintelligence against Japanese espionage in the United States was at an end.

Edouard Eugene Henri Arnaud was born in Marseilles, France, on September 29, 1885.[18] In November 1944, Arnaud, code-named "Pep" by the FBI, first approached the SIS's Frank Siscoe in Madrid to volunteer his services in the United States as an agent against the Japanese. Arnaud told Siscoe a vague story involving a reception at the Japanese embassy where a German official named Schultz or Schluss suggested that he start work for the Germans as an agent in the United States. When he later asked his Japanese host about the approach, he was urged to pursue it, not for the Germans but for the Japanese. Later he was informed that the mission involved collecting secret Japanese funds not known to the U.S. officials. A contact in New York would meet him in connection with a mission that would last a matter of months and include a trip to Argentina. With little else to go on, skeptical Washington officials expressed interest in using him against the Japanese and then ordered Siscoe to send Arnaud alone to the United States with the family to follow at a later date.[19]

At Siscoe's urging, Arnaud returned to the Japanese embassy on December 11, 1944, where he met with Yakichiro Suma. A career diplomat and a wily intelligence officer with previous service in Washington, Suma was, in the words of one historian, "one of the primary movers in instigating Japanese espionage activities against the Allied powers during the Second World War." Suma outlined for Pep Japan's extensive financial investments in Latin America and asked him about any contacts he had in Mexico. Suma told Pep that tight restrictions on the movement of funds to the Western Hemisphere prevented his financing his travel, instead promising to deposit $20,000 ($266,000 in 2012) in a Spanish bank for him as there was no possibility of paying him while in the United States. Despite these uncertainties, Ladd and Tamm authorized the Bureau's underwriting of his travel and began efforts to obtain an emergency temporary entry.[20]

A look into Pep's sketchy background led to some interesting revelations. Arnaud had visited the United States in November 1937 with his family when he was working as the president of the Asiatic Mining Company partnering with an American named Jules Rosen, a fifty-two-year-old commodities broker based in Cleveland and New York. For twenty-five years the company had supposedly purchased Japanese goods and acted as a broker for a Tokyo-based firm named Mitsui and Company. As for Rosen, he had gotten into the commodities business in 1925 starting with the importation of Chinese and Japanese products and later serving as president and treasurer of the Dai Ichi Raw Silk Corporation. Later he worked as a commodities broker with Hartman Pacific Company, which imported Japanese products for May's Department Store in Cleveland and Gimbel Brothers and Macy's in New York City. In 1942 Rosen was reportedly working as a manager for a company called Leonard J. Buck and Company in Caracas, Venezuela, brokering the sale of industrial diamonds and metals.[21]

During the war Pep tried to sign on with the OSS, which turned him down for "security reasons." His rejection was based in large part on his claims that from 1909 to 1919 he worked for the General Secretariat of the Bank of France as an advisor and organizer of the foreign department and later as a technical advisor for a private French bank from 1921 to 1932.

Other questionable claims involved his employment as a financial consultant, Director of Propaganda for the Minister of France, and economic representative for the French Ministry of Colonies. OSS's investigation revealed that he was seventeen years old when he was employed by the Bank of France as a low-level clerk. New suspicions arose when it was discovered that Asiatic Mining and Trading Company also had a poor reputation with very little credit extended to it. FBI records acquired from MI5 indicated that Arnaud had a reputation as "pro-Nazi or pro-Vichy," surmising further that his "enterprises have been questionable and only profitable to him, having defrauded individuals of sums of money. He is believed to be the type of individual who would greatly exaggerate his capabilities and is regarded as being unreliable."[22] Ladd and Tamm then warned Siscoe and Flinn to be "particularly cautious and alert when dealing with Pep," as files in Washington indicate that he exaggerated his capabilities and that he was a flim-flam artist who had defrauded people in the past and has been regarded as "unreliable."

While rushed arrangements were underway for his visa, Arnaud started pressuring Siscoe for additional visas for his wife and children. Siscoe promptly turned him down, insisting that if his mission was successful than permanent arrangements would be made for his family to follow. Siscoe was ordered to avoid any commitments to Pep about traveling alone, but if he insisted on his family coming with him, consideration "would then be given to the facilitating of temporary visas for Pep's wife and children."[23]

Joseph Lynch, the FBI legat in London, was ordered to acquire a Navicert (a British-issued exemption from search and seizure by blockade patrols) for Arnaud. In a memorandum to Hoover, Tamm made no effort to hide the fact that considerable risk was involved in arranging for Arnaud's travel to the United States under FBI control. "We are taking a calculated risk . . . in trying to bring to the United States Edouard Arnaud as a double agent, a Frenchman who was a collaborator during Nazi occupation of France." Having no sources against the Japanese and desperately in need of them, Tamm explained that the goal was the establishment of a "real, honest-to-goodness double agent, ostensibly working for the Japanese and this man presents our best bet to date."[24] Despite these concerns, the British offered assurances that the Navicert would be issued for Arnaud's passage and would not interfere in any way with his transit.[25]

On January 13, 1945, Pep related Suma's instructions that he leave for the United States with his family for "permanent residence," fearing that

FBI suspicion would fall on him if he traveled alone. Siscoe also learned that the Japanese were unable to pay him in the United States but would deposit a sum of $20,000 ($266,000 in 2012) in a Portuguese bank for his use. Suspecting a ruse, Siscoe instructed Pep to meet again with them, this time reminding them that his visa was now in hand but that arranging visas for his family's travel would significantly delay his departure.[26]

After eight days of silence Pep again met Siscoe, insisting that he take his family, this time as far as Venezuela while he proceeded onto the United States alone. Siscoe reluctantly agreed to this change with a warning that if his mission failed, there remained a "distinct possibility that his family would have to remain in Venezuela."[27] After three weeks of more silence, Pep again surfaced with a new plan. He told Siscoe that he would send his family to France while he proceeded to the United States alone through Venezuela. Without inquiring, Siscoe wondered why suddenly the Japanese would countenance placing their agent in danger from the FBI after insisting that he travel to America with his family. Nevertheless, Siscoe agreed to the move with the proviso that he use his own funds, which the FBI would reimburse once he arrived in New York City.

By March, Siscoe's confidence in Pep was at an end when he suddenly reported that his Japanese contacts had cooled on the idea of Pep's mission and then, only weeks later, again ordering him, in true cloak-and-dagger fashion, to travel to New York to collect some mysterious Japanese funds.[28] As for underwriting his trip, he told Siscoe that as he proceeded through Lisbon he was to visit the Japanese Legation, where funds would be provided to him upon presentation of his passport. As for this new mission, he was told to stay at New York's Hotel Roosevelt where someone would contact him by telephone or in person between May 15 and May 31. The recognition signal required the mystery man to give him a number under fifty, to which Pep would respond with a corresponding number that when added to the first would sum to fifty. This individual would then place Pep in contact with someone else.[29]

For a matter of weeks, contact between the Japanese and Pep was broken, which Siscoe attributed to the sudden break in diplomatic relations between Spain and Japan on April 10, 1945. Despite this setback, plans remained underway for Pep to leave for the United States on or about May 1, 1945. The FBI's thinking was that in view of the extraordinary lengths they went to get the temporary visa for Pep, they should let him proceed to Lisbon to negotiate with the Japanese over his money. If they refused, Flinn could discuss the matter with the British, who could quickly cancel the Navicert for Pep's transit. Further consideration was also given to the idea that if Pep was denied transit, the case could still carry on with someone, perhaps an undercover agent, posing as Pep at the hotel.[30]

In anticipation of Pep's departure from Lisbon, Hoover received authority to tap Arnaud's telephone at the Hotel Roosevelt. While these efforts were underway, new information about the foxy Arnaud was coming to light. He made a practice of selling fictitious companies that purportedly owned land in Venezuela rich in minerals and metals. An equally bogus engineer working for Arnaud confirmed the quality of the load, which prompted the sale to a bamboozled buyer who then went to Venezuela only to find the land worthless. As for Asiatic Mining and Trading Company, it also was a fraud. FBI investigators in Paris in May 1945 had tracked down the former manager of the Chase Bank there who described Pep as an "imposter" and a "crook with whom all relations should be avoided." Finally, a search of French police records showed that Arnaud had cleverly escaped from custody after having been arrested for embezzling 18,000 francs. The new FBI legat in Paris reported that Pep, the man the FBI hoped would be its gateway into Japanese espionage, had a penchant for starting companies, all fictitious, with shares sold to the public that he used for personal benefit.[31]

By May no progress had been made for his travel to the United States, largely due to his procrastination and dallying. As for FBI plans in the United States, the New York office had reviewed his file and concluded that the use of an undercover agent posing as Pep to meet the unknown subject would pose considerable risk and thus deserved serious discussion. First, Pep had lived in New York, opening the possibility that his contact man at the Hotel Roosevelt would be someone he knew, which would immediately expose the ploy. Another concern was what step to take after the undercover agent staying at the hotel under Pep's name met the contact person. Should a surveillance be started to identify him and other possible ring members? In the end the New York office recommended a prompt interview of the person be conducted, with pressure applied on him to identify the rest of the ring.[32]

With a clear picture of the miscreant Pep now in hand, Siscoe nevertheless continued to play along with him on the possibility of getting something worthwhile out of the case. It did not take long before Pep described for him a telephone call from someone named Tamura, Suma's secretary, conveying the news that his contact in New York would be available until

June 30, 1945, and that Pep should first meet the Japanese representative in Switzerland for reasons not explained before moving on to the United States.

By June 1945 the FBI had ceased any further interest in him. Siscoe summed it up in a cable to Washington on August 4, two days before the atomic bomb was dropped on Hiroshima. Siscoe had "little confidence in Pep who may be trying to come to the United States for personal ends," at the same time acknowledging that Pep's zeal to help the Allied cause had a "very flimsy basis if in fact it ever existed."[33]

By this time Pep and his family had returned to Paris, where they quietly moved into a new life in a flat on the Boulevard Haussman. There he was forgotten by the FBI and lost to history.[34]

CHAPTER THIRTEEN

ND98

Less than a month after the FBI arrest of the Duquesne ring, a short, stocky Latin man with black hair, graying at the temples, slipped quietly into the American embassy in Montevideo, Uruguay, with an intriguing story to tell. He was greeted by Selden Chapin, a First Secretary and experienced diplomat with years of State Department service. The stranger identified himself as Jorge Mosquera, a German spy sent to South America on an intelligence mission. He had been recruited in Germany with orders to locate a wireless operator who would set up a radio station somewhere in Uruguay while he proceeded to the United States to collect military intelligence that he would mail to Uruguay for transmission to Germany.[1]

As evidence of his story, he produced a series of microphotographs containing his instructions together with a collection of letters from the Abwehr for use in seeking help from three Americans. Within a month, the State Department informed the FBI about Mosquera's eagerness to assist U.S. authorities against the Germans. "Mosquera places himself and his information at our entire disposal," State Department official William Dawson told the FBI, "and is willing to carry on with the communications scheme if we think fit and would even be willing to feed false information."[2]

Hoover's technical experts found Mosquera's information consistent with German intelligence procedures. His secret writing chemicals matched those in other cases, as did his radio instructions that conformed "in all respect with the systems used by genuine German agents." His precarious financial situation also offered credence to his story. The Abwehr routinely held funds of agents, the FBI reported, as a means of control and assurance of retaining loyalty to the mission. "In previous cases such personal funds are known to have even been used by German authorities in paying for the services of active agents in the United States." Chapin further reported that all indications point to his honesty and "perfect discretion" during his stay in Montevideo. Despite some lingering uncertainty, Edward Tamm asked the State Department to quickly arrange for Mosquera's travel to the United

States where the FBI would take responsibility for him.[3] On November 18, 1941, nineteen days before the Pearl Harbor attack, the SS *Argentina* slipped into New York Harbor with the FBI's new double agent on board. Waiting at the pier were FBI agents who immediately whisked him to their office at Foley Square in Lower Manhattan, where they began a series of interviews lasting days. The principal FBI interrogator was William G. Friedmann, a seasoned veteran and German linguist who had recently played a central role in the Duquesne case by secretly eavesdropping on conversations when ring members delivered intelligence to the office of the FBI's double agent. As Mosquera spoke only Spanish, German, and Italian, their conversations were held in German.

Mosquera was born to Spanish immigrants in Rosario, Santa Fe, Argentina, on June 30, 1895. He was the youngest of ten children in a family made up of seven girls and three boys. His father was a retailer. With only a tenth-grade education, Jorge was issued a draft number at the age of eighteen but was never called for military service. Following in his father's footsteps, he began a sales career buying and selling agricultural products in Buenos Aires, which led him to start his own business importing German products into Argentina.[4]

In 1925 the thirty-year-old businessman made his first trip to Europe to examine the German side of the import-export business. Within months he had acquired a new and untested business partner who quickly asked him for a loan to cover unexpected debts. When Mosquera insisted on a security payment, his offended friend claimed a family relationship with a prominent German industrialist that he said made such guarantees unnecessary. After learning that no such well-heeled relative existed, Mosquera confronted him with a revolver in his pocket, which got him eight hundred German marks and a promise that the balance in goods would be shipped to Argentina. When Mosquera returned to Argentina, the agreed upon shipment of products arrived and more than made up the balance due. Mosquera permanently returned to Hamburg in 1927, where he opened a new business importing and exporting goods between Germany and Latin America.[5]

By 1936, changing economic and political conditions in Germany led Mosquera to liquidate his business for $40,000 ($661,000 in 2012). It was then that a friend in the chemical export business, Herbert Krug, introduced him to a Hamburg Nazi party official named Julius Steinert, who began the slow process of recruiting him into espionage by describing him as a "good friend of the Germans" who could be called upon to assist the party in its time of need. In September 1939 he finally accepted Steinert's offer by agreeing (probably as a test of his competence and loyalty) to deliver two letters to someone in Amsterdam and then assess the person's views about Germany.[6]

A month later Mosquera received an unexpected letter from a stranger calling himself "F. W. Boewig," inviting him to Berlin at Steinert's suggestion so that he may "learn to know him." Boewig soon dispatched him to the Canary Islands on an assignment to determine the existence of a British submarine base in the region. A year passed before Boewig again asked him to undertake another mission, this time to Africa to collect information on British activities, but Mosquera promptly rejected the request, claiming poor English-language ability. To appease Boewig, Mosquera suggested a permanent move to Lisbon to set up a German cover company using his own savings blocked from transfer out of the country by German law. Ignoring his offer, Boewig instead sent him to Czechoslovakia, where an "SS Division" officer would give him further instructions. In Prague he was ordered to begin explosives training at the Bruenner and Skoda munitions works in anticipation of an assignment to Mexico or Cuba. Terrified by the prospects of sabotage, he fled back to Berlin, this time claiming a lack of technical knowledge.[7]

After more months of inactivity, he received an unexpected call one day in March 1941 from Hans Blum, an old friend from his business days. Revealing for the first time his rank as a major in the German army, Blum bluntly asked him to spy in the Western Hemisphere for the Abwehr. Seizing on the offer as a chance to get out of Europe, Mosquera agreed and even suggested as a possible contact Ricardo Gioscia, an old friend and owner of a Montevideo music store.[8] Blum's new source soon found himself at an espionage school in Hamburg studying secret inks, codes, radio construction, and telegraphy. Six weeks later he received microdots containing Abwehr requirements and additional encouragement to pursue anything of value beyond the list. Blum warned him, however, that he was embarking on a long-term mission that demanded patience and extreme caution, as detection would have fatal consequences for him. He must "be careful of the FBI," Blum cautioned, "since they have already arrested some individuals in America." Funds for his espionage would come through agents already in the United States, he was told, with his personal savings and a substantial reward awaiting him in Germany at the end of the war.

Jorge Mosquera. Abwehr source dispatched to the United States with orders to acquire information about the American atomic bomb program. His revelations to the FBI became a pivotal factor in the U.S. decision to pursue the Manhattan Project. *FBI*

Blum then raised another consideration, atomic research, ordering Mosquera to search out any information concerning "experiments performed in the United States relative to shattering of atoms." The German military was anxious to develop high explosives from atom sources that they believed would weigh no more than a pound to a pound and a half. In what was almost a premonition of the future five years hence, Blum speculated that the nation which "will be victor in this war will be the one which has accomplished the task of shattering the atoms and applying the results thereof."[9] With training behind him and instructions in hand, Mosquera left Hamburg by train on June 15, 1941, bound for the Hotel Excelsior in Bilbao,

Spain. Two days later he met an Abwehr agent named Jose Boogen, his espionage cutout, who would receive his cables and secret writing messages for passage to Blum. Within a week he was just another passenger aboard the *Cabo de Esperanza* bound for Uruguay.[10]

Mosquera's microphotographs held a gold mine of information for both the FBI and Allied policy makers. Complete details for the construction of his radio station, along with broadcast times, sending and receiving frequencies, call letters, emergency keys, and transposition code, were all there. In an unimaginable blunder, the Abwehr also included the names of sixteen espionage agents located in Spain, Portugal, Switzerland, Sweden, Germany, Argentina, and, most importantly, New York City. There were demands for all sorts of statistics on raw materials, fabricated products, canons, optical instruments, and specialty products like machine tools made in the United States and Canada. Abwehr interest also focused on the delivery schedules for fighter aircraft, artillery shell production by the Bethlehem Steel Corporation, factory numbers on aircraft parts, monthly aircraft production figures, and a final ominous request to "deduce artificially the uranium or other alloy which may be substituted therefor [*sic*] as an atom constructor."[11]

The microphotographs, the complex series of radio instructions, the codes, the letters from high German authorities, and Mosquera's background, all tracked with previous cases, were solid evidence of his truthfulness and the accuracy of his information. Other encouraging elements in his story included his receipt in December 1941 of a letter from Freidel Schlosser, his former secretary in Hamburg, a member of the Nazi party, and an acquaintance of Julius Steinert, and finally the three American names that Mosquera carried with him: Alexander Semmler, Elmer Carleton, and Max Rudloff.[12]

Alexander Semmler was born in Dortmund, Germany, on November 12, 1900. A musical prodigy who began performing as a concert pianist at age fifteen, he studied piano under Joseph Pembaur, professor of musicology at the University of Marburg, and composition with the great Gustave Jenner, Johannes Brahms's only composition student. He was living in Bremen when he immigrated to the United States, arriving in New York on October 23, 1923, aboard the SS *Muenchen*. In 1927 Semmler joined the Columbia Broadcasting System's symphony orchestra as a pianist and later worked for RKP-Pathe Film Company scoring the music for radio programs and films. By his own estimate, Semmler had composed over a thousand scores throughout his life for dramatic broadcast and film use, much of it for major network programs. Six years later, he married Eleanor Bell, a twenty-nine-year-old American from Baltimore. On July 17, 1930, with his wife by his side and Lulu Mayer, a concert pianist and family friend acting as a witness, he became an American citizen at a ceremony in New York City.[13]

Nine days after the Pearl Harbor attack, Mosquera visited Semmler's New York City studio at 51 West 53rd Street, and after a few minutes of light conversation in German they moved on to lunch at a nearby restaurant. After mentioning Hans Blum, Semmler fondly recalled how they originally met while sailing to Germany with his family in 1936. Later they socialized regularly with Blum and his wife, dining with them often at their home in Hamburg. Mosquera assessed Semmler as "pro-German" and someone who concealed his true feelings for fear of risking his personal and business interests. After agreeing to assist Mosquera and asking him if his needs were commercial in nature, Mosquera told him that he would provide full details at a later date. He then cryptically explained that any information Semmler provided would be sent to Europe through a friend in a South American consulate. Surprised and suspicious, Semmler changed his tone abruptly, claiming that he was very busy with music commitments which prevented him from offering Mosquera any help. Semmler never responded to Mosquera's inquiries again.[14]

Mosquera's next contact was Elmer H. Carlton, owner of Remle-Carlton Company (Remle is Elmer spelled backward), a manufacturer's representative and chemical import/export company in midtown Manhattan. The American-born Carlton, six feet tall, around fifty years old, and fluent in six languages, had served as a foreign service officer in Oslo and Copenhagen during the First World War; he later moved to Berlin where he spent much of the next twenty years. Sources who knew him unanimously commented on his open Nazi sympathies; co-workers snidely called him the "Fuehrer" behind his back. He was a regular guest at the German embassy in Washington and the consulate in New York. When not hosting German businessmen and diplomats, he could be found at local German restaurants in Manhattan's Yorkville section, greeting patrons with the stiff-armed "Heil Hitler" salute. Remle-Carlton imported uniforms from Germany for his friend, Fritz Kuhn, the notorious antisemite and leader of the German-American Bund who was imprisoned for tax evasion in 1939. Carlton also had major financial interests in Germany through his close friendship with Hjalmar Schacht, Hitler's finance minister.[15]

Under Friedmann's direction Mosquera, now assigned the code name

Benson House with "Clifford," the dog, circa 1942. *James R. Millen*

"ND98," met Carlton at his New York City office on December 18, 1941. Following some perfunctory conversation, Mosquera mentioned Blum and his Hamburg firm Remy and Blum. Carlton immediately sensed that Mosquera was in the United States on an intelligence mission, "but at no time did he ask me or anything further," nor did he "ask me anything because he never wanted to know any more about the matter." Carleton gradually closed the door on any future cooperation, explaining that he "regretted very much to tell me that he would not be able to help me at all" while at the same time offering Mosquera assurances "that his sympathies for Blum, as well as all of his friends in Germany, are still the same and will remain such." Then he offered Mosquera the clincher. "The situation here has been radically changed," Carlton warned, "and in view of this [I want] to remain loyal." Moving to another tack, Mosquera acknowledged Carlton's dilemma but then asked for his help with introductions to people who could assist him in his work. Carlton "immediately replied not." He trusted no one sufficiently with such matters and then warned ND98 "not to talk to any person in this country about such a matter, and even less to confide such a matter in any other person."[16]

After these two failures, Mosquera was turned down a third time on January 13, 1942. Max Fritz Ernst Rudloff was a Brooklyn resident, a naturalized American citizen born in Germany in the 1890s, married and the owner of a chemical import/export firm with offices at 59 Pearl Street in Manhattan. When they first met at Mosquera's room at the Governor Clinton Hotel, the suspicious Rudloff questioned how he acquired his name. When he mentioned Blum, Rudloff immediately responded, "I thought that was it." The remainder of their stiff and formal conversation was laced with Mosquera's effort to discuss Blum, which Rudloff curtly "cut off," steering the conversation back to business matters. Mosquera later told Friedmann that Rudloff "smelled a rat" and would have no further dealings with him.[17]

Indians had lived on the tiny speck of land along the North Shore of Long Island for hundreds of generations, surviving off the abundant wild game that roamed the forests, as well as modest farming and the bountiful sea life offered up by the rivers and freshwater streams that flowed in and out of Long Island Sound. Digging a few inches beneath the water's surface they found abundant quahogs, a hard-shelled clam-like creature, and periwinkles, a type of freshwater snail that were also staples in the local diet. Supplementing their seafood and meat diet, they cultivated a variety of shoreline herbs such as skunk cabbage, tall meadow rue, and "lysimachia terrestis," known to the locals as "swamp candles." They called the little spit of land hanging one hundred feet over the sound Pauquaconsuk, "the place where we wade for thick, round-shelled clams." The first record of white settlement in 1671 described eight families who carved out farms and built homes from the thickets of red maple, oak, and hickory. They called their tiny community "wading in the river," later changing it to "Wading River."[18]

During the American Revolution the region was a hotbed of intrigue. With the British in firm control of the entire 110-mile stretch of Long Island, local residents, often in the same family, divided their loyalty, some supporting the British crown, others backing the rebels, the rest sitting on the fence patiently waiting for an outcome. Just a few miles west of Wading River sat the equally sleepy settlement of Setauket, where the famed Culper ring, a group of rebel spies, gathered intelligence in New York City and then sailed it seventeen miles across Long Island Sound to Connecticut where a waiting express rider carried the precious material to Benjamin Tallmadge, George Washington's intelligence chief in Tarrytown, New York.[19]

Wading River had changed very little by the start of the Second World War. It was situated eighty miles east of New York City, with another twenty-nine miles along the North Fork to Orient Point and the Atlantic Ocean. Local fishermen and farmers still made up the year-round population of five hundred living within its ten-square-mile area. Nassau and Suffolk Counties, composed of 1,373 square miles or 878,720 acres, were inhabited by less than a quarter of a million people—one person for every four acres. The two counties were four times larger than New York City but with four percent of the population.[20]

Development of Long Island was discouraged by an odd combination of working-class locals suspicious of outsiders and robber barons living on grand estates that dotted the landscape. Long Island's beautiful North Shore, called the Gold Coast, stretched from Glen Cove, where Pierpont Morgan kept his magnificent yacht *Corsair* for weekend sojourns on the sound with New York Yacht Club friends, east to Wildwood, a crumbling Stanford White–designed stone castle on the North Fork. Over the decades, the plutocrats with adjoining estates, ranging from fifty to several thousand acres, worked hard to ensure that their idyllic world remained undisturbed from intrusion by the squalid masses living in cramped New York City tenements.[21]

Their money filtered into the pockets of local politicians in return for assurances that Long Island access remained as difficult as possible. The few narrow unpaved roads that did exist were intentionally kept in poor condition, with crater-like potholes so deep and wide that travel became a supreme test of courage for any driver willing to chance it. The situation only worsened as one drove further east. "One encountered unpaved roads which with rain cars became mired, bringing the endless line behind them to a halt. If the earth was dry, thick clouds of dust hung over unpaved stretches."[22]

Train travel offered no relief. The Long Island Railroad, extending from Manhattan to Montauk Point along the South Shore and Orient Point on the northern line, was a slow and painful adventure for passengers willing to endure seemingly endless hours journeying from one end of the line to the other, stopping at dozens of stations along the way. Hoping to cut off even this means of access, a group of financiers led by Charles Pratt and Stephen Harkness, business partners of oil magnate John D. Rockefeller, bought controlling interest in the railroad to ensure that the North Shore line would remain "especially antiquated and rickety."[23]

Richard Millen was a physicist, former college professor, and FBI agent who worked in the Laboratory Division. A year after joining the Bureau in 1938 he was assigned to the radio engineering section. Since February 1940 he had worked on clandestine communications, first building and then supporting the secret site in Centerport, New York, which the FBI used for eighteen months during the Duquesne espionage investigation. Shortly after Christmas 1941 Millen, together with Sam Foxworth, made the arduous trek out to Wading River, where they found their treasure, a vacant house owned by a local fisherman in a remote, densely wooded area more than two miles from the nearest road. Arrangements were quickly made for Special Agent Donworth Johnson, a tall, lean FBI agent who moved from Chicago with his wife and baby daughter, to manage the site. Johnson was chosen because his "tubercular" appearance could explain his avoidance of the wartime draft. Isolation and remoteness coupled with decent atmospheric conditions for clear radio transmissions made the Benson House, as it was known, ideal for the new secret FBI wartime operation.[24]

The house was a spacious three-story wood frame structure situated about one hundred feet from a bluff that dropped sharply down to a narrow beach. Its wide porch overlooking the sound captured delightful summer breezes off the water and panoramic views that extended to the Connecticut shoreline on clear days. The sweeping circular dirt driveway brought visitors to the back of the house, which opened into a small pantry adjacent to a large and fully equipped kitchen capable of handling three meals a day for the half-dozen FBI technicians assigned there. Everyone ate in the formal dining room with coffee and cake served in the parlor or on the porch in good weather. The second floor served as the staff dormitory with the off-limits third floor crammed with bulky radio transmitters and receivers, back-up equipment, a maintenance shop, and a cramped storage area filled with everything from vacuum tubes and wires to paperclips and pencils. Perched on desks along the wall were banks of radios, where technicians wearing earphones and with pencils in hand hunched over keys tapping out messages while struggling to discern the often faint signals coming in from Germany. Within weeks the FBI's "tubercular family man," along with his wife and infant and their large snarling dog Clifford (whose job was to discourage visits from curious locals), moved into the house. For the remainder of the war the couple occupied the first floor while the others settled upstairs. To allay suspicions, Millen erected the radio antenna deep in the woods, well out of sight from casual observers. Electricity for operating the power-sucking transmitters (to avoid questions from suspicious electric meter readers) was supplemented by a gasoline engine quieted by an oversized Buick muffler installed in a corner of the basement, which vented outside through pipes in the walls.[25]

The ND98 channel sprang to life with its first broadcast to Hamburg on January 28, 1942. Turning Blum's guarantee of assistance from his three American sources against him and the Abwehr, the Benson House technicians were soon radioing Mosquera's frantic desperation. "On Carlton, Semmler and Rudloff I cannot rely. First one refused entirely. The others too. But they appear to me to be unsuitable." Hinting at the sudden spike in security with America now at war, he warned his handlers of the growing anxieties among Axis sympathizers in the wake of the mass internment of Germans, Italians, and Japanese in the weeks following the attack on Pearl Harbor. There was "ever increasing activity of the FBI and the almost daily arrests," such that "Axis people are very apprehensive." After outlining the enormity of the challenge facing him, he began pleading for help. "I need the assistance of two or at least one important good worker. German, if possible, but they naturally must be reliable people. At least one known to you. Do everything you can to execute my wishes. It is necessary. Many thanks."[26]

Less than three months after radio contact began with Hamburg, a problem arose which threatened to derail the case. Richard McNutt, the radio technician posing as Mosquera's recently hired radioman, suddenly resigned from the FBI. A radio operator's unique "fisting" technique (singular style of tapping out the message key) is like a fingerprint, instantly recognizable to an experienced operator receiving his message. While McNutt could be easily replaced, the FBI's horror was that the Germans had recorded McNutt's messages, which they could easily compare to new American transmissions. Any changes, even imperceptible, could still be detected. Some consideration was given to telling Hamburg that Mosquera's radioman got cold feet, forcing him to go off the air until new arrangements could be made. The problem was solved when Benson House informed Hamburg that his radioman had been suddenly drafted into the army. No interruption in service would occur as a close friend, sympathetic to the German cause, would continue to transmit for the same money. Replacing McNutt was Loren Tannenhaus, who continued to send uninterrupted Mosquera messages from May 1942 until the end of war.[27]

In an amazing display of audacity, the Abwehr took the great risk of once again reminding him of the importance of collecting atomic research

Antenna hidden in the woods adjacent to the Benson House used for communicating with Hamburg, Germany. *James R. Millen*

information. Within days of its first broadcast Benson House received startling instructions to collect "whatever information . . . relative to experiments being conducted in the United States with Uranium 235," especially "all types of information dealing with atomic experiments." For Friedmann, the goal was to obtain genuine passage information that would "undoubtedly more firmly establish [Mosquera] in the eyes of the Germans." Having virtually no knowledge of atoms, atomic fission, or Uranium 235, nor access to the secret, high-level government discussions then underway about atomic weapons development, FBI agents in New York began scouring public journals and newspapers for any scraps of data on the subject. By March 1942 they had found one lengthy *Fortune* magazine article on atomic fission, which the military cleared for passage to the Germans.[28] At the same time, Mickey Ladd, the National Defense Division boss, turned to Ed Coffey, the head of the Laboratory Division, who in turn reached out to the scientific community for help. Coffey's efforts produced a *Washington Evening Standard* article describing a speech given by the Nobel Prize–winning physicist Ernest O. Lawrence, the head of the physics department at the California Institute of Technology, explaining his invention of the cyclotron, a gigantic particle accelerator capable of exploding atoms. Next they got a copy of a November 1940 Westinghouse Research Laboratory press release marked "Not for Re-Publication" that reported that scientists were examining "all proposed methods of uranium separation, and have experimented with some untried ways." One of the best bets, the release noted, was "a device called the Ultracentrifuge" that separates Uranium 235. "There is no doubt that it will work," the release continued, but the "only hitch is in building one." Other useful information came from a November 1941 edition of *Review of Scientific Instruments,* which contained the "complete plans of an electrostatic generator for nuclear research at the Massachusetts Institute of Technology."[29]

New York agents struggling to locate feed material on atomic research were unknowingly facing a pivotal moment in world history. Decades later a historian and expert on the history of the American atomic bomb described the single question hanging over the decision to develop an atomic weapon. A "single lurid fear," he wrote, "brought the American decision to undertake the vast effort and expense required to build the atomic bomb—the fear that Hitler's Germany would do it first." Even before Pearl Harbor, leading American scientists agonized over the possibility that Hitler had a six-month head start in atomic research which may have been widening.

Their concerns were not unreasonable: German scientists had dominated the new field of atomic physics in the 1920 and 1930s, Europe's only uranium mines were in located Czechoslovakia, now controlled by Germany, and in May 1940 German armies had seized the world's only heavy-water plant in Norway.[30]

In 1938 the physicist Leo Szilard fled his native Hungary, traveling first to England and then on to the United States, where he joined the staff of New York's Columbia University as a researcher. Szilard had grown increasingly fearful that Hitler was trying to corner the uranium market by purchasing exclusive leases on uranium ore found in vast quantities in the Congo, then a colony of Belgium. Szilard took his concerns to an old friend, Albert Einstein, considered the world's most famous scientist and the winner of the 1921 Nobel Prize for his discovery of the photoelectric effect. After convincing Einstein that world survival depended on the United States beating the Germans in an atomic weapons race, he urged him to warn President Franklin Roosevelt of the danger of this lethal science falling into the wrong hands. In his now famous letter, which reached the president on October 11, 1939, Einstein described the possibility of setting up "a nuclear chain reaction in a large mass of uranium, by which vast amounts of power and large quantities of new radium-like elements would be generated" leading to "bombs . . . extremely powerful bombs of a new type." Hoping to spur prompt White House action, Einstein warned that the Germans might already be pursuing such research. Wasting no time, Roosevelt ordered the creation of an ad hoc committee chaired by Dr. Lyman Briggs, director of the National Bureau of Standards (NBS), the nation's physics laboratory, to examine the question. After nearly two years of inaction, a new group called the Office of Scientific Research and Development (OSRD) was formed on December 6, 1941, to study the matter under the chairmanship of Vannevar Bush, an electrical engineer and founder of the predecessor of the Raytheon Corp., assisted by Harvard University president James Conant and former MIT president Arthur Compton.[31]

There is no known paper trail recording the details of the Abwehr's demands for information on U.S. atomic research progress ever reaching OSRD officials. There is little doubt, however, that the instructions given to ND98 before he left Germany and the demands for information about uranium contained in a microdot mailed to Tricycle in April 1942 were conveyed by Coffey to Conant and Bush. On March 9, 1942, Bush told the president that while Germany may be pursuing an atomic bomb, "I have no indication of the status of the enemy program, and have taken no definite steps toward finding out." Facts, however, soon began emerging without Bush's active pursuit of them. At a May 23, 1942, meeting Conant assembled the nation's leading experts in an attempt to decide which of several methods of bomb construction should move to the pilot plant and industrial engineering stages. Conant used an arms-race argument to identify the point of decision:

> While all five methods [centrifuge, gaseous barrier diffusion, electromagnetic, graphite, heavy water plutonium pile] appear to be equally promising, clearly the production of a dozen bombs by the five routes will certainly not be the same but might vary by six months or a year because of unforeseen delays. Therefore, if one discards one or two or three of the methods now, one may be betting on the slower horse unconsciously. To my mind the decision as to how "all out" the effort should be might well turn on the military appraisal of what would occur if either side had a dozen or two bombs before the other.[32]

Conant described for the group the latest evidence of a German bomb program, which now included new indications of espionage activity. There were British reports that the Germans had heavy water. Dr. Peter Debye, the former head of Berlin's Kaiser Wilhelm Institute (KWI), Germany's leading scientific research center, came to America eighteen months earlier with reports that the German army had taken control of the institute and was hard at work on a bomb. Conant then added a new and more startling factor, which he described cryptically in a top-secret letter to Arthur Compton: "Recently intercepted instructions to their agents in this country [that] shows they are interested in what we are doing." In his book *The Making of the Atomic Bomb,* Richard Rhodes wrote that "Conant thought that this last evidence was the best."[33]

Not surprisingly, Coffey hit a stone wall when he sought NBS and OSRD help for feed material. Officials described it as so delicate that only a personal letter from J. Edgar Hoover would be considered, with little chance that even his request would be honored. Coffey warned Ladd that the critical importance of atomic research to the nation's security required extreme caution in the "preparation of the material that should be transmitted to the New York Office," adding that "care should be exercised that absolutely no worthwhile information be transmitted."[34]

By the fall of 1942, Joint Security Control of the Military Intelligence

Alexander Semmler. Jorge Mosquera unsuccessfully approached Semmler, a German pianist and NBC Radio orchestra conductor, for espionage assistance on orders from Abwehr officer Hans Blum. *New York World Telegram & Sun Collection, Library of Congress*

Division, created the previous summer to tighten military security, began adding a central deception staff to its portfolio for both military services. According to its own directive, "cover" was defined as "planned measures for disguising or concealing an operation against an objective such measures being directed against an enemy and as desired against friendly forces." The objective was to encourage enemy action on a belief that something true was actually false. The art of deception was a separate discipline, defined as "planned measures for revealing or conveying to the enemy true information (or false information which could be evaluated as true) regarding our strategic plans, strength, dispositions, operations or tactics with the purpose of causing him to reach false estimates and to act thereon." The purpose of deception was making the enemy believe that something false was true. As Thad Holt wrote, cover conceals truth, deception conveys falsehood. Cover induces non-action while deception induces action.[35]

JSC's first head of strategic deception planning was an army colonel named Newman Smith. The fifty-three-year-old Smith came from Dothan, a southeast Alabama lumber town, where he was educated by a series of private tutors and academies. Joining the army at the age of eighteen, Smith distinguished himself in combat over the next two years against the Moros in the Philippines before returning to Alabama's Howard College (now Samford College). In 1916 he joined the Alabama National Guard as a captain in the "Old Fourth," one of the Army of Northern Virginia's storied Civil War regiments that saw continual combat from First Manassas to Appomattox. Smith's unit later merged into New York's famed 42nd "Rainbow" Division before shipping out in November 1917 to Europe, where it fought at the Battle of the Marne, St. Mihiel, and the Meuse-Argonne offensive. After the war he worked for Guaranty Bank in New York (later Morgan Bank), Constantinople, and Brussels before joining the Motor Dealers Credit Corporation financing Studebaker and Erskine automobiles. When the Depression forced the company's closure of its European operations in 1933, Smith returned to the United States as a sales manager in New York and later at the company's southern division in Atlanta.[36] Throughout the 1920s and 1930s Smith kept his reserve army commission until retiring at the age of fifty. On November 19, 1942, as Allied troops began racing across North Africa, he returned to uniform reporting to General George Strong, the army's head of military intelligence. Two days before Christmas he was commissioned a lieutenant colonel and assigned to the JSC a month later.[37]

Smith soon took personal charge of JSC's "Special Section," which put him in direct contact with the FBI on a routine basis. His many and varied duties included monitoring the activities of double agents, coordinating and creating information passed to the enemy through these channels, pursuing new sources of information, analyzing public sources for suitable passage material, and keeping careful record of information passed through all American deception channels. Smith liaised with Robert Cunningham, the head of the FBI Espionage Section, signing off personally on proposed messages sent through FBI double agents.

Another first for Smith was coordination with forty-eight-year-old John H. "Jonny" Bevan, the head of the London Controlling Section (LCS), who coordinated British deception schemes for every wartime operation as well as those involving Churchill's overseas travels with the title "Controlling Officer." Bevan, also an army lieutenant colonel, had previously been a well-connected City of London stockbroker whose circle of friends included General Hastings "Pug" Ismay, Churchill's military chief of staff; Stewart Menzies of SIS; and Field Marshal Sir Alan Brooke, the Chief of the Imperial Staff, a fellow bird watcher and regular dining companion. As an agency of the War Cabinet, LCS operated from the Central War Room in London, with Bevan serving from May 1942 until the end of the war.[38]

Bevan arrived in Washington for his first meeting with JSC officials on December 23, 1942. Over the next few weeks Bevan and Smith produced a series of secret agreements, defining their individual responsibilities for worldwide deception against enemy forces. The British would create the deception strategies for Europe, North Africa, India, and the Middle East, with the Americans in a supporting role. JSC, in turn, assumed primary responsibility for deception coordination against the Japanese in the Pacific, China, and Australia. The particular controlling section or theater commander who initiated a deception plan was responsible for its implementation, and no other controlling section or theater could implement a plan unless requested to do so. At the same time everyone recognized that constant "coordination of plans was an absolute necessity." One illustration of this new JSC/LCS arrangement concerned the HMS *Nelson,* which was scheduled to depart for the Pacific Theater following repairs at the Philadelphia Navy Yard. When Smith requested British permission to leak this information to the Germans through FBI double agents code-named "Koehler" (see chapter 15), LCS gave its approval but "not [repeat] not desirable to indicate her destination."[39]

Unlike the chronic Abwehr problems in getting funds to other FBI double agents, there was little difficulty concerning Mosquera. Following his agreement to cooperate, FBI agents in Montevideo recruited Ricardo Gioscia as the money funnel from the Germans to an FBI bank account in New York. Money was either wired from Europe to Gioscia or delivered to him by German consulate officials who would then send it to an FBI bank account in New York City.[40]

In January 1942, Mosquera settled into a new and relaxed New York lifestyle as the owner of La Plata Commercial Company, a phony business created by the FBI, and began a romance with a no-talent vocalist bedazzled by dreams of becoming an opera diva. Bored and with little to occupy his time, Mosquera soon began pestering Friedmann for money to pay for his girlfriend's voice lessons, publicity photos, a manager, entrée to well-connected theater people who could arrange for auditions, and the purchase of a house for her and her family in Yonkers, New York. FBI agents soon found themselves running around the New York City Theater District trying to arrange high-profile auditions for a singer with no reputation and even less artistry. Mosquera's anger over money soon bubbled over into a heated meeting with Friedmann, which produced admissions that he had lied to agents in 1941 when he claimed that the Abwehr kept his $40,000. Now he acknowledged that before leaving Germany he gave the money to his then-mistress, Franciska Halle. Extortion became the watchword when he cabled Gioscia in Montevideo to no longer send his funds to the FBI's bank account without first getting his permission.[41]

The large sums of money sent by the Germans were clear reflections of Mosquera's importance to them as a source. From May of 1942 to March 10, 1944, he was paid a total of $46,875.90 (more than $612,000 in 2012), beginning with $5,954.02 and ending with $16,000. When the FBI considered dropping him as a source and running the case without him, JSC raised serious objections. The rapidly approaching invasion of Europe made him an essential deception channel against the Germans. His communications with the Germans were "highly regarded by them," Smith wrote, making it critical that the FBI employ every effort to "maintain the good will of Mosquera and keep him under control." Facing little choice, Hoover ordered the New York office to give him a salary of $500 a month ($6,642.05 in 2012) and pay his federal and New York State income taxes as well.[42]

Beginning in April 1942, FBI deception strategy called for the expansion of his access to a wide variety of material without raising any German suspicions about how one man could acquire such unique intelligence. The JSC assisted in this effort by creating a simple alphabetic priority system for messages sent by double agents under FBI control. The most important were "A" messages. These were both true and false reports jointly created by JSC/LCS as part of the larger deception campaign that Allied planners wanted to put over to the Germans. The messages jointly coordinated and approved by London and Washington were then supplied to the FBI for passage by a double agent who would most logically have access to such information. A second category was the "B" message, carefully crafted by the FBI for administrative purposes (money, security, radio problems, etc.) or information culled from public sources and then approved by JSC before transmission to Hamburg. Typical of the "B" messages was a carefully reworded newspaper article sent in August 1942: "Built and delivered and ready for service in July nineteen forty two, sixty nine cargo ships of about seven hundred and gross tons and six tankers of about sixty three thousand ditto." Twenty days later, a very pleased Hamburg jokingly teased ND98 regarding his lack of nautical knowledge: "Your two two six [previous ND98 outgoing message] [is] unfortunately propaganda from newspapers. Besides tonnage not gross tons but dead weight tons parenthesis dwt parenthesis. Navy ought to get correct July figures for you. Never mind old boy don't be downhearted."[43] Mosquera occasionally used the FBI as an excuse for slow production. "I have already been in designated places in German district in these and other places and one cannot obtain anything of value for even drunkards [who] do not have confidence to speak of war matters for all who frequent there know that agents of the FBI swarm there in civilian and military uniforms."[44]

Gradually "A" and "B" messages began arriving in Hamburg describing the nature of La Plata Commercial Company and Mosquera's need to travel regularly to Washington, D.C., the epicenter of important military secrets. ND98 soon began introducing Hamburg to his four new (imaginary) sources. One was a well-placed civilian, a War Department employee in Washington code-named "Wasch"; another, called "Nevi," was a New Yorker working at the Brooklyn Navy Yard. To further expand his range of access, ND98 was soon touting Nevi's new source, "Osten," and a fourth named "Rep" who was working in a critical department at the Republic Aviation Company on Long Island. JSC and the FBI officials began meeting regularly to coordinate the use of these sources for radio passage of intelligence to Hamburg, based on overall direction and guidance from LCS in London.[45]

Building up a source in the enemy's mind required the incremental passage of information that was both valuable and capable of verification by the enemy. At the same time great care had to be employed to assure the enemy of the double agent's loyalty to them while not being so successful as to raise suspicions that he was under American control. In order to strengthen ND98's bona fides JSC, the FBI, and LCS began sending reports through his channel from his sub-sources, starting in November 1942 with an "A" message from Wasch concerning British Air Marshall John Slessor. The forty-five-year-old Slessor was a veteran of the First World War, seeing action as a pilot in the Middle East and earning the Military Cross. As a warrior scholar he was well known to the Luftwaffe, having written a study on the effectiveness of air power over the battlefield and behind enemy lines. From the start of the Second World War he handled a variety of senior air assignments leading up to April 1942, when he was promoted to Air Vice Marshall and Assistant Chief of the Air Staff and worked closely with American military officials on combined air offensives over Europe. In January 1943 the Combined Chiefs of Staff (CCS) meeting with Churchill and Roosevelt at Casablanca officially assigned Slessor to head the all-important Coastal Command, which was responsible for protecting Allied shipping from menacing U-boats along thousands of miles of ocean from Iceland to West Africa. For Admiral Doenitz, the commander of Hitler's U-boat fleet, Slessor's appointment was particularly important. In January 1942 the German navy introduced a specially designed Enigma machine into the U-boat service, rendering the vessels impregnable to decryption by Bletchley Park, which had been monitoring them since June 1941. They remained unreadable for the next year, followed by another six months of sporadic success during a period when Doenitz was expanding the number, size, and range of his U-boats into the western Atlantic and Gulf of Mexico. By the late summer the alarming increase in attacks on vital convoys soon placed Allied losses, in the words of Churchill's official biographer, at "unprecedented levels."[46]

ND98 leaked the transfer in November 1942. "An important new contact advises me that after Air Marshall Slessor's return from Washington he is to replace Air Marshall Joubert as A.O.C. in C. (Air Officer Commanding-In Chief, Coastal Command)." He cautioned the Germans that "this information will not be known in London for a couple of days and when it becomes known it will be of great interest. If it becomes known through a German radio broadcast it will probably be a bombshell to English." Slessor replaced Joubert less than three months later.[47]

JSC's use of ND98 began to intensify in April 1943 when the CCS appointed Lt. General Frederick Morgan, a British army officer, as the Chief of Staff to the Supreme Allied Commander (COSSAC), with orders to begin planning for an early 1944 invasion of Europe. Supporting Morgan was Lt. Colonel John Jervis Read, handling physical deception (phony tanks, troop dispositions, false radio traffic, etc.), and Roger Hesketh, managing "Special Means" or controlled leakage. Having no troops of his own, COSSAC was forced to rely on the fighting forces or other agencies for support in the execution of any deception plans. For controlled leakage, any information that the Allies wanted the enemy to know was channeled through the LCS. In the event, at the time the COSSAC sponsored only one deception plan, code-named "Cockade," which required COSSAC's Special Means deception needs to be submitted to a LCS subcommittee known as Twist, which Bevan also chaired. Twist then decided which channel would be the most appropriate for conveying the misinformation to the enemy and would be dispatched accordingly.[48]

What was Cockade? When Morgan was appointed chief of staff to the future Supreme Commander in April 1943, he also received a directive ordering him to prepare an "elaborate camouflage and deception scheme extending over the whole summer with a view to pinning the enemy in the West and keeping alive the expectation of a large-scale cross-Channel operation in 1943." It also included a ruse in the form of a large-scale amphibious feint to provoke an air battle that would employ both British air assets and the U.S. Eighth Air Force. The deception's objective was twofold: containment of German forces in the west preventing them from being used on other active battlefronts, and the destruction of German aircraft.[49]

Starting in July 1943, Smith and Bevan began using Mosquera in the Cockade deception operation. On July 29, Wasch in Washington described some solid "closed circle rumors" that a large part of the 101st Airborne Division had been sent to England together with the First Army headquarters "under great secrecy." Two days later the Germans replied appreciatively: "Your last message very interesting. Hope to hear more from you." Cunningham quickly informed Smith about the "quite unusual" speed of the response and feedback, which rarely occurred. A month later Wasch's "well informed source" described "great activity along the East Coast" involving training and troop preparations for use in the "invasion of Europe." To allay any lingering German questions concerning their destination, Mosquera reported that "drivers of all types of vehicles are being trained for left-hand driving." Reinforcing his messages about East Coast troop buildups, he alerted the Germans that Major General Roscoe B. Woodruff had been appointed head of a "recently organized" army task force on the East Coast. During July Woodruff was in London with intentions to stay until some type of emergency circumstance forced his return "in great haste," leaving his senior staff members behind to continue the development of some unknown plans. Woodruff, in fact, took command of the VII Corp in England in the fall of 1943. Another warning came on October 10, 1943, when he described the award of a contract to an American firm for the production of aluminum-built C-46 transport planes, as the army "needs all transport planes of greater capacity and longer range."[50]

When General Eisenhower arrived in London in January 1944 to assume overall command of the planned invasion of Europe, Morgan's COSSAC organization was absorbed into Supreme Headquarters Allied Expeditionary Force (SHAEF) with orders to concentrate on Fortitude, the code name for the plan to deceive the Germans as to the date and location of the invasion of Europe. Taking its instructions from both Smith in Washington and Bevan in London, the FBI began in January 1944 to send dozens of JSC-LCS inspired messages designed to mislead and misdirect the enemy. The deception topics that ND98 fed to the Abwehr were many and varied. Some targeted enemy morale with graphic descriptions of growing American airpower. One February report described a "remarkable new technique" in aircraft engine design, enabling planes to carry "greater bomb loads [and] heavier armor and armament and more gasoline," vastly increasing range, speed, and maneuverability. The Germans also learned about newly invented infrared devices capable of seeing through heavy clouds and fog and advanced guided missiles attached to the nose of a plane that could seek out targets emitting heat "such as steel mills and vessels at sea." As German air combat capability deteriorated, leaving ground troops and war industries increasingly vulnerable to Allied air superiority, ND98 began sending a series of reports concerning the powerful new B-29 Superfortress bomber. It weighed 100,000 pounds with a 10,000-pound payload, a tactical radius of 1,000 miles, and a cruising altitude of 30,000 feet. The plane's engine and production problems, he next warned them, had been "overcome," leading to tests in the Caribbean and South Atlantic preparatory to "the assignment of the first B-29 survey ship from here to England."[51]

Part of the Fortitude deception was Bodyguard. This aspect of the plan was designed, in the words of one its key planners, "to induce the enemy to make faulty strategic dispositions in relation to operations by the United Nations against Germany."[52] On February 21, 1944, less than four months before D-Day, ND98 learned from Wasch that an "acquaintance" reported that several thousand soldiers scheduled to depart for Europe had been issued "new winter clothing." One feature of the original features of the Bodyguard plan was the encouragement of German belief in postponement of the invasion due to an assortment of problems in the United States. Over the next few months double agents in England and America fed the Abwehr a diet of truth and lies about acute shortages of landing craft and British criticism of American force preparedness, which made the exaggerated scale of the attack appear more difficult to attain than was the case. The most useful ploy was convincing the enemy of delays in landing craft due to labor unrest and strikes in America. In London, the Double Cross agent code-named "Tate," a confessed Nazi dropped into England by parachute in September 1940 and then turned by B1(a), radioed on January 20, 1944, that "labor troubles have curtailed production of invasion barges to such an extent that the dates of future operations may be affected."[53]

Dozens of carefully crafted JSC messages conveyed this same theme from America. Just six days into the year, Wasch learned about a staggering War Department order for the production of "85000 landing craft of all types." More than 4,000 contractors and 20,000 subcontractors had received "urgent instructions to expedite" production, which "should be built by next spring or summer." Weeks later, conflicting reports from both Wasch and Nevi described unexplained troop movements together with hints of serious production delays, which should push back the invasion date. One from the ever-reliable Wasch deepened the mystery by revealing "secret consultations" between American labor leaders and Roosevelt administration officials "concerning interference with production, particularly of invasion craft occasioned by recent strikes in key plants." Two days later, Wasch overheard an angry conversation about War Department officials in London who were the butt of "very critical" British criticism for the slow buildup of American forces with "little or no training on the organization and tactics of the Germans." On May 2, 1944, ND98 offered further confusion when he reported Eisenhower's fury that vitally needed landing craft, already in short supply, were being diverted to the Pacific area, seriously delaying British initiation of their "forthcoming operations in the Balkans," which Wasch described as "predominant." Just four days before the invasion, Mosquera offered new emergency intelligence designed to ease German fears about the imminence of attack: "Wasch has just reported information appearing of highest importance and possibly indicating some plan change. It appears that a force consisting of a number of infantry and armored divisions originally scheduled for U.K. are being diverted for special operation." He went on to note "that force consists of four infantry and two armored divisions not having undergone amphibious training and scheduled for use as follow up to initial assault."[54]

In the days and weeks following the invasion, with Allied forces struggling to break out of Normandy, JSC/LCS continued to rely on Mosquera's channel to help hold German forces at the Pas de Calais for the main attack the Germans still expected. Two reports on June 12, possibly pointing to a second invasion in southern France, described four U.S. infantry and two armored divisions undergoing special training in river crossings and bridging operations. The second warned the enemy of "strong indications" of a major attack through Norway, the Mediterranean, and the Balkans. Within hours Hamburg frantically replied: "Please rush more details."[55] Ramping up the stupefaction even more to a German high command now facing a rapidly shrinking two-front war, Wasch offered further dispiriting news that Russian Lend-Lease deliveries for the first four months of 1944 was two million tons, including 1,200 planes, 400 tanks and tank destroyers, 210,000 trucks, 900,000 miles of telephone wire, and 2.8 million tons of food. A month later Berlin learned that troop concentrations setting up in a U.S. staging area "are follow[ing] up for another large scale landing." By September, however, with the immediate pressure in France's Contentin Peninsula eased, the increasingly dispirited Germans were told that military supplies moving over the Normandy beaches were approaching 100,000 tons per day.[56]

As Allied troops neared the German frontier in the first week of December, an opening occurred that suggested the use of ND98 as a direct channel with the Japanese. The opportunity presented itself when the Germans radioed a question to Mosquera over some confusion involving Wasch and Nevi. The FBI told the Germans that Wasch's friend with access to military information working on the West Coast and in desperate need of money was willing to broadcast military information to Japan in exchange for a $1,000 monthly payment. "Have Tokyo supply code," Mosquera insisted, "or if agreeable to you I shall furnish Wasch with my code using a different key." Hamburg quickly rejected the offer, fearing the danger to Mosquera and his sources.[57]

ND98 also assisted in the deception campaign formulated for Admiral Chester Nimitz's (the Commander in Chief of Pacific Forces) invasion of the Gilbert and Marshall Islands. Anticipating that the Germans would pass ND98's information to the Japanese, JSC supplied "sufficiently true" intelligence that Nimitz was planning his main attack against the Kurile Islands in the Northern Pacific, when in fact the main thrust would come at Japan's easternmost perimeter in the Gilbert and Marshall Islands. The deception was designed to keep the bulk of the Japanese navy in its home waters. At the request of the CCS, the following information was radioed to Hamburg through the Mosquera channel on November 2, 1943.[58] "Nevi reports for Tokyo the following: Recently at a gathering a high ranking U.S. Naval officer made an inadvertent remark from which Nevi believes that there is now being planned a large scale attack against the northern Kurile Islands. The probable day of the attack was not disclosed but he believes that it will happen soon and in conjunction with a large scale feint attack later this month."[59]

Despite the German rejection of ND98's new Japanese source, JSC imperceptibly began moving the FBI's source toward the Pacific theater of operations. Initial ND98 messages offered Wasch and Nevi observations on the tough fight that Japanese forces were waging in the Philippines and the abundant supply of railway freight cars available for moving cargo to West Coast ports. Four days before the start of the Battle of the Bulge, they placed B-29 production at more than 150 a month, which military planners believed "will provide much larger groups for strikes against Tokyo once the Navy reaches the China coast." Again, in December he radioed that the navy had completed the first principal phase of their photo reconnaissance of the main islands of Japan, the China coast, and Formosa.[60]

By the fall of 1944 Nimitz had cleared the central Pacific area with the liberation of the Marianas and then faced the question of where next to move. Formosa and China were favored by the navy, while General Douglas MacArthur pushed for the liberation of the Philippines and Luzon. The navy also considered going into the Bonins and Okinawa in the Ryukus. A JSC team that visited the Pacific theater from October 10 through December 19, 1944, soon designed a deception code-named "Plan Bluebird" and sent it on to Washington for approval on November 21, 1944.[61]

Bluebird, the most extensive and elaborate all-American deception yet mounted, was designed for the planned invasion of Okinawa. The idea was to "convince [the Japanese] of [American] intention of invading the Island of Formosa and the south coast of China between Formosa and Hainan Island in the spring of 1945, and to continue this threat through the summer of 1945, if, and as necessary." The JSC put over the story that the invasion was designed to relieve pressure in China, gain bases on the Asian mainland in anticipation of blockading Japan, seize the China coast from Hong Kong to Amoy in order to open supply routes to China, and isolate Japanese forces in Southeast Asia and the East Indies. The object of the plan was to provoke a redeployment of Japanese forces away from Iwo Jima and Okinawa, the real target of U.S. forces.[62]

JSC began using ND98 in the project starting with a message from Wasch, whose supply officer friend on the West Coast "states emphatically that conflicting views among high officials as to next move against

Japan" had prompted Admiral William Leahy, the president's naval aide, to issue a press release announcing that Roosevelt would not countermand the decisions of the Joint Chiefs of Staff. Ten days later Wasch reported the delight of high officials that increased B-29 production would mean larger bomber groups for strikes against Tokyo when bases were secured in China. Together with a South American source, ND98 was soon reporting on the success of the "rubber model project" which depicted "in great detail the islands of the Formosa area and the adjacent China coast." To further confuse the Japanese as to timing of the invasion, Wasch learned in January that army supplies, destined for the invasion of Formosa, had been rerouted to help block the German offensive in the Ardennes. Just days later Wasch's friend learned that deliveries of supplies to the Soviets may have been delayed also but this time due to navy demands for China operations. To enhance ND98's credibility with Japanese leaders, JSC had him send a series of reports between February 22 and March 2, 1945 (the month-long battle of Iwo Jima began on February 19), with details of a planned Washington conference in March involving Nimitz, General Albert Wedemeyer, commanding general of the China Burma India Theater, and the American ambassador to Chungking. Later, Magic intercepts (the American code name for decryption of coded Japanese diplomatic messages) of the weekly intelligence circular of the Army General Staff in Tokyo revealed a Japanese assessment of the American forces that "points strongly to a landing on the China coast some time in June or later."[63]

In the aftermath of the Battle of Iwo Jima, ND98 reported to the Germans that heavy fighting on the island had forced the American high command to take control of additional covering airfields in the vicinity of the Ryuku Islands before moving on to the invasion of Formosa and China. Supporting this idea was another ND98 report two days later revealing the formation of a new Tenth Army at Hawaii under the command of General Simon Bolivar Buckner, formerly of the Alaskan Command. By the end of April, ND98 was still reporting "on high authority" that continued harassment from Japanese aircraft operations were forcing American commanders to pursue subsidiary targets, thus further delaying the Formosa-China operation. One of his last messages to the Germans, just days before the German surrender, reported that a general and his aide who met with Wasch had complained that if the war in Europe had ended at the New Year, "the Okinawa landings would have been made at the same time as the invasion of Formosa and South China coast."[64]

In the end, ND98's true value to the Allied war effort was summed up by Newman Smith, who described his contributions as an "important part in the successful operations of the Allies on the Coast of Normandy." In the weeks following the invasion Smith recalled that "even if the Germans realize that he was double-crossing them, he has more than proved his value" to the war effort. Between November 1943 and the final surrender in May 1945, ND98 sent more than 150 "A" messages and a similar number of "B" communications that were routinely accepted by the Abwehr. In the closing days of the Third Reich, as the British closed in on Hamburg, German officials were still offering payments of $40,000 for information from ND98. German faith in ND98 never wavered.[65]

CHAPTER FOURTEEN

Gaston DeChant

On May 2, 1945, President Truman issued an executive order appointing Robert Jackson, Associate Justice of the Supreme Court, as the representative of the United States and chief of counsel to an international war crimes tribunal. Jackson's mandate was the preparation and prosecution of "charges of atrocities and war crimes against such of the leaders of the European and Axis powers . . . as the United States may agree with any of the United Nations to bring to trial before an international military tribunal."[1]

One person who was directly affected by Truman's decision was a French flying ace and FBI double agent who made the first transatlantic flight from Europe to North America in 1930, just three years after Charles Lindbergh's successful crossing in *The Spirit of St. Louis* in the other direction. His name was Dieudonné Costes, born on November 4, 1893, at Septfond, Tare-et-Garonne, in France's Gascony region. As a youngster he attended the Ecole des Arts in Metier, where he took a three-year engineering course before abruptly dropping out at sixteen to take pilot training. Next came two years of compulsory military service and advanced flight training at St. Cyr before his reassignment at the start of World War I to Rheims, where he dug trenches due to an oversupply of pilots. As the fighting quickly expanded, Costes found himself on the Balkan front flying combat missions for the French Air Service. By war's end he had earned a reputation as a wounded ace, chalking up eight enemy kills and losing two fingers from a shell burst while skimming over enemy lines.[2]

He resumed civilian life, flying mail throughout Europe for Latecoere Airlines, and then joined Breguet Aeronautics Company as a pilot testing new aircraft. During the infancy of flight when aircraft companies made their reputation by chasing long-distance and speed records, Costes did his part admirably in placing Breguet front and center on the world stage. In 1925 he scored a first with a round-trip flight from Paris to Assuan, Egypt. A year later he broke a world record by flying 5,396 kilometers from Paris to Iran, then on to India before returning to Paris. In 1927 Costes scored another first, flying from Paris to Argentina, Brazil, the United States, and, later, non-stop across the South Atlantic from Senegal to Natal, Brazil. When poor weather forced an end to his first westbound Paris to New York crossing, he turned east instead, flying from Paris to China, a distance of nearly 8,000 kilometers, setting a new world distance record in the process. His famous trip from Paris to New York on September 1–2, 1930, with his copilot, Maurice Bellonte, in just over thirty-seven hours was greeted with a ticker-tape parade along Fifth Avenue and a White House meeting with President Hoover.[3]

During the 1930s his fame led him from testing aircraft and chasing records to the more complex and lucrative side of management in the aircraft industry. By the start of the Second World War, Costes was the president of Hispano-Suiza, an aircraft manufacturing company with factories employing 14,000 workers in Grantham, England; Tarbes, France; and Paris. The Tarbes plant produced engines for French aircraft in Europe and North Africa, while his two facilities in Paris made parts and motors for Mercedes-Benz, producing revenue of 20 million francs per month.[4]

Costes first came to the FBI's attention in October 1942, when he unexpectedly walked into the American embassy in Lisbon to report his recruitment by the German military intelligence, an espionage relationship that began just weeks after German forces stormed across France in the summer of 1940. When the European war started, Costes joined French forces as a colonel stationed as the technical director at the Versailles School of Aviation, where he prepared cadets for combat flying. In February 1940 he returned to Hispano-Suiza, which was then developing new and more powerful aircraft motors desperately needed by the French military. The collapse of France led to a move to Paris where he did everything, he later claimed, to "delay all work which would benefit the Germans," a move that landed him a three-day prison sentence for mismanagement and sabotage. His release was followed by constant surveillance, harassment, repeated interrogations, and a German prohibition on resumption of work with his company. Months later, his agreement to collaborate with German civil authorities led to reinstatement with his company and a seat on the board of directors, which he allegedly used to frustrate German ambitions. Charging that obvious opposition would have led to imprisonment or execution, he entrusted himself with the "very delicate mission" of outward collaboration while secretly delaying "to a maximum the manufacture of the necessary equipment for mass production." His sabotage, he later argued, was so cleverly concealed from the onsite German observers that no one caught on to production delays and the gradual increase in faulty products shipped to German forces. In later interviews with the FBI he frequently became emotional, expressing pride in delaying German armament production for many months while at the same time voicing remorse for the "painful moments, moments of physical and moral fatigue, [when] I often hoped that a few well aimed bombs would help me succeed in my task. I was not so lucky. It never came."[5]

After two years of collaboration and supposed resistance, Costes eventually caught the eye of the Abwehr. The original approach was made in May or June 1942, when German engineers overseeing the Mercedes-Benz work suggested that he move to the United States where he could obtain valuable secrets about mechanical and industrial development. The Germans were "so deceived," he boasted, that "they had decided to offer me very special work in the United States: in straight language this is called 'espionage.'" When the wary Frenchman agreed, secret planning meetings soon began with intelligence officers at different Paris apartments.[6]

Over a period of weeks Costes and his handlers concocted a scheme in which he and his wife, Maria, would travel first to Madrid and then on to Lisbon, where they would book passage on a ship bound for Buenos Aires and then on to New York. In Madrid he was to contact American officials with an offer of assistance as a pilot, engineer, and aviation consultant for the Allied war effort. The Abwehr believed that his fame and reputation would give Costes high-level access to the latest advances in U.S. aircraft design and technologies which he could then report back to German authorities. Once permanently situated in America, a German agent named Paul Jean Marie Cavaillez would leave for Buenos Aires or some other South American capital to set up a wireless radio for transmission of Costes's information to Germany.

Born on July 28, 1902, in Blois, France, Cavaillez finished high school with a degree in electrical engineering. During the 1930s he lived at 2 Place Marechal Petain with his mother in the town of Antibes, where for two years he worked on the construction of the Antoplois Theater and later managed a garage before mustering into the French army in September 1939 as a sergeant and later as a lieutenant in the French air force. A year later he moved into a Paris apartment with Noelle Lacabanne, whose husband, Maurice, a French army officer, had been captured and imprisoned by the Germans. In these years of German occupation Cavaillez survived on his wits, investing

Dieudonné Costes. World renowned French flier who faked cooperation with the Germans and later served as a double agent for the FBI. After the war he returned to France where he was imprisoned and tried for treason. *New York World Telegram & Sun Collection, Library of Congress*

in shady deals by buying and selling on the black market. When not struggling to put food on the table, he occupied his time improving his invention, which would enable planes to land in low visibility.

Cavaillez first came to Abwehr attention in late 1940 when he struck up a conversation with a stranger in a Paris bar. Through so-called business contacts his new friend soon arranged for an "Ausweiss," a hard-to-get travel permit which allowed him to travel from Paris through Vichy France to visit his mother still living in Antibes. Their meetings led to a December 1941 introduction to Abwehr officers in Paris who offered him a job as a radio operator for an agent then assigned to Africa. When he refused the assignment, he later claimed, they warned him that rejection was not an option now that he knew so much about Abwehr intelligence practices. After a year-long lapse Cavaillez was suddenly sent to Hamburg to undergo training in radios and codes, followed by his return to Paris where he had little contact with the Abwehr for another eighteen months. In December 1943 the Abwehr suddenly issued Cavaillez emergency instructions to depart for the United States to act as Costes's radioman. These hasty and unexpected arrangements, he later recalled, came about as result of "very good information [which] had just been received from the agent in the United States," making it "essential that radio contact be established between this agent and German Intelligence officers in Germany." It was only then that he learned Costes's identity as the agent, a man he had never met but had seen many times in the past at aviation shows.[7]

Before he left Paris for Madrid, Costes had received training in secret inks along with a list of 650 words corresponding to types of aircraft production, which he was to memorize for transmission in secret writing format to mail drop addresses in Spain and Portugal. Consistent with Abwehr practice, he was also supplied with three microphotographs containing instructions for encoding and decoding his messages and a reagent for developing secret writing messages hidden in a cigarette lighter and the base of a cold cream jar. As for where in America he should settle, this question the Germans left to Costes.[8]

Costes first met with Lieutenant Colonel Dorsey Stephens, the assistant military attaché at the American embassy in Madrid. After outlining his tale he supplied Stephens with his espionage paraphernalia along with seven mail drop addresses, the names and descriptions of his German contacts, and an offer to serve as a double agent in America. "I am willing to go the United States and put myself entirely at your disposal," sending back "as per your instructions all the information which you might choose . . . false or exaggerated." Selling himself further to Stephens, he bragged that "through me you can have a greater possibility to uncover the German Agents, to counteract their plans and to arrest them if the occasion presents itself or if such action is opportune."[9]

Following a flurry of cables to Washington and FBI acceptance of his services, Costes and his wife boarded the SS *Cabo De Hornos* at Lisbon and sailed for Argentina. Waiting for them in Buenos Aires on January 11, 1943, was William H. Doyle, the Bureau's SIS man at the American embassy. The local publicity surrounding the arrival of an international hero proved useful in deflecting attention away from Doyle's discreet investigation of his activities. First he arranged a full-time surveillance of Costes, followed by checks with local sources. Wary Free French emigrés warned Doyle to be careful in his dealings with Costes; he was a French national hero with close ties to Vichy officials and unusual access to German-occupied Paris. Adding to Doyle's suspicions was the ease of his sudden departure from occupied France for a visit to the Western Hemisphere.

Doyle's concerns only deepened when inconsistencies and omissions bubbled up during his interviews of Costes. The Frenchman repeated the story he told Stephens but neglected to mention recent correspondence with friends in France as well as a Mercedes-Benz business acquaintance named Karl Abt, the German manager of Hispano-Suiza who later proved to be an Abwehr officer. Another problem was Seroussi Nessin, whom Costes cabled and failed to disclose to American or British authorities. Nessin was a French businessman who had passed through Trinidad on his way to Montevideo in October 1942. A British record noted that for years he had lived in Italy before moving to France in March 1941, where he was placed in a concentration camp in the city of Nice. A year later he was suddenly released for reasons unknown and permitted to leave France for South America. When British authorities questioned him in Trinidad, he named Costes as a friend who had voiced doubts about the German chances of victory, a statement that led British and FBI officials to suspect Nessin's collaboration with "[Costes] in his plans to act as an agent."[10]

Eleven days later Costes and his wife departed Buenos Aires for Miami, Florida, where they met Earl Connelley and his mysterious assistant, "Robert Marchand," a French Canadian smuggler and black market racketeer, who would act as the Frenchman's personal assistant for the rest of the war. Marchand was, in fact, Robert Aime Maheu, a twenty-six-year-old FBI agent fluent in French. Maheu grew up in a French Canadian household in Waterville, Maine, a mill town situated in the southwest corner of the state on the edge of the Kennebec River where the main industry was the Hathaway Company, maker of fine men's dress shirts for generations of Americans. His ambitious parents owned a grocery business along Water Street in front of a barn that also served as the headquarters for the family's carbonated beverage business called the Elm City Bottling Company. Recalling his childhood many decades later, Maheu pointed fondly to a sign with the company's name hanging in his Las Vegas office, which he described as his

Mary Costes. Wife of Dieudonné Costes who accompanied her husband to the United States unaware of his Abwehr espionage mission. After the war she remained in America to pursue a singing career in Hollywood, California. *New York World Telegram & Sun Collection, Library of Congress*

personal "Rosebud." During the summer months, when not delivering soft drinks to local vendors, Bob could be found on one of the many streams and brooks around Waterville rowing a bark canoe, which he also found handy for delivering newspapers to outlying farmers living along the river.[11]

Maheu was raised with a strong Roman Catholic family tradition. He attended Sunday Mass at St. Francis Catholic Church, joined the Knights of Columbus, and received his early education at Notre Dame Parochial School. His father taught him how to shoot rifles and handguns. Old Waterville friends many decades later still recalled his skills with a pistol and one field day event in which he put on a shooting demonstration. Following Maheu's death, childhood friend Wilfred Chamberlain could still describe that day: “He was amazing, the trick shots he could do with a mirror and all kinds of things.” Another old chum named Clayt LaVerdiere knew him as soft-spoken with an easy-going courteous personality who never lost the common touch, “even though his business has brought him in contact with some of the more prominent individuals in the country.” As a teenager he learned to fly a plane, a hobby that he continued through college and certainly helped him when he began working with Costes.[12]

Waterville was the home to Morgan Business College on Main Street, which trained accountants and secretaries on three floors over the F. W. Woolworth store. It also boasted Colby College, the twelfth-oldest independent liberal arts college in the United States and one of America’s first coeducational institutions, founded in 1813. Continuing his Catholic tradition Maheu set off for Worcester, Massachusetts, after high school, enrolling in the College of the Holy Cross, the oldest Jesuit college in New England and one of the oldest in the nation. Despite extra jobs to earn needed money for tuition and expenses and the discipline of campus life, Maheu found these years “idyllic.” He made many friends, some life-long, like Edward Bennett Williams, who later became one of the nation’s most influential lawyers and owner of the Washington Redskins football team. After earning an economics degree in 1935 he enrolled in law school at Georgetown University, attending classes at night while working full-time for the Agriculture Department analyzing aerial photographs of crops and fields to ensure that farmers were actually growing crops subsidized by the federal government.[13]

In December 1940, at the age of twenty-three, Maheu suddenly abandoned law school and his day job to join the FBI, which was looking for translators. Following training school and a brief stint in Arizona he was assigned to the Seattle Division working as the Resident Agent for the Aberdeen, Washington, area. Settled in a new career with a regular salary, he married his high school sweetheart, Yvette Doyon, who crossed the country by train and bus for their tiny wedding in Aberdeen. In June 1943 Hoover suddenly ordered him back to the East Coast, where he began his strange new life as Robert A. Marchand, crook, confidence man, and secretary to Frances’s most famous aviator. Maheu’s alias was a simple matter of security to prevent someone “checking back to his hometown and learning of his association with the FBI.” As for Yvette, she returned to Waterville with their year-old son, Peter, knowing nothing of her husband’s assignment except that he was living and working in New York. Contact between them was limited to occasional telephone calls or letters transmitted through an FBI agent in Maine. Maheu's mission was simple: ensure that Costes did not "get away from us by ideas he may develop."[14]

In New York, Costes and his wife moved into the Waldorf Astoria Hotel until more suitable living arrangements could be made. The hard-nosed Connelley quickly sized up his new source as haughty, stubborn, arbitrary, and temperamental with an "unusually high opinion of himself and his ability." Reminiscent of Popov, Costes's expensive tastes soon became another full-time FBI headache for the next two years of the war. Mrs. Costes, who was accustomed to a lavish European lifestyle, believed that her husband's American visit was business-related with no idea about his Abwehr relationship or FBI double-agent role. Her refusal to live anywhere except an "apartment-hotel" with suitable maid service soon became a major source of frustration for Connelley and his staff. Among the residences selected and rejected were the Ritz-Carlton, Del Monico's ($3,580 per year, $47,000 in 2012), the Ritz Towers ($6,500 per year, $85,538 in 2012), and the Hotel Pierre ($4,800 per year, $63,167 in 2012). Eventually the exasperated Connelley arranged for a three-bedroom furnished apartment at the Park Lane, adjacent to the Waldorf, at a rate of $4,200 per year ($55,270 in 2012).[15]

Another problem was Mrs. Costes's financial assets. When she arrived in Miami she had hidden in her wardrobe a cache of jewelry valued at $345,000 ($4,540,000 in 2012). Under wartime rules, only Americans and citizens of Allied nations could carry jewelry and uncut gems in a safe place before entering the country in order to avoid paying duty. Adding to Connelley's woes was Mrs. Costes's fury when the Treasury Department's Foreign Funds Control Unit seized and held her jewelry until she could rightfully establish her ownership claim. Compounding her rage was the near impossibility of an alien from an occupied country proving that the funds were not acquired through German activities.[16]

Costes shared his wife's demands for the return of her jewels, a desire he believed to be perfectly reasonable. In the meantime his own list of requirements for their basic monthly needs were equally eye-popping. It included $600 for food, $100 for English lessons, and $150 for his wife's musical accompanist, whom she recently hired in anticipation of her planned opera debut in the winter of 1943. He also expected the FBI to cover an additional $100 monthly payment for his wife's sister, a widow living in Algiers with two children, and another $600 for "diverse expenses such as taxis, theaters, clothing et cetera." As British and American troops slogged it out with Hitler's Afrika Corp. across Tunisia and Egypt, the now exasperated Connelley minced no words with his Washington bosses, calling Costes a "well fed Axis collaborator who has become a great French patriot who is here now to serve his country if this can be done with the greatest degree of comfort and luxury to himself." Connelley grudgingly settled on FBI compensation of $1,600 a month, which Costes would have to rely on to cover his own expenses.[17]

Mrs. Costes played her American role as a glamorous French refugee to the hilt, splashing her photo across New York's society pages and taking every opportunity to record her unique views on the situation in Europe. "As she sat in the salon of her suite at the Park Lane she looked as if she had just come from the Rue de la Paix," one reporter noted, as she described the eagerness of Paris courtiers to continue designing as they did when Paris "was at its gayest." All in an attempt, she proudly charged, to keep up the "spirit of France."[18]

Behind the glamour and glitz, however, the couple's domestic relationship was in turmoil. FBI microphones in their Park Lane apartment continually recorded only long hours of uninterrupted silence between the two, suggesting a strain in the marriage which undoubtedly started long before their departure from Europe. Through wiretaps, FBI eavesdroppers soon learned of Maria's secret romance with Gregory Ratoff, a Russian-born stage actor then living and working in California. Ratoff was a forty-five-year-old Russian immigrant born in Samara in 1897 who came to America in 1922. Over the years he became a prominent actor and director with more than seventy-five films to his credit. In 1944 he won additional notoriety for his direction of the pro-Soviet film *Song of Russia.* Over the next two years Maria traveled frequently to the West Coast, staying with Ratoff while pursuing her own movie career.[19]

What did the boss think of Connelley's deal with Costes? His response was swift and clear. Exploding in paroxysms of rage, Hoover was "stunned at this case" and demanded to know "just how did we ever come to bring this fellow here" and who "approved the acceptance of this 'lemon.'" Hoover noted that Costes had not "*delivered* a thing & yet we have obligated ourselves to pay him $1600 per mo. It is beyond my comprehension. Take steps *at once* to get him out of U.S. and terminate his salary as soon as that is effected not later than Oct. 31 and sooner the better."[20]

The FBI director's problem with Costes was seemingly solved when the mercurial Frenchman suddenly decided that he wanted to fly combat missions rather than remain in the United States deceiving the Abwehr. Over the next four months he began pressuring the Free French Committee of Liberation in Washington to send him to North Africa as an officer in the French forces. What ensued was a complex series of negotiations involving the Free French, the FBI, the army, and the British concerning French acceptance of his services, London's willingness to give him a transit visa, and General Eisenhower's authorization for his entry into the North African theater. By December it was clear that Costes was going nowhere. The British refused him a visa to pass through Bermuda and the French closed the door, claiming that he was too old for military service in an active war zone.[21]

Costes vented his anger at the FBI over his rejection, blaming Hoover for conspiring with British authorities to deny him the chance to fight for the Free French Forces. The blunt Connelley soon set him straight, explaining that the FBI had nothing to do with his problem and, in fact, was "anxious for him to go." It was in this atmosphere of suspicion and hostility that Costes and Marchand began forging a cooperative relationship in an attempt to enhance the value of the man whom the Abwehr viewed as its most valuable aviation source in the United States.

In the months before Hoover's explosion, Costes, now carrying the FBI code name "Tom X," sent a number of secret writing messages to German mail drop addresses in Portugal and Spain. The open cover letters with chatty and breezy missives signed "Gaston DeChant" contained secret messages, all prepared in collaboration with Marchand. Costes gloated over his successful arrival in the United States and the attendant newspaper publicity that followed. "Generally speaking the American press received me well. All the newspapers were favorable except one, *PM,* a newspaper of the extreme left," he wrote. He reported his successful recruitment of an airline employee who agreed to smuggle his letters aboard the Pan Am Clipper for posting in Lisbon. The Pan American courier was, in fact, Dennis Flinn, the FBI's legal attaché in Lisbon who received them from Washington through the diplomatic pouch. Through Ostrich, Art Thurston tracked Berlin's receipt of Costes's letters, confirming both their arrival and the Abwehr's delight over his success.[22]

After whetting German appetites with hints about visiting the French cruiser *Richelieu* docked for repairs at the Brooklyn Navy Yard and a possible army source in Panama, he fired off a series of complaints about the constant danger that he faced, his need for faster communications, and a

Robert Maheu. A young FBI agent posing as "Robert Marchand," a French-Canadian smuggler who acted as confidential assistant to Dieudonné Costes throughout the war. Decades later Maheu would gain fame as confidential assistant to reclusive billionaire Howard Hughes. *FBI*

pressing need for funds. "Living here is very expensive," he warned, and "if I wish to live in a normal fashion and have the possibility of keeping up good connections I must expect a monthly expenditure of $3,000 [$39,000 in 2012]. My means are terribly limited if I wish to live and pay for the services which will be given to me." Touching on his employment possibilities, he warned that consulting jobs in the aircraft industry were impossible without a special permit; "therefore I am expecting you to help me without delay."[23] Costes began ramping up the pressure for radio help by insisting that the volume of information that he was collecting could not be handled by secret writing alone. He told the Abwehr that when he departed Buenos

Aires, "Paul's [Cavaillez] papers to enter Argentina were in order. Since, I have no advice concerning his voyage or his arrival or an explanation why he has not come." Almost plaintively he noted that "our communications by radio would be very important and profitable and we should finally establish them."[24]

With Abwehr confidence in Costes now supreme, the JSC used him for the first time on August 12, 1943, as a deception channel with a message based on the recent Allied invasion of Sicily hinting that a separate French attack was planned for Corsica.

> From a certain source it has been established that at the time of his departure from Washington, General Giraud received from Roosevelt the plan of a general proclamation to address to the French people. Giraud was charged with delivering it to Churchill. It is believed that that signifies the development of an action that will take place in the very near future. The plan of the Roosevelt and Churchill meeting with the Allied chiefs seems to confirm it.[25]

Over the course of the war Costes and Marchand sent dozens of "A" and "B" secret writing messages that covered everything from the latest jet aircraft research to military activities in the Middle East, the Mediterranean, and Europe, all in an effort to confuse the enemy. Writing in January 1944 they hinted at a possible Allied invasion of Southern France. "Activities in mobilizing all able bodied Frenchmen for service in Africa and elsewhere have involved me to such an extent I have not had opportunity for some time to contact my friends who made visits possible in certain plants."[26] One "A" message sent in April 1944, designed to signal a delay in the upcoming invasion of Europe, warned that "Republican members of Congress are actively spearheading an anti-administration Fourth Term presidential drive in the form of legislative pressure designed to retard or prevent the expected forthcoming invasion of the European continent."[27]

After months of delay, Cavaillez arrived in Madrid on April 25, 1944, where he contacted U.S. officials, saying nothing about his Abwehr role but claiming that he had escaped from France with plans for an invention that he wished to offer to the American military for use in combat aircraft. When told to prepare a resumé covering his past two years in France, he haughtily replied, "I do not hide from you that I shall be very distressed if, after waiting three years to leave France, in order to bring to you an invention whose great value I know because I have tested it myself." With an FBI agent now in

Madrid sidestepping procedural niceties, Cavaillez sailed from Vigo, Spain, on September 11, 1944, aboard the SS *Magallane* after conveniently receiving his Navicert from British authorities. While he was at sea Washington alerted the FBI SIS men in Trinidad and Havana about Cavaillez, ordering them to take no action that would alert his suspicions. SIS in Havana in turn told the Cuban police that it was "imperative that nothing be done to arouse suspicions of [Cavaillez] and let him go through uninterrupted" to the United States.[28]

Upon Cavaillez's arrival in New Orleans on October 12, 1944, the attorney general ordered "blanket authority . . . for installation of microphone and technical coverage of John Y [FBI code name assigned to Cavaillez] at his various addresses."[29] His bags were confiscated and sent to Washington where laboratory analysis found no evidence of espionage. During a routine customs interview he claimed he had no funds but hoped to secure subsistence from a "friend" while he settled into the Hampshire House Hotel in New York City in anticipation of marketing his aircraft invention. Four days later under FBI surveillance, he left for New York by train on the Piedmont Limited, arriving on October 18, taking a room at the Hotel Pierre.[30]

Six days later the French Military Mission in Washington informed Hoover that Cavaillez had contacted them, claiming that he came to America to develop an invention that American military authorities were keenly interested in exploring. To make his task easier he sought their assistance in securing an apartment and employment in Washington while he pursued his business venture. At the FBI's urging, French officials rejected the request in the hope that confining him to New York would improve the chances of his meeting Costes. While under surveillance, FBI agents observed Cavaillez signaling his arrival in the United States to the Germans with a postcard signed "Pablo" to a known German mail drop in Lisbon. Investigation in Lisbon soon uncovered a bank account in Cavaillez's name at the Credit Franco Portugais S.A. with the equivalent of $26,000 on deposit. Another discreet check revealed his instructions to bank officials for an immediate $1,000 transfer to him followed by a monthly transmittal of $500 ($6,600 in 2012) through Chase National Bank in New York.[31]

For the next several weeks the FBI continued to track his every move between New York and Washington. In Washington he mailed a postcard to his mistress in Paris at 22 rue de Ranelagh, visited the Library of Congress where he read books on electronics, and met with Free French officials. While he moved around the city, searches of his hotel room and briefcase

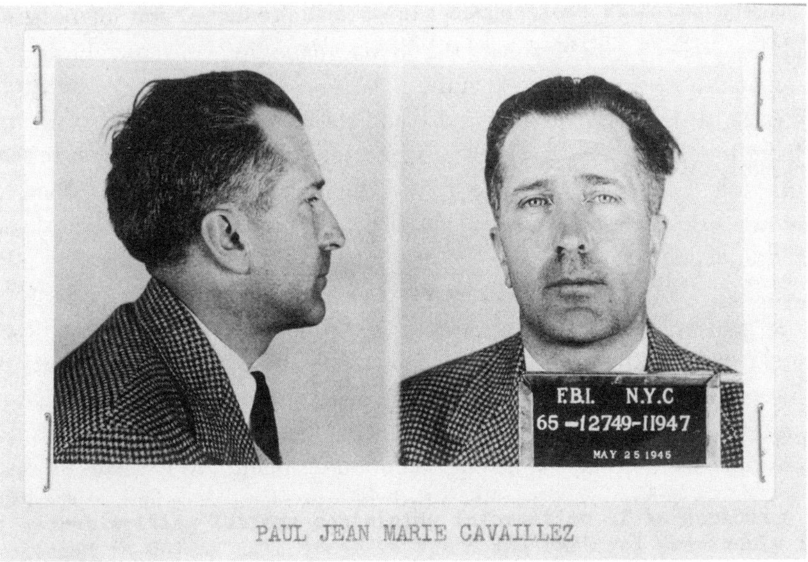

Paul Cavaillez. French radio operator sent to the United States to transmit Costes's intelligence to the Abwehr in Europe. *FBI*

produced nothing of value.[32] Free French liaison with the Bureau reported that Cavaillez expressed interest in military service as an officer but showed no desire for an assignment in France for what he only described as "political reasons." His plan was to remain in the United States, traveling around the country, inspecting army camps, and studying aviation engineering. In conversations with a French officer who was also an FBI source, Cavaillez expressed interest in visiting the RCA Laboratories in Edison, New Jersey, site of one of the nation's leading military research centers, where he could discuss his invention with other engineers and scientists. As a French army officer, he confidently explained, security checks would be minimal, giving him greater freedom of movement. During the conversation about aviation, when the source casually raised Costes's name (at the FBI's suggestion), Cavaillez expressed surprise, cautiously describing him as a man with a reputation for spending "a lot of money" who he believed was living in South America. As an afterthought, he indicated that peace would soon come to Europe as Germany had already lost the war.

While there was never any consideration of his joining the army, French officials played along with the FBI by offering him a pre-induction physical exam together with completing reams of application forms. A few weeks later he learned of his acceptance into the French Army, but his advanced age ruled out service as a pilot. Instead he was ordered to report to Bolling Field in Washington for inoculations in preparation for an assignment to French North Africa. Upon hearing the startling news, the now "dumbfounded and greatly disappointed" Cavaillez quickly appealed to French and U.S. military intelligence officials in the hope of reversing the decision.[33]

With Cavaillez making weekly trips to Washington and Costes in New York eagerly awaiting contact, Ostrich reported two important pieces of information on November 13, 1944. First, Berlin had deposited more than $20,000 in a Madrid bank for Cavaillez's use and, second, demanded explanations concerning why nothing had been received from him since receipt of his safe arrival postcard. Impatient Berlin authorities ordered Madrid to cable Cavaillez demanding answers. "Please give babies news. Nothing received since letter 13th October," which would signify the commencement of his scheduled wireless transmissions on "the times and frequencies agreed upon" between January 1 through January 5, 1945.[34]

Now that Paris had been liberated and Allied forces were roaring toward the German frontier, Costes began pestering the FBI to permit his return to Paris. After assuring him of the need for his continued cooperation even in these closing days of the war, Marchand secured Costes's agreement to meet Cavaillez. The FBI's plan called for Costes to extract sufficient evidence for an arrest that could then be used as leverage to turn Cavaillez into a double agent. The challenge, however, was putting the two Frenchmen together without arousing Cavaillez's suspicions. After much debate it was decided that Costes should directly approach his radioman.[35]

On December 13, 1944, two days before the start of the massive German counteroffensive in Belgium's Ardennes Forest region, Cavaillez received an unannounced visit from Costes at his room at the Hotel Pierre. While preparing for the confrontation, the now nervous Costes worried that the pressure of such a meeting could result in his forgetting important details of their discussions that could diminish the value of the plan. To ensure accuracy and a complete transcript, he urged Connelley to secretly record their conversations. Keeping him in the dark that the meeting would be recorded, he told Costes that any benefit from such a recording was offset by the fear of discovery of the microphone. As they sat down in his suite, Cavaillez became deeply suspicious of Costes's sudden appearance at his door. When asked how he got his room number without checking with the desk clerk, Costes cleverly replied that he was so conscious of security for them both that he got Cavaillez's address from the French mission in order to go directly to his room. It was a response that completely satisfied his new radioman.[36]

For the next three hours both men spoke in hushed tones, making FBI microphone coverage practically worthless. Cavaillez claimed he arrived alone in the United States and did not contact Costes, fearing that he was "under surveillance." When Costes offered him his telephone number and address he expressed relief that he now had someone to rely on. The remainder of the discussion was operational in nature, centering on their movements in the United States, how to work out a radio code for communication with Germany, Costes's financial situation, timing for transmissions, and future contact arrangements between them. When Cavaillez revealed that he had brought no radio and asked about the availability of a transmitter capable of reaching Europe, Costes agreed to purchase one. Next he described the full array of parts required for the transmitter which Costes began listing on a sheet of paper. After completing half a page Costes turned the list over to Cavaillez, who proceeded to jot down an additional three full pages of notes.[37]

Over the next few weeks Cavaillez's resolve increasingly strengthened with Costes's support. When he later raised suspicions about the mysterious Marchand, Costes vouched for him completely. He explained that they had worked closely together since his arrival in the United States two years earlier; it was Marchand who moved through the city buying the necessary radio parts, and it was Marchand who had a home on a secluded site along Long Island's North Shore which could prove useful for communicating with Hamburg.[38] At their next meeting at the Russian Tea Room in New York, Marchand accompanied Costes. After some general conversation Cavaillez accepted him and then asked him to bring the radio equipment to his new apartment at the San Carlos Hotel. On April 9, 1945, Marchand delivered the radio to Cavaillez's apartment, where he tested it with German-supplied frequencies.[39] Three days later, not satisfied with the radio's strength, Marchand again visited the San Carlos apartment with one hundred feet of copper wire that Cavaillez had requested for use as an antenna.[40]

Three weeks before the end of the war in Europe, the case was significantly strengthened when Marchand invited Cavaillez to his Long Island estate (actually the home of an FBI contact) in Locust Valley, New York, for two days in an attempt to contact Hamburg. There on April 21, 1945, he quickly set up his Halicrafter receiver and spent the rest of the day listening to random shortwave transmissions. Early the following morning wearing earphones supplied by Costes the French radioman once again began carefully searching for Hamburg's signals. As the morning wore on with no success, Marchand was instructed to shut off the main power in the house in order to eliminate outside interference. Then, using only battery power and with Marchand and Costes watching his every move, the radio came to life, with Cavaillez moving the dial between the two frequencies in accordance with a daily receiving schedule: from 10:00 to 10:05, 10:10 to 10:15, 10:20 to 10:25, and 10:30 to 10:35. After thirty-five minutes no contact was reported.[41]

By April, FBI discussions were underway with Costes concerning his future trial testimony against Cavaillez. After voicing fierce reluctance to testify in open court, Costes was assured that every effort would be made to keep him off the stand and out of public view. Now that France was liberated, he was anxious to end his involvement in the case and get back to Paris. Hoping to sway his FBI bosses, Costes then came up with a hare-brained scheme to return to France where he would somehow involve Cavaillez in a German underground organization that would surface in the future. His idea was ignored without comment.[42]

With arrest only days away and Cavaillez once again growing increasingly wobbly about the possibility of discovery, he told Costes of his plan to destroy anything that could link him with spying, including his personal diary containing incriminating entries. From the FBI's standpoint, the diary was critical for two reasons: it could offer useful tidbits of evidence that would strengthen the case, and it would serve as an excellent reference for his later interrogation. After gradually calming him down and continually urging him not to lose his head, Costes took him to Bethpage, Long Island, on the evening of May 17, where they golfed for the next two days to ease his anxiety.[43]

Connelley planned Cavaillez's arrest for May 24 while the two men golfed. At the last moment, however, he decided to wait one more day in the hope that Costes could extract even more useful information.[44] FBI agents Alfred H. Cote and Maxwell J. Wallace, both fluent in French, together with Wendell Stoops and Wynn Bennett, arrested Cavaillez in the early morning of May 25 at his San Carlos Hotel apartment in Manhattan. After searching his room, the agents took him to the twenty-ninth floor of the United States Court House where Connelley, assisted by Cote and Wallace, interviewed him for the next eight hours. As the day wore on he slowly laid out the details of his intelligence assignment, his travel to the United States to serve as Costes's radioman, his meetings with Costes, and Abwehr bank deposits in Lisbon totaling $26,000 worth of Portuguese escudos that he later converted to dollars. By 5:00 Cavaillez had initialed and signed a 156-page confession (in French) acknowledging his illegal entry into the United States with $23,000 (more than $290,000 in 2010 dollars), which for unknown reasons was not found during the initial search of his luggage. After arraignment before Judge Francis G. Caffey and his plea of not guilty, Cavaillez was jailed with bail set at $50,000. Over the next several days he was reinterviewed for corrections of his statement and to open two envelopes that he had previously turned over to an attorney in Washington for safekeeping. The two envelopes contained $14,000. Later the FBI confiscated additional funds totaling $16,000 ($204,000 in 2012), which Hoover told Assistant Attorney General Tom Clark had arrived in the United States through the Spanish diplomatic pouch.[45] By June 2 Cavaillez had acquired an attorney who promptly informed him that under no circumstances should he sign any more statements without counsel present.[46]

Problems for the Department of Justice and the U.S. Attorney's Office in New York defining specific charges against Cavaillez arose during the summer of 1945. While no one doubted that he came to the United States under German orders to conduct spying operations and conspired with Costes and Marchand, Cavaillez in fact never committed an overt act of espionage. After much soul-searching, the original espionage charge was dropped. In the end, however, the funds he managed to smuggle into the United States and could not explain resulted in guilty pleas on September 25, 1945, to charges of trading with the enemy (sending two postcards to German mail drops) and violating the government's order of freezing funds ($15,000) in which Germany had an interest. For these acts he was sentenced to five years in prison.[47]

As for Costes, he quietly sailed alone for France the following month while his wife moved on to Hollywood to live with Ratoff. The two would marry four years later after his divorce from his first wife, the actress Eugenie Leontovich.[48] A year and a half later on June 26, 1947, Costes was arrested by French military authorities at his Paris home and charged with collaborating with the Germans before his dispatch to America. After a two-year imprisonment and a lengthy trial, he was acquitted of treason, having convinced the court that his collaboration was simply a ploy to escape from France in order to betray the Germans as an FBI double agent. Costes remained in France, living quietly in Paris for the next twenty-five years until his death at the age of eighty on May 19, 1973. He is buried at the Cemetaire du Passy in Paris.[49]

CHAPTER FIFTEEN

Koehler

As Arthur Thurston arrived in London and Dusko Popov left New York for Spain in November 1942, an Abwehr agent code-named "Koehler" was dispatched to the United States on an espionage mission with the following instructions contained in a microdot:

> American scientists are working on atom-smashing uranium. Stages of these requirements important for us. Names of professors are: Prof. FERMI, PUPIN PHYSICS LABORATORY, COLUMBIA UNIVRSITY, NEW YORK CITY is an Italian emigrant. Prof. DEYBE [*sic*] Dutch emigrant, formerly director of KAISER WILHELM INSTITUTE BERLIN, address unknown, probably New York, however. Prof. LAWRENCE, address unknown. Koehler should make contacts very carefully, through a third person whenever possible, without mentioning the purpose for the time being. As soon as radio connections are established he will receive definite instructions and questions in this matter from here.[1]

Koehler's real name was Alfred Meiler. He was a Jew, born on October 1, 1891, in the ancient city of Nijmegen, Holland, near the German border. Together with his two older brothers, Paul and Max, he spent his younger years in Amsterdam working in the family business selling electrical supplies. When the First World War broke out, he supplemented his income serving the ever-watchful Dutch police as a double agent against the belligerents who were using neutral Holland as a center of espionage. Meiler first volunteered to the French, and after they turned him down he walked into the German embassy, where his services were eagerly accepted. Throughout the war they paid him two hundred guilders a week for low-level information he cleared through Captain Boallard, a Dutch counterintelligence officer posing as a journalist.[2] In 1919 he received an award of sorts from the Dutch government for his wartime service when his eighteen-month prison sentence for theft was reduced to six in consideration of his counterespionage work. In the early 1920s he joined the Catholic Church before marrying

Elizabeth Nathan in 1925 in a Jewish ceremony in Munich, Germany. The couple then settled down, with Alfred following in the family tradition and opening Venlo-Meiler, a small electric shop in Venlo, Holland, which he operated until 1941.

During the late 1920s he became active in right-wing politics, joining the Dutch Nazi Party in 1932 and later becoming a trustee for the Schulverein, the German Language School Society in Holland (Meiler was fluent in Dutch, English, and German). During the 1930s as Nazi antisemitism grew, Meiler resigned or was expelled from the Schulverein, probably because of his wife's (and secretly his own) Jewish background.[3] While working for the German Language School Society he befriended Udo von Bonin, an influential Nazi and head of the Abwehr Abstelle in Amsterdam who later became the head of German intelligence in France. Hoover's men were all too familiar with von Bonin, having been embarrassed by him just four years earlier following the espionage arrest in February 1938 of an American army deserter named Gunther Rumrich. Von Bonin was a key figure in the ring, traversing the Atlantic from America to Germany armed with intelligence information while providing his American agents money and instructions. Following Rumrich's arrest, von Bonin quickly fled the United States for Germany while under FBI investigation. In the summer of 1940, with German troops in control of Holland, Meiler approached his old friend von Bonin for help in fleeing to a neutral country. Von Bonin agreed to his safe passage in exchange for an agreement to spy for the Abwehr. Meiler had few options. His parents were deceased but he still had two brothers living in Holland who could be forced to serve as hostages in exchange for his loyalty. As for his wife, she had no one in Europe but did have extended family living in the New York City area. Facing little choice, Meiler began basic agent training in The Hague at the end of 1940 under von Bonin's direction and later in Paris, where he lived at the Hotel Bristol while taking advanced espionage courses at Abwehr headquarters in the Hotel Lutetia. With his education complete and a new German passport in the name of Alfred Koehler to ease cross-border travel, he returned to Venlo where he sold his business, settled his affairs, collected Elizabeth, and then returned to Paris to await his assignment.[4]

In January 1942 the Meilers left Paris bound for Madrid, where they were instructed to book ship passage for Argentina. Having secured travel visas through von Bonin at the Spanish embassy in Paris, Meiler and his wife made their way across the Spanish border at Irun-Hendaya, where a waiting Abwehr agent took back their German documents and replaced them with their original Dutch passports in their true names. While the facts are still unknown today, it seems likely that the Meilers dithered in Madrid for three months before executing their plan to seek sanctuary in the United States. After supposedly failing in their attempts to get a ship for South America as ordered, the couple reported their plight to the Free Dutch consulate, expressing interest in working for American authorities in the United States.[5] Following a series of cables between Madrid and Washington, the Meilers received U.S. visas and tickets for the *Guine,* which departed for America from Lisbon on May 5, 1942. A month later the ship was spotted off the coast of Florida by the Coast Guard, which took custody of the vessel and escorted it into New Smyrna Beach, Florida, for inspection. Under questioning in Sunny South Hospital and Sanitarium, where he was admitted for pneumonia and typhoid, Meiler told his complete story to ONI officers who then turned him over to FBI agents.[6] After a month, his condition improved sufficiently for travel to New York under FBI escort, where he was ensconced in a suite at the Hotel Mayflower to continue his recovery and begin plans for his new life as a wartime double agent.[7]

One piece of information that Meiler mentioned to agents was a newspaper article that he read while hospitalized, about the recent FBI arrest of Herbert Karl Friedrich Bahr on charges of espionage. Meiler believed that Bahr was identical to a young man he had observed acting suspiciously on the train from Madrid to Lisbon. Through conversations he learned that the stranger was an American who had attended a technical school in Germany and spoke fluent German. Later, after identifying a photo of Bahr as the stranger on the train, he described another encounter with him in Madrid, this time in the company of a young Swiss woman named "Siegfried" who was en route to America to marry an unknown "German Jew residing in Chicago."[8] Later in Lisbon their paths crossed again with Bahr, who was in the company of another woman named "Mrs. Krieger," an American returning to the United States after a lengthy assignment at the American embassy in Madrid.[9]

Meiler's one-on-one training in The Hague focused on shortwave radio construction, communication, and secret writing. What must have unnerved his FBI interrogators were a description and a brief conversation with a Dutch sailor, possibly from The Hague, who was also receiving instruction in the building where he was studying. Over a glass of beer one evening the man told Meiler that he would soon leave for America to

Benson House. The house as it appears today, overlooking Long Island Sound in a secluded section of Wading River, New York. FBI technicians used it as a radio plant to send and receive double-agent messages with Hamburg, Germany, from January 1942 to May 1945. The house and surrounding property are currently owned by the Episcopal Diocese of Long Island. *Episcopal Diocese of Long Island*

coordinate "short-wave radio activities from New York to Europe." Aside from his physical description, Meiler could offer no further information about him. During his training he learned of a large radio receiving and transmission station on the seventh floor of the Hotel Lutetia that communicated with a ring in West Africa code-named "Pila."[10] If sent to Argentina, he was to set his radio and correspond with Pila on a scheduled basis.

Upon arrival in New York, he sent a letter on August 10, 1942, to a mail drop at the Hotel Continental in San Sebastian, Spain, reporting his safe arrival. Over the next two months efforts focused on Meiler's physical recovery, analysis of his instructions, and repeated questioning about his background, which included cross-checking his tale against diaries, letters, and telephone books (including the name of a woman he casually romanced behind his wife's back in Spain) confiscated by the U.S. Customs Service when he arrived in Florida.[11]

Within weeks another radio transmitter was installed at Benson House, with radio operator Samuel O. Smith assigned to simulate Meiler's transmissions. To make his story more believable he later told the Germans about a close friend working for General Electric who could arrange for the purchase of necessary parts for the radio. The Abwehr had issued him a copy of a Dutch bible and the Dutch national anthem, "Wilhelmus," for use in encoding and decoding his messages. Pressure grew quickly to activate Meiler's radio, as the Germans planned to begin contacting him in early July. Evidence soon mounted that the Paris station was trying to contact him when the Canadian Monitoring Service in July, then the Coast Guard in August, and later the FBI's Clinton station began intercepting radio signals using his call sign L.L.U. on 14,180 kilocycles. Meiler cautioned the FBI that the Paris radio operators knew his keying style and that he typed a maximum of eighty letters a minute. Careful not to arouse suspicions, Meiler's fisting technique was recorded by the FBI for study by Smith, now assigned to Wading River.[12]

"Fermi" in Meiler's microphotograph was Enrico Fermi, a forty-one-year-old Italian born in Rome on September 29, 1901. After graduating with honors in mathematics and physics from the University of Pisa at the age of twenty-five, he joined the faculty of the University of Rome as a full professor of theoretical physics. Eight years later he leaped onto the world stage when he developed what one biographer called the "major theoretical work of his life," a quantitative theory for beta decay, the nucleus's creation and expulsion of high-energy electrons in the course of radioactive change. Life for Fermi during the 1930s was a blend of teaching mixed with international conferences and meetings throughout Europe and America, where the world's leading physicists exchanged ideas about the exciting new field of atomic physics. In 1935, for instance, he participated in a summer program at the University of Michigan and later taught thermodynamics at Columbia University.[13]

By the second half of the 1930s Fermi's world experienced dramatic changes with the growth of fascism and the increasing threat to his family from Mussolini's new racial laws. Fermi and his wife, Laura, had two children. While the threat to their children was minimal because Fermi was Catholic, his wife was in danger because of her Jewish background. In 1938 the family traveled to Stockholm where he accepted the Nobel Prize and then stunned the world by resettling in America after accepting a professorship at Columbia University. In the winter of 1942 he left Columbia for the

University of Chicago, where he devoted himself to the creation of an atomic weapon. Later that year he and his staff produced the first nuclear reactor, known as Chicago Pile-1, which went critical for the first time on December 1, 1942—less than six months after Koehler's arrival in the United States.[14]

"Lawrence" was Ernest Orlando Lawrence, a full professor of physics at the University of California, Berkeley. The forty-one-year-old South Dakota native, the son of a school superintendent and a teachers college president, began teaching at Berkeley after receiving his doctorate in physics at Yale University. In 1939 he was awarded the Nobel Prize for his 1929 invention of the cyclotron, the first particle accelerator to achieve high energies. Due to wartime conditions in Europe, the prize was awarded to him by the Swedish consul general in February 1940 at a ceremony on the University of California campus. When America entered the war, Lawrence, like hundreds of other American physicists and engineers, plunged into war work; his radiation laboratory, known as the "Rad Lab," became a major center for atomic research.[15]

Unlike Fermi and Lawrence, Abwehr interest in "Deybe" was grounded on firsthand information about him and his past. Born Josephus Wilhelmus Debije in 1884 at Maastricht, Holland, he was always referred to as Peter Debye. After receiving a doctorate in physics in 1908 at the University of Munich, he taught chemistry and physics throughout Europe before his appointment as the new head of the Kaiser Wilhelm Institute of Physics (KWI), which opened in Berlin in 1938 with funds provided by the Rockefeller Foundation. In 1936 Debye won his own Nobel Prize in chemistry for his investigations of X-rays and light scattering in gases. Over the next two years, as Hilter continued to gobble up larger chunks of Europe, pressure mounted on Debye to defend the institute's independence from increasing Nazi military encroachment. Complicating his difficulties were his behind-the-scenes efforts to help his many Jewish colleagues escape from Germany while fending off government insistence that he renounce his Dutch citizenship and become a naturalized German. By the end of 1939 Debye decided to emigrate to America, privately explaining to Warren Weaver, a Rockefeller Foundation official, that the army had taken over the KWI for research into the construction of an "irresistible offensive weapon." Following his arrival in the United States, ostensibly to take a temporary teaching position at Cornell University, Debye supplied U.S. authorities with full details of the work then underway on atomic research in Germany.[16]

The Abwehr wrongly believed that Debye's international prestige as a

Nobel Prize winner and former head of KWI would naturally place him among the top rungs of the scientists working on an atomic weapon. Faced with OSRD's absolute refusal to authorize ND98 to pass any atomic research intelligence to the Abwehr, the FBI sought to stall them by describing the airtight security surrounding America's weapons programs. In a February 3, 1943, message Meiler described the handicaps posed by military security regimens in place, adding that a "foreigner," particularly with his "accent," made it "dangerous to make contacts and secure information." To soften the blow he boasted of his success at having located Debye, noting that he was not at Columbia as the Nazis suspected but at Cornell in rural New York, hours away from Manhattan, thus making contact "for the time being . . . impossible."[17] Eight days later Hamburg signaled its favorable assessment of Meiler's work: "Uncle is highly pleased. He declares his approbations and well wishes." Then in a warning that surely eased FBI anxieties, the Abwehr instructed Meiler to "henceforth please use caution and discretion in fulfilling assigned tasks." On February 21, 1943, while U.S. and British troops fought their way into Tunisia to trap Rommel's Afrika Corp, Hamburg signaled Meiler again to "put off contact with DeBye until you yourself feel safe" and refocus attention to the Allies' next move. "At this time the landing intentions of Americans in Europe is important. We desire information as to the strength and time element together with the source of your information."[18]

Over the next two months Hamburg urged Meiler to secure employment that would offer him "as much freedom as possible" to pursue anything that could glean insights into American war plans. His radio messages were laced with complaints about Abwehr's insensitivity to the danger he faced, as evidenced by their occasional failure to respond to radio messages: "I succeeded in establishing contact with you after much effort, danger and expense. Your seeming lack of interest discourages me. If you have no interest in the matter advise me so that I will no longer endanger myself needlessly." Three days later Hamburg apologized, explaining that his work "is important and gratefully acknowledged"; to reduce his risk they proposed limiting his transmissions to once a week. Next he explained that opening an electric shop was out of the question due to acute shortages of electrical products, which were being diverted for war use. Instead, he had started studying diamond cutting, which he hoped would lead to opening a business that would give him ample time for espionage. Hamburg agreed, noting that while studying he should seek out information from public sources such as journals, magazines, and the daily press. "We are interested in all details about new equipment and methods for directional finding of ships, U-Boats and airplanes." Included in the message was a list of seven technical magazines such as *Aeronautics, Electrical Engineering, Flying* and *Aero Progress,* which they encouraged him to read for useful intelligence.[19]

By May 1943 the FBI began ramping up pressure on the Abwehr in the hope of drawing out other agents, either in the Western Hemisphere or luring them from Europe. Meiler constantly pestered Germany for funds, complaining about living and travel expenses, lessons to improve his English, his diamond-cutting course, and the purchase of the radio equipment. After cushioning his demands with a description of radar as "ultra-high frequency radio waves to determine the location of U-Boats, planes, and ships," he insisted on $2,000 to ease his financial straits and make it easier to continue uninterrupted espionage. Radar information struck a nerve with German naval officials, who were suffering appalling submarine losses in the Atlantic after so much success against Allied shipping just a year earlier. Within days they were demanding answers about the use of infrared for locating large submarines and anti-submarine apparatuses "based on telescopic systems." American war planners learned how desperate the German navy had become when the Germans insisted that the "importance" of this information "is great as well as the faith of Uncle (Abwehr) in you and your proficiency." Concerning his money: "Uncle will do everything to back you up. All friends wish you a happy Pentecost especially your faithful Uncle."[20]

During the Second World War, New York City was the epicenter for war production, ship building, and port facilities. The New York Naval Shipyard, universally known as the Brooklyn Navy Yard, was the largest warship facility in the world, employing more than 100,000 people. Brooklyn was also the headquarters for both the Brewster and Todd shipyards, where workers toiled around the clock building transports and tankers. Just across the East River in Manhattan, where the Norden Company on Lafayette Street was turning out thousands of secret bombsights, ship captains regularly assembled at Battery Place for intelligence briefings on the submarine menace they would face just days later in the Atlantic. Over the course of the war more than 1,400 convoys with troops and equipment would sail to Europe and the Mediterranean from New York. The war also pivoted thousands of companies away from everyday consumer manufacturing to making unconventional items for military use. In Brooklyn, the Charles Pfizer Company began producing tens of thousands of penicillin vials; in Staten Island, the S.S. White Dental Company turned from dental instruments to manufacturing tachometer needles; while the venerable Steinway & Company did its part for the war effort by redirecting its piano craftsmen to producing glider wings.[21]

Like the Mosquera channel, the JSC/LCS also used Meiler's radio for deception, starting in the summer with the support of Cockade. In July 1943 he sprinkled demands for funds to buy diamond-cutting equipment with a report from a "business acquaintance" that his son, trained in mountain warfare, had shipped out to Iceland with his unit. Hamburg immediately expressed "many thanks for the valuable information," insisting on more details about the port and date of his departure for Iceland and where he was trained. A week later Meiler reported that he was assigned to the 29th Division, which left for Iceland in July and had trained as some type of specialist in the "North-eastern part of the country." Through casual eavesdropping "on subway" between two army officers, he learned "that recently a large number of gliders have been shipped from the U.S. to the United Kingdom." Building on these tidbits about troop movements to Iceland and gliders to England, he next described a group of Brooklyn Navy Yard workers grumbling about a sudden spike in security that required special permits for movement in certain areas. Days later the Germans sent a panicky reply, asking him how this new regimen would impact his spying: "Can you now observe outgoing ship traffic in the Harbor or secure reliable information with time element concerning this." Meiler warned that the situation in New York was grave and becoming more ominous following the recent FBI arrest of two German spies, making movement around the navy yard increasingly dangerous: "Harbor regulations here are becoming more severe each day, and one needs a special permit to be in this area. If I were found by authorities and questioned it could spoil everything." Meiler, again cautioned to be careful, was told to pay attention as he made his way through New York City streets for army vehicles of all types, recording the number and letter designations on the bumpers and fenders. Starting in October 1943, Benson House began filling the airwaves with streams of numbers both real and fictitious in support of Morgan's camouflage and the Cockade lie: "Here are additional numbers of Army motor vehicles observed in New York City on Nov. 7th 4305855, 3129688, W229839, MVP770, 113772."[22] Throughout the fall Abwehr interest also focused on U.S. ship-building statistics for 1944: "Instigate further investigation concerning 'son' known USA ship building program 1944 includes 1036 Victory ships. Newspaper information advised that 350 turbines will be on hand in 1944 for these ships."[23]

In January 1944, with all eyes now focused on the invasion of Europe, Meiler, like Mosquera and all British Double Cross agents, was redirected toward the Fortitude deception. While Mosquera contributed his support to the myth of Fortitude South and the imaginary First U.S. Army Group (FUSAG) poised to invade the Pas de Calais, Meiler bolstered Fortitude North, the Allied scheme to convince the Abwehr of an imaginary Fourth British Army based in the Scottish highlands poised to strike against German forces somewhere along the coast of Norway, Denmark, or southern Sweden or possibly link up with Russian forces in the Baltic region. British intelligence had reason to suppose that the Germans already believed three things: first, that the Fourth Army existed or at any rate existed in the autumn of 1943 as an offshoot of Scottish Command with its headquarters near Edinburgh; second, that the 52nd Lowland Division was in eastern Scotland, a myth fed to them by British controlled agents and intercepted by their own wireless service; and, third, that the 55th United States Division was in Iceland, a lie supported in the autumn of 1943 by Meiler and reinforced by MI6 double agents COBWEB and BEETLE, both in Iceland.[24] Adding to German confusion was a JSC/LCS inspired message that Meiler sent on March 3, 1944, briefly describing a conversation he heard in a Manhattan bar on February 27 among a group of officers who were "drinking and conversing quite loudly." In reply to a joking remark about service in Iceland, one officer cautioned his buddies not to "laugh too soon." Meiler described their shoulder patches as a "five sided blue and gold device of a kind I had never seen before." In fact, the shoulder patch was the emblem of the 55th Infantry Division, an imaginary unit that would become part of the Fourth Army's order of battle. He concluded that this same officer warned that because "it is entirely possible that some of them [55th Division troops] might also be sent there as prior to his departure housing facilities were being prepared for a large number of troops."[25]

Ten days later, after applauding Meiler for spotting this "five cornered emblem," Hamburg urged him to look for more shoulder patches along with any information about the shipment of troops "in the direction of Europe." Over the next three months in the lead-up to the Normandy invasion, Meiler bombarded Hamburg with an wide assortment of intelligence details. On March 17, supporting an earlier Mosquera message, he reported a conversation with a friend who visited a Kansas military base where B-29 crews with considerable experience operating heavy bombers were wearing campaign ribbons from the European and African campaigns. Another, designed to confuse the Germans about the date of the invasion, offered details about labor strikes involving 3,000 workers at a Detroit plant producing landing craft.[26] On May 26 his visit to local hotels and clubs led to conversations with American GIs on "embarkation leave" who were fairly closed-mouthed but did reveal that they had to be "back at their respective camps on or before June first." Meiler apologized for his failure to obtain the place, date of departure, and destination, explaining that even the troops are kept in the dark regarding such details. Four days later, again on the subway sitting next to two British merchant seamen, he learned that the massive French ocean liner *Ile de France,* in service as a troop transport, was sitting idle at the Brooklyn Navy Yard despite its having been ready to sail for a number of weeks.[27]

At the end of June as Allied troops struggled to break out of Normandy, Meiler continued pitching his lies about a second invasion with a new round of shoulder patch sightings. One was a "green round badge with a white wolf on it," symbolizing the 104th Infantry Division, the "Timberwolves," which left New York on August 27 and entered the fight in Europe two months later. In July he sent a JSC message describing the alarming growth of combat troops in New York certain they would soon be going overseas. Others included the badge of the III Corp, Second U.S. Army, and the 92nd Division.[28] In August, as American GIs streamed across France, Meiler sent a JSC message reporting Allied troop losses as very light compared to large numbers of German casualties and considering the large scale of the operation. The Abwehr offered their thanks along with continued demands for more information.[29]

In September 1944 Meiler introduced the Germans to a new imaginary source named Holtz, a worker at the Brooklyn Navy Yard whose greed, spending habits, and desperate need for money made him ideal as a "good source of information" on ship movements. Within weeks Benson House began sending a flood of Holtz-inspired intelligence on all matter of naval information. Illustrative of his work were U.S. Merchant Marine statistics calculating a total inventory of more than 3,400 ships with a cargo capacity of 35 million tons along with a report that repairs on the troop ship *Normandie* berthed at the Todd Shipyards had been discontinued.[30]

The Abwehr's ability to pay British and U.S. Double Cross agents was always difficult during the war due to the Bletchley Park wizards, the aggressive work of MI5, censorship, tight travel restrictions, and extremely long distances, making the delivery of funds to America even more problematic. As the European war entered its fourth year, routine civilian travel across the Atlantic became impossible, with all aircraft and shipping devoted to high-priority military personnel and cargo. Neutral ships from Portugal and Spain still sailing to the Western Hemisphere underwent close scrutiny from British counterintelligence and from U.S. authorities once they arrived in U.S. ports. Careful questioning of travelers often led to denial of entry to the United States or worse if their answers proved questionable. The same was true for money transfers from Europe to American banks. No spy could simply walk into a bank and withdraw transferred funds from his account.[31]

This was the situation in the summer of 1943 when Benson House received an Abwehr message assuring Meiler that they were desperately trying to send him funds, not in cash, check, or wire transfer, but rather in the form of postage stamps he could convert to cash. Over a seven-month period between September 1943 and March 1944 as the Allies prepared for the European invasion, Hamburg radioed a series of conflicting messages assuring him that stamps were on the way, that they had been shipped either directly to him from Spain or Portugal or through a South American city, but at the same time asking Meiler for a secure post office box where he could receive mail. In the end, despite his fury he received nothing.[32]

On March 3, 1944, after receiving all these mixed messages about money and stamps, Meiler was instructed to expect jewelry instead. His German bosses radioed that they "have a chance of bringing to you men's jewelry by a trustworthy person probably in March. Suggest a ring and tie pin." Next they asked him for the identity of a trusted contact who could handle the transfer. Before he could respond he received another series of messages informing him that the exchange would take place "in your country" and he was to introduce himself to the contact man only as "Koopman" working for a business called "Kornfeld Fox Film." Shortly after this radio message he received another instructing him to contact Maurice Van Gelder, owner of Biological Raw Products Company at 415 Lexington Avenue in New York, for the jewelry.[33]

The fifty-two-year-old Van Gelder was a Dutch citizen and a Jew, born on August 3, 1892, in Harlingen, a small fishing and shipping village in northern Holland. His father died in 1920; he had no idea about the fate of his eighty-three-year-old mother, Eva Van Messel, at the hands of the

Nazis. He later told the FBI that relatives in neutral countries had learned of her arrest and murder by the Germans.[34] Van Gelder's decision to leave Holland grew out of his many travels throughout Europe during the late 1930s, which convinced him that war was coming and would force him to turn to the United States to ensure his family's safety. Together with his wife, Caroline, also a Dutch citizen, born in Tilburg, Holland, in 1894, and his three children he fled Europe, arriving in New York on November 6, 1939, just two months after the German invasion of Poland. The Van Gelders' two older children were doing war work, with the daughter assigned as an editor on South African affairs for the Office of War Information and the son serving as a radio operator for the Dutch air force somewhere in the Pacific. The youngest child, also a son, was still in school and living at the family home on 230 Rockingham Avenue in Larchmont, New York.[35]

In Holland he had owned G. Van Gelder and Company, an Amsterdam-based import-export company with his partner, Erich Pintus, a German Jew from Berlin, who he believed was murdered by the Germans along with his wife and children. Van Gelder's share of the company when liquidated amounted to $25,000 ($413,000 in 2012), which he later used for ship passage, housing, and establishment of his current business.[36]

When Meiler, posing as Koopman, first telephoned Van Gelder on May 10, 1944, with the German-supplied cover story, the bewildered Van Gelder had no idea what he was talking about and turned him away. Meiler quickly radioed his fury to Hamburg, accusing them of foolishly placing him in jeopardy, threatening to end his service to the Fatherland, and demanding answers. As Allied soldiers stormed the beaches of Normandy on June 6, 1944, the Abwehr offered desperate apologies for the confusion while speculating that Van Gelder's instructions, which left Lisbon on a "neutral ship" in April, probably had not yet arrived: "Van G does not know your position. He only has instructions from a friend to pay Koopman. In as much as the route is long, these instructions probably have not yet reached him. Friend will repeat instruction telegraphically next week." Meiler was then urged to be patient and "wait quietly now until we confirm." Within weeks the authorization for Van Gelder to pay him had been confirmed and Hamburg radioed him to retrieve the funds.[37]

The FBI had a unique advantage at this point as Meiler had never met Van Gelder. On June 12, 1944, Meiler, using the name Koopman, again telephoned Van Gelder, who acknowledged having the funds that he would supply to Meiler's acquaintance as his work schedule prohibited a personal meeting. The conversation also confirmed Hamburg's warnings that Van Gelder, who knew nothing about "Koopman's espionage, was performing a business related service." Special Agent Carter Evans Jones, a four-year FBI veteran who had previously lived in Holland and spoke Dutch, was chosen to pose as John Lugt, Meiler's friend. By the time Jones and Van Gelder met, FBI agents, probably through a mail cover, had confirmed Van Gelder's receipt of the payment authorization from a person named Israel Van Messel who lived at the Hotel Ritz in Barcelona, Spain. On June 16, 1944, Jones met Van Gelder at his office, where he received $2,000 ($26,000 in 2012) for his friend Koopman.[38]

Later investigation revealed that Van Gelder's actual involvement in this case started in November 1943 when he began receiving postcards and letters from Israel (possibly Isador; Van Gelder couldn't recall the correct name) Van Messel, his first cousin, known as "Is" or "Izzy," whom he had not seen for more than a decade. Van Gelder, who cooperated fully with FBI agents, claimed that Van Messel lived in Barcelona, worked in the wine business, and talked about his parents' delicate health and his fear for his wife and children still living in southern France under German control. Van Messel next suggested the possibility of a business partnership with Van Gelder, claiming that a contact in Venezuela who owed him $3,000 would forward funds to Van Gelder to hold for Van Messel. Van Gelder agreed to help but never received any funds. In the spring of 1944 Van Messel wired him that a coffee firm called Machado Company at 115 Broad Street in New York would provide him with the funds and additional instructions for him to pay $2,000 to a man named Koopman. Van Gelder knew of no purpose for the additional $1,000, denied any previous knowledge of Koopman, Lugt, or Machado, and he did not know of anyone else who was to receive funds from Van Messel.[39]

Adding to this already murky story of intrigue and money transfers was information from the FBI's London office that the Free French had actually recruited Israel Van Messel, then living in Barcelona, as a double agent against the Germans based on his romantic relationship with a woman then in French hands in Algiers. When questioned, Van Messel told the French that his Abwehr bosses in Paris had ordered him to arrange the transfer of funds to his unwitting cousin, Maurice, in New York for passage to someone described only as "Jan Koopman." MI5 also supplied Van Messel's personnel file, which was forwarded to Washington.[40]

The Van Messel file revealed the identity of another Dutchman named

Jan Letch who had recently walked into the American embassy in Madrid offering his services to the British. Letch, who would soon become "Mike," the central figure in the FBI's MICASE, had been originally dispatched from Paris by the Germans to carry the jewelry for payment to Meiler. After learning his story the FBI agreed to use him as a double agent, arranged for his travel to the United States, and, after his arrival in New York in November 1944, learned that his assignment was to pose as a film company executive (for Kornfeld Fox Films) carrying two pieces of jewelry for a German agent named Alfred Meiler. Feigning ignorance of anyone named Meiler and wanting to confirm Letch's trustworthiness, FBI agents instructed him to keep his rendezvous with Meiler in the lobby of New York's Astor Hotel. The actual encounter was almost farcical when an FBI agent, posing as Meiler, gave Letch the agreed-upon password, grabbed the jewels, and then disappeared into the street with hardly a word spoken between them. When the nonplussed Letch returned to the FBI in failure, agents consoled him with assurances that he had done well and that sometimes "these are the breaks of the game." The operation was in fact a success. The jewelry, a stick-pin and brooch worth about $2,000, were now in FBI custody, as was the $2,000 in cash that Van Gelder had given to Lugt. Weeks later Benson House radioed to Hamburg that Meiler had gotten a "trustworthy person to get the jewelry from L and have it in my possession."[41]

Beginning in January 1945, Meiler turned his attention toward the war in the Pacific. Sprinkled with new demands for funds he began supplying intelligence which JSC hoped would go to the Japanese. Until Hamburg was overrun by British forces in May 1945, the Germans continued their unquestioning acceptance of reports from Meiler's imaginary subagent Holtz and two new equally fictitious sources, "Otto" and "Herman," working along the East Coast. Holtz, who had turned into an essential source for the Germans, was now reporting shocking data on the accelerated construction pace of the *Kearsarge, Oriskany,* and *Reprisal,* three new aircraft carriers at the Brooklyn Navy Yard, and the new *Coral Sea* and *Midway* at Norfolk, Virginia. Otto and Herman, who seemed to be everywhere, reported on repairs of the light cruiser *Marblehead,* the planned construction of two new Essex class carriers 850 feet in length and capable of carrying fighters, dive bombers, and torpedo bombers, and the carrier *Bon Homme Richard* in Bayonne, New Jersey, with engine problems. At the Philadelphia Navy Yard they spotted the aircraft carriers *Antietam, Princeton, Guam,* and *Midway,* the cruisers *Chicago* and *Los Angeles,* seven submarines along with five old destroyers recently returned by the British, and the cruiser *Atlanta*, which was then in the final stages of readiness for a late march departure "to join the fleet in the Pacific." In addition to naval intelligence, the Germans also learned that the 119th Infantry Division (a ghost division that never existed) had recently returned from Alaska. A close friend of Holtz who had visited San Francisco was amazed at seeing dock areas filled with ships loading and unloading while hundreds of others idled in the harbor because of "insufficient space." Walking near one dock area, Holtz's source could hardly move due to "street stacked so high with jeeps, tanks, motors and other supplies." Hamburg appreciated Holtz's information and was eager to keep him in play. Even in the closing days of the war, one FBI agent reported that "Germany was insisting that when Holtz travels he should look around for further friends who can furnish him information and should set up a means of communication with them." Recognizing his value, the FBI continued to use him to wheedle money out of the Germans. "He is doing good work for us," Meiler reported, but "I must take care of him and as you know it costs money to operate."[42]

Like Mosquera, the Germans maintained complete faith in Meiler until the very end. On April 24, 1945, he gloomily concluded that "although things do not look so good I think, I can assume that Uncle knows that I am not one of those people who do not keep their promises. I'll hold out until the last moment . . . but as I advised you before I need funds."[43] A week before the Germans surrendered, Hamburg sent a final heartfelt message to its loyal and courageous source: "Because of present situation we must consider the temporary disruption of our connection. Uncle will protect your interests in the future as before and will care for you. He thanks you many times for that which you have done up to present time."[44]

CHAPTER SIXTEEN

Peasant

In the months before the start of the war in Europe, Admiral Wilhelm Canaris, the head of the Abwehr, completed the reorganization of his service on October 18, 1939. The new structure consisted of three main branches covering all aspects of intelligence. Branch I, the largest unit, conducted foreign espionage through a vast network of outposts scattered throughout various enemy areas in Europe. Next was Branch II, which focused on sabotage, and Branch III, the Abwehr's counterintelligence apparatus. Branch I had seven espionage groups, two of which were assigned to specific areas: IH Ost and IH Oest (I army east and west). The other five chased military technical intelligence with designations such as IHt (responsible for army technical matters), IL (the Luftwaffe), and IM (naval intelligence).[1]

In November 1941 IM officers at the Abwehr's Netherlands field outpost recruited an agent whom they planned to send to the Western Hemisphere on a mission to set up a wireless radio for transmission of military information to Germany. Following espionage training, the agent left Bremen accompanied by two officers who took him across France and over the Pyrenees Mountains, crossing the Spanish border in the trunk of a car. After a night in a local hotel he pressed on across Spain to the little town of San Sebastian on the Portuguese border, where he discovered that the guide assigned to take him the rest of the way had been arrested by Spanish police for smuggling. After two idle weeks in Madrid he set out again, this time with a new guide who spirited him across the Portuguese frontier near the border village of Guarda. On May 28, 1943, both men quietly boarded a train for Lisbon where another Abwehr contact returned his Dutch passport, together with $5,000 ($66,000 in 2012) in exchange for a receipt he signed using his new code name—Muth.[2]

Later, certain that he was alone, Muth made his way to the Dutch consulate where he told his story to Neils Gestramus, a Dutch security official. Within hours he was in the hands of MI6's John de Sallis, who had him signal his successful contact with Dutch officials and their offer of a consular position in Argentina. Until he reached South America he would communicate by secret ink letters, adding that his new assignment first required a detour to England to apply for his Argentine visa. Ten days later, Muth was in London undergoing MI5 interrogation.[3]

Muth was a Dutch Jew, born Hellmuth Siegfried Goldschmidt on January 3, 1895, in Groningen, Holland. The record of his early years is obscure. His parents divorced when he was a child; he attended school in Wiesbaden, Germany, and lived for a time in Munich with his stepfather, a German named Augustus Blum. For eight months in 1913 he attended Oxford University before returning to Holland, where he joined the army as a junior officer and later studied law at the University of Leiden. For the next twenty years he traveled the world off and on, developing fluency in English, Spanish, German, and French while working as a finance inspector in the Dutch East Indies; a roustabout; a clerk in Tulsa, Oklahoma, with the Royal Dutch Shell Company; and another clerk job in The Hague and Colombia, South America, with the International Trading Consortium.[4] While his work performance records are scant, some insight can be gathered from the mixed reviews he received during his two years with Shell Oil in Tulsa. When he first started with Shell a company official described his "mental training" as "very good." He had traveled "far and wide, is a likeable gentleman and should prove satisfactory to everyone in connection with this work." A year later he was fired after expressing no "interest in accounting or detail work," still owing the company $130 with no indication of any repayment.[5] By April 1939, as war clouds once again darkened Europe, Goldschmidt was back in Holland mobilizing into a Dutch air regiment and then the cavalry on the headquarters staff of the 4th Hussars in Ede, where he served until his desertion in the wake of the German invasion of Holland in May 1940.

His introduction into espionage began a year later while living quietly in southern Holland when he ran across an old friend and business colleague named Mathias Janssen. The two men first met in 1932 when they formed a brief business partnership selling gold extracted from metals using a special apparatus invented by Janssen. Goldschmidt soon learned that Janssen had survived the First World War by smuggling rubber from Holland to Germany and planned to make it through the present conflict by conducting "economic espionage" for the Abwehr.[6] Goldschmidt later told MI5 interrogators that he was initially skeptical of his friend's boasts until one day, when both were stopped by German police, Janssen produced papers allowing them to proceed without interference. Their friendship eventually led to

Goldschmidt's introduction to some Abwehr officers who turned him down for intelligence work after learning of his Jewish background. Undeterred, Janssen turned to the Abwehr's Netherlands Abstelle, which recruited him to spy for Branch I M (Marine).[7]

Following his acceptance as a source, he underwent an extensive series of interviews concentrating on his many travels, with particular emphasis on his activities in North and South America, his work for Shell Oil, people he met, and his chances of finding useful work offering access to valuable intelligence in the Western Hemisphere. After aptitude testing for a foreign espionage assignment, he moved to Bremen for a concentrated course of study on secret writing, codes and ciphers, radio systems, and the complexities of international radio communications. Day after day, for hours on end, he tapped out encrypted messages in Morse code while practicing cipher techniques using special books filled with lists of numbers and letters that his instructors later critiqued. Branch I M officers quizzed him on the identification of Allied ships by displaying seemingly countless photographs of British and American vessels.

Never far from Goldschmidt's mind was the growing desperation of Holland's Jews at the hands of their German occupiers. Ever eager to ingratiate himself with his new masters and fully aware of the fatal consequences that awaited him if he failed his training, Goldschmidt worked especially hard, even going so far as to suggest ideas for improved Abwehr intelligence collection. In one case he described an old friend from his days in Colombia named Max Gertz as a potentially useful source. Gertz, born in Colombia to German parents, served in the kaiser's army during the First World War and remained loyal to Hitler and the Nazi cause after returning to South America. The greedy Gertz, he told his tutors, was the port captain at Baranquilla who would take payoffs for valuable shipping data, which he could then send to Germany. When his bosses expressed no interest, Goldschmidt concluded that the Abwehr was already in contact with him.[8]

In August 1943, while Goldschmidt was still in Portugal, MI5 officers briefed Arthur Thurston about him and his willingness to assist the Allies as a double agent either in Latin America or the United States. They cautioned him, however, that the MI6 station in Lisbon had some doubts about Abwehr commitment to the case based on how loosely they handled him, raising some questions about his potential value as a double agent.[9] Since arriving in Spain in May 1943 he still had acquired no radio. His secret writing capabilities were primitive, correspondence with Portugal was

W. Mark Felt. FBI agent who supervised the Peasant case. Six decades later he would reveal himself as "Deep Throat," journalist Bob Woodward's Watergate source. *FBI*

unpredictable, and there was no guarantee that his letters would ever reach the Germans.[10]

After interviewing Goldschmidt and satisfying himself as to his truthfulness, Thurston quickly and, as it turned out, prematurely vouched for him. He urged Washington to accept him as a useful deception channel for the SIS in Argentina.[11] Another option was keeping him in the United States where he could pass bogus naval information, while helping to identify an unknown Abwehr paymaster who had been mentioned to him during his training in Hamburg. Another consideration was Goldschmidt's service with two different sections of Branch I M, leading certain FBI officials to ponder the thought of gaining "control of the Abwehr."[12] His authentic credentials with the Dutch government-in-exile could also support any travel he would undertake in pursuit of his intelligence objectives. At the same time, however, the painful hangover from the Popov calamity a year earlier still lingered in the minds of Ladd and Tamm. Their question for Thurston was why the British were suddenly and uncharacteristically keen to turn Goldschmidt over to the FBI. For his part, Thurston saw MI5's offer as wholly logical, based on the "inherent nature of the case rather than because the British believe or fear that he is compromised."[13] The enormity of the war raised the stakes of every decision involving the use of human sources in the complex web of deception against the Abwehr, not to mention the great risk involved in accepting an unknown and untested source from another counterintelligence service. Yet as one FBI supervisor noted, the gamble was worth taking: "Only by attempting to handle these matters and taking our chances will we be able to progress in the area of counterespionage and gain further control of the Abwehr's activities."[14]

Day-to-day FBI management of the Goldschmidt case in Washington fell to Special Agent W. Mark Felt, a thirty-year-old native of Twin Falls, Idaho, who had joined the FBI in January 1942. A 1935 University of Idaho graduate with a law degree from George Washington University in 1940, Felt briefly worked in Texas before transferring to the National Defense Division as a supervisor on the Major Case Desk under Harry Kimball.[15] Felt quickly laid down some stringent requirements for the FBI's acceptance of Goldschmidt, which included MI5 assurance that the Germans still had "continued faith in him," the FBI would dictate payments for his services (simmering recollections of Popov), and that his double-agent work carried no guarantees of U.S. citizenship at the completion of his service. Thurston assured Felt of MI5's belief that the Germans still had complete trust in Goldschmidt while challenging his insistence on acquiring clear proof as "excessive" and "wasteful.[16] By the end of the month, with no further information on Goldschmidt's background available, Felt accepted him as a counterintelligence source in Argentina.

Over the next several weeks while arrangements proceeded for Goldschmidt's transfer to the United States, Thurston and MI5 began having second thoughts about their hasty support for this new operation following the receipt of alarming reports on the Dutchman's behavior in London. His litany of misconduct included unreasonable demands for money, a sudden romance with a woman working for the "United States Army Paymaster" at the American embassy, his forced removal from an MI5 safe house after propositioning a chambermaid, and, most egregious, his arrest by local police for engaging in sex with a woman in a public park. Adding to these headaches was a recent Dutch report confirming his May 1940 desertion charges. Faced with these new realities, a somewhat chastened Thurston conceded that moving Goldschmidt to America would pose unacceptable problems for FBI agents responsible for his day-to-day handling. Managing such a "greedy character," he cabled, with an overweening "desire for self-aggrandizement" and an "appetite for women that is excessive and catholic," would end in a calamity both for the FBI and the larger war effort. Mincing no words, Thurston called him a "completely worthless and irresponsible individual" who agreed to assist the FBI in the United States in order to pursue "other adventures once he arrives on U.S. shores." So grave were Thurston's concerns that he even urged Washington to have an FBI agent escort Goldschmidt to the United States just to ensure his safe arrival.[17]

After further consultation with MI5, Thurston offered Washington an alternative plan that could still salvage Goldschmidt's usefulness without concern about the daily handling nightmare. His idea was to use him as a fictional source in the United States while keeping him bottled up in England under the watchful eye of the British police. Mindful of the eight Nazi saboteurs who had landed from U-boats on the coasts of Long Island and Florida in June 1942, he warned Felt that one of Goldschmidt's assignments was pinpointing landing sites for future sabotage teams, and the equally important task of identifying the mysterious Abwehr paymaster and his network. A plausible cover story for his travel to the United States could be concocted for the Germans, with the FBI laboratory carefully replicating his secret ink and wireless communications. "The scheme . . . might quite possibly be productive on a short term basis," Thurston urged, "and of course once the plan is in operation a decision could be made from the results obtained as to whether the deception should be continued."[18]

Ladd and Tamm finally accepted Thurston's novel proposal, and by November 1943 work was underway on creating a non-existent Goldschmidt in the United States, now code-named "Peasant." A post office box was quickly rented in New York City for secret ink correspondence, while an FBI radio operator began practicing his distinctive transmitting style using recordings supplied by MI5. As Goldschmidt was a very inexperienced radio operator, his FBI substitute filled his messages with errors common to amateurs. By using his left hand, with the radio key placed on the edge of a table so that the hand and arm had no support, the technician found that he could easily produce scores of unintentional and intentional mistakes. At the same time, FBI radio stations in South Natick, Massachusetts, Wading River, New York, and Clinton and Waldorf, Maryland, started listening on

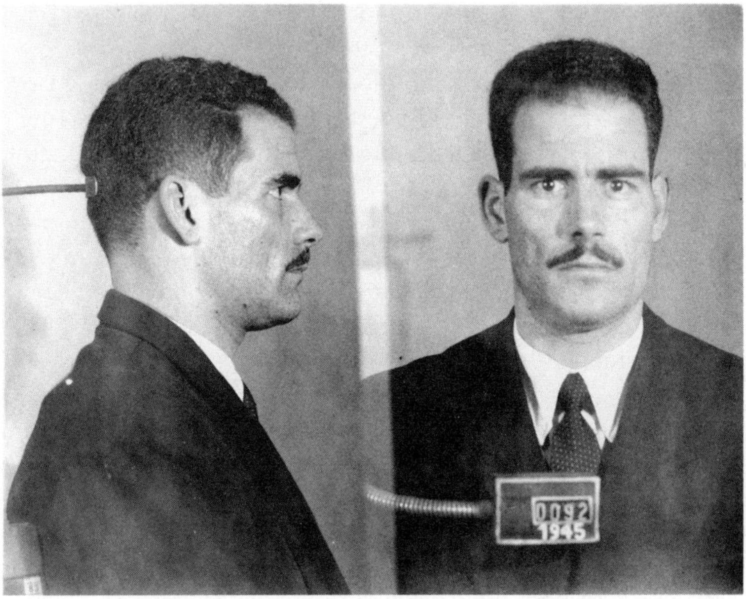

Augusto Strecht Ribeiro. An Abwehr agent, identified by Ostrich, who secretly traveled from Portugal to Brazil where he was arrested in Rio de Janeiro on espionage charges. *FBI*

a twenty-four-hour-a-day basis for the call signs given to Goldschmidt by the Germans. At the same time, an intensive search began for an FBI agent matching Peasant's description who could meet with a German agent if the necessity arose.[19] On November 13, 1943, an FBI-prepared letter was sent from London to a mail drop in Lisbon reporting that he was still in England awaiting a new assignment that could take him to the United States. "Because attitude of the Argentine government not very liberal," he warned, "Mr. van Kleffen [the Dutch foreign minister] thinks more desirable not to send me there. Unhappily my name not Dutch and not Aryan. Possibly two or three weeks in North America."[20]

Three weeks later, Felt sent Peasant's signal of both his safe arrival in the United States and a new predicament in a secret ink message sent to Portugal: "Upon arrival found that position which Van Kleffen promised was no longer open here. Have no job and no money. Can your New York man still contact me?" To soften the blow, the FBI offered encouraging news that a "transmitter is available in New York" and that he was looking for a suitable bungalow but "can't do much without funds." With a sense of urgency he ended his desperate message with a plea to the Germans: "Please hurry. My mailing address is John Gold, PO Box 720, New York City."[21]

No response to Felt's gamble was received until February 12, 1944, when the FBI's South Natick radio station intercepted a twenty-three-minute German transmission, probably from Hamburg, using the call sign DFO and frequency assigned to Peasant. A day later South Natick again picked up Hamburg's broadcast, but then nothing was heard for months.[22]

Frustrated by the silence, Felt tried again to alert the Germans to Peasant's presence in New York in April through a series of open text letters and cables to his Lisbon mail drops. Ramping up the gamble another notch, he ordered the transmission of a clear-text letter signed in Peasant's true name on April 14, less than two months before D-Day, addressed to Augusto Strecht, his cover address in Oporto, Portugal, with his return address as Hotel Governor Clinton, New York City. Felt then ordered the FBI's legal attaché in Lisbon, Dennis Flinn, to verify receipt of the letter, with no success. Then suddenly, a week before the Normandy invasion, both the South Natick and Clinton stations sprung to life when Hamburg began signaling Peasant twice a day, in the afternoon and evening, but again with no messages attached.[23] With the Abwehr frantically searching for Peasant, Felt raised the stakes even higher by dispatching a second clear-text letter to Peasant's Lisbon cover address on July 31, 1944, in the hope of provoking a response: "Informed your samples received by cable 22nd. Acknowledge receipt. Helmut Goldschmidt."[24]

While FBI and Abwehr radio technicians groped through the ether for each other, serious questions arose concerning Peasant's access to the valuable shipping information that he could easily acquire by simply living in New York. Felt worried about Peasant's spy skills. He was not just some poorly trained German agent but an Abwehr's marine branch source capable of easily identifying all types of Allied ships from specific combat vessels to cargo ships and tankers entering and departing the Port of New York. As the Germans would expect him to transmit such details, it would be difficult for the JSC to produce critical feed material consistent with his naval knowledge. Failure to produce decent intelligence could raise Abwehr questions about Peasant's loyalty, commitment, or, even worse, his control by the FBI. Furthermore, Hoover already had ND98, a double agent with no naval training working at the Brooklyn Navy Yard in New York and transmitting information to the Germans from his notional sub-source code name

"Nevi." The final and perhaps most important consideration was the strategically vital nature of the Port of New York and the Brooklyn Navy Yard, which were then operating at full capacity in support of the Allied ground offensive in France and Holland. The fear was that too much vital information would have to be sacrificed in exchange for a counterintelligence reward that wasn't worth the risk. These concerns soon forced Ladd's decision to move Peasant away from New York. In a memorandum to Tamm, Ladd warned that Peasant "will not logically have access to urgent information such as the departure of convoys in which his principals, the section I-M (Naval) of the Hamburg Division of the German Intelligence, would be interested, whereas if he were placed in a coastal port from whence convoys depart, Navy would naturally not clear information on departure of such convoys and it would be difficult for [Peasant] to explain to his principals."[25]

Now that Peasant was conveniently out of New York, the next question was finding a suitable location where he could do the most good for the Allies. During the Second World War, oil and specialized oil-based lubricants were essential Allied components for victory. "The truth is," in the words of one expert, "oil was an indispensable product, in all its forms, to the Allied campaigns around the world. Without it World War II could never have been won."[26]

By August 1944 oil had become, according to one historian, "Germany's Achilles heel." From 1942 to 1944 Berlin's refineries produced 23 million tons of fuel, compared with more than 600 million tons produced by the Allies during the same period. Growing fuel shortages even before the Normandy invasion forced German leadership to take radical steps to conserve oil. Military training was reduced, fleets of vehicles powered by wood-burning motors were manufactured, oxen were used to tow Luftwaffe aircraft on runways rather than waste fuel taxiing, and German scientists began desperate efforts to extract synthetic oil from acorn and grapes.[27]

As Peasant had previously worked for Shell Oil Company, consideration was now given to his rejoining his old firm in a position offering him logical access to useful intelligence. Shell officials offered three possibilities. One, which was immediately ruled out, was an assignment at the company's headquarters in Manhattan. Next, consideration was given to placing him at the company's main terminal in Sewaren, New Jersey. Sewaren had become important in the war effort following the completion in October 1943 of the Big Inch and Little Big Inch pipeline, which pumped hundreds of thousands of gallons of oil daily (without fear of U-boat attack) over 2,000 miles from Texas to the Sewaren terminal, where tankers lined up to carry fuel across the Atlantic to newly liberated Dutch and French seaports. Peasant could theoretically pick up sensitive data, not just about specialized lubricants, but military plans for "extremely secret engines and machinery used in war equipment." Except for the ship captains, Shell employees and crew members never knew the destination of these products, a security requirement which offered Peasant the chance to "cultivate" a captain for such information. The third option, which was selected for Peasant, stationed him in Washington. Working at the epicenter of war planning offered the imaginary source access to important connections. At the time, most Shell Oil employees in the capital had been transferred to two government agencies: first, the Petroleum War Council, made up of industry leaders who bridged the divide between industry and the government, and, second, the United States Petroleum Administration for War, which managed worldwide wartime petroleum supply, transportation, foreign petroleum operations, foreign relations, and oil policy. Having worked for Shell years earlier (the Germans were aware of this fact), his rehire would appear plausible to the Abwehr, it would be consistent with his previous work experience, and it would offer him logical access to a mixture of valuable information, rumors, and other tidbits picked up from soldiers and sailors in local bars and from senior military and civilian officials on the Washington cocktail party circuit. In the end Ladd hoped that Peasant's Washington job would afford him "access to restricted and confidential information concerning almost every phase of the uses and needs of petroleum by the Army and Navy."[28]

At the same time that FBI plans were underway for Peasant's move to Washington in August 1944, Ostrich decrypted a message from the Lisbon's Abstelle to Berlin. Having finally received Felt's desperate letters and cables, Abwehr intelligence officers now began pressuring their headquarters for funds to support Peasant's work. Equally revealing was the identification of his case officer, Wilhelm Hamann, an Abwehr naval officer, code-named "Lembach," who was then preparing some type of package for shipment to him in the United States. Just days later, another Ostrich decrypt to Berlin described plans for the August 31, 1944, Lisbon departure for Brazil of the Spanish ship *Cabo de Buena Esperanza* carrying an unidentified German agent. Under orders from Felt, Flinn secretly examined the ship's manifest where, buried among the dozens of passengers, he discovered the name Augusto Strecht Ribeiro—Peasant's Portuguese mail drop. On August 24, further encouraging news arrived from the U.S. Office of Censorship: an intercepted cable sent from Lisbon by someone named Antonio Concalves to Peasant's New York mailbox informing him that ways of delivering a payment to him were being pursued. Two days later, South Natick and Clinton reported Hamburg's renewed radio activity but yet again with no messages.[29] Finally, on August 30, more than a year after crossing the Spanish frontier in the trunk of a car, Peasant made his first successful radio contact with Hamburg: "Well located Washington. Have excellent possibilities through Shell employment and other contacts. . . . Can you arrange payments?"[30]

Now with communications successfully established, FBI strategy focused on creating the persona of a fiercely loyal and well-placed German spy with access to important military secrets, struggling with his homemade radio equipment and battling transmission problems, together with encoding and decoding errors caused by a combination of inexperience and daily terror of discovery by the FBI. As the case progressed, FBI technicians enhanced Peasant's image using the Abwehr's own radio techniques against them. In a letter addressed to the Washington field office, one Bureau official described the tactic as follows:

> During the course of the contact it was observed that ONB [Abwehr—Hamburg] is still using very high power, indicating his desire to maintain contact. Likewise he continually attempts to "break" *Peasant* during procedural stages. This is interpreted as his belief that *Peasant* is able to work "break in" and his desire to have Peasant restrict his transmissions to a minimum, probably in order to reduce his chances of detection by U.S. monitors. *Peasant* has not acknowledged his attempt to 'break' and has continued his transmissions as though he was not able to work duplex. The ability to work this type of contact is indicative of good operating ability, which *Peasant* may later develop, but which at the present time, is not commensurate with his present state of advancement, as reflected by his actual recordings. In time *Peasant* will become a little more proficient in this operation, which will result in more traffic being handled in less time. This is in keeping with the general plan to have *Peasant* so gradually improve his sending and operational ability as to be hardly recognizable to the German operator. In fact it is the purpose to make the improvement so imperceptible as to cause the German to believe that the improvement is his own ability to handle *Peasant,* rather than any definite improvement on the part of *Peasant.*[31]

On September 1, 1944, the day after Peasant proudly radioed Germany about his new Washington assignment, Hamburg responded. After congratulating him "most heartily," they again reassured him that they were

J. Edgar Hoover. Hoover receiving an award for his wartime service in December 1945 from New York City mayor Fiorello La Guardia. Looking on from left to right are the FBI's E. S. Conroy and Attorney General Tom Clark. *New York World Telegram & Sun Collection, Library of Congress*

"taking steps with regard to money."[32] On September 6 Peasant got to work, first by extending his sincere disappointment over the success of Allied advances in France and then demanding new instructions: "Have good contacts here. What information is urgent?" Without waiting for a reply, he reported the next day that a "friend" in the Patent Office had learned that the Boeing Company in Seattle was producing a four-engine double-deck cargo plane similar to the B-29 with a larger fuselage.[33] Forty-eight hours later Hamburg radioed a request for details on aircraft manufactured by the Douglas, Curtiss, and Republic aircraft companies, specific requirements for the new B-29 bomber and its armaments, together with confirmation of reports that the Chrysler Corporation was supplying parts for the new super bomber. Signaling their growing fear of the bomber's use against the German homeland, the Abwehr asked for information regarding "how they are being navigated across the Atlantic." A day later Peasant responded with intelligence that only added to their anxieties. The oil industry was producing "over 700000 barrels of 100 octane aviation gasoline daily" with a large part "in excess of 100 octane for use in B-29 and B-32."[34]

These sudden and unexpected series of Abwehr questions about the new B-29 were particularly intriguing to JCS planners. The B-29 Superfortress program which began in 1942 had been plagued from the start with serious design problems, particularly engine overheating and fires that resulted in a numerous accidents and crew deaths during its many months of testing. Its first introduction into combat occurred on June 5, 1944, when a large-scale force launched from India bombed Japanese railroad shops in Bangkok, Thailand. Ten days later another B-29 group launched from Chengdu, China, and conducted the first bombing raid on the Japanese home islands since the famed Doolittle Raid in April 1942, attacking the Imperial Iron and Steel Works in Yahata, Japan. Adding to the Japanese misery was the aircraft's large payloads of bombs and unique ability to fly at altitudes well beyond the range of both ground-based anti-aircraft weapons and fighter planes. So frustrated had the Japanese become even during these early stages of the plane's use that in desperation a plane piloted by Sergeant Shigeo Nobe rammed his fighter into one B-29, resulting in the loss of two aircraft.[35]

Peasant's new Shell Oil job, his established radio contact with Hamburg, German interest in the B-29, and the encouraging revelations from the Ostrich source all prompted Ladd to open discussions with the JSC using this unique source as a deception channel. In addition to a background briefing on the case, Ladd provided a list of fourteen categories of information that Peasant was to acquire in the United States, such as details of East Coast defenses and the use of aircraft carriers and aerial coastal patrols in anticipation of the arrival of more U-boat saboteurs. Other requirements included oil storage figures, plans for new factories, and any hints of "American plans for the Middle East."[36]

On September 18, 1944, Ladd's briefings led the JSC to consider redirecting Peasant away from the Germans to the Japanese as a double agent. Fueling this interest was an FBI message sent just weeks earlier suggesting the possibility of Peasant's transfer with Shell to the West Coast with an increase in salary. JSC was so keen on the possibility that they assured Felt that they would provide deception traffic calculated to establish Peasant's value to the Japanese if the Germans "care to release [Peasant] to their remaining Axis partner."[37]

Until the end of the war in Europe an FBI double agent's outgoing messages were categorized as "A" or "B." "A" messages containing a blend of accurate and fictitious information were created by JSC deception planners for passage to Hamburg. "B" messages, culled by agents of the Washington Field Office from open sources, were sent to Felt in the form of suggested messages, with the actual source of the information separately identified. All proposed "A" and "B" messages were first discussed with translators assigned to the FBI's Cryptanalytic Section, who assisted in assuring that the Abwehr operators made no mistake in deciphering the information.[38] Strict deadlines were imposed on message approval, with all suggested messages arriving at FBI headquarters no later than ten o'clock in the morning, three days preceding the planned transmission date. To ensure promptness, special messengers carried the proposed messages between headquarters and the Washington Field Office (WFO), the only exceptions being emergency JSC deception considerations. Following JSC and FBI headquarters approval, the translated message was then handed to the Cryptanalysis Section of the Laboratory Division for encryption. Next, the text went to the radio operator, always the same person at Waldorf, who used an English translation of the message while transmitting to assist his understanding of the nature of the material he was sending. Incoming traffic from Germany picked up at Clinton and Wading River was immediately transmitted to the Cryptanalysis Section for decryption and translation and then on to the JSC with an attached request for an appropriate reply. After JSC clearance, the messages were returned to Felt, who sent them to the WFO for transmission to the Germans. His responsibility was particularly difficult in ensuring that Peasant's unique words, phrases, or expressions used in one message remained consistent in all following outgoing messages. Routine administrative messages, covering the operation's management, financial support, and radio frequencies, were prepared by WFO with no role for the JSC.[39]

Robert Cunningham, the FBI Section Chief in charge of the FBI's deception program, working with JSC's Newman Smith, began sending specially prepared radio messages to Hamburg in September 1944. Typical of these outgoing messages was one describing "Klein," Peasant's new money-hungry sub-source working at Chrysler. Klein had learned that the Northrup Corporation was manufacturing the P-61, the largest night-fighter aircraft ever produced, powered by two Pratt & Whitney engines capable of producing a thrust of 2,000 horsepower. As a test the JSC inserted some information for the Japanese in a signal dated September 22, which, as usual, included a plea for funds: "Overheard former flying employee, friend of [Klein], say that Pratt and Whitney twenty eight cylinder R dash four three six zero developed at least three thousand horse power."[40] Another hinted at revolutionary rocket experiments allowing aircraft to take off "in very short distances." In December, after congratulating the Germans on their surprise offensive in the Ardennes, Peasant introduced them to "Triptane," a new anti-knock chemical recently introduced into aircraft fuel for improved engine performance. When the Germans demanded more information he described it as a "C-seven branch paraffin and that only small quantities are being made. Very small quantities triptane used in one fifteen to one forty five octane gasoline. Probably not sufficient to identify by analysis."[41]

Peasant then closed the door on any German hopes for more triptane data with regrets that such information was so closely held that he would be unable to "verify gas as high as one fifty octane."[42] In keeping with his notional cover of a terrified German agent ever fearful of discovery, he often lashed out at the Abwehr for their indifference to the danger he faced by having him pursue reckless tasks that would compromise his mission. In one message he rebuked his Abwehr bosses for questioning his report on war production statistics, warning them that his "WPB [War Production Board] friend was greatly incensed when I questioned the accuracy of his report. At great risk to himself he removed records from WPB files to show me and I was able to learn the production totals which I sent you."[43]

As Allied forces continued sweeping across Europe toward the German border, the JSC began feeding Peasant new deception data targeted for use of the Japanese.[44] One startling report claimed that he was "endeavoring to check rumor current in Washington that Joseph Stalin will be White House guest on December seventh next." Another, designed to demoralize both German and Japanese planners, claimed that even in the final months of the war in Europe his War Production Board source still reported that "so far as he knows there are no export restrictions of shipments to Soviet Russia." Another series of JSC-inspired Japanese misdirection originated with Peasant's new and equally imaginary source named Wave, a secretary working for a highly placed naval officer. Wave began describing the recent "launchings of the submarines, *Quillback* and *Argonaut* at Portsmouth Navy Yard and the *Capitaine* at Groton, Connecticut," which are part of a much larger navy program "to keep total number of submarines increasing at rate of two or three new submarines for each one lost."[45] Mixed with Wave's information was scuttlebutt that Peasant overheard in the bar of the Statler Hotel between two army officers, complaining that the U.S. Navy's plan for future Pacific operations was better than the army's concept. Peasant also gleaned some tidbits from an unnamed source that the "B-29 program is to double the production within the next twelve weeks," followed just weeks later by new intelligence from Wave that completion and commissioning of the 13,000-ton cruiser *Chicago* had been postponed for several weeks "because of the need for using navy yard workers for the repair of other naval ships returning from long-term sea duty." Toward the end of the year Peasant expressed puzzlement over Wave's lengthy unavailability followed by her sudden reappearance. "When I finally saw her last night," he cryptically radioed, "she remarked that she wished that she could be assigned to the Alaska forces." Then on January 23, 1945, the Japanese learned of a dramatic increase in the military draft "by the first of the year [requiring] nine hundred thousand men."[46]

In the wake of the surprise German winter counterattack through Belgium's Ardennes region, Wave began sending a series of "very urgent" JSC-inspired warnings for passage to the Japanese. Wave had been present at meetings where high-level officers insisted that the problems in Europe would have no impact on Pacific operations. Despite the setback to the Allied forces in Europe, navy officials "are putting forth their strongest efforts to maintain their own operations schedules even if it has the effect of slowing other operations in the nearby Southwest Pacific." Supporting this message was another that identified Admiral Royal E. Ingersoll, who had served as commander of the Atlantic Fleet since January 1942. Ingersoll had recently been promoted to the combined posts of Deputy Chief of Naval Operations and Deputy Commander of the U.S. Fleet, coupled with a sudden transfer to San Francisco as the commander of the Western Sea Frontier. As a 1905 naval academy graduate, Japanese naval strategists knew of Ingersoll's close familiarity with Pacific operations, having previously worked with the British some years earlier on joint planning operations against the Japanese as the head of the navy's War Plans Division. His new job commanding all naval forces engaged in coastal shipping encompassed the protection of supplies shipped from West Coast ports to task forces and war zone ports in the western Pacific Ocean. Wave again hinted to the Japanese that major changes were underway in the Pacific Theater. Her officer "had gone to San Francisco that morning to attend a conference at Admiral Ingersoll's office. She said this conference resulted from sudden changes in plans in the Pacific."[47]

By the end of January 1945 the JSC apparently began to assemble impressive evidence that Peasant's deception material, passed to Germany for transmission to the Japanese, had been accepted as genuine. Military communications intercepts revealed that Japanese military planners were factoring his reports into their plans while analysis of Ostrich proved that the "Germans had placed faith in Peasant." The JSC also reported to Ladd that the "Germans had believed the information reported by Peasant to be correct and had relayed this information on to the Japanese, who also believed it to be correct." Despite these positive updates by mid-January 1945, however, WFO's Peasant case agent, Maurice Taylor, began complaining to Felt that after five months of radio exchanges with Hamburg nothing had occurred that led him to suspect that the enemy was in any way "suspicious of his genuineness or that such faith that they may have had in him has lessened." At the same time he expressed frustration at his difficulty estimating "the degree of confidence" the Germans had in Peasant. Taylor asked Felt for his help in comparing the Peasant case with other double-agent operations as well as "various sources and from the nature and importance of questions and assignments received by various agents in incoming traffic." Ladd's frustration stemmed from JSC's refusal to share the contents of these messages with the FBI, a factor that made a complete picture of Peasant's relationship with his German bosses impossible to determine. Such information could have also proven useful in developing future plans and directions for the FBI's small stable of double agents. One flummoxed FBI supervisor at the time described his unit as "somewhat in the dark" about German faith in Peasant, a problem of critical importance "to the Bureau of receiving Japanese intercepted radio messages which is undoubtedly the source of [JSC] information." Venting his disappointment to Ladd he went on to explain that "if such information was made available to the Bureau, we would then be in a position to better judge the standing of our double agents and also the type of information which is considered to be of value to the Japanese as well as the Germans." There is no indication that such information was ever provided to the FBI.[48]

From the start of communications with Hamburg in August 1944, Peasant constantly harassed the Germans for funds. His financial situation was always precarious, he pleaded, and his employment, which barely covered his personal expenses, could not offset the costs of his additional intelligence activities. His unpaid invoice included funds to pay his sources throughout the government, his radio purchase, rental on the remote bungalow that he used as his radio site, travel costs (gasoline rationing was in effect), and lost wages. His German handlers responded constantly with reassurance that everything was being done to get money to him, even revealing that a courier sent from Europe had not been heard from since he left. "We find no explanation for failure of your remittance to appear," they radioed him in February 1945. "We await the daily return of agent and clarification. We can't do anything at present."[49]

Just weeks later the issue of funds suddenly sprang to life again when Hamburg signaled that they were as "amazed as you (Peasant) at the failure of transmittal to arrive and we're still awaiting explanation of whereabouts of two thousand." Hamburg suddenly asked him for suggestions concerning safe methods for passage of funds while at the same time hinting at Abwehr use of Strecht as the courier. "How can means be safely sent to you *from Brazil*?"[50] Peasant described a business acquaintance who traveled regularly to Rio de Janeiro where he worked with the head of the Standard Oil of Brazil, a man who did favors for friends by receiving packages and gifts which he carried back to the United States. The Brazilian oil manager, a forty-seven-year-old lawyer named Wingate Man Anderson, was a Minnesota native, a lawyer, a Marine Corp veteran of the First World War, and the president of Standard Oil of Brazil since 1936. After a briefing on the Peasant operation by Heber Clegg, an SIS officer and the legal attaché in the Brazilian capital, Anderson agreed to serve as the conduit for Peasant's funds between Brazil and the United States.[51]

Hoover's SIS men in Rio de Janeiro had been closely watching Accacio Augusto Strecht Ribeiro ever since he disembarked from the *Cabo Buena de Esperanza* on October 10, 1944. Within a month of Strecht's arrival, Special Agent George A. Van Noy had placed him under continuous surveillance. Van Noy was considered an old South America hand with a year in his current assignment and another fifteen months in Bolivia surveying factories for evidence of espionage and sabotage. Van Noy's local informants closely watched Strecht's activities, focusing particular attention on his movements and behavior patterns. His mail and cable traffic were copied and read, his contacts were identified, and his room at the Hotel Palacete was secretly searched—all in an effort to assess his susceptibility to recruitment as a potential double agent. A number of interesting new facts made up Van Noy's new profile on Strecht. He spoke only Portuguese and worked as a draftsman for Concreto Armado Contruecoes, a Rio de Janeiro engineering firm specializing in reinforced concrete construction. He came from a prominent family in Portugal and had a brother named Carlos Augusto Strecht Ribeiro, a physician on the medical teaching staff at the University of Oporto. One source reported a suspicion that Strecht may harbor "strongly pro-British" sentiments.[52] By February 1945 Van Noy had placed a double agent in contact with Strecht, who slowly gained his confidence and befriended him. After a series of meetings, Strecht showed his true colors when he began asking Van Noy's source for American military and technical journals having nothing to do with concrete. In Washington, the SIS Division began assembling JSC-cleared military and technical magazines for passage to Strecht through Van Noy's source. Based on the source's information, together with Strecht's probes for military information, which deflected attention away from Peasant, Van Noy sought Washington's authority to recruit Strecht as a double agent. Before any decision could be taken, however, the war in Europe ended. Kit Carson, the head of the SIS, no longer needing sources against the Abwehr, instead recommended Strecht's arrest by the Brazilian police so more information could be quickly learned about his Abwehr role. To deflect attention away from Peasant, Van Noy told Brazilian authorities that Strecht's identification as a German spy surfaced from the arrest of a spy in Portugal named Mario Ferreira Pinheiro, who confessed to working for the Germans and later incriminated Strecht. Rio police arrested him at eight o'clock on the evening of July 17, 1945, with Van Noy remaining in the background as an unseen observer. Under questioning Strecht admitted spying for the Germans and also gave a complete description of his three months of training at Bremen for his mission to Brazil to set up a wireless transmitter capable of reaching Hamburg. While denying any actual espionage in Brazil (he never mentioned Peasant), he produced a series of microdots containing radio instructions which the police quietly turned over to Van Noy. After a lengthy period in police custody he was turned over to Brazil's Supreme Military Tribunal for prosecution.[53]

In the final months of the war in Europe, both the FBI and JSC contained efforts to establish direct contact between Peasant and the Japanese. On April 15, 1945, in one of its final messages, Hamburg asked Peasant about the impact of President Roosevelt's death on the American people. Not expecting a reply they signaled the end of the operation with a warning that he was now on his own. All these efforts in the end were to no avail. British forces were closing in on Hamburg, spelling the end of any future radio transmissions. Furthermore, German efforts to contact Strecht in Rio de Janeiro were futile due to his address changes and the Portuguese consulate's failure to keep current on his whereabouts. In the end Peasant never received a dime from the Germans for his work.

While the Peasant channel ended when British forces entered Hamburg on May 2, 1945, questions still lingered about the possibility of German resistance groups taking to mountain redoubts to fight on in Bavarian Alps. Credence to these suspicions was heightened when Peasant received his final message, that "in view of the situation you must figure on temporary suspension of supervision. Nevertheless please stand by further to receive. In case you cannot hear us transmit messages on hand to us blind each group double. We will try to confirm."[54] The FBI continued "blind" broadcasting until June 3, 1945, with no response. Independent army, FBI, and FCC monitoring of German channels during this period only confirmed the assessment that the Abwehr was permanently out of business. As for Goldschmidt, who still languished in London, MI5 warned him that he too was now on his own, and for his safety he should remain forever silent about the entire affair. In August 1945 the Peasant affair ended when Felt sent a final communiqué to the British informing them that the FBI "considered [the case] closed and the British may dispose of Peasant as they see fit."[55]

CONCLUSION

Rheims is a medieval French city near the Belgian border, eighty miles northeast of Paris. Located in the Champagne-Ardennes region, it was the traditional site of the crowning of the French monarchs and is famed for the production of world-renowned champagne. On May 7, 1945, it was the site of the headquarters of General Dwight Eisenhower, supreme commander of all Allied troops in Europe. In the very early hours that morning, General Admiral Hans-Georg von Friedeburg, a former Hitler aide and the head of the German navy, together with Field Marshall Alfred Jodl, a former chief of staff under Wilhelm Keitel and head of German troops in Europe, entered the room with stone-faced expressions and glumly sat down at a table. Sitting opposite them was the equally stoic General Walter "Beetle" Smith, Eisenhower's chief of staff, who had orders to accept the signed Articles of Military Surrender. Friedeburg and Jodl's signatures, affixed to the documents at 2:41 in the morning on May 7, 1945, meant an end to the fighting at midnight on May 8, 1945. Considering the carnage, sacrifices, tragedies, and countless lives lost on both sides over the previous six years, the brief ceremony, which took place in a standard prefabricated army building, had almost a surreal and somber quality about it. Smith later described this remarkable moment in history as simply a "strange thing." Everyone was silent. None of the Allied officers around the table "displayed any emotion. . . . It was a moment of solemn gratitude."[1]

On May 8 Hoover shared Smith's feelings of gratification that the killing in Europe had ended. For most Americans the war began on December 7, 1941, with the Japanese attack on Pearl Harbor. Hoover's war started twenty months earlier when the director jumped into the unknown by taking the first tentative steps to link the FBI and U.S. counterintelligence to the British cause. Over the next five years he led an unprecedented transformation that grew the agency he loved so dearly from a small continental law enforcement force into a counterespionage service, a counterintelligence agency, and then a worldwide intelligence service, in the process building his own lasting international reputation.

What is odd about Hoover's personal stature as an international figure is his absence of curiosity about the world beyond America's borders. There is no evidence that he ever left the continental United States except, perhaps, for a brief trip to Cuba in the late 1930s. Nor did he ever travel abroad during the war despite numerous opportunities to do so. He had no background in foreign intelligence. Yet he built a formidable foreign espionage service that operated from July 1940 to May 1947, when it closed down in the wake of the passage of the National Security Act which, in turn, gave birth to the Central Intelligence Agency. The Special Intelligence Service helped create the model for the CIA's Cold War Clandestine Service with FBI agents assigned to embassies and consulates servicing other FBI agents and sources acting under business cover in foreign countries. They worked with local police officials, recruited penetration agents in local governments, collected secret political, economic, military, and industrial information, ran locally recruited surveillance teams, and for the first time established its own clandestine communication system with Washington, often in violation of local law. After the war Hoover gave his SIS personnel the option of returning to conventional FBI work, remaining with their cover company, or joining the new CIA. Many chose the CIA, and by 1950, three years after it came into existence, every CIA station chief in Latin America had previously served in Hoover's SIS.

For almost four decades before the Second World War, the FBI had forged strong relations with Canadian police officials, particularly the Royal Canadian Mounted Police. Policing both sides of a common 3,000-mile border, hunting fugitives, smugglers, bank robbers, murderers, and criminals of every variety, often along hundreds of miles of uninhabitable, untamed, and unforgiving land, was a daunting task that required constant cooperation and coordination. Agents and mounties worked well together pursuing informal "cross-border" operations that got the job done and built mutual trust in the process. The same could not be said for the British. When they first met in April 1940 Hoover viewed his relationship with Stephenson as an opportunity for FBI growth in the counterintelligence and foreign intelligence field, a chance to learn the tactics and strategies of both crafts, and the hope of acquiring a partner who could help him prosecute the war that he knew was coming. Before America entered the war, British

Security Coordination oversaw censorship of mail which proved so valuable to Hoover in identifying German agents in the United States and Latin America. Hoover reciprocated by supplying BSC with insights into new technical advances and providing its only means of secure communication with London for almost a year. Hoover was, in the words of the BSC's own secret history, "its licensor" and "in a very real sense, its patron."[2]

But then Stephenson miscalculated: rather than carefully modulating his diplomacy, he exercised a blinding act of political ineptitude by aligning himself with William Donovan, who he believed had President Roosevelt's ear and so turned over his American sources to him, an action one knowledgeable British observer called a "gross blunder."[3] Adding to this debacle were Wyndham Bruce's confidential remarks about BSC to Thurston, Ladd, and Kimball, made not out of malice but on RCMP's similar experiences with BSC and Bruce's lengthy history of cooperation with Hoover.

What was the price of Stephenson's miscalculations? After winning his knighthood in 1944, Stephenson was ushered out of MI6 and quietly disappeared. He never grasped the longer view of history that "good [British] relations with Hoover after the war," as Guy Liddell wrote in June 1943, were going "to be of great importance and that even if we do not get a very good return for our money now, it is essential to try to build for the future."[4] Liddell clearly saw the future; Stephenson did not. Instead of playing a balanced role as the representative of all British intelligence agencies in America by carefully crafting equally strong alliances with both the FBI and OSS, he unnecessarily sowed the seeds of Hoover's antagonism and suspicion that cost MI6 dearly in the years following the war when the treachery of Kim Philby and Donald Maclean was exposed.

The Hoover–Stephenson controversy had its positive results. There was Liddell's May 1942 fact-finding visit to the FBI in Washington which opened his eyes to the extent of the rift and the reasons behind it. He introduced FBI officials to the British Double Cross System of exploiting MI5 double agents for use in strategic deception against the Germans. Both Liddell and Ladd initialed, for the first time, an exchange agreement between the two services. Liddell's visit led to Hoover's decision to send Harry Kimball to London on his own fact-finding mission two months later. MI5 officials showed him their full array of tactics and methods, including an examination of the Double Cross System from both a strategic and tactical perspective, lessons he later applied to FBI double-agent operations. Kimball's visit coincided with the arrest of the eight German saboteurs, a fact that raised the keen interest of Victor Rothschild in examining firsthand everything connected with their plans, tactics, and explosives. Kimball's visit led to Rothschild's controversial trip to Washington where he aired the deep-seated grievances between MI5 and MI6 to startled FBI officials. Rothschild's presence in Washington coincided with Hoover's fury over BSC's authorization of Tricycle to pass (without FBI concurrence) to the Germans the names of three prominent Americans (including the head of an important congressional committee) with claims that they were his sources of information in America. And finally at that same moment there was Hoover's refusal to have any further dealings with Colonel Charles Ellis, Stephenson's deputy, despite his plaintive appeals to the director.

Having lost all faith in Stephenson, Hoover dispatched Arthur Thurston to London as his personal representative, a move that stunned British officials, yet opened a direct pipeline of communications with MI5 and its boss, David Petrie. Overnight, Thurston emerged as a singular confidential conduit between the FBI and MI5, a move quietly embraced by Petrie and one that quickly forced Menzies to brief the new FBI man in London on Ultra and its successes against Abwehr ciphers. Within a month, a second FBI man, John Cimperman, was ordered to the British capital to begin the complicated (and often dangerous) task of reviewing Ultra product, which now carried the FBI code name Ostrich.

The Ostrich revelation was a groundbreaking moment in FBI counterintelligence history. Never before had Hoover used foreign-produced communications intelligence for counterintelligence purposes. Until the end of the war it provided invaluable information that Hoover later cited as one of the FBI's most important wartime intelligence sources. Ostrich also laid the basis for postwar systems of blending conventional investigation and cryptology. In 1947 the FBI signed a top-secret memorandum involving the Venona revelations that the Army Security Agency was extracting from Russian one-time pad messages. Thurston's pressure for stronger FBI security of Ostrich material led to his insistence that no FBI interviews of suspects should be based on Ostrich alone, and no mention of it should be made to other government agencies. The same policy was later applied to the joint FBI/ASA handling of Venona.

Encouraged by this new opportunity that Thurston offered MI5 for direct contact with Hoover, Petrie began pressuring his own higher-ups for a reciprocal arrangement with his own man embedded with the FBI in Washington. Despite Hoover's strong endorsement of the proposal, the effort failed, following MI6's insistence that any liaison outside the British Empire remained their exclusive domain.

Notwithstanding Stephenson's shenanigans, Hoover owed a great debt of gratitude to the British, particularly MI5. Highly skilled British technicians, steeped in the counterintelligence art and science of secretly removing, copying, and then returning documents to diplomatic mail bags (what MI5 called Triplex), taught FBI personnel these dark arts, which it later called "Flaps and Seals." Particular appreciation went to John Masterman, the chairman of the Double Cross Committee, Guy Liddell, Victor Rothschild, and Tar Robertson for a thorough education in counterintelligence, counterespionage, and counter-sabotage. Robertson and his staff received special attention for providing Kimball with the equivalent of an advanced tutorial on the role of double agents in deceiving the enemy. Before December 1941, FBI agents thought of double agents as useful only for identifying German spies. After Pearl Harbor, with Liddell's introduction of the strategic benefits of the Double Cross concept to Ladd and Kimball, FBI focus underwent a seismic shift away from their use in arrests and convictions to deceiving the enemy about Allied plans and intentions.

Organizationally, FBI use of double agents was also a first when agreement was made between the U.S. military and the British calling for LCS control of all deception operations in the European theater with the JSC in a support role and the United States serving as the primary planner for western Pacific operations. Beginning around January 1943, British deception planners first began employing them as part of Cockade, the successful deception plan to convince the Germans to freeze their forces in northwest Europe in anticipation of an invasion planned for some time in 1943. Starting in January 1944 the FBI stable of sources turned their attention to the support of the Fortitude deception with a steady stream of reports about fictitious army divisions, labor strikes, senior military appointments, newly built encampments, and specialized training, all to confuse the enemy about Allied military strength, timing, and location of the European invasion. By December 1944, with victory in sight in Europe (sudden readjustments when the Battle of the Bulge erupted), JSC began turning FBI sources westward in the hope of confusing the Japanese military about where America would strike next.

What were the contributions of these sources to the war effort? As early as December 1941 ND98 offered the chilling revelation about German eagerness for information concerning American atomic research. They demanded the locations of Enrico Fermi and Ernest Lawrence (both Nobel Prize winners in physics) and U-235, a rare uranium element essential for the construction of an atomic weapon. U.S. nerves were further frayed when the Germans radioed Koehler to investigate the whereabouts of Peter Debye, also a Nobel Prize winner and a professor of chemistry at Cornell University who had earlier supplied government scientists with information concerning German military progress in atomic fission while serving as the head of the Kaiser Wilhelm Institute in Berlin. Richard Rhodes, author of *The Making of the Atomic Bomb,* wrote that it was German espionage in the United States that convinced James Conant to recommend that President Roosevelt fund the development of an atomic weapon. While this writer believes that the tipping point for Conant's decision to recommend pursuit of atomic bomb development was the information gleaned from ND98, Koehler, and Tricycle, it is hoped that this new insight will provoke a reexamination of the decision made by Conant, Vannevar Bush, and Arthur Compton.

From a counterespionage standpoint they were especially valuable. Careful examination of FBI files suggests the sophistication of the FBI agents handling these sources and the often ridiculous problems involved in the use of human sources. The Peasant case was a classic first-time example of joint FBI/MI5 cooperation and counterespionage deception, which convinced the Abwehr that their source was reporting valuable intelligence from the United States while remaining bottled up in England under the watchful eye of the British. Other features, such as the use of separate radios for transmission of messages from each double agent and the insights from analysis of German radio traffic, all proved useful to U.S., Canadian, and British counterintelligence officials. Koehler, ND98, Peasant, and Costes contributed important insights into German difficulties of all types. Allied military officials also learned how little the Germans knew about the U.S. military production and deployment of forces and material. Even such mundane German requests as the insistence on receiving barometric pressure readings reflected the large blind spots in German intelligence coverage in North America. They also surfaced other agents such as Paul Cavaillez, Jan Letch, Israel van Berg, and Ribeiro Strecht, who was later arrested in Brazil. ND98 identified Semmler, Rudloff, and Carlton, who refused to cooperate with him. While Japanese intelligence failed to mount any meaningful espionage apparatus in the United States, efforts to counter them continued until the end of the war as evidenced by the decision to use the unscrupulous Pep in the closing months of the European conflict.

What we do not know even today is the impact that these double agents had on German military decision making. We do know, however, that as part of the larger team of combined U.S. and British Double Cross agents they passed information that did contribute to the success of Cockade and Fortitude and later against the Japanese as part of Plan Bluebird. From a counterintelligence perspective we know from a number of pieces of evidence that they were important to the Germans right up to the end of the war in Europe. All the imaginary sources created by the FBI were accepted completely by the Germans, who in some cases urged especially careful treatment of them to ensure their continued cooperation. The Germans maintained radio and secret writing contact with them until April 1945. During the war they received large sums of money, a strong indicator of their importance. The record is clear that in the face of overwhelming difficulties the Germans tried desperately to supply their American agents with funds, in one case promising a source payment in the form of stamps and eventually sending him jewelry through another German agent who happened to already be on the FBI payroll.

May 8, 1945, was a Tuesday. Like every American, Hoover was elated at the news of Germany's unconditional agreement to end the bloodshed in Europe. But unlike his countrymen who basked in the belief that the Allied nations would go forward together to peacefully rebuild the world, the FBI director held a different view of the future. Despite contentions with the British, the high level of cooperation that had evolved played a key role in Allied success. Hoover had no such relationship with America's other wartime partner, the Soviet Union. On the contrary, while all of the FBI's investigative and intelligence assets focused on defeating fascism, Hoover kept a frustrated eye on Stalin's agents quietly plying their espionage trade under the cover of Allied cooperation. An anonymous letter sent to Hoover in 1943 identified Russian intelligence officers and their spying activities in the United States. Investigation had also uncovered troubling evidence of Russian interest in the atomic bomb. In a few months, the names Elizabeth Bentley and Igor Gouzenko would reverberate across the Atlantic, rocking the new and still fragile Anglo-American relationship. In two years army code breakers would lift the lid on Soviet atomic espionage, revealing the vast extent of Stalin's treachery against his wartime partners.

The war in Europe was at an end. But as the exhausted Hoover quietly breathed in the fresh clear air of peace and victory after forty-one months of relentless battle, he could already see darkening skies on the horizon filled with a new and more terrifying threat that would last for decades. Sitting alone in his private office on May 8, 1945, this man, who had played such a magnificent role fighting one war on a world scale, suddenly faced an icy realization: one war had ended, and now he faced another.

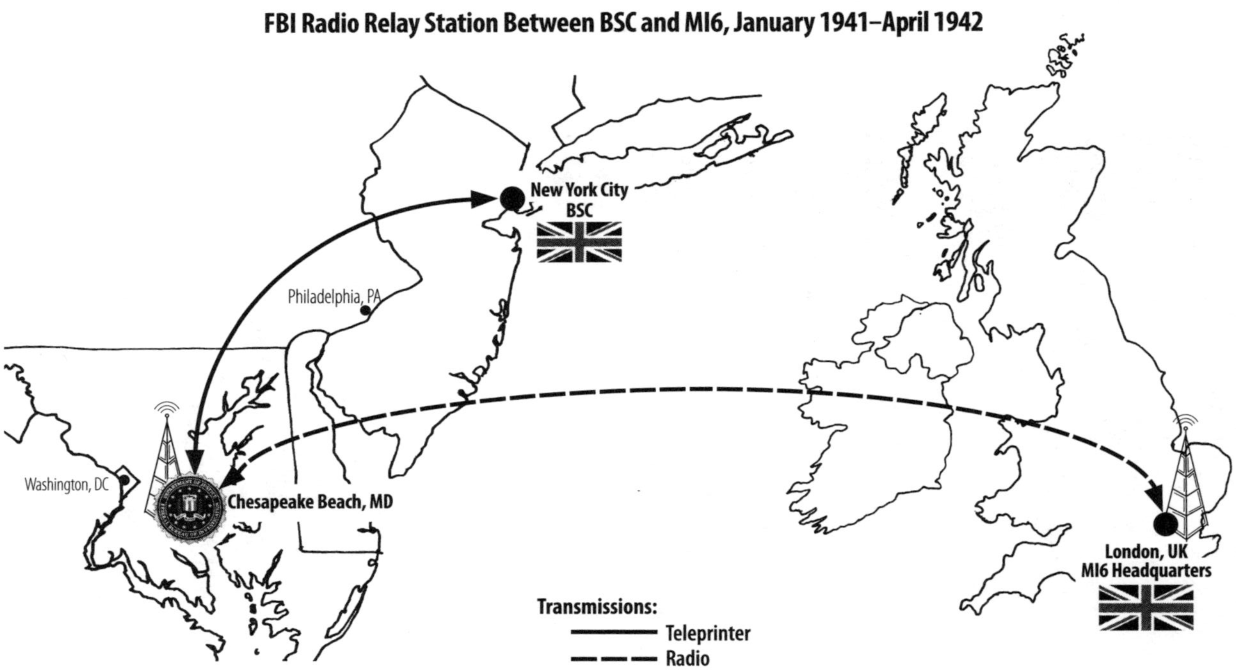

Appendix A. FBI Radio Relay Station between BSC and MI6

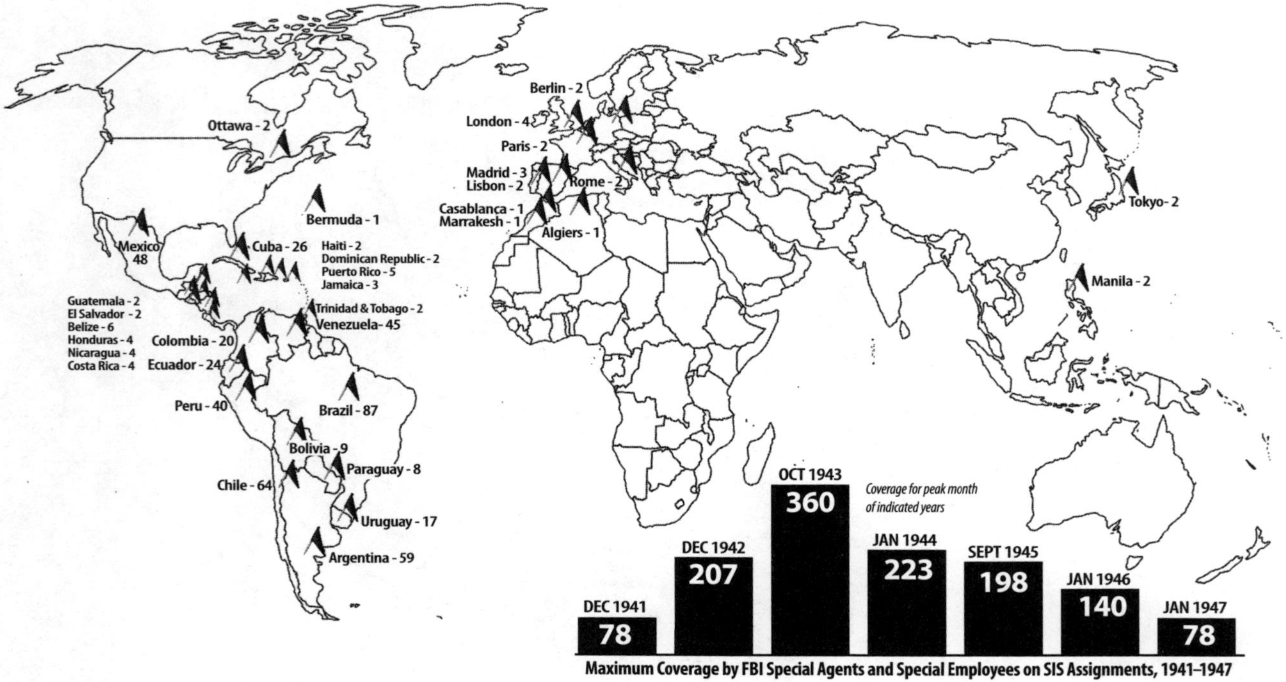

Appendix B. FBI Special Intelligence Service Coverage

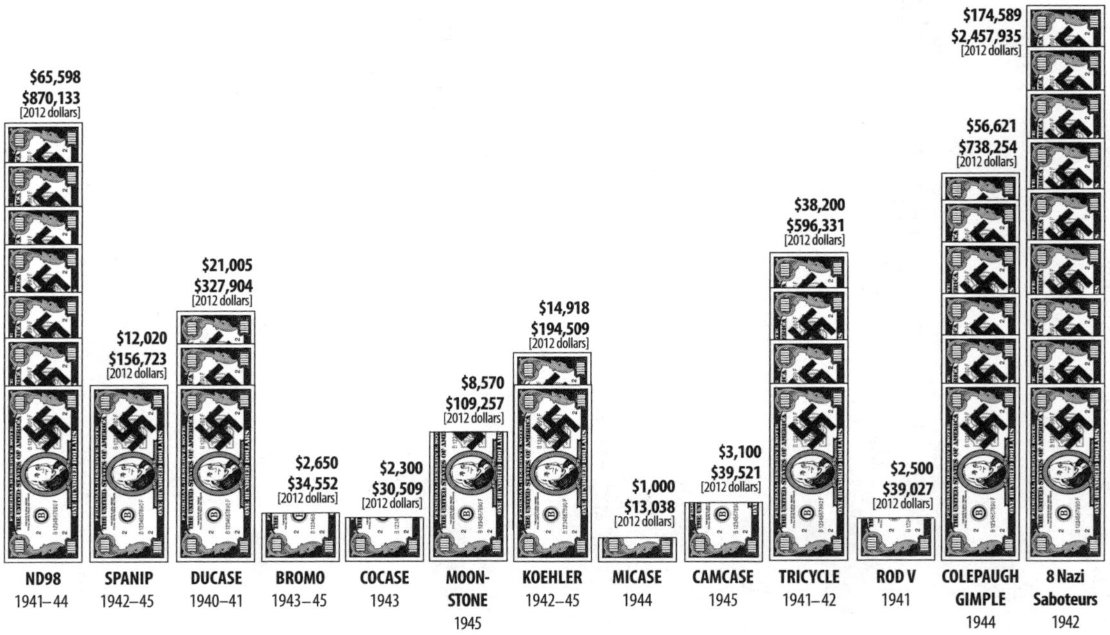

2012 inflation figures from http://www.bls.gov/data/inflation_calculator.htm/

Appendix C. Money Given by the German Nazis to Its Agents Operating in the United States

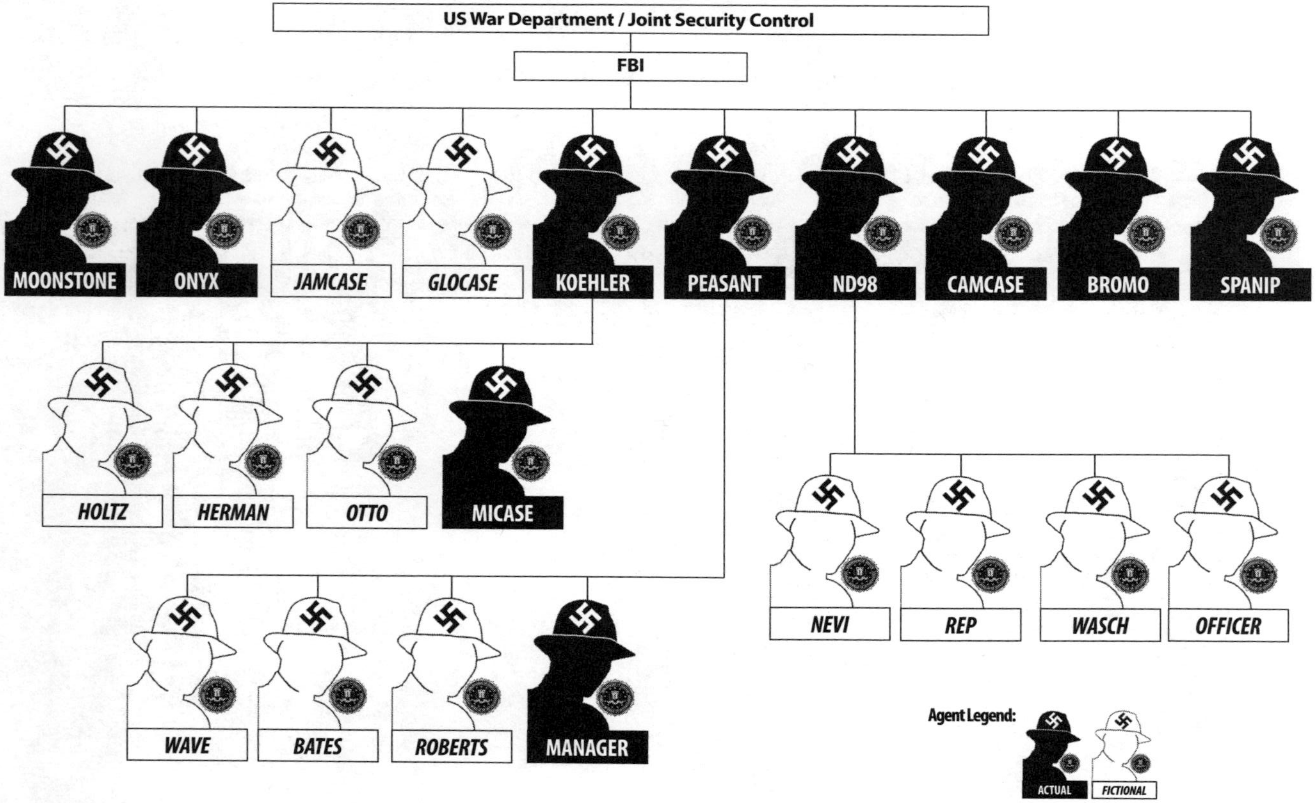

Appendix D. Genuine and Fictional FBI Double Agents

NOTES

ABBREVIATIONS

DDP	Dennis DeBrandt Papers (privately owned)
FDRL	Franklin D. Roosevelt Library, Hyde Park, New York
FOIPA	Freedom of Information and Privacy Act
GLD	Guy Liddell Diaries
GLUD	Guy Liddell Unpublished Diaries
HHL	Herbert Hoover Library, West Branch, Iowa
KV	British National Archive for British Security Service Files
LOC	Library of Congress, Washington, D.C.
NA	National Archives, Kew, England
NARA	National Archives and Records Administration, College Park, Maryland
RG	Record Group
THP	Thad Holt Papers, U.S. Army Historical Institute, Carlisle, Pennsylvania
USAHI	U.S. Army Historical Institute, Carlisle, Pennsylvania

INTRODUCTION

1. Nigel West, ed., *The Guy Liddell Diaries* (London: Routledge, 2005), vol. 1, 1.
2. GLUD, October 23, 1943.
3. While this study focuses only on the "hot war" against the Axis powers, there was another FBI counterespionage war, far smaller in scale, underway in the United States against America's ally the Soviet Union. This should be the subject of another in-depth examination.

CHAPTER 1: A REMARKABLE WEEKEND

1. Lynn Olson, *Citizens of London* (New York: Random House, 2010), 67.
2. Author interview of William Adair, April 10, 2011.
3. Author interview of Jean King and Marion Ramey, Lusby, Md., June 5, 2009.
4. Special thanks are extended to FBI historian John Fox for arranging an extended afternoon tour of Hoover's Department of Justice office suite. For artistic understanding of the interior space of Hoover's office, the author expresses his sincere appreciation to Bill Adair of Washington, D.C.

5. Tour of Hoover's office suite.

6. Ibid.

7. Memorandum to Hoover, July 17, 1917, RG 60, Box 20, NARA.

8. Bruce W. Bidwell, *History of the Military Intelligence Division, Department of the Army General Staff, 1775–1941* (Frederick, Md.: University Publications of America, 1981), 42.

9. For helpful background on this period of FBI counterintelligence development, see Raymond J. Batvinis, *The Origins of FBI Counterintelligence* (Lawrence: University Press of Kansas, 2007).

10. Ibid.

11. Paul Kavieff, *The Life and Times of Lepke Buchalter* (New York: Barricade Books, 2006).

12. Curt Gentry, *J. Edgar Hoover: The Man and the Secrets* (New York: W. W. Norton, 1991), 242; Ronald Spector, *Eagle against the Sun* (New York: Vintage Books, 1995), 59.

13. Thomas Fleming, *The New Dealers' War* (New York: Basic Books, 2001), 1–2.

14. Ibid.

15. J. Edgar Hoover Office Visitor and Telephone Logs, available at the FBI Reading Room, J. Edgar Hoover Building, Washington, D.C., and online. Hereafter referred to as "Hoover Office Visitor and Telephone Logs."

16. Tamm letter to Donovan, December 5, 1941, William J. Donovan Papers, USAHI.

17. Previous biographies have claimed that Hoover and Tolson traveled to New York City together on December 6, 1941, returning to Washington the following day. Hoover's Office Visitor and Telephone Logs for the period contradict these claims. The last recorded meeting of the two men in Hoover's office before the attack took place on December 2, 1941. The logs record no Tolson visits to Hoover's office from December 1 to December 10 during this period. They include calls from Tolson on December 5 and 6 from his hometown in Cedar Rapids, Iowa. Their first personal meeting after the attack occurred on the morning of December 10, 1941. Hoover Office Visitor and Telephone Logs.

18. Don Whitehead, *FBI* (New York: Random House, 1956), 182.

19. Ibid.; Hoover Office Visitor and Telephone Logs for December 7, 1941, reflects a telephone call from Hoover in New York City to his office fifty-one minutes before the attack at 12:09 and three calls later in the afternoon at 2:50, 2:59, and 3:40.

20. Milton Ladd memorandum to Tamm, December 7, 1941, John Toland Papers, Box 126, FDRL; John Toland interview of Charles Fahy, John Toland Papers, Box 117, FDRL. Hereafter referred to as "Fahy interview."

21. Milton Ladd memorandum to Tamm, December 7, 1941, John Toland Papers, Box 126, FDRL.

22. Memorandum entitled "Arrest Plans," "History of the FBI in World War II," Record Group 65, Box 92, NARA.

23. Fahy interview; Hoover Office Visitor and Telephone Logs.

24. Hoover Office Visitor and Telephone Logs.

25. Hoover letter to Adolf Berle, December 8, 1941, Adolf Berle Papers, Box 4, FDRL; Hoover Office Visitor and Telephone Logs.

26. Hoover Office Visitor and Telephone Logs.

27. Ibid.; John E. Schmitz, "Enemies among Us: The Relocation, Internment, and Repatriation of German, Italian, Japanese Americans during the Second World War" (Ph.D. diss., American University, Washington, D.C., 2007), 262.

CHAPTER 2: JONES AND STOTT

1. J. Edgar Hoover, *Persons in Hiding* (Boston: Little, Brown, 1941), 189–208; Batvinis, *Origins*, 52–68.

2. Charles Ager, *Report on Visit to England,* internal FBI monograph, 1938.

3. Batvinis, *Origins*, 61–64.

4. Gill Bennett, *Churchill's Man of Mystery* (London: Routledge, Taylor and Francis, 2007), 67–69.

5. A serious limitation for MI6 was the Foreign Office's refusal to provide "cover" at embassies around the world except for the role of Passport Control Officers responsible for the issuance of visas. Robert Cecil, "Five of Six at War: Section V of MI6," *Intelligence and National Security* 9, no. 2 (April 1994): 348.

6. Bennett, *Churchill's Man of Mystery*, 256.

7. R. P. Kramer memorandum to Tamm, March 19, 1940; Berle memoranda, March 26, 1940, April 4, 1940; Berle letter to Hoover, April 1, 1940; Hoover letters to Berle, March 22, 1940, April 10, 1940; Berle memorandum to Dunn, April 18, 1940, DDP.

8. R. P. Kramer memorandum to Tamm, March 19, 1940.

9. Berle's attitudes about the emerging American relationship with the British were summed up in a private diary note he recorded on October 11, 1940: "The matter of handling the English seems to me to require some thought. In the World War we came so into the British camp that we became virtually an adjunct to the British war machine. They kept that position after the war and the result of that was that we got not one single thing that we really desired in the ensuing peace. This time it seems to me that the thing should be the other way around. We have the ultimate strength. We also have the ultimate consistency of principle; we are the inevitable economic center of the regime which will emerge—unless of course we all go under. This is troublesome. There are so many men around here . . . who take the British whole without developing a strictly American point of view, that it becomes difficult." Beatrice Bishop Berle, ed., *Navigating the Rapids* (New York: Harcourt, Brace Jovanovich, 1973), 341–342.

10. Berle letter to Hoover, April 1, 1940, DDP.

11. Department of State memorandum, April 4, 1940, DDP; Kehler was convicted of Engelberg's murder on March 11, 1940, and sentenced to ten years in prison. "Engelberg Slayer Convicted by Jury," *New York Times,* March 12, 1940, 9:2.

12. Christopher Andrew, *Defend the Realm* (New York: Alfred A. Knopf, 2009), 227.

13. Memorandum entitled "Note on the Work of Sir Eric Holt-Wilson in the Creation of the Imperial Security Service, 1912–1940," RG 59, Box 80, NARA; David Stafford, *Churchill and Secret Service* (New York: Overlook Press, 1999), 33, 183–184.

14. Hoover letter to Warren, March 17, 1941; Johnson letter to James Dunn, August 11, 1940; Holt-Wilson letter to Johnson, July 19, 1940, RG 84, Box 3, NARA.

15. Bill MacDonald, *The True Intrepid* (Vancouver, B.C.: Raincoast, 2001), 61–62.

16. Hoover's only known foreign trip before the Second World War was a brief vacation to Cuba. Batvinis, *Origins*.

17. MacDonald, *The True Intrepid*, 43–51.

18. Ibid., 104.

19. Bennett, *Churchill's Man of Mystery*, 193.

20. Ibid., 193–195.

21. MacDonald, *The True Intrepid*, 43–51.

22. Bennett, *Churchill's Man of Mystery*, 252–254.

23. Ibid.

24. Starting before American entry into the war, Hoover began recording an internal topical diary of the FBI's relationship with William Stephenson and the British Security Coordination entitled "British Intelligence Service in the United States [Running memorandum]." This top-secret document, which was only available to Hoover, Edward Tamm, Crawford Carson, and D. Milton Ladd, offers a fascinating 300-page look at the tumultuous relationship between the services as seen through the eyes of the FBI; the author obtained it through FOIPA. Hereafter referred to as "Running memorandum."

25. Ibid.

26. Bennett, *Churchill's Man of Mystery*, 254.

27. Running memorandum.

28. "A History of CW Radio Communications Activities in the FBI, 1940–1975," 2nd ed. with photographs (n.p., n.d.), 17–23.

29. The author offers special appreciation to James Millen for background information on his father. The FBI's neighbor was the Naval Research Laboratory (NRL) on Randall Cliff. "'Commuting' for the researchers back then meant a bus from NRL [Washington office] on Monday morning over narrow winding roads, improvised sleeping arrangements, and return to NRL at the end of the week. There was radio contact back to the lab, but otherwise no means of communication. And gasoline was rationed, so there was no alternative travel option." In the words of one long-time resident, "There was nothing but summer cottages, unwinterized and many with only a hand pump for water." "NRL Science Faces Forward; CBD Vets Recall Rich History," *Town of Chesapeake Beach Newsletter,* Summer 2006, 11–12. Courtesy of Joan Kilbon, Calvert County, Maryland, Library System, Twin Beaches Branch, Chesapeake Beach, Md.

30. Ibid.

31. Ibid.

32. Ibid.

33. Batvinis, *Origins*, 190, 220–221.

34. It has been a long-held belief that Hoover chose the term British Security Coordination as the cover for Stephenson's New York operation. The Running memorandum records that this title was chosen by either Stephenson or his British superiors in the weeks before his return to America in January 1941.

35. Batvinis, *Origins*, 197–202. World War II History of the Special Intelligence Service, RG 65, Box 80, NARA.

36. Bennett, *Churchill's Man of Mystery*, 256.

37. H. Montgomery Hyde, *Room 3603* (New York: Farrar, Strauss, 1962), x–xi.

38. Bennett, *Churchill's Man of Mystery*, 256.

39. Running memorandum; William S. Stephenson, ed., *British Security Coordination: The Secret History of British Intelligence in the Americas* (New York: Fromm International, 1999), 59–65.
40. Ibid.
41. Ibid.
42. Ibid.
43. There is compelling evidence that Hoover maintained wiretaps on members of Stephenson's staff. In one instance John Pepper, a senior BSC officer, discussed with his wife, then in Cleveland, Ohio, the possibility of his transfer back to London. Foxworth letter to Hoover, December 1, 1942, DDP.
44. Running memorandum; Stephenson, *British Security Coordination*, 188–206.
45. Bennett, *Churchill's Man of Mystery*, 256.
46. Douglas Waller, *Wild Bill Donovan* (New York: Free Press, 2011), 62–63, 71–72.

CHAPTER 3: THE BALLOON WENT UP

1. Memorandum of Conversation, February 18, 1942, RG 59, Box 4930, 841.20211/361/2, NARA.
2. *Oxford Dictionary of National Biography* (New York: Oxford University Press, 2004), 60: 87.
3. Ibid.
4. Robert Sherwood, *Roosevelt and Hopkins* (New York: Harper & Brothers, 1948), 247.
5. Ibid., 483.
6. Cordell Hull, *The Memoirs of Cordell Hull*, vol. 2 (New York: Macmillan, 1948), 1135–1136; U.S. Senate, Senate Resolution 2399, 77th Cong., 2nd sess., April 2, 1942.
7. Running memorandum.
8. U.S. Senate Resolution 2399, 77th Cong., 2nd sess., April 2, 1942.
9. Running memorandum.
10. Ibid.
11. Memorandum of Conversation, March 5, 1942, entitled "Activities of British Intelligence Here," RG 59, Box 4930, 841.20211/36, NARA.
12. Ibid.
13. Running memorandum, Berle Memos, February 26, 1942, and February 28, 1942, Adolf Berle Papers, Box 213, FDRL.
14. Berle memorandum, February 28, 1942, Berle Papers, FDRL.
15. Ibid.
16. After leaving the embassy meeting, Biddle observed to Berle that "somebody has been doing some tall lying here," referring to Stephenson fabricating information to the ambassador, while the ambassador, for his part, was "to say the least 'fuzzy' in dealing with the situation." Memorandum of Conversation, March 10, 1942, RG 59, Box 4930, 841.20211/36.
17. *Oxford Dictionary of National Biography*, 46: 383. Additional information concerning Reid's connection with MI5 was supplied by Nigel West.

18. GLD, 1.
19. Ibid.
20. GLUD, March 31, 1942.
21. John C. Masterman, *The Double Cross System* (New Haven, Conn.: Yale University Press, 1972), 60; *Oxford Dictionary of National Biography*, 33: 728–729; GLD, 3–5.
22. "On the Confirmation of Nomination of Edward Allen Tamm to Be a Justice of the District Court of the District of Columbia," Hearings Before the Subcommittee on the Judiciary, U.S. Senate, February 18, 1948; "501 at Georgetown University Are Given Diplomas as Rain Drives Assemblage of Spectators to Shelter," *Washington Post*, June 10, 1930, 4.
23. Liddell was fully aware of this, noting later in his diary that he imagined this information is "wirelessed back and then goes to the submarines by ZPT but I could not of course tell the Americans about this." GLUD, June 14, 1941.
24. FBI file 77-70444, "Daniel Milton Ladd, aka, FBI Reading Room"; "D. Milton Ladd Dies; FBI Agent for 25 Years," *Washington Evening Star*, July 12, 1960.
25. GLUD, June 4, 1942.
26. "Two Seized on Ships as Italian Spies," *New York Times*, April 19, 1942, 10; GLUD, June 4, 1942.
27. GLUD, June 4, 1942.
28. Ibid.
29. Ibid.
30. Background on Bruce provided by RCMP historian Sophie Chevalier-Forget. Forget letter to author, February 9, 2011.
31. GLUD, June 4, 1942.
32. GLUD, June 11, 1942.
33. GLUD, June 10, 1942
34. Weber and his family remained interned for the remainder of the war. GLD, vol. I, 247, 251, 255; GLD, June 4, 1942.
35. GLUD, June 16, 1942.
36. GLUD, June 16, 1942, June 18, 1942.
37. McDonald, *The True Intrepid*, 287–289; GLD, July 5, 1942.
38. Gordon Welchman, *The Hut Six Story* (Shopshire: M & M Baldwin, 200), 171.
39. GLUD, June 18, 1942.
40. GLUD, July 5, 1942
41. GLUD, July 8, 1942.

CHAPTER 4: ROTHSCHILD IS COMING

1. Liddell had even more headaches when he learned that Pujol's wife was threatening to expose her husband's cooperation with the British to Spanish embassy officials in London if she were not allowed to return to Spain. How Liddell's staff shut her up is a fascinating story. Ben Macintyre, *Double Cross* (New York: Crown Publishers, 2012), 142–143; GLUD, July 13, 1942.

2. Nigel West, *Garbo* (London: Grafton Books, 1986).
3. GLUD, August 21, 1942.
4. Ibid.
5. Ben Macintyre, *Operation Mincemeat* (New York: Harmony Books, 2010), 25.
6. GLUD, August 25, 1942.
7. Ibid.
8. Ibid.
9. Ibid.; Masterman, *The Double Cross System*, 103.
10. GLUD, August 25, 1942; Masterman, *The Double Cross System*, 63.
11. For complete details concerning Camp 020 see Oliver Hoare, *Camp 020* (London: Public Records Office, 2000); Andrew, *Defend the Realm*, 248, 250–251.
12. Andrew, *Defend the Realm*, 249.
13. Ibid.
14. John C. Masterman, *On the Chariot Wheel* (Oxford: Oxford University Press, 1975), chaps. 7–21. After the war President Harry Truman awarded Robertson the Legion of Merit for his remarkable service to the United States. Geoffrey Elliott, *Gentleman Spymaster* (London: Metheun, 2011), 33–85; author's records.
15. Masterman, *The Double Cross System*, 8–9.
16. Andrew, *Defend the Realm*, 260–262.
17. Hoover wrote on Kimball's memorandum as follows: "This is a lie as far as the FBI is concerned. [See that Capt. Liddell and Lord Rothschild are so informed.] H." He went on to write: "Indicate to Lord Rothschild informally that we are just as dissatisfied with Stephenson's outfit as he is. H." Kimball memorandum to Ladd, November 2, 1942, DDP.
18. GLUD, August 26, 1942, September 12, 1942. After carefully studying the saboteurs' cache, FBI laboratory technician Donald Parsons, one of the top explosives experts in the country, concluded that there was "enough material . . . to do millions of dollars' worth of damage to the American war industry." Michael Dobbs, *Saboteurs: Nazi Raid on America* (New York: Vintage, 2005), 114–115.
19. GLUD, September 12, 1942, September 13, 1942.
20. Kimball memorandum to Ladd, November 2, 1942, DDP.
21. Kimball memorandum to Ladd, "British Liaison," November 2, 1942, DDP. Rothschild prepared for the private use of the FBI a six-page, single-spaced memorandum on November 2, 1942, entitled "MI-5 Counterespionage Organization." Bureau officials restricted its distribution with this heading at the top of the memorandum: "This memorandum is strictly confidential and is under no circumstances to be shown to anyone outside of the FBI, and within the FBI only to those to whom it will be of interest." Rothschild memorandum, DDP.
22. Andrew, *Defend the Realm*, 239.
23. Rothschild memorandum; "MI5–5 Counterespionage Organization."
24. Kimball memorandum.
25. Ibid.
26. Ibid.
27. Ibid.
28. Ibid.

29. Running memorandum.
30. Ibid. Biographical information on Walter Bell from Nigel West letter to author, March 14, 2007; Stephenson letter to Hoover, November 14, 1942, DDP.
31. Nigel West letter to author, March 14, 2007.
32. Chapman Pincher, *Too Secret Too Long* (New York: St. Martin's Press, 1987), 440–456.
33. Pincher identifies Zilenski as Ellis's brother-in-law, while Costello describes him as the father-in-law. Pincher, *Too Secret Too Long*, 440–441; Costello, *Mask of Treachery* (New York: William Morrow, 1988), 384.
34. Stephenson letter to Hoover, November 14, 1942, DDP; Ellis letter to Hoover, November 23, 1942; Helen Gandy letter to Ellis, November 30, 1942, DDP.
35. Tamm memorandum to Hoover, December 2, 1942, DDP.
36. Ellis letter to Hoover, November 23, 1942; Helen Gandy letter to Ellis, November 30, 1942, DDP.
37. "I dined with Victor Rothschild and Walter Bell. There was a very frank discussion about British Security Co-ordination. Bell thought that the position was quite irretrievable and that the only thing for us to do was to have a direct link with the FBI. J. Edgar Hoover had made it plain to him before he left. He said, moreover, that if Bill Stephenson did not discontinue his undesirable activities in Washington, DC he would run him out of town." GLUD, December 1, 1942.

CHAPTER 5: ART GOES TO LONDON

1. Amy Thurston Bertheaux letter to author, March 20. 2007.
2. Author interview of Arthur Thurston in Shelbyville, Indiana, November 4, 1995; Bertheaux letter to author, January 15, 2007.
3. Thurston interview.
4. Ibid.
5. Ibid.
6. It was Thurston who provided to ONI the Abwehr questionnaire to Dusko Popov requesting information regarding the U.S. naval base at Pearl Harbor (see chapter 10). Thurston letter to parents, July 22, 1940; Bertheaux letter to author, January 15, 2007.
7. Hebert M. Clegg telegram to Mrs. W. Eden Thurston, November 21, 1943; Bertheaux letter to author, January 15, 2007.
8. Thurston letter to parents, November 22, 1942; Bertheaux letter to author, January 15, 2007.
9. Olson, *Citizens of London*, xiv.
10. Ibid., 79.
11. John Gilbert Winant, *Letters from Grosvenor Square* (New York: Houghton Mifflin Company, 1947), 2; Olson, *Citizens of London*, 69.
12. Olson, *Citizens of London*, 104.
13. Ibid., 382.
14. Ibid., 374.
15. Thurston letter to Hoover, November 23, 1942, DDP.
16. Ibid.

17. Ibid.
18. Ibid.
19. Ibid.
20. Thurston letter to Hoover, December 1, 1942. DDP.
21. *Oxford Dictionary of National Biography*, 43: 919–920.
22. Ibid.
23. Andrew, *Defend the Realm*, 236–237.
24. Ibid., 237.
25. Ibid.
26. Ibid., 238–239.
27. Winant letter to Petrie, December 1, 1942; Thurston letter to Hoover, December 5, 1942, DDP.
28. Thurston letter to parents, November 21, 1943, November 29, 1942, December 20, 1942; Bertheaux letter to author, January 15, 2007.
29. A decade later Thurston would marry DePrez's daughter. "Alumni in High Command," *Culver Alumnus* 13, no. 3 (July 1932): 20–21.
30. Thurston letter to parents, November 21, 1943; Bertheaux letter to author, January 15, 2007. Information on Fred Chadburn was provided by his son, Ian, in an email to the author, February 15, 2007.
31. Thurston indicated that Walter Bell was the only officer that the Bureau trusted. Bell was the only MI6 officer trusted by FBI officials. After arriving back in London on November 30, 1942, Bell described a meeting he had with Menzies in which he described Stephenson as having "surrounded himself . . . with a staff that can generally be characterized as low caliber and irresponsible." Bell went on to note that "proper control has not been exercised over this staff" and "very emphatically that a number of these men must be relieved of office." Thurston letters to Hoover, December 5, 1942, December 8, 1942, December 14, 1942, DDP.
32. Norman Sherry, *The Life of Graham Greene, 1939–1955*, vol. 2 (New York: Penguin Books, 1995), 84.
33. Ibid.
34. Brown describes the philosophy at Eton as follows: "Since Eton was a royal college, the place to which, in general, went the sons of nobles, the clergy, the established oligarchy, it regarded all change as being for the worst, for it implied change in the established order. Thus it also deplored the American Revolution because it established republicanism, and the kings and the established order feared that republican ideas would spread to the lower classes in the empire, as they had spread to France and served to ignite the French Revolution less than twenty years after the colonists 'secession.'" Alexander Cave Brown, "C" (New York: Macmillan, 1987), 34.
35. Ibid.
36. Ibid.
37. Ibid.
38. Thurston letter to Hoover, December 14, 1942. DDP.
39. Ibid.
40. Thurston letter to parents, December 27, 1942; Bertheaux letter to author, January 15, 2007.

41. Thurston letter to parents, December 27, 1942.
42. Ibid.

CHAPTER 6: OSTRICH

1. David Kahn, *Seizing the Enigma* (Boston: Houghton Mifflin, 1991), 25–26; Ronald Lewin, *Ultra Goes to War* (New York: Pocket Books, 1978), 34–35.
2. Penelope Fitzgerald, *Brothers Knox* (Washington, D.C.: Counterpoint, 2000).
3. Ibid.
4. Graham Keeley, "Nazi Enigma Machines Helped General Franco in Spanish Civil War," *Times of London,* October 24, 2008, 47. Just weeks before the start of the Second World War in Europe, Polish military officials invited a group of French and British cryptographic experts to a secret meeting in a forest near Warsaw where they displayed a fully assembled Enigma machine, details of its wiring mechanism, and successful results of their efforts to break its cipher. Knox was a member of the British team. Jozef Garlinski, *The Enigma War* (New York: Charles Scribner's Sons, 1979), 42.
5. Keith Jeffery, *The Secret History of MI6* (New York: Penguin, 2007), 432.
6. Andrew, *Defend the Realm*, 254–255; Jeffery, *Secret History of MI6*, 486.
7. Thurston cable to Hoover, January 10, 1943, DDP.
8. Ibid.: "Got Winant's OK so fast."
9. Costello, *Mask of Treachery*, 426–427.
10. "In view of the conditions under which the material contained therein was obtained, it is urgently requested that it be treated strictly confidential." Thurston letter to Hoover, December 15, 1943; "The Ostrich Story," FBI file entitled "Ostrich," obtained by author through FOIPA.
11. There was a certain irony in Cowgill's absurd efforts to protect the secret of ISK and ISOS from possible leaks by MI5, the American military, and the FBI. For some time his deputy in Section V's Iberian Desk was Harold Adrian "Kim" Philby, one of the so-called Magnificent Five agents recruited by the Soviet intelligence service while students at Cambridge University. The secrets produced by the geniuses at Bletchley Park routinely passed across Philby's desk, with the interesting ones turned over to Moscow. Costello, *Mask of Treachery*, 415–416; GLD, November 18, 1941; Genrikh Borovik, *The Philby Files* (Boston: Little, Brown, 1994), 196; Thurston letter to parents, January 11, 1943; Bertheaux letter to author, January 15, 2007.
12. Thurston letter to parents, January 30, 1943; Bertheaux letter to author, January 15, 2007.
13. One of Thurston's closest friends in the FBI was Special Agent John Williams, who served on the German espionage desk in the National Defense Division. Decades later Williams still remembered Thurston's request in the telegram for his assignment to London to handle the Ostrich material. Unfortunately for Williams other matters interceded, preventing him from taking the assignment. Author interview of John Williams, April 30, 2007.
14. "In Memory," *Assembly: United States Military Academy* 4, no. 6 (June 1947), internal army biographic record, U.S. Army History Center, Washington, D.C.
15. Joseph Persico, *FDR's Secret War* (New York: Random House, 2001), 183–184.

16. "Ostrich Story."

17. In his memorandum for Ladd, Burton concluded with his opinion that Strong "apparently feels about Stephenson as we do and does not want any information of a military nature or which is intended for the military establishment to pass through Stephenson's hand." Burton memorandum to Ladd, April 16, 1943. Hoover, in his letter to Strong acknowledging Burton's conversation, assured the general that he had no "desire to interfere with the flow of material of material of military nature through regular military channels from British Military Authorities to you. Copies of the material which is obtained from the British under this new arrangement will be transmitted to you personally. The fact that this material will be transmitted to you will not be made known to the British Intelligence." R. R. Roach memorandum to Ladd, April 16, 1943; Thurston telegram to Hoover, January 10, 1943, DDP.

18. Burton memorandum to Ladd, April 16, 1943.

19. While Hoover was struggling to get FBI access to Ultra, Kim Philby was supplying it to Moscow through his London handler. Nigel West, *Triplex* (New Haven, Conn.: Yale University Press, 2009), 108; Hoover letter to Strong, April 30, 1943, DDP.

20. Thurston letter to Hoover, August 26, 1943, DDP; "Ostrich Story."

21. "Ostrich Story."

22. Ibid.

23. Ibid.

24. Ibid.

25. Ibid.

26. Ibid.

27. Ibid.

28. Ibid.

CHAPTER 7: A FOOL'S ERRAND

1. Rick Atkinson, *The Day of Battle* (New York: Henry Holt, 2007), 434.

2. Thurston letter to Guy Liddell, February 6, 1943, KV 4/206, NA.

3. *Oxford Dictionary of National Biography,* 38: 263–264.

4. "On two occasions I [Mills] memorized the Commissioner's (Stuart Wood) words. These are as follows. 'Stephenson's organization is wrong, is rotten! I have told my Minister that Stephenson's organization has double-crossed me.'" Mills letter to Liddell, February 18, 1943, March 3, 1943, KV 4/206, NA.

5. Ibid.

6. Andrew, *Defend the Realm*, 254–255.

7. Mills letter to Robertson, January 26, 1943, KV 4/206, NA.

8. Liddell report, "The Security Service and the FBI," March 18, 1943, NA; Petrie letter to Vivian, March 14, 1943, KV 4/206, NA.

9. Petrie letter to Vivian, March 14, 1943, KV 4/206; GLUD, January 22, 1943, and February 9, 1943. A chastened Thurston later acknowledged to Liddell that "he may have said more in his cable than was said to him." Petrie letter to Cooper, February 23, 1943, KV 4/206; Draft letter to Thurston, Undated, KV 4/206, NA.

10. *Oxford Dictionary National Biography,* 13: 263–264.

11. Andrew, *Defend the Realm*, 239.

12. Final Minutes April 9, 1943, KV 4/206, NA. Liddell confided, "Quite clearly Bill Stephenson does not intend to resign and the farce of British Security Co-ordination will continue. It would be far better if they wiped the whole lot out and started again." GLUD, April 8, 1943.

13. "Franz Bopp and Baron Schack to Answer Federal Charges in San Francisco," *New York Times*, February 16, 1916; Petrie letter to Hoover, April 21, 1943, KV 4/206, NA.

14. Atkinson, *The Day of Battle*, 5.

15. Thurston memorandum to Ladd, May 27, 1943, FBI File 62-64178, FBI-British Relations, FOIPA.

16. Denham letter to Petrie, July 8, 1943, KV 4/206, NA.

17. Ibid.

18. Ibid.

19. *Oxford Dictionary of National Biography*, 56: 580–581.

20. Ibid.

21. Tamm memorandum to Hoover, June 24, 1943, 62-64178, DDP.

22. Denham letter to Petrie, July 843, KV4/206, NA.

23. Ibid.

24. GLUD, August 10, 1943.

25. GLUD, July 26, 1943.

26. *Oxford Dictionary of National Biography*, 26: 672–673; *Times of London*, June 7, 1973, June 11, 1973, June 14, 1973.

27. GLUD, August 13, 1943, November 21, 1943.

28. Petrie later wrote to Cooper concerning his cable to Stephenson as follows: "I confess I am still at a loss to see how my cable of 7th June to Stephenson, which was only to remind him of his understanding, to make 'necessary adjustments with Vivian' to help smooth and speedy transfer marked any departure. I hold this the more firmly as, transfer having been decided on, delay had nothing to commend it; the F.B.I. had declined to deal further with Stephenson and we are in the middle of a world war." Petrie memorandum to Cooper, August 10, 1943, KV 4/206, NA; Butler Note for Mr. Duff Cooper, August 10, 1943, KV 4/106, NA; Thurston letter to Petrie, August 13, 1943, KV 4/206, NA; GLUD, July 5, 1943.

29. Cooper letter to Petrie, August 11, 1943, KV 4/206, NA.

30. Hoover cable to Thurston, August 13, 1943, DDP.

31. Cooper draft cable to Denham, August 9, 1943, KV4/206, NA.

32. GLUD, August 4, 1943.

33. Memorandum entitled "Conclusions Come to a Meeting of Sir David Petrie, 'C,' and Mr. Duff Cooper," September 27, 1943, KV 4/207, NA.

34. Denham cable to Cooper, August 8, 1943, KV 4/206, NA. Stephenson later told Liddell over lunch that if MI5 acquired its own liaison with the FBI, "he would resign." GLUD, August 2, 1943.

35. It is interesting to note how sensitive this issue was as evidenced by the line Petrie placed in the text and later crossed out before dispatch. In referring to Mills as the MI5 representative who would meet with the FBI, he wrote, "I have told Mills that he should make regular visits to you as often as may prove to be possible." The line was scratched out. Petrie letter to Hoover, October 2, 1943, KV 4/207, NA.

36. Petrie letter to Hoover, October 2, 1943, KV 4/207, NA.

37. To emphasize his sincerity Hoover gave Petrie the sixteen-volume FBI file on the Ernest Lehmitz and Roberto Lanas Vallecilla espionage cases, which were originally uncovered through British censorship at Bermuda. Petrie letter to Hoover, October 2, 1943, KV 4/207, NA. Hoover letter to Petrie, October 21, 1943, KV 4/207, NA; GLUD, August 14, 1943.

38. Denham cable to Petrie, October 22, 1943, KV 4/209, NA. Liddell met with Cooper to discuss what procedure should be followed when Mills has had a need to visit the FBI. Cooper told Liddell that he is "very anxious that you [Mills] should avoid trouble as much as possible, but there was no reason whatever why you should be accompanied to the F.B.I. by anyone from B.S.C. If when you notify them that you are proposing to visit Washington, this suggestion is made to you, the proper course for you to adopt is to say that you do not require the assistance from anyone from B.S.C. at your interview." Butler letter to Mills, October 7, 1943, KV 4/207, NA.

39. Denham letter to Hoover, October 26, 1943, KV 4/209, NA; Burton memorandum to Ladd, November 2, 1943, FBI File 62-64178, "FBI-British Relations."

CHAPTER 8: SOUTH OF THE BORDER

1. Batvinis, *Origins*, 210.

2. Ibid.

3. "History of the S.I.S. Division," RG 65, NARA. This is a comprehensive five-volume internal review of the FBI's intelligence service prepared in 1947. It examines the administration of the service, relationships with other government departments and foreign governments, expenses, cases, organizational structure, and so on. It is a candid look at every aspect one could think of for such a history with appraisals of strengths and weaknesses, failures and successes. It also includes eight annual reports, ranging from 1940 to1947, covering activities for each year of the service's existence.

4. Ibid., 104.

5. Ibid., 3.

6. Gus Jones, *The Nazi Failure in Mexico,* unpublished memoir. The author expresses his appreciation to Robert Heibel for this manuscript. George Ellis, *A Man Named Jones* (New York: Signet Books, 1963), 35–45.

7. Jones, *Nazi Failure in Mexico*, 22.

8. Batvinis, *Origins.*

9. "History of the S.I.S. Division," 6.

10. Ibid., 7.

11. Ibid., 8.

12. Ibid., 16.

13. Ibid., 12.

14. Spruille Braden, *Diplomats and Demagogues* (New Rochelle, N.Y.: Arlington, 1971), 245.

15. Ibid.

16. On May 4, 1940, M. Clair Spear received emergency orders from Hoover to join Carl Norden, the inventor of the famed bombsight that bore his name, and serve as his bodyguard while he sailed from New York to Genoa, Italy. Spear's assignment was to

protect Norden from possible kidnapping by the British, the Germans, or the Italians, all of whom were anxious to acquire the secrets of the bombsight. While at sea Spear received a radiogram from Hoover warning him that German forces had invaded France, that Norden was in extreme jeopardy, and that every effort should be made to return him safely to the United States. After convincing Norden of his perilous situation and the need to abandon his plans to visit his family in Switzerland, Spear took possession of his personal papers, which included blueprints for the bombsight, and threw them overboard before the ship reached Gibraltar. When the ship reached Genoa, its final destination, Norden and Spear remained on board until it returned to New York a week or so later. Full details of Spear's adventure can be found in Batvinis, *Origins*, 160–166; Braden, *Diplomats and Demagogues*, 245. Special Intelligence Service Personnel List prepared by the FBI in 1947 and provided to the author by Kenneth C. Crosby. Hereafter referred to as "SIS Personnel List."

17. "History of the S.I.S. Division"; SIS Personnel List, author's copy.

18. "History of the S.I.S. Division," 42.

19. Ibid., 53.

20. Ibid., 74.

21. Ibid., 112.

22. Ibid., 134.

23. Ibid., 212.

24. After the war Roberts formed Cinerama Productions, a movie production company that pioneered a revolutionary new technology which "altered the way we experience movies by putting the viewer in the film." Most Cinerama movies were travel adventures that took audiences around the globe to faraway places. Among his most famous productions was the 1962 epic western *How the West Was Won,* starring Debbie Reynolds, James Stewart, and John Wayne, with narration by Spencer Tracy. In spite of his physical handicap, Roberts was also a world-class sports fisherman and only the second American to receive a commercial pilot's license. During the late 1950s he also served for four years as the president of the Maidstone Club in East Hampton, New York. Author interviews of Linda James and Sally Jenkins, East Hampton, New York, September 29, 2009; "Deaths: Roberts, Dudley Devore, July 7, 2000," *New York Times;* special appreciation to Paul Rickenbach, mayor of East Hampton, for his assistance.

25. Certified copy of an entry of birth, September 6, 1928, United Geophysical Company Brochure, undated, Herbert Hoover III Collection, HHL.

26. Biographical sketch of Herbert Hoover Jr., June 1967, Herbert Hoover III Collection, HHL.

27. "History of the S.I.S. Division," 319.

28. Jones, *Nazi Failure in Mexico*, 4.

29. Oral history interview with Joseph Campisi, June 7, 2003; online transcripts of oral histories conducted by retired special agents of the FBI under the sponsorship of the Society of Former Special Agents of the FBI and currently held by the National Law Enforcement Museum, Washington, D.C.; "History of the S.I.S. Division," 138.

30. "History of the S.I.S. Division," 210.

31. Ibid., 310.

32. Author interview of Kenneth McCorkle Crosby, November 25, 1999.

33. "History of the S.I.S. Division," 311.
34. Ibid., 312.
35. Ibid., 311.
36. Ibid., 314.
37. Ibid., 316.
38. Ibid., 317.
39. Ibid., 320; Crosby interview.
40. Raymond J. Batvinis, "The Strange Odyssey of Louis Beck," www.fbistudies.com.
41. "History of the S.I.S. Division," 318.
42. "A History of CW Radio Communications Activities in the FBI 1940–1975," 2nd ed. with photographs.
43. Ibid.
44. Years later, one of the operators of the Santiago station admitted that concern for security was so serious that he broadcasted only between midnight and 6 a.m., "with a pistol lying on top of the receiver." "History of CW Radio Communications Activities."
45. Nichols memorandum to Glavin, April 4, 1943, courtesy of Ernest Porter.
46. Ibid.
47. Crosby interview; Don Whitehead, *The FBI Story* (New York: Random House, 1956), 221–222.
48. "History of the S.I.S. Division," 420.
49. Ibid., 443.
50. Ibid., 435.
51. Ibid., 349.
52. Jones, *Nazi Failure in Mexico*.
53. "History of the S.I.S. Division," 418.
54. Ibid., 402.
55. Ibid., 343.
56. Ibid., 377.
57. Ibid., 298.
58. Ibid., 303.
59. Ibid., 307.
60. Ibid., 333.
61. Ibid., 394.
62. Ibid., 401.
63. Ibid., 498.
64. Ibid., 505.
65. SIS Personnel List; "History of the S.I.S. Division," 169.

CHAPTER 9: THE MAN FROM BUFFALO

1. Richard Dunlop, *Donovan: America's Master Spy* (Chicago: Rand McNally, 1982), 13.
2. Donovan's brother, Vincent, became a Roman Catholic priest. Thomas Troy, *Wild Bill and Intrepid* (New Haven, Conn.: Yale University Press, 1996), 15.
3. Dunlop, *Donovan*, 25.

4. Ibid., 35–43.

5. Ibid., 44–46.

6. Ibid., 107.

7. "'Wild Bill' Donovan, A.E.F. Hero Now Makes War on Federal Offenders," *New York Times,* February 23, 1922, 3; Dunlop, *Donovan,* 144.

8. "Colonel Donovan Made Aide to Stone," *New York Times,* August 15, 1924, 4; Dunlop, *Donovan,* 153–154.

9. "Wheeler Acquitted on a Single Ballot after Ten Minutes," *New York Times,* April 25, 1925, 4; Troy, *Wild Bill and Intrepid,* 58–62.

10. "Called to Attend Embargo Parley," *New York Times,* September 19, 1939; Stephenson, *British Security Coordination,* 442.

11. Stephenson, *British Security Coordination,* 442.

12. Ibid.

13. Ibid.

14. In a memorandum to Hoover, Hugh Clegg wrote of a recent meeting where Donovan claimed that he told President Roosevelt that "if he accomplished nothing else of value during the present World War . . . that one thing which could be placed to his credit was his helping pave the way in England for the FBI representatives to obtain valuable information concerning most confidential matters." In the margin of Clegg's memorandum, Hoover scrawled, "If I recall correctly I think we were there before the Colonel arrived." Clegg memorandum to Hoover, December 10, 1941, DDP; "U.S. Survey of Hitler Conquests Reveals 'Fifth Column' Spearhead," *New York Times,* August 20, 1940; "Germans Said to Spend Vast Sums to Pave the Way Abroad," *New York Times,* August 23, 1940; Troy, *Wild Bill and Intrepid,* 62; Tamm memorandum to Hoover, June 11, 1941, DDP. Donovan briefed Hoover on August 6, 1940. FBI Donovan File, Washington, D.C.

15. Stephenson, *British Security Coordination,* 446–447.

16. Ibid.

17. Troy, *Wild Bill and Intrepid,* 70

18. Ian Fleming thought the new service should be centered in the FBI, a notion that Stephenson and Godfrey quickly dispelled. Troy, *Wild Bill and Intrepid,* 229; Tamm memorandum to Hoover, June 11, 1941, DDP.

19. Troy, *Wild Bill and Intrepid,* 69.

20. Batvinis, *Origins,* 69–98; Roosevelt letter to Biddle, July 14, 1941, DDP.

21. Memorandum of Establishment of Service of Strategic Information, June 10, 1941, DDP.

22. "Donovan Is Named Information Head," *New York Times,* July 12, 1941, 5; "Designating a Coordinator of Information," *New York Times,* July 14, 1941; Roosevelt letter to Biddle, July 14, 1941, DDP.

23. There was one experienced investigator who was blackballed. A month after the president's decision, Hoover informed Donovan about a "story current in Washington" that Leon Turrou was seeking a position with the COI. Turrou was the FBI agent who investigated the Gunther Rumrich espionage investigation in 1938 and was later "dismissed with prejudice" for selling information about the investigation to the press. "A considerable amount of political pressure was developed, Hoover explained, to have this dismissal removed, but the facts against Turrou were so overwhelming that

Departmental authorities have consistently declined to alter the dismissal." Hoover letter to Donovan, August 1, 1941; Tamm memorandum to Hoover, August 20, 1941; Foxworth memorandum to Hoover, September 13, 1941, DDP. Douglas Waller described Downes as was "one of Donovan's true oddballs." Waller, *Wild Bill Donovan*, 73, 93, 123.

24. Foxworth memorandum to Hoover, September 4, 1941, DDP.

25. Douglas Waller, in his excellent biography of Donovan, claims that Hoover had a "mole" working at the message center inside the COI who regularly fed him information. Waller, *Wild Bill Donovan*, 76.

26. John Haynes, Harvey Klehr, Alexander Vassiliev, *Spies* (New Haven, Conn.: Yale University Press, 2009), 293–329. A very revealing study of wartime Soviet espionage in the United States.

27. Dunlop, *Donovan*, 353–354.

28. Stephenson, *British Security Coordination*, 38.

29. Robin W. Winks, *Cloak & Gown* (New York: William Morrow, 1987, 153).

30. Ibid., 155–159.

31. Ibid., 159–166.

32. Ibid., 168.

33. Cuneo and Tamm remained friends for decades after the war as evidenced by the correspondence between the two men contained in the Ernest Cuneo Papers at the FDRL. Ibid., 167.

34. Ibid.

35. Ibid., 172–173.

36. This was the famed "Cynthia" case which involved Amy Elizabeth Thorpe Pack, the daughter of a Marine Corps major and divorced wife of an abusive British diplomat who plied sex for secrets in an attempt to steal codes from Vichy France's Washington embassy in the months before the North Africa invasion. Pack, previously a BSC source, had been turned over to Donovan, who assigned her to Downes. Winks, *Cloak & Gown*, 171; Waller, *Wild Bill Donovan*, 122–123.

37. Winks, *Cloak & Gown*, 173.

38. Downes and his burglary team managed to steal away before the police arrived. Later, he wrongly claimed that the sirens he heard were from FBI vehicles, which only amplified Donovan's hatred for his FBI rival. Author interview of Douglas Waller, May 9, 2012; Waller, *Wild Bill Donovan*, 127.

39. Batvinis, *Origins*, 251–252.

40. Ovakimian, Mikail Gorin, and Japanese spy Itaro Tachibana were released from custody and departed the United States in June 1941. Ibid.

41. Waller, *Wild Bill Donovan*, 224.

42. Ibid.

43. Ibid.

44. Haynes, *Spies*, 529–530.

45. Ibid., 445–456.

46. History of the Federal Bureau of Investigation, Special Intelligence Service, RG 65, NARA.

47. Waller, *Wild Bill Donovan*, 338.

48. Ibid.

CHAPTER 10: BREACH OF FAITH

1. In the days before Warren and Foxworth first discussed the British proposal, two German agents arrived in the United States with an offer of service to the FBI. The first was Adrina Otero, an American citizen who worked for years in Europe as a professional dancer. In the years before the war she worked as a double agent for the French intelligence service until the fall of France, when the Germans ordered her to start spying in the United States. She arrived in New York on May 12, 1941, and offered her assistance as a double agent. Possessing what one FBI agent called a "superlative artistic temperament," Otero soon demanded that the FBI secure a contract for her to dance in New York at a leading hotel for which she is "unqualified." On January 20, 1942, she inquired of the Germans in a secret writing message about continuing her work, which they positively affirmed. The FBI was working with her to further these plans. The other German agent was Rafael Romero Soto, who arrived in New York City from Buenos Aires on June 3, 1941. Soto volunteered to work as an Abwehr spy in the United States in consideration of his release from a Spanish prison. After espionage training in Barcelona the Abwehr papered him as a Costa Rican citizen named Pedro Rodriguez Valiente. From Spain he was sent to Argentina as the first step to moving on to the United States. After arriving in Buenos Aires he walked into the American embassy and volunteered his assistance as a double agent; and on June 3, 1941 he arrived in New York City. After collecting $500 ($7,800 in 2012 dollars) from the Germans, he fled to Mexico and was later returned to FBI custody from Cuba. Under FBI questioning Soto admitted that he was an escapee from the Colorado State Penitentiary who made his way to Spain, where he was again imprisoned for unspecified criminal activities. He claimed that he made contact with his German bosses in Mexico, telling them that he had arranged for a radio operator who was available for contact at any time. In the hope of renewing contact with the Germans, the FBI set up a radio station to keep in contact with the Germans. Foxworth memorandum to Hoover, June 5, 1941, Dusko Popov, Records of FBI Files, FBIHQ, RG 65, NARA, "FBI Popov File."

2. Russell Miller, *Operation Tricycle* (New York: Pimlico, 2005), 13–33.

3. Ibid.

4. Ibid.

5. Ibid.

6. Ibid.

7. Ibid.

8. Macintyre, *Double Cross*, 33.

9. Popov received the new code name Tricycle for his "fondness for three-in-a-bed sex." Andrew, *Defend the Realm*, 253.

10. Miller, *Operation Tricycle*, 63–65.

11. Ibid.

12. Ibid.

13. In May 1940, British code breakers had cracked the Abwehr's hand cipher system known as ISOS and by December 1941 were reading its machine cipher as well, known as ISK. Andrew, *Defend the Realm*, 249–255.

14. One author described a young married woman named "Gwennie" (full name

redacted from Popov MI5 file) who carried on a passionate affair with Popov while her husband was away from London on business. Theorizing that she was an MI5 informant he lauded her as "one more unsung hero, performing sterling though unconventional wartime service for her country." Macintyre, *Double Cross*, 64–66.

15. Miller, *Operation Tricycle*, 67–89.

16. Ibid.

17. Ibid.

18. For background on Connelley see Batvinis, *Origins*, 232.

19. He was instructed to purchase a radio receiver in the United States and he produced one half of a postcard given to him by the Germans in Lisbon. The other half would serve as the recognition signal for the person supplying his transmitter. NYO Report of SA Charles Lanman, September 17, 1941, FBI Popov File, 65-36994.

20. Ibid.

21. Ibid.

22. Connelley letter to Hoover, August 19, 1941, FBI Popov File.

23. Claiming ignorance of Plan Midas, Popov cautioned Connelley against informing the British about their discussion of the funds. Days later FBI suspicions of British motives deepened when Popov changed his original story about the origins of the money and Ellis's anger at him for mentioning it to the FBI. "Hell, you shouldn't have told them that," Ellis fumed, "that's none of their business." After instructing Ellis to provide him with the full story of Plan Midas, Connelley reported to Hoover that this British scheme may be the reason why the FBI had not received the second half of Popov's history. Connelley letter to Hoover, August 25, 1941, Carson memorandum to Foxworth, August 21, 1941, FBI Popov File.

24. Ellis insisted that the British were "leaving his [Popov's] future activities in your hands." Connelley letter to Hoover, August 19, 1941, FBI Popov File.

25. Connelley letter to Hoover, August 20, 1941, FBI Popov File.

26. Ibid.

27. Ibid.

28. Ibid.

29. NYO Report of SA Charles Lanman, September 17, 1941, FBI Popov File.

30. Thurston memorandum to Ladd, October 3, 1941, FBI Popov File.

31. Ibid.

32. Ibid.

33. Ibid.

34. After discussing the need for passage material, ONI agreed "to pick out one particular item from this questionnaire and [FBI] request ONI to furnish on this one particular item." Fletcher memorandum to Ladd, October 25, 1941, FBI Popov File.

35. NYO Report of SA Charles Lanman, October 14, 1941, FBI Popov File.

36. NYO Report of SA Charles Lanman, December 24, 1941, FBI Popov File.

37. Ibid.

38. Ibid.

39. Running memorandum. Hoover noted on Ladd's memorandum, "See no more butterfly trays are allowed to enter at any US port." Memorandum for Ladd, December 29, 1941, FBI Popov File.

40. NYO Report of SA Charles Lanman, December 24, 1941, FBI Popov File.

41. Annual Reports, 1941–1943, Special Intelligence Service, FBI, United States Department of Justice, 1942, 25–26, RG 65, NARA.

42. Ibid.

43. New York teletype, April 2, 1942, FBI Popov File.

44. Ibid.

45. C. F. Lanman memorandum to Foxworth, March 14, 1942, FBI Popov File.

46. Weeks later Stephenson supplied Hoover with a copy of a decrypted Abwehr radio message to Engels, warning him that "since there is suspicion that Ivan (Popov) is working for both sides, we recommend extreme caution in dealing with him." [No title,] *New York Times,* April 22, 1942; Stephenson letter to Foxworth, March 25, 1942, FBI Popov File; Coffey memorandum to Tracy, May 7, 1942, FBI Popov File.

47. Foxworth letter to Hoover, April 13, 1942, FBI Popov File.

48. Foxworth letter to Hoover, April 9, 1942, FBI Popov File.

49. Thad Holt, *The Deceivers* (New York: Scribner, 2004), 247; Foxworth letter to Hoover, April 22, 1942, FBI Popov File.

50. Foxworth had his own suspicions of possible British duplicity concerning the original purpose for Popov's assignment to America, telling Ladd that "about the possibility of the British having brought Popov over for some other purpose than actually to operate as a double agent for us." Little memorandum to Ladd, July 6, 1942, FBI Popov File.

51. Ibid.

52. Foxworth letter to Hoover, April 9, 1942, FBI Popov File; "Igor Cassini, Hearst Columnist, Dies at 86," *New York Times,* January 9, 2002.

53. Lisbon memorandum, FBI Popov File.

54. Kimball memorandum to Ladd, October 19, 1942, DDP. Hoover wrote the following on Kimball's memo: "Until we have some further explanation no further information is to be given & contact N.Y. specifically about this and let Stephenson know how we consider this a breach of faith. H." Kimball memorandum to Ladd, October 23, 1942, FBI Popov File. Elvira Chaudoir, code-named "Bronx," was a British double agent. To impress the Abwehr, MI5 had her reveal that Oliver Stanley, former British war minister and peers Lord Lovit and Lord Mountbatten numbered among her friends. "Of course they had no idea Bronx was attributing some splendid indiscretions to them. If they'd known they'd have been furious." Similarly, Victor Rothschild was "somewhat put out to discover" that another double agent, code-named "Artist," had MI5 orders to describe his assistance to the German source in gaining him entry into the British Isles. Rothschild worried that if the story leaked out people would get the wrong impression. "It might appear unnecessarily finicky on my part but it might be as well to have permanently on record that the whole Lord Rothschild-Artist saga is imaginary." Macintyre, *Double Cross*, 133, 212.

55. "Representative Sol Bloom Dies of Heart Attack at 78," *New York Times,* March 8, 1949.

56. Lisbon memorandum, FBI Popov File.

57. Kimball memorandum to Ladd, October 23, 1942, FBI Popov File.

58. Popov may have been safely back in London free of the FBI but not of his American creditors. When the Keystone Debt Collection Agency learned of his employment with

the British government they sought payment through diplomatic channels for monies he still owed to a company named Trivett's Tested Seeds. MI5 eventually paid the bill. Macintyre, *Double Cross*, 146; Hoover letter to Foxworth, November 3, 1942, FBI Popov File.

CHAPTER 11: THE COUNT FROM NEW YORK

1. Wilhelm Albrecht Von Rautter, with aliases, Espionage—G, World War II Headquarters Files, 66–1723-Sub I, Section II, History of FBI Activities in World War II, RG 65, Box 126, NARA. Hereafter referred to as "Rautter with aliases."
2. Wilhelm Albrecht Von Rautter, KV2/3004–3005, NA.
3. Batvinis, *Origins*, 201–202.
4. Ibid.
5. Fred Lewis was eventually identified as Ernst Fritz Detlev Heinrich Lehmitz, a naturalized U.S. citizen of German birth. He was arrested by the FBI for espionage on June 28, 1943, and later sentenced to a lengthy prison term. Batvinis, *Origins*, 202.
6. Rautter with aliases.
7. Ibid.
8. Ibid.
9. Ibid.
10. Ibid.
11. Ibid.
12. Ibid.
13. Ibid.
14. Ibid.
15. Ibid.
16. FBI undated memorandum obtained under FOIPA. Hereafter referred to as "FBI memorandum."
17. Ibid.
18. Clay Lancaster, *Old Brooklyn Heights* (New York: Dover Books, 1979).
19. "Cork Dealer as Agent of Nazis," *New York Times*, November 4, 1944, 44.
20. Batvinis, *Origins*, 226–256.
21. Rautter with aliases; Batvinis, *Origins*, 226–256.
22. Rautter with aliases.
23. Ibid.
24. Ibid.
25. Ibid.
26. Ibid.
27. FBI memorandum.
28. "German Held Here as Spy," *New York Times*, January 12, 1944, 44. Ten days later a Manhattan doll shop owner named Velvalee Dickinson was charged with passing national defense information contained in antique dolls to the Japanese through agents in Buenos Aires. Dickinson pleaded guilty to violating the censorship act and on August 14, 1944, was sentenced to a ten-year jail term at the Federal Correctional Facility at Alderson, West Virginia.
29. "Ex-Count Escapes the Noose in Spy Plot," *New York Times*, October 11, 1944, 23.

CHAPTER 12: JAPS, ASPIRIN, AND PEP

1. FBI memorandum.
2. Ibid.
3. Robert Wilcox, *Japan's Secret War* (New York: William Morrow, 1985), 69–71.
4. Ibid., 69–71.
5. Andrew, *Defend the Realm*, 259–262.
6. FBI memorandum.
7. Ibid.
8. Wilcox, *Japan's Secret War*, 67–71.
9. SIS Personnel List, in author's collection.
10. Wilcox, *Japan's Secret War*, 67–71.
11. The British were already aware of Kobbe's mission through Ultra. "We [MI5] then discussed the Chinchilla Kobbe case. Valentine Vivian thought that the action we suggested might prejudice the security of BJ [diplomatic intercept]. . . . It seems fairly clear now we will have to let Kobbe go through to Vancouver and then make some approach there through the Canadians." MI6 continued to deny BJ material to the FBI. GLUD, November 18, 1942, June 4, 1943, and June 28, 1943.
12. "I saw Arthur Thurston . . . about the Chinchilla Kobbe case. Thurston will ascertain from Washington whether they would be prepared to send Aladren up to Vancouver on some pretext to make contact with Kobbe." GLUD, July 21, 1943.
13. Graeme Mount, *Canada's Enemies* (Toronto: Dundurn Press, 1993), 102.
14. Jeffery, *The Secret History of MI6*, 402–403.
15. FBI memorandum.
16. Ibid.
17. Ibid.
18. Hoover teletype to Siscoe, November 29, 1944; B.P. Shetter memorandum to Ladd, December 12, 1944, FBI file entitled "UNSUB, Informant, Eduard Arnaud, Espionage G, 100–201548." Obtained from FBI under FOIPA. Hereafter referred to as "Pep Case."
19. Siscoe teletype to Hoover, November 19, 1955; Hoover teletype to Siscoe, November 22, 1944; memorandum to Ladd, April 24, 1945, Pep Case.
20. Tony Mathews, *Shadows Dancing* (New York: St. Martin's Press, 1993), 32; Siscoe teletype to Hoover, December 12, 1944, Pep Case.
21. FBI Washington Field Office report, January 3, 1945; NYO report, January 6, 1945, Pep Case.
22. B. P. Shetter memorandum to Ladd, December 12, 1944. Shetter later warned Ladd, "From the information thus far developed concerning Pep it would appear that Pep is not the type of individual that the Bureau would normally want to develop into a double agent. However, in view of the Bureau's urgent desire to establish Japanese double agents and the difficulty that has been encountered it would appear that even in view of the derogatory information, further consideration should be given toward using Pep." B. P. Shetter memorandum to Ladd, January 9, 1945, Pep Case.
23. Hoover teletype to Siscoe, December 15, 1944; Hoover letter to Flinn and Siscoe, December 13, 1945, Pep Case.
24. B. P. Shetter memorandum to Ladd, January 9, 1945, Pep Case.

25. Siscoe teletype to Hoover, December 24, 1944, Pep Case.

26. Shetter memorandum to Ladd, January 9, 1945, Pep Case.

27. Siscoe wrote in his next two cables to Washington that "developments to date do not inspire confidence," pointing to his "previous background, the indefiniteness of his mission, lack of financial arrangements, his obvious desire to get permanent visa for himself and family to enter the United States, his dilatory attitude toward departure and his constant change of plans." He went on to note that "while there is no evidence of bad faith on the part of Pep, due caution has been and will continue to be used in handling him." In response, Hoover warned Siscoe to "be particularly cautious in dealing with Pep to prevent Japs from learning our interest in double agents and thus endangering the Double Agent Program." Siscoe cables to Washington, March 7, 1945, March 14, 1945, and Hoover teletype to Siscoe, March 10, 1945, Pep Case.

28. Hoover confirmed the decision, noting on the memo, "I think we should take the risk. OK. H." Tamm memorandum to Hoover, January 11, 1945, Pep Case.

29. Hoover letter to NYO, April 25, 1945, Pep Case.

30. NYO report, January 6, 1945, Pep Case.

31. E. E. Conroy letter to Hoover, May 8, 1945, Pep Case.

32. Hoover letter to NYO, May 24, 1945, Pep Case.

33. Siscoe teletype to Hoover, August 4, 1945, Pep Case.

34. Horton Telford letter to Hoover, August 4, 1945, Pep Case

CHAPTER 13: ND98

1. Over the years confusion has arisen concerning the title of this case. It started as an FBI file entitled "Jorge Mosquera, with aliases," 65-37233, when Mosquera first came to the FBI's attention in 1941. The newness of these types of matter caused the FBI to eventually title the case "Rudloff with aliases" when Max Rudloff was identified as a possible espionage suspect. It is also worthy of note that when Chapin began interviewing Mosquera, he used the services of an MI6 officer stationed in Montevideo who reported his meeting to London, characterizing the new source as "Minaret." Report of SA William G. Friedman, December 4, 1941. File was obtained under the provisions of the FOIPA. Hereafter referred to as "FBI Mosquera File."

2. Ibid.

3. Ibid.

4. Ibid.

5. Ibid.

6. Ibid.

7. Ibid.

8. Ibid.

9. Ibid.

10. Ibid.

11. Ibid.

12. Ibid.

13. E. Ruth Anderson, *Contemporary American Composers* (Boston: G. K. Hall, 1982),

89; Certificate of Arrival, Declaration of Intentions, May 10, 1926, Petition of Citizenship, July 17, 1930, Bureau of Immigration, U.S. Department of Labor, Municipal Records Center, New York, New York; "Alexander Semmler, 76, Composer of Music for TV, Radio and Film," *New York Times*, April 25, 1977, 34.

14. Foxworth letter to Hoover, December 30, 1941, FBI Mosquera File.

15. NYO report of SA J. C. Fellner, March 20, 1942, FBI Mosquera File; War Department General and Special Staffs Name Index to Correspondence of the Military Intelligence Division of the War Department, General Staff, 1917–1941, M1194, Box 40, NARA.

16. NYO report of SA J. C. Fellner, March 20, 1942; J. W. Carlsen memorandum, February 18, 1942, FBI Mosquera File.

17. Foxworth letter to Hoover, January 14, 1942, FBI Mosquera File.

18. Robert Caro, *The Power Broker* (New York: Knopf, 1974), 148–149.

19. Alexander Rose, *Washington's Spies* (New York: Bantam Books, 2006), 38–43.

20. Caro, *The Power Broker*, 148–149.

21. Ibid., 153.

22. Ibid., 157.

23. Ibid., 151.

24. Author interview of James Millen, April 10, 2013, and of Kathleen Loomis Ward, September 23, 2009, along with author visit to Benson House. John Fox and the Society of Former Special Agents of the Federal Bureau of Investigation provided biographical data on Millen and Johnson.

25. Author interview of Kathleen Loomis Ward and author visit to Benson House, September 23, 2009. John Fox and the Society of Former Special Agents of the Federal Bureau of Investigation provided biographical data on Millen and Johnson.

26. NYO Report of SA J. C. Fellner, April 11, 1942, FBI Mosquera File.

27. NYO teletype, April 28, 1942; Johnson memorandum to Ladd, April 28, 1942, FBI Mosquera File.

28. Johnson memorandum to Ladd, April 28, 1942, FBI Mosquera File.

29. NYO Report of SA J. C. Fellner, April 11, 1942, FBI Mosquera File.

30. Richard Rhodes, *The Making of the Atomic Bomb* (New York: Simon & Schuster, 1986), 406; Thomas Powers, *Heisenberg's War* (Boston: Little, Brown, 1993), vii. Alexander Sachs, a friend of Einstein who delivered the letter to Roosevelt, recalled years later the president saying, "Well Alex, what you are after is to see that the Germans don't blow us up." Walter Isaacson, *Einstein* (New York: Simon & Schuster, 2007), 474–477.

31. Rhodes, *The Making of the Atomic Bomb*, 406.

32. Ibid., 407.

33. Ibid., 408.

34. Coffey memorandum to Ladd, May 1, 1942, FBI Mosquera File.

35. Holt, *The Deceivers*, 53.

36. Ibid., 54–55.

37. Ibid., 289.

38. Andrew, *Defend the Realm*, 284; Holt, *The Deceivers*, 289. H. M. O'Connor memorandum to JSC, January 25, 1945, THP.

39. H. M. O'Connor memorandum to JSC, January 25, 1945, THP; FBI memorandum.
40. FBI memorandum.
41. Ibid.
42. Ibid.
43. William H. Crawford memorandum to Ladd, September 3, 1942; Memorandum for the Record, July 12, 1944, THP; G. R. Levy memorandum to Ladd, September 2, 1942, FBI Mosquera File.
44. "I as well as my people are doing the best we can. The control and watchfulness of everything that has to do with the Government Administration of military and war production has become very acute. Even the activity of the FBI in comparison to the time of my arrival has increased five hundred percent." On November 9, 1942, ND98, in response to a German message questioning his ring's courage, furiously insisted that "not one of our reports came from the newspapers." As if to challenge the Abwehr on this point of honor he insisted that they "check continuously the information from Wasch and Nevi even though I have absolute confidence in both as well as in the radio man." November 19 and November 21, 1942, messages, Rudloff A and B Messages, Box 11, THP.
45. William H. Crawford, memorandum to Ladd, September 3, 1942; FBI memorandum.
46. Martin Gilbert, *Winston Churchill: Road to Victory, 1941–1945* (Boston: Houghton, Mifflin 1986), 68–69.
47. "Slessor Goes with Eaker," *New York Times,* January 9, 1944. Hoover letter to Edwin Watson, December 3, 1943, Of10b File, Box 22, FDRL.
48. Frederick Morgan, *Overtures to Overlord* (Garden City, N.Y.: Doubleday, 1950), 29; FBI memorandum.
49. Roger Hesketh, *Fortitude: The D-Day Campaign* (New York: Overlook Press, 2000), 1.
50. Rudloff A and B Messages, Box 11, THP.
51. Ibid.
52. Hesketh, *Fortitude*, 17.
53. Ibid., 59.
54. Rudloff A and B Messages, Box 11, THP.
55. Ibid.
56. Ibid.
57. Ibid.
58. Hoover letter to Edwin Watson, December 30, 1943, Of10b, FDRL.
59. Ibid.
60. Holt, *The Deceivers*, 670.
61. Ibid., 672.
62. Ibid., 730.
63. Ibid.
64. Ibid. Buckner and the Tenth Army were then engaged in the fighting on Iwo Jima.
65. Ladd memorandum to Hoover, March 20, 1945, entitled "Double Agents and Financial Transactions." Contained in FBI file number 65–20026 entitled "Cocase," obtained from the FBI under FOIPA.

CHAPTER 14: GASTON DECHANT

1. Telford Taylor, *The Anatomy of the Nuremberg Trials* (New York: Alfred A. Knopf, 1992), 39.

2. In May 1945, following publicity about Costes's work for the FBI, a childhood acquaintance reported that Costes had been arrested as a teenager for a number of petty crimes including prostitution. "Dieudonne Costes, Pioneer Flyer, Dies," *New York Times*, May 20, 1973, 64.

3. Ibid.

4. Interrogation Report, Trinidad Travelers Censorship, December 16, 1942, 64-20026, Department of State memorandum dated December 16, 1942. FBI investigative file number 65-20026 entitled "Dieudonne Costes, Espionage—G," obtained from the FBI under the FOIPA. The title of the case was later changed to "Cocase." Hereafter referred to as "Cocase."

5. Ibid.

6. F. S. Penney memo to Ladd, March 13, 1943, and March 29, 1943, Cocase.

7. FBI Johnson report, December 19, 1942, Cocase.

8. Little memorandum for Ladd, January 16, 1943, Cocase.

9. FBI Report of SA Richard Johnson entitled "Paul Cavaillez and Tom X," dated July 23, 1943, FOIPA Johnson FBI report. After interviewing the couple, Doyle urged his use as an agent, at which point Tamm authorized the necessary funds for their travel to the United States to begin work as a double agent. Tamm ordered that the case be designated a "Special under E. J. Connelley." Ladd memo to Tamm, March 15, 1943, Cocase.

10. Robert Maheu, *Next to Hughes* (New York: HarperCollins, 1992), 10.

11. Author interview of Peter Maheu, August 10, 2010; "Waterville's Robert Maheu Never Lost Touch with Home," *Kennebec Journal*, March 18, 2009.

12. Maheu, *Next to Hughes*, 20; "Robert Maheu, FBI Agent and CIA Fixer Who Became Howard Hughes Bagman," *Guardian*, August 20, 2008, 33; "Robert Maheu, 90; Tycoon's Aide, CIA Spy," *Washington Post*, August 6, 2008.

13. Author interview of Peter Maheu, August 10, 2010; Connelley letter to Hoover, May 7, 1943, Cocase.

14. Connelley letter to Hoover, May 7, 1943, Cocase.

15. Costes's total monthly demands including rent amounted to $1,900. Accounting for inflation, this amounts to $25,000 per month in 2012. Since assuming responsibility for the case in March 1943, the FBI had incurred a total of $4,165 in expenses ($55,000 in 2012). Ladd memorandum to Hoover, August 3, 1943, Cocase.

16. After the war Paul Cavaillez told FBI agents that the Abwehr gave Costes a "small fortune before he departed France." NYO report of SA Albert H. Cote, 1016, 1945, Cocase; Routing Slip, Undated, FBI File 64–20026–355, Cocase.

17. F. S. Penny memo to Ladd, December 3, 1943; Ladd memorandum to Cunningham, December 14, 1943; Hoover letter to Connelley, December 31, 1942, FBI File 64–200226, Cocase. "I told Connelley that in his talk with Tom X this morning he should stress the fact that he should go to South America that once he gets out of this country he will never get back. Connelley stated that this is the only thing we can do now and

will see what we can do into talking him into going to Argentina." Ladd memorandum to Tamm, December 21, 1943, Cocase.

18. "Desire to Keep Up the Spirit of France Is Motivating Force," *New York Times,* July 14, 1943.

19. "Ratoff Burial Here: Russian Actor Will Be Cremated in Switzerland," *New York Times,* December 15, 1960.

20. "Of course nothing is to be put in writing." Then as an afterthought he wondered, "How many others are playing us for such suckers." Ladd memorandum to Cunningham, December 14, 1943.

21. NYO report of SA Albert H. Cote, October 16, 1945, Cocase; Routing Slip, Undated, FBI File 64-20026-355, Cocase.

22. These were the messages that prompted the Abwehr to initiate Cavaillez's mission to the United States. Wendell Stoops report, August 30, 1943, Cocase.

23. Siscoe letter to Hoover, May 19, 1944, Cocase.

24. What was discovered was the name Jean Louis Poivrel residing at 442 East 52nd Street in New York City. Poivrel was a French citizen born in Rennes in 1901 who arrived in the United States by ship from Lisbon in August 1940. Investigation was immediately instituted on him. Hoover teletype to Connelley, October 13, 1944; Connelley letter to Hoover, February 23, 1944, Cocase.

25. While this money would be available within two or three weeks, the Bureau was at a loss to understand what money he was then currently using for living expenses, as he claimed only having $50 when interviewed upon his arrival in New Orleans. Speculation extended to the Spanish Consulate providing him funds when he received a telephone call at his hotel room that was intercepted by the FBI, or possibly loans from fellow passengers aboard the SS *Magallanes.* Connelley began concentrating on the funds he was expending until his funds arrived from Lisbon. Connelley letter to SAC, Washington, November, June 1944, Cocase.

26. Connelley letter to Hoover, January 25, 1944; Hottel letter to Hoover, November 14, 1944, Cocase.

27. NYO report of SA Robert Maheu, May 3, 1944; SAC, WFO to Hoover, December 5, 1944; Washington Field Office teletype to Bureau and NYO, November 18, 1944, Cocase.

28. Hoover to Connelley, November 30, 1944. It is also important to note that the Bureau had an informant inside the Spanish embassy in Washington who had access to the diplomatic bag and could watch it being filled and emptied and could offer the FBI insights into its contents. One suggestion made to WFO was that they alert the source to the identity of John Y and urge the source to keep an eye peeled for any evidence of his name in the bag. Part of this idea was based on information that many Spaniards in the United States send letters to the Spanish embassy which, when opened, contain another addressed to friends and relatives in Spain and elsewhere, which the embassy sends back to Madrid for mailing in the diplomatic pouch. Hoover to Connelley, November 28, 1944. When he visited Washington the FBI followed him to a meeting with Roberte Rocherte at her home at 2021 O Street, Washington, D.C., which she shared with her mother, Marguerite Fellrath. Rocherte was then serving as a temporary employee with the Military Intelligence Division of the War Department at the Pentagon, where she

performed translation work, and she had previously worked at the American embassy in Paris. Sources indicated that he was working with Rocherte, who he claimed was working in the air section of the army to get a letter from General Arnold that would allow him to remain in the country as a military observer. Intercepted conversations provided insight into the close friendship between the two and her interest in getting the letter. WFO report of SA George Davis, December 16, 1944, Cocase.

29. NYO memorandum entitled Cocase, December 15, 1944.

30. Ibid.

31. FBI Laboratory letter to NYO, December 20, 1944. What is of further significance is that the list of parts is in the handwriting of Cavaillez, which Connelley believed would be very useful and compelling evidence if prosecution of Cavaillez was considered. Penny memorandum to Ladd, December 21, 1944, Cocase.

32. WFO teletype, February 1, 1945, Cocase.

33. NYO teletype, February 27, 1945, Cocase.

34. Ibid.

35. NYO teletype to Hoover, April 23, 1945, Cocase.

36. Ibid.

37. Penny memorandum to Ladd, May 19, 1945, Cocase.

38. Ibid.

39. See Hoover memorandum to Clark, June 1, 1945, Cocase.

40. Report of SA Wendell Stoops, June 14, 1945, Cocase.

41. "Ratoff Burial Here: Russian Actor Will Be Cremated in Switzerland," *New York Times,* December 15, 1960.

42. NYO teletype to Hoover, April 23, 1945, Cocase.

43. Ibid.

44. Penny memorandum to Ladd, May 19, 1945, Cocase.

45. Ibid.

46. Hoover memorandum to Clark, June 1, 1945, Cocase.

47. "Cavaillez Pleads Not Guilty," *New York Times,* July 21, 1945; "Paul Jean Marie Cavaillez Sentenced Here," *New York Times,* September 28, 1945.

48. "Ratoff Burial Here: Russian Actor Will Be Cremated in Switzerland," *New York Times,* December 15, 1960.

49. "Dieudonne Costes, Pioneer Flier Dies," *New York Times,* May 20, 1973; New York teletype to Bureau, June 27, 1947, Cocase.

CHAPTER 15: KOEHLER

1. Report of SA E. R. Landnaes, August 4, 1942; report of SA Peter Hoehl, August 27, 1943. FBI File number 65–41274 entitled "Alfred Meiler, alias Alfred Koehler; Elizabeth Meiler, with aliases: Elsa Meiler, Else Koehler, Elizabeth Koehler, Esp.-G." File obtained from the FBI through the FOIPA. Meiler was later assigned the code-name "Pat J" by the FBI. Hereafter referred to as "Alfred Meiler with alias."

2. Report of SA E. R. Landnaes, August 4, 1942, Alfred Meiler with alias.

3. For a detailed account of the Rumrich case and Von Bonin's role, see Batvinis, *Origins*, 3–28.

4. Report of SA E. R. Landnaes, August 4, 1942, Alfred Meiler with alias.

5. Ibid.

6. Meiler told FBI agents that he originally had a total of 30,000 guilders from the sale of his home and business, which the Germans confiscated. They then gave him $15,000 ($211,000 in 2012), which represented a portion of the proceeds. After his ship was stopped by the Coast Guard, Meiler attempted suicide by ingesting a drug called neumotol. He was taken off the ship and taken to a hospital in New Smyrna Beach, Florida, where he quickly recovered. Months later after questioning, Mrs. Meiler turned over another $10,000 that they apparently had hidden from the Abwehr and attempted to smuggle into the United States. The FBI had nagging suspicions of the Meilers based on discrepancies in Alfred's background information and their attempt to smuggle the $10,000 into the country, which the FBI discovered when Mrs. Meiler and her friend from New York, Jadwiga Light, traveled back to Florida for a vacation and while there recovered the money from a safe deposit box that the couple had taken in a local Miami bank. The FBI was also suspicious given the background of the money received in Spain, Mrs. Meiler's attempted suicide, Light's knowledge of the Meilers' connection with the FBI, and the burial of the money in a lot near the hospital in New Smyrna Beach. Report of SA E. R. Landnaes, December 21, 1942; report of SA Howard Hawkins, May 14, 1943, Alfred Meiler with alias.

7. An attorney general authorized microphone and telephone taps that were installed on Meiler's hotel suite to monitor their private conversations and identities of any callers. The early use of microphones by the FBI is not recorded in detail. Following the issuance of President Roosevelt's May 21, 1940, memorandum, microphone surveillances were used in cases involving matters affecting the defense of the nation. Throughout World War II and until 1965 the use of microphones was initiated upon the authority of the FBI director. The unsettled state of law regarding admissibility of evidence obtained from microphones was of continuing concern to FBI officials. Under existing policy the Bureau was installing and using microphones on its own authority. On the other hand, the use of these techniques was dictated by considerations of national security that were clearly of concern to President Roosevelt and his successors. Although the Department of Justice was not being informed of the installation of microphone coverage, it was clearly aware of this practice by the FBI. In connection with prosecutions of communist leaders under the Smith Act, extensive discussions were held between Bureau representatives and officials of the department concerning the use of microphones, particularly the question of admissibility of evidence derived from such coverage. Memorandum entitled "June Warrantless Electronic Surveillance by the FBI," September 11, 1975, Do Not File (Frederick, Md.: University Publications of America, 1988), microfilm call no. 90/7006, LOC.

8. Report of SA E. R. Landnaes, December 21, 1942, Alfred Meiler with alias.

9. Ibid. FBI investigation of Siegfried is redacted.

10. Ibid.

11. Ibid.

12. Report of SA E. R. Landnaes, November 4, 1942; Alfred Meiler with alias.
13. Rhodes, *The Making of the Atomic Bomb*, 205–208, 242–243.
14. Ibid., 146.
15. Ibid.
16. Powers, *Heisenberg's War*, 430. Report of SA D. J. Williams, October 1, 1940, in FBI case entitled "Dr. Peter J.W. Debye, Special Inquiry, National Defense Research Committee," THP.
17. Report of SA Howard Hawkins, March 1, 1943, Alfred Meiler with alias.
18. Report of SA Howard Hawkins, May 14, 1943, Alfred Meiler with alias.
19. Report of SA Howard Hawkins March 2, 1943, Alfred Meiler with alias.
20. Report of SA Howard Hawkins, May 25, 1943, Alfred Meiler with alias.
21. Special thanks to the staff of the New-York Historical Society for their assistance on New York and World War II.
22. Lehmitz was arrested for espionage on June 28, 1942. Batvinis, *Origins*, 202; Report of SA Howard Hawkins, November 19, 1942, Alfred Meiler with alias.
23. Report of SA Peter Hoehl, November 27, 1943, Alfred Meiler, with alias.
24. Hesketh, *Fortitude*, 72.
25. Report of SA Howard Hawkins, June 3, 1944, Alfred Meiler with alias.
26. That same day Garbo responded to German concerns about troop movements in Scotland and how much time would be lost from the moment the 52nd British Lowland Division departed. The division was scheduled to lead the attack on Narvik with follow-up from the 55th Infantry Division in Iceland, sailing directly to Narvik immediately after the initial assault. It was to be strengthened by three imaginary Ranger battalions coming from the United States to Iceland before the attack was launched. A Norwegian contingent in Scotland was also to be included in the force. No real corps being available to command the Northern force, an imaginary one was created. This came into being in March 1944 and was known as the 7th British Corps, which would oversee the 55th Infantry Division and the three Ranger battalions. Garbo offered his assurances that the invasion fleet was still in the Clyde River and another important British division had not moved.
27. Report of SA Howard Hawkins, June 3, 1944, Alfred Meiler with alias.
28. Report of SA Peter Hoehl, September 27, 1944, Alfred Meiler with alias.
29. Ibid.
30. Report of SA Howard Hawkins, October 27, 1944, Alfred Meiler with alias.
31. Batvinis, *Origins*, 98–119.
32. "Proposal for transmitting money. You can receive something like four weeks eight postage stamp collections in two letters containing 4 each having a total value of $2000." These types of messages were exchanged for much of the life of the operation. The stamps were never received. Report of SA Howard Hawkins, June 3, 1944 Alfred Meiler with alias.
33. Ibid.
34. Report of SA Peter Hoehl, July 25, 1944, Alfred Meiler with alias.
35. Ibid.
36. Ibid.
37. Ibid.

38. Ibid.
39. Report of SA Peter Hoehl, September 14, 1944, Alfred Meiler with alias.
40. Ibid.
41. Report of SA Howard Hawkins, June 3, 1944, Alfred Meiler with alias.
42. "Further money shipment possible over South America to a bank there. Have you anyone who can receive at his bank an amount up to $20000 and what would be the reason therefore." Report of SA Howard Hawkins, March 5, 1945. From February 25 to May 1, 1945, a total of ninety-three messages were exchanged, averaging more than one per day. "In any event please continue contact with Holtz also if he is transferred." Report of SA Peter Hoehl, July 10, 1945, Alfred Meiler with alias.
43. Ibid.
44. Ibid.

CHAPTER 16: PEASANT

1. The boundary between I H Ost and I H West was an imaginary line running east of Norway and Italy, according to the countries in which the agents worked, not the countries the information concerned. David Kahn, *Hitler's Spies* (New York: Macmillan, 1978), 238.
2. Arthur Thurston letter to Hoover with attachment entitled "Helmuth Siegfried Goldschmidt," August 6, 1943, 65-51317, FOIPA. Hereafter referred to as "FBI Goldschmidt File."
3. Ibid.
4. Thurston letter to Hoover with attachment entitled "Career of Helmuth Siegfried Goldschmidt," August 6, 1943. Hereafter referred to as "Goldschmidt Career." FBI Goldschmidt File.
5. NYO report of SA W. Willis Fisher, August 25, 1943; WFO teletype, August 29, 1943, FBI Goldschmidt File.
6. Goldschmidt Career, FBI Goldschmidt File.
7. Ibid.
8. Ibid. Later investigation confirmed that Max Gerdts Pochet was born in Colombia to German parents and served in the German army during the First World War. He was fired from his job as port captain at Puerto Colombia around June 1940 and later secured employment as a customs inspector at Barranquilla, Colombia. "He was reported to have obeyed orders emanating from the Nazi Party while acting as a port captain. Believed to have been contacted in 1938 and to have been in the pay of German Intelligence Service." Bogota, Colombia report of SA Joseph F. Campisi, June 28, 1944, FBI Goldschmidt File.
9. Goldschmidt Career.
10. Thurston letter to Hoover, October 23, 1943, FBI Goldschmidt File.
11. Ibid. In his memoir W. Mark Felt claims that he conceived the idea for keeping Goldschmidt, code-named "Peasant," in England while convincing the Germans that he was spying for them in the United States. "What to do with Gold," Felt wrote, never identifying him, offering only the name created by the FBI for his New York post box that was used for letters and cables from the Abwehr. Because "he had been trained by

Nest Bremen the question was referred to me for recommendation. I recommended that we take the case but leave Gold in England in protective custody. We would create a fictitious Gold who would come to Washington and set up an espionage operation. Thus we would not only control what information went to the Nazis but also use the bogus Gold to ferret out the spies he was to work with. Hoover agreed." The file contains no Felt memorandum to Hoover. The idea originated with Thurston in London and was supported by Tyler and Fletcher in Washington. W. Mark Felt, *The FBI Pyramid* (New York: G. P. Putnam's Sons, 1979), 36.

12. Ibid.

13. Goldschmidt gave Thurston, who knew him only as "Mr. McDuff" from the U.S. embassy, written permission to use his name in a fictional double-agent operation in collaboration with MI5 and waived his rights to any funds received from the Germans. L. Tyler and R. G. Fletcher memorandum to Ladd, November 18, 1943, Thurston letter to Hoover, November 18, 1943, FBI Goldschmidt File.

14. L. Tyler and R. G. Fletcher memorandum to Ladd, November 18, 1943, FBI Goldschmidt File.

15. Felt, *FBI Pyramid*, 17–24.

16. L. Tyler and R. G. Fletcher memorandum to Ladd, November 18, 1943, FBI Goldschmidt File.

17. Thurston cable to Hoover, October 24, 1943; Thurston letter to Hoover, October 23, 1943, FBI Goldschmidt File.

18. Thurston letter to Hoover, October 23, 1943; Hoover teletype to Thurston, November 4, 1943; Ladd memorandum to Hoover, December 3, 1943. Hoover wrote on the margin of Ladd's memo, "Are we sound in not having this man sent to U.S.? Can we effect the contact without him here?" FBI Goldschmidt File.

19. Hoover letter to NYO, November 30, 1943; Hoover letter to London, December 1, 1943; Ladd memorandum to Coffey, December 3, 1943, FBI Goldschmidt File.

20. Translation from German, October 16, 1943, FBI Goldschmidt File.

21. Hoover letter to Thurston, January 5, 1944, FBI Goldschmidt File.

22. Boston teletype to Hoover, February 8, 1944; R.E. Thornton memorandum to Coffey, February 15, 1944. FBI Goldschmidt File.

23. Hoover letter to Flinn, May 18, 1944, FBI Goldschmidt File.

24. R. E. Newby memorandum to Ladd, March 7, 1944; Hoover letter to NYO, March 9, 1944, FBI Goldschmidt File.

25. Two years earlier MI5 experienced a similar problem with "William Gerbers," Garbo's imaginary informant who lived in the major port city of Liverpool. Had Gerbers existed, he would have been able to supply volumes of information about ship readying in the Mersy River for the anticipated invasion of North Africa. Any failure to report his observations would have brought Abwehr suspicion on Garbo and his entire network. British deception planners solved the problem by infecting Gerbers with a "lingering malady" that later proved fatal. Macintyre, *Double Cross*, 126. NYO letter to Hoover, August 17, 1944, FBI Goldschmidt File.

26. Keith Miller, "How Important Was Oil in World War II," George Mason University, History News Network, July 5, 2000.

27. NYO letter to Hoover, August 17, 1944, FBI Goldschmidt File.

28. I. W. Conrad was suspicious of a leak in London to the Germans concerning this case. I. W. Conrad memorandum to Coffey, July 22, 1944, FBI Goldschmidt File.
29. Hoover letter to WFO, September 1, 1944, October 2, 1944, FBI Goldschmidt File.
30. C. F. Downing memorandum to Coffey, September 23, 1944, FBI Goldschmidt File.
31. Felt memorandum to Ladd, August 29, 1944; C.F. Downing memorandum to Coffey, September 1, 1944, FBI Goldschmidt File.
32. Memorandum, September 7, 1944, FBI Goldschmidt File.
33. Hoover letter to WFO, September 13, 1944; FBI Goldschmidt File.
34. Miller, "How Important Was Oil in World War II."
35. Hoover letters to WFO, September 1, 1944, October 2, 1944, FBI Goldschmidt File.
36. Felt memorandum to Ladd, September 18, 1944, FBI Goldschmidt File.
37. WFO report of SA Maurice Taylor, November 9, 1944, FBI Goldschmidt File.
38. Felt memoranda to Ladd, October 2, 1944, October 4, 1944, and memorandum, January 17, 1945, FBI Goldschmidt File.
39. WFO Report of SA Maurice Taylor, November 9, 1944, FBI Goldschmidt File.
40. Ibid.
41. Ibid.
42. Report of SA Maurice Taylor, February 1, 1945, FBI Goldschmidt File.
43. Ibid.
44. Ibid.
45. Hoover letter to WFO, January 16, 1945, FBI Goldschmidt File.
46. WFO letter to Hoover, January 1, 1945; report of SA Maurice Taylor, February 1, 1945, FBI Goldschmidt File.
47. WFO letter to Hoover, January 17, 1945, R.A. Newby memorandum to Ladd, January 26, 1945, FBI Goldschmidt File.
48. Untitled memorandum, February 17, 1945, FBI Goldschmidt File.
49. G. R. Levy memorandum to Ladd, March 8, 1945, FBI Goldschmidt File. Emphasis added.
50. "Plan Oil Plant," *Miami News,* October 2, 1945; "W. M. Anderson, 57, Oil Executive Dies," *New York Times,* March 22, 1952; Hoover letter to WFO, March 29, 1945; FBI Goldschmidt File.
51. Felt letter to Cimperman, August 19, 1945, FBI Goldschmidt File.
52. Rio de Janeiro report of SA George Van Noy, August 29, 1946, FBI Goldschmidt File.
53. Coffey memorandum to Ladd, April 16, 1945, FBI Goldschmidt File.
54. TAR Robertson, ever concerned about the expense of running his stable of Double Cross agents, complained to Liddell that the FBI should reimburse MI5 for the £150 it had cost him for taking care of Peasant. Liddell diplomatically responded to his premier agent runner that "it is far better that we should pay the 150 pounds and hope that in the end we shall get a dividend from the FBI. I would much rather do this than create a slightly awkward atmosphere of haggling with an ally." That same day Robertson was again reminded that "although it is true that PEASANT has costs us over 150 pounds I hardly think that in view of Lend-Lease & the fact that PEASANT has given us a good deal of information we can reasonably claim this from the FBI." Liddell memorandum to

Robertson, November 11, 1943, KV2/467, NA; R. T. Reed memorandum to Robertson, November 43, 1943, NA; Felt memorandum to Ladd, August 15, 1945, FBI Goldschmidt File.

55. Felt cable to M. J. Lynch, August 2, 1945, FBI Goldschmidt File.

CONCLUSION

1. Carlo de Este, *Eisenhower: A Soldier's Life* (New York: Henry Holt, 2002), 703.
2. Stephenson, *British Security Coordination*, 4.
3. GLUD, April 2, 1943.
4. GLUD, June 10, 1945.

SELECTED BIBLIOGRAPHY

ARCHIVES

American Institute of Physics, College Park, Maryland
  Peter Debye Papers
Federal Bureau of Investigation Reading Room, Washington, D.C.
  Alfred Meiler, 65-41274
  British Intelligence Service in the United States, 65-5004
  Dieudonné Costes File, 65-20026
  Dusko Popov File, 65-36994
  FBI-BSC Liaison File, 62-64178
  Jorge Mosquera File, 65-37233
  Ostrich File, 65-49714
  UNSUB, Informant, Eduard Arnaud, Espionage G, 100-201548
  Wilhelm von Rautter, 66-1723
Federal Records Center, New York, New York
Franklin D. Roosevelt Presidential Library and Museum (FDRL), Hyde Park, New York
  Adolf Berle Papers
  Charles Fahy Papers
  Ernest Cuneo Papers
  Frank Schuler Papers
  Harold Smith Papers
  Harry Hopkins Papers
  Henry Morgenthau Papers
  James Rowe Papers
  John Toland Papers
  John Winant Papers
  President's Map Room File
  President's Official Files
  President's Safe File
  President's Secretary File
  Sumner Welles Papers
  Whitney Shepardson Papers
Georgetown University, Washington, D.C.
  Francis Biddle Papers
  Fulton Oursler Papers

Herbert Hoover Presidential Library and Museum (HHL), West Branch, Iowa
  Herbert Hoover III Papers
Library of Congress (LOC), Washington, D.C.
  Archibald MacLeish Papers
  Carl Spaatz Papers
  Cordell Hull Papers
  Frank Knox Papers
National Archives and Records Administration, College Park, Maryland
National Law Enforcement Officers Museum (NLEOM), Washington, D.C.
  Alex Rosen Papers
  Joseph Campisi Oral History
Royal Canadian Mounted Police, Ottawa, Canada
United Kingdom National Archives, Kew, England
University of Hawaii, Manoa
  John Burns Papers
University of Maryland, College Park, Maryland
  Gordon Prange Papers
U.S. Army Military History Institute, Carlisle, Pennsylvania (USAMHI)
  Thad Holt Papers
  William J. Donovan Papers

INTERVIEWS BY THE AUTHOR

Barrett, Melvin, October 4, 2010 (telephone)
Bertheaux, Amy, March 8, 2008
Crosby, Kenneth, October 14, 1998, November 25, 1999, and March 3, 2001
Edwards, Sally, September 9, 2009
Eskridge, Ron, August 8, 2011 (telephone)
Flinn, Dennis, May 7, 1993, and June 8, 1993
James, Linda, September 9, 2009
Lercari, Leann, August 21, 2011 (telephone)
Maheu, Peter, August 10, 2010 (telephone)
Ramey, Marion, and King, Jean, October 30, 2010, and February 2, 2011
Semmler, Ileana, May 3, 2010
Thurston, Arthur, March 2, 1995
Williams, John, April 30, 2007

ORAL HISTORIES

John Burns, University of Hawaii, Manoa
Joseph Campisi, National Law Enforcement Museum, Washington, D.C.

PRIVATE PAPERS

Dennis DeBrandt Papers
Richard Millen Papers, courtesy of James Millen, Vernon, Connecticut

PERIODICALS

Assembly
Collier's
Culver Alumnus
East Hampton Star
Experimenter
Grapevine
Guardian
Honolulu Advertiser
Honolulu Star Bulletin
Investigator
Kennebec Journal
Miami Herald
Miami News
National Geographic
New York Times
Pittsburgh Post-Gazette
QST
Short Wave Craft
Town of Chesapeake Beach Newsletter
Washington Evening Standard
Washington Post
Washington Star

FILMS

The First Battle. Dir. Tom Coffman. Honolulu, 2006.
John A. Burns: The Man and His Times. Honolulu: EMME Productions, 2000.

BOOKS AND ARTICLES

Abramson, Rudy. *Spanning the Century: The Life of W. Averell Harriman*. New York: William Morrow, 1992.

Ackerman, Kenneth D. *Young J. Edgar*. New York: Carroll & Graf, 2007.

Alcazar de Velasco, Angel. *Memorias de un Agente Secreto*. Barcelona: Plaza & Janes, 1979.

Allason, Rupert. *The Branch.* London: Secker & Warburg, 1989.

Alvarez, David. *Secret Messages.* Lawrence: University Press of Kansas, 2000.

Anderson, E. Ruth. *Contemporary American Composers.* Boston: G.K. Hall, 1982.

Andrew, Christopher. *Defend the Realm.* New York: Macmillan, 2009.

———. *For the President's Eyes Only.* New York: Harper Perennial, 1995.

———. *Her Majesty's Secret Service.* New York: Penguin, 1987.

Atkinson, Rick. *An Army at Dawn.* New York: Henry Holt, 2002.

———. *The Day of Battle.* New York: Henry Holt, 2007.

———. *Guns at Last Light.* New York: Henry Holt, 2013.

Ayer, Frederick. *Yankee G-Man.* Chicago: H. Regnery, 1957.

Bascomb, Neal. *Hunting for Eichmann.* New York: Houghton Mifflin, 2009.

Bassett, Richard. *Hitler's Chief Spy.* London: Cassell, 2005.

Batvinis, Raymond. "The Minutes Were Like Hours." *Intelligencer* (Winter/Spring 2013).

———. *The Origins of FBI Counterintelligence.* Lawrence: University Press of Kansas, 2007.

———. "The Strange Odyssey of Louis Beck." FBIstudies.com.

Beesly, Patrick. *Very Special Admiral: The Life of Admiral J. H. Godfrey.* London: Hamilton, 1980.

Bennett, Gil. *Churchill's Man of Mystery.* London: Routledge, Taylor & Francis, 2007.

Benson, Robert Louis. *A History of U.S. Communications Intelligence during World War II: Policy and Administration.* Ser. 4, vol. 8. Fort Meade, Md.: Center for Cryptologic History, 1997.

Berle, Beatrice Bishop, ed. *Navigating the Rapids.* New York: Harcourt Brace Jovanovich, 1973.

Bessel, Richard. *Germany 1945.* New York: Harper, 2009.

Best, Nicholas. *The Greatest Day in History.* New York: Basic Books, 2008.

Biddle, Francis. *In Brief Authority.* Garden City, N.Y.: Doubleday, 1962.

Bird, Kai, and Martin J. Sherwin. *American Prometheus.* New York: Vintage, 2006.

Borovik, Genrik. *The Philby Files.* Boston: Little, Brown, 1994.

Boyd, Carl. *Hitler's Japanese Confidant.* Lawrence: University Press of Kansas, 1993.

Boylan, Dan, and T. Michael Holmes. *John A. Burns: The Man and His Times,* Honolulu: University of Hawaii Press, 2000.

Braden, Spruille. *Diplomats and Demagogues.* New Rochelle, N.Y.: Arlington, 1971.

Breuer, William. *Hoodwinking Hitler.* Westport, Conn.: Praeger, 1993.

Brinkley, Alan. *The Publisher: Henry R. Luce and His American Century.* New York: Knopf, 2010.

Brinkley, David. *Washington Goes to War.* New York: Ballantine, 1988.

Bristow, Desmond. *A Game of Moles.* London, 1993.

Brown, Alexander Cave. *"C."* New York: Macmillan, 1987.

Burns, Jimmy. *Papa Spy.* New York: Walker, 2009.

Burrough, Bryan. *Public Enemies.* New York: Penguin, 2004.

Bush, Vannevar. *Pieces of the Action.* New York: William Morrow, 1970.

———. "Lyman J. Briggs and Atomic Energy." *Scientific Monthly* 78 (May 1954): 275.

Calvocoressi, Peter. *Top Secret Ultra.* New York: Pantheon, 1980.

Canadine, David. *Andrew Mellon.* New York: Knopf, 2006.

Caro, Robert A. *The Power Broker.* New York: Knopf, 1974.
Cecil, Robert. "Five of Six at War." *Intelligence and National Security* 9, no. 2 (April 1994): 345–353.
Chapin, Helen Garacimos. *Shaping History.* Honolulu: University of Hawaii Press, 1996.
Charles, Douglas "Before the Colonel Arrived: Hoover, Donovan, Roosevelt and the Origins of American Central Intelligence." *Intelligence and National Security* 20, no. 2 (December 2004).
Clark, Ronald. *The Man Who Broke Purple.* Boston: Little, Brown, 1977.
Colville, John. *The Fringes of Power.* New York: W. W. Norton, 1985.
Compton, Arthur. *Atomic Quest.* New York: Oxford University Press, 1956.
———. *The Cosmos of Arthur Holly Compton.* New York: Knopf, 1967.
Conant, James B. *A History of the Development of an Atomic Bomb.* Unpublished manuscript, Office of Scientific and Research and Development (OSRD), Bush-Conant File, Folder 5, NARA.
———. *My Several Lives: Memoirs of a Social Inventor.* New York: Harper & Row, 1970.
Conant, Jennet. *The Irregulars.* New York: Simon & Schuster, 2008.
———. *Tuxedo Park.* New York: Simon & Schuster, 2007.
Costello, John. *Mask of Treachery.* New York: William Morrow, 1988.
Coyle, Brendan. *War on Our Doorstep.* Surrey, B.C.: Heritage House, 2002.
Culver, John, and John Hyde. *American Dreamer.* New York: W. W. Norton, 2000.
D'Este, Carlo. *Eisenhower: A Soldier's Life.* New York: Henry Holt, 2002.
Dobbs, Michael. *Saboteurs: Nazi Raid on America.* New York: Vintage, 2005.
Dorril, Stephen. *MI6.* New York: Simon & Schuster, 2000.
Dunlop, Richard. *Donovan: America's Master Spy.* New York: Rand McNally, 1982.
Eisenhower, Dwight D. *Crusade in Europe.* New York: Doubleday, 1948.
Elliott, Geoffrey. *Gentleman Spy.* London: Methuen, 2011.
Ellis, George. *A Man Named Jones.* New York: Signet, 1963.
Erskine, Ralph, and Michael Smith, eds. *Action This Day.* New York: Bantam, 2001.
Farago, Ladislav. *The Broken Seal.* New York: Random House, 1967.
Feldman, Noah. *Scorpions.* New York: Twelve, 2010.
Felt, Mark. *The FBI Pyramid.* New York: G. P. Putnam's Sons, 1979.
Fitzgerald, Penelope. *Brothers Knox.* Washington, D.C.: Counterpoint, 2000.
Fleming, Thomas. *The New Dealers' War.* New York: Basic Books, 2001.
Flynn, Peter A. *Intercepted in Bermuda: The Censorship of the Transatlantic Mail during World War II.* Chicago: Collectors Club of Chicago, 2005.
Fowler, Blond. *FBI Woman.* N.p., 1976.
Fuchs, Lawrence. *Hawaii the Excellent.* Honolulu: Bess, 1992.
Gaddis, John Lewis. *George F. Kennan: An American Life.* New York: Penguin, 2011.
Garlinski, Jozef. *The Enigma War.* New York: Charles Scribner's Sons, 1979.
Gellman, Irving. *Secret Affairs.* Baltimore: Johns Hopkins University Press, 1995.
Gentry, Curt. *J. Edgar Hoover: The Man and the Secrets.* New York: W. W. Norton, 1991.
Gilbert, Martin. *Winston Churchill: Road to Victory, 1941–1945.* Boston: Houghton Mifflin, 1986.
Grombach, John V. *The Great Liquidator.* New York: Doubleday, 1980.
Groves, Leslie R. *Now It Can Be Told.* New York: Harper & Row, 1962.

———. "The Atom General Answers His Critics." *Saturday Evening Post*, May 19, 1948.
Hack, Richard. *Puppetmaster.* Beverly Hills, Calif.: New Millennium, 2004.
Handel, Michael, ed. *Strategic and Operational Deception in the Second World War.* London: Frank Cass, 1987.
Hardie, Robert. "History of Converter M-134-C Top Secret, Chapter XVIII, The Zero Machine." *History of Converter M-134-C*, vol. 1, part 2. Washington, D.C.: Army Security Agency, n.d.
Harrington, Dale. *Mystery Man.* Washington, D.C.: Brassey's, 1999.
Harrison, E.D.R. "British Radio Security and Intelligence 1939–1943." *English Historical Review* 124 (February 2009).
Harrison, Richard. *The CID and the FBI.* London: Frederick Muller, 1956.
Haufler, Hervie. *Codebreakers' Victory.* New York: New American Library, 2003.
Hayes, Carleton. *Wartime Mission in Spain.* New York, 1945.
Haynes, John Earl, Harvey Klehr, and Alexander Vassiliev. *Spies.* New Haven, Conn.: Yale University Press, 2009.
Hershberg, James. *James B. Conant: Harvard to Hiroshima and the Making of the Nuclear Age.* Stanford, Calif.: Stanford University Press, 1995.
Hertig, Katherine L. "American Strategic Deception in the Pacific, 1942–1944." *Intelligence & National Security* 2, no. 3 (July 1987).
Hesketh, Roger. *Fortitude: The D-Day Campaign.* New York: Overlook, 2000.
Hoare, Samuel. *Ambassador on Special Assignment.* London, 1946.
Hodge, Andrew. *Alan Turing: The Enigma.* New York: Simon & Schuster, 1983.
Holmes, Richard. *In the Footsteps of Churchill.* New York: Basic Books, 2005.
Holt, Thad. *The Deceivers.* New York: Scribner, 2004.
Hoover, J. Edgar. "Enemy's Masterpiece of Espionage." *Reader's Digest*, April 1946.
———. *Persons in Hiding.* Boston: Little, Brown, 1941.
———. "The Spy Who Double-Crossed Hitler." *American Legion*, May 1946.
Howard, Michael, and F. H. Hinsley. *The History of British Intelligence in the Second World War.* 5 vols. Cambridge: Cambridge University Press, 1979–1990.
Hunt, John Gabriel, ed. *The Essential Franklin Delano Roosevelt.* New York: Portland House, 1996.
Hyde, H. Montgomery. *Room 3603.* New York: Farrar, Straus, 1962.
Irving, David R. *The German Atomic Bomb.* New York: Simon & Schuster, 1968.
Isaacson, Walter. *Einstein.* New York: Simon & Schuster, 2007.
———. *The Wise Men and the World They Made.* Boston: Faber and Faber, 1986.
Ismay, Hastings. *The Memoirs of General Lord Ismay.* New York: Viking, 1960.
Jeffery, Keith. *The Secret History of MI6.* New York: Penguin, 2010.
Jones, Gus. *The Nazi Failure in Mexico.* N.p., August 30, 1944.
Jones, R. V. *Most Secret War.* London: Penguin, 1978.
Kahn, David. *The Codebreakers.* New York: Scribner, 1996.
———. *Hitler's Spies.* New York: Macmillan, 1978.
———. *Reader of Gentlemen's Mail.* New Haven, Conn.: Yale University Press, 2004.
———. *Seizing the Enigma.* New York: Houghton Mifflin, 1991.
Kavieff, Paul. *The Life and Times of Lepke Buchalter.* New York: Barricade, 2006.
King, Daniel. "Trip to Camp X." *Intelligencer* (Summer/Fall 2012).

Knight, Amy. *How the Cold War Began.* New York: Carroll & Graf, 2005.
Kotani, Ken. *Japanese Intelligence in World War II.* London: Osprey, 2009.
Lancaster, Clay. *Old Brooklyn Heights.* New York: Dover Books, 1979.
Lewin, Ronald. *Churchill as Warlord.* New York: Scarborough House, 1973.
———. *Ultra Goes to War.* New York: Basic Books, 1978.
Liddell, Guy. Unpublished diaries, 1939–1945.
MacDonald, Bill. *The True Intrepid.* Vancouver, B.C.: Raincoast, 2001.
Macintyre, Ben. *Agent Zigzag.* New York: Harmony, 2007.
———. *Operation Mincemeat.* New York: Harmony, 2010.
MacPherson, Nelson. *American Intelligence in Wartime London.* London: Frank Cass, 2003.
Maheu, Robert, and Richard Hack. *Next to Hughes.* New York: HarperCollins, 1992.
Mahl, Thomas. *Desperate Deception.* Washington, D.C.: Brassey's, 1998.
Malkin, Lawrence. *Krueger's Men.* Boston: Little, Brown, 2006.
Masterman, John C. *The Double-Cross System.* New Haven, Conn.: Yale University Press, 1972.
———. *On Chariot's Wheel.* Oxford: Oxford University Press, 1975.
Mathew, Tony. *Shadows Dancing.* New York: St. Martin's, 1993.
Meier, Andrew. *The Lost Spy.* New York: W. W. Norton, 2008.
Miller, Russell. *Codename Tricycle.* New York: Pimlico, 2005.
Montague, Ewen. *The Man Who Never Was.* London: Evans Brothers, 1953.
Moore, Jeffrey M. *Spies for Nimitz: Joint Military Intelligence in the Pacific War.* Annapolis, Md.: Naval Institute Press, 2004.
Morgan, Frederick. *Overture to Overlord.* Garden City, N.Y.: Doubleday, 1950.
Morley, Jefferson. *Our Man in Mexico.* Lawrence: University Press of Kansas, 2008.
Mount, Graeme Stewart. *Canada's Enemies.* Toronto: Dundurn, 2002.
Neitzel, Sonke, ed. *Tapping Hitler's Generals.* Yorkshire: Pen & Sword, 2007.
Nelson, Anne. *Red Orchestra.* New York: Random House, 2009.
Okihiro, Gary. *Island World.* Berkeley: University of California Press, 2008.
Olson, Lynne. *Citizens of London.* New York: Random House, 2010.
Persico, Joseph. *Imperial Rockefeller: A Biography of Nelson A. Rockefeller.* New York: Simon & Schuster, 1982.
———. *Roosevelt's Secret War.* New York: Random House, 2001.
Philby, Harold A.R. *My Silent War.* New York: Grove, 1968.
Pincher, Chapman. *Too Secret Too Long.* New York: St. Martin's, 1987.
Powers, Thomas. *Heisenberg's War.* Boston: Little, Brown, 1993.
Prados, John. *Combine Fleet Decoded: The Secret History of American Intelligence and the Japanese Navy in World War II.* New York: Random House, 1995.
Prange, Gordon W. *At Dawn We Slept.* New York: McGraw-Hill, 1981.
Preston, Paul. *Franco.* New York: Harper Collins, 1993.
Ratcliff, R. A. *Delusions of Intelligence.* Cambridge: Cambridge University Press, 2006.
Reich, Cary. The *Life of Nelson A. Rockefeller: Worlds to Conquer, 1908–1979.* New York: Doubleday, 1996.
Reiding, Jurrie. "Peter Debye: Nazi Collaborator or Secret Opponent." Ambix 57, no. 3 (November 2010): 275–300.

Rhodes, Richard. *The Making of the Atomic Bomb.* New York: Simon & Schuster, 1986
Rings, Werner. *Life with the Enemy.* Trans. J. Maxwell Brownjohn. Garden City, N.Y.: Doubleday, 1982.
Rivas, Darlene. *Missionary Capitalist: Nelson A. Rockefeller in Venezuela.* Chapel Hill: University of North Carolina Press, 2002.
Rose, Alexander. *Washington's Spies.* New York: Bantam, 2006.
Rudgers, David F. *Creating the Secret State.* Lawrence: University Press of Kansas, 2000.
Sakamaki, Kazuo. *I Attacked Pearl Harbor.* New York: Association Press, 1949.
Schmitz, John E. "Enemies among Us: The Relocation, Internment, and Repatriation of German, Italian, and Japanese Americans during the Second World War." Ph.D. diss., American University, Washington, D.C., 2007.
Schoonover, Thomas. *Hitler's Man in Havana.* Lexington: University Press of Kentucky, 2008.
Secrets and Spies. Pleasantville, N.Y.: Readers Digest Association, 1964.
Sherry, Norman. *The Life of Graham Greene, 1939–1955.* Vol. 2. New York: Penguin, 1995.
Sherwood, Robert. *Roosevelt and Hopkins.* New York: Harper Brothers, 1948.
Sibley, Katie. *Red Spies in America.* Lawrence: University Press of Kansas, 2005.
Simpson, B. Mitchell. *Admiral Harold R. Stark: Architect of Victory, 1939–1945.* Columbia: University of South Carolina Press, 1989.
Smith, Michael. *Six.* London: Biteback, 2010.
Spector, Ronald. *Eagle against the Sun.* New York: Vantage, 1985.
Stafford, David. *Churchill and Secret Service.* New York: Overlook, 1999.
———. *Secret Agent.* New York: Overlook, 2001.
Stephens, Robin W.G. *Camp 020: MI5 and the Nazi Spies: The Official History of MI5's Wartime Interrogation Center.* Richmond, England: Public Records Office, 2000.
Stephenson, William S., ed. *British Security Coordination: The Secret History of British Intelligence in the Americas, 1940–1945.* New York: Fromm International, 1999.
Stevenson, William. *Intrepid's Last Case.* New York: Villard, 1983.
———. *A Man Called Intrepid.* New York: Harcourt Brace Jovanovich, 1976.
Stout, Mark. "The Pond: Running Agents for State, War and the CIA." *Studies in Intelligence* 48, no. 3 (2004).
Strauss, Lewis. *Men and Decisions.* New York: Doubleday, 1962.
Taylor, Telford. *The Anatomy of the Nuremberg Trials.* New York: Knopf, 1992.
Thomas, Evan. *The Very Best Men.* New York: Simon & Schuster, 1995.
Thurlow, Richard. "Soviet Spies and British Counterintelligence in the 1930s: Espionage at Woolwich Arsenal and the Foreign Office Communications Department." *Intelligence and National Security* 19, no. 4 (December 2004).
Toland, John. *Infamy.* Garden City, N.Y.: Doubleday, 1982.
Troy, Thomas. *Wild Bill and Intrepid.* New Haven, Conn.: Yale University Press, 1996.
Vanderbilt, Cornelius. *Man of the World: My Life on Five Continents.* New York: Crown, 1959.
Vaughn, Hal. *Sleeping with the Enemy.* New York: Knopf, 2011.
Waller, Douglas. *"Wild Bill" Donovan.* New York: Free Press, 2010.
Welchman, Gordon. *The Hut Six Story.* Shopshire, U.K.: M & M Baldwin, 2001.

West, Nigel. *Garbo.* London: Grafton, 1986.
———. *Mask.* New York: Routledge, 2005.
———. *MI5.* London: Triad Panther, 1984.
———. *The SIGINT Secrets.* New York: William Morrow, 1988.
———. *Venona.* New York: HarperCollins, 2000.
———, ed. *The Guy Liddell Diaries.* Vols. 1–2. London: Routledge, 2005.
West, Nigel, and Madoc Roberts. *Snow.* London: Biteback, 2011.
West, Nigel, and Oleg Tsarev. *Triplex.* New Haven, Conn.: Yale University Press, 2009.
Whitehead, Don. *The FBI Story.* New York: Random House, 1956.
Wilcox, Robert. *Japan's Secret War.* New York: William Morrow, 1985.
Williams, Robert V., and Ben-Ami Lipitz. *Covert and Overt Recollecting and Connecting Intelligence Service and Information Service.* Medford, N.J.: Scarecrow, 2005.
Winks, Robin. *Cloak & Gown.* New York: William Morrow, 1987.
Winterbotham, Frederick W. *The Ultra Secret.* New York: Harper & Row, 1974.
Wires, Richard. *The Cicero Spy Affair.* Westport, Conn.: Praeger, 1999.
Yoshikawa, Takeo, and Lt. Col. Norman Stanford. "Top Secret Assignment." *United States Naval Institute Proceedings* 86, no. 2 (December 1960).

INDEX